CONTENTS

INTRODUCTION

Are you looking for a new smart Air Fryer oven that will help you cook all sorts of meals? Well, you are about to get lucky, as we are introducing you to the amazing Kalorik Digital Maxx Air Fryer oven. We all know Kalorik due to its variety of kitchen appliances. From the first toasted, they presented to the latest Air Fryer ovens; all came with quality and durability offered by Kalorik. As of today, there is a range of innovations that Kalorik introduced in the tech world. The smartest Kalorik Digital Maxx Air Fryer oven is having proven to be the most successful model of this range due to its smart features. In this cookbook, you can learn all about this new Air Fryer Oven and will get to know various recipes that you can cook using its smart cooking functions.

Being a Kalorik appliance is already a pretty big reason to bring this beauty home. But there are actual cooking advantages that this efficient Maxx Air Fryer Oven offers you.

1. Modern Design

The design of the Maxx Air Fryer oven is something that makes it stand out among the rest of the air fryer ovens in the market. Its size and shape make a complete balance; you can manage cooking space and your countertop space at the same time. Since this oven can replace multiple food appliances due to a variety of its cooking functions, it can be easily placed anywhere in the kitchen.

2. Multifunctional

This one appliance can replace most of the cooking appliances in your kitchen as it provides a number of cooking functions in one place. This Air Fryer oven can be used to bake food, toast, grill, roast, braise, rotisserie, broil, and dehydrate all sorts of food items. The versatility of its cooking function increases when you count the temperature and timer settings, which can also be adjusted manually to cook according to your own preferences. There are several accessories that come with the oven, and they all help to cook on a specific cooking mode. There is a total of 21 preset given in the appliance which allows you to cook all variety of meals.

3. Modern French Door System

One of the most interesting features of this Air fryer oven is its French door system, which opens from the center with a single-hand opening. Due to this feature, there is no dripping and scalding on its door during each cooking session. The French door system also makes it easy to check the food or to handle it during cooking. Moreover, it provides you complete space to insert a large tray or pan inside the Air Fryer oven.

4. Family Size

The 26-quart Maxx Air fryer oven is known for its large size and all the capacity suitable for cooking all portion sizes. So, whether you have a large family or a small family, this Air fryer oven can serve the needs of all. Now baking a turkey and roasting a whole chicken or a duck is not a problem, as you can not only adjust them all in this Air Fryer oven, but you can also add side ingredients along with them.

5. Simple and Smart Control Panel

Another good feature of this Air Fryer oven is its easy and simple control panel, which is completely user friendly. There are two main buttons to choose between the Air Fryer options or baking options. And the control dial is used to select the mode of cooking in each option.

Kalorik Digital Maxx Air Fryer Oven Deconstructed

The modern glass French door design of the Maxx Air Fryer is fairly simple and easy to handle. When you unbox the appliance, you will find the following parts and components inside:

Parts and Components

Firstly, there is this base unit, which has dimensions equal to 15.75" width x 12.5" length x 14" height, and inside the unit, there is 26-quart volume to hold your food items. This oven unit has sturdy built, and it must be placed on a flat, rigid and strong base. The glass door is attached to the front, and on top of the glass doors, there is a control panel and display screen. Inside the oven, there are four grooves on each sidewall to fix baking trays, dripping pans, and Air fryer basket.

The Nine Accessories

Besides the base unit, there are nine accessories that are provided with the oven to aid different cooking functions. These accessories include the following:

- Air frying basket
- Baking pan
- Air rack
- Crumb tray
- Bacon tray
- Steak/dehydrator tray
- Rotisserie spit
- Rack handle
- Rotisserie handle

All these accessories are dishwasher safe, can be removed and washed after the cooking session.

Control Panel and Cooking Functions

The control panel is fixed on the front of the appliance, on top. And it has a dial, five buttons, and a display screen. On this screen, you can see all the 21 presets written on the screen indicating different food types like:

- Chicken
- Fish
- Ribs
- Steak
- Wings
- Bacon
- Eggs
- Fries
- Corn
- Shrimp
- Vegetables
- Pizza
- Pastry etc.

Then there are other cooking modes like:

- Air Fry
- Bake
- Broil
- Roast
- Toast
- Defrost
- Reheat

The lowermost rectangular button on the control panel is labeled as START/STOP, so you can press the button to initiate or stop your cooking operations. Above this button, there are two buttons, which light up when they are pressed:

- Air Fry: When it is pressed, the appliance converts into an Air Fry. The dial is then used to select the required preset to select the time and temperature according to the recipe.
- Oven: When this button is pressed, you can use the appliance like an electric oven, and with the help you the dial, you can use the presets for an oven function.

Above the Air Fryer button, there is a button for Convection, which can be pressed to circulate the heat inside the oven through Convection. The other button on its right side is for the Light inside the oven. It can be pressed to see the condition of the food.

How to use Kalorik Digital Maxx Air Fryer Oven

Here are a few simple steps to use your Kalorik Digital Maxx Air Fryer Oven:

1. Getting Started

At first, place the appliance at an appropriate place in the kitchen. The back and top of the oven should be kept open for ventilation. Check all its accessories and then plug it in. The lights of the display screen will light up.

If you are using the oven for the first time, make sure to wash all the accessories with water or soap water and allow them to dry and keep them at a place where they are safe from the dirt and grease.

2. Setting Up the oven

The crumb tray is placed at the bottom of the oven, and it is important to use this tray to protect the floor of the oven. So always fix the crumb tray in the lowermost portion of the oven. You can now select the accessories according to the recipe and the type of food. The air fryer basket is used to Air Fry variety of food items, so use this basket to keep the food inside the oven. The baking pan and tray can be used for a variety of purpose:

- To bake food
- To roast items
- To Broil
- To toast

The Rotisserie rod and handle are provided to cook on the chicken, or duck, etc. on the rotisserie. In this way, the chicken or duck is heated properly from all sides as the rod rotates and gets an even brown color on all sides.

The dehydrator tray is used for dehydrating meat, fruits, and vegetables. And there is also a bacon tray that is used for cooking crispy bacon in the oven. You can use the accessories according to your needs. There is also an Air Rack, which you can use for Air frying as well as for roasting or baking etc.

Cooking and Adjustment

Now that you have selected the desired accessories for cooking. Prepare your food and keep it ready for the oven. The oven quickly attains the required heat for cooking, so it is suggested to not to preheat the oven and directly place the food inside and then select the cooking functions. You can adjust the settings according to the given recipe. Generally, it is best to select after your food is placed inside.

Once the food is set inside, close the French glass doors to seal the oven and then select any of the two options: AIR FRY or OVEN, then use the dial to select the required preset to adjust the time and temperature.

When the appliance starts actual cooking, the timer starts ticking, and you will notice the magic happening inside the oven through its glass doors. If you want to flip or toss the food inside the oven, then simply press STOP to pause the cooking function and flip or toss the food. Close the doors again and resume cooking by pressing the START button. You can always use the LIGHT function to check the status of your food and prevent it from burning, overcooking, or undercooking.

Once the operation is completed, the appliance will indicate so by a beep or a blink on the screen. It is wise to leave the food for 5-10 minutes in the oven and then dish out for safe and easy handling. When you are done cooking, remove the food from the oven along with all the accessories used.

Cleaning and Maintenance

No cooking appliance can work for long if it is not cleaned or maintained properly, especially an Air Fryer oven like this oven needs all the care and attention to keep it suitable for cooking clean and hygienic food. Inside the oven, when food particles or dirty accessories are left without cleaning, it can cause bacterial growth, which can then contaminate the food placed inside. So, here are few simple steps to clean the appliance after every cooking session.

1.   First, unplug the appliance and remove all the trays or pans placed inside. Make sure to wear gloves or oven mittens while handling the hot trays. It is important to clean the tray and pan while they are hot to prevent all the grease and food particles stuck on them from hardening.

2.   Leave the cooking appliance with its door open and allow it to cool completely.

3.   Use this time to wash all the accessories used in the cooking operation. You can either wash them by lightly rub them with soap water or wash them in the dishwasher. Avoid using hard material to scrub these accessories, as they could damage their outer surface.

4.   Once the accessories are washed, leave them to dry completely.

5.   Now that the oven is cooled from inside out, you can take a lightly damp cloth and wipe off all the grease and food particles from the inner walls of the Air Fryer oven.

6.   Use another lightly wet cloth to wipe off the doors, door handle, the control panel dial, its buttons, and the displace screen.

7.   Never immerse the unit water and keep it away from liquids as well.

APPETIZERS AND SIDE DISHES

1. Roasted Brussels Sprouts

Servings: 6
Cooking Time: 30 Minutes
Ingredients:
- 1-1/2 pounds Brussels sprouts, ends trimmed and yellow leaves removed
- 3 tablespoons olive oil
- 1 teaspoon salt
- 1/2 teaspoon black pepper

Directions:
1. Start by preheating toaster oven to 400°F.
2. Toss Brussels sprouts in a large bowl, drizzle with olive oil, sprinkle with salt and pepper, then toss.
3. Roast for 30 minutes.
- **Nutrition Info:** Calories: 109, Sodium: 416 mg, Dietary Fiber: 4.3 g, Total Fat: 7.4 g, Total Carbs: 10.4 g, Protein: 3.9 g.

2. Easy Home Fries(2)

Servings: 4
Cooking Time: 20 Minutes
Ingredients:
- ½ medium white onion; peeled and diced
- 1 medium green bell pepper; seeded and diced
- 1 medium jicama; peeled.
- 1 tbsp. coconut oil; melted
- ½ tsp. pink Himalayan salt
- ¼ tsp. ground black pepper

Directions:
1. Cut jicama into 1-inch cubes. Place into a large bowl and toss with coconut oil until coated. Sprinkle with pepper and salt. Place into the air fryer basket with peppers and onion.
2. Adjust the temperature to 400 Degrees F and set the timer for 10 minutes. Shake two or three times during cooking. Jicama will be tender and dark around edges. Serve immediately.
- **Nutrition Info:** Calories: 97; Protein: 1.5g; Fiber: 8.0g; Fat: 3.3g; Carbs: 15.8g

3. Browned Ricotta With Capers And Lemon

Servings: 4 To 6
Cooking Time: 8 Minutes
Ingredients:
- 1½ cups whole milk ricotta cheese
- 2 tablespoons extra-virgin olive oil
- 2 tablespoons capers, rinsed
- Zest of 1 lemon, plus more for garnish
- 1 teaspoon finely chopped fresh rosemary
- Pinch crushed red pepper flakes
- Salt and freshly ground black pepper, to taste
- 1 tablespoon grated Parmesan cheese
- In a mixing bowl, stir together the ricotta cheese, olive oil, capers, lemon zest, rosemary, red pepper flakes, salt, and pepper until well combined.

Directions:
1. Spread the mixture evenly in the baking pan.
2. Slide the baking pan into Rack Position 2, select Air Fry, set temperature to 380ºF (193ºC), and set time to 8 minutes.
3. When cooking is complete, the top should be nicely browned. Remove from the oven and top with a sprinkle of grated Parmesan cheese. Garnish with the lemon zest and serve warm.

4. Air Fry Broccoli Florets

Servings: 2
Cooking Time: 10 Minutes
Ingredients:
- 1 lb broccoli florets
- 1/2 tsp chili powder
- 1/4 tsp turmeric
- 2 tbsp plain yogurt
- 1 tbsp chickpea flour
- 1/2 tsp salt

Directions:
1. Fit the Cuisinart oven with the rack in position 2.
2. Add all ingredients to the bowl and toss well.
3. Place marinated broccoli in a refrigerator for 15 minutes.
4. Place marinated broccoli in an air fryer basket then places an air fryer basket in a baking pan.
5. Place a baking pan on the oven rack. Set to air fry at 390 F for 10 minutes.
6. Serve and enjoy.
- **Nutrition Info:** Calories 114 Fat 1.5 g Carbohydrates 20.5 g Sugar 5.7 g Protein 8.5 g Cholesterol 1 mg

5. Savory Chicken Nuggets With Parmesan Cheese

Servings: 4
Cooking Time: 25 Minutes
Ingredients:
- 1 lb chicken breasts, cubed
- Salt and black pepper to taste
- 2 tbsp olive oil
- 5 tbsp plain breadcrumbs
- 2 tbsp panko breadcrumbs
- 2 tbsp grated Parmesan cheese

Directions:
1. Preheat Cuisinart on Air Fry function to 380 F. Season the chicken with salt and pepper; set aside. In a bowl, mix the breadcrumbs with the Parmesan cheese.
2. Brush the chicken pieces with the olive oil, then dip into breadcrumb mixture, and transfer to the Air Fryer basket. Fit in the baking tray and lightly spray chicken with cooking spray. Cook for 10 minutes, flipping

once halfway through until golden brown on the outside and no more pink on the inside. Serve warm.

6. Mom's Tarragon Chicken Breast Packets

Servings: 2
Cooking Time: 15 Minutes
Ingredients:
- 2 chicken breasts
- 1 tbsp butter
- Salt and black pepper to taste
- ¼ tsp dried tarragon

Directions:
1. Preheat Cuisinart on Bake function to 380 F. Place each chicken breast on a 12x12 inches foil wrap. Top the chicken with tarragon and butter; season with salt and pepper. Wrap the foil around the chicken breast in a loose way to create a flow of air. Cook the in your Cuisinart oven for 15 minutes. Carefully unwrap and serve.

7. Tasty Bok Choy Crisps

Servings:2
Cooking Time: 10 Minutes
Ingredients:
- 2 tbsp olive oil
- 4 cups packed bok choy
- 1 tsp Italian seasoning
- 1 tbsp yeast flakes
- Sea salt to taste

Directions:
1. In a bowl, mix olive oil, bok choy, yeast, and Italian seasoning. Dump the coated kale in frying basket. Set the temperature of Breville toaster oven to 360 F on AirFry function and press Start. Cook for 5-8 minutes until crispy. Serve sprinkled with sea salt.

8. Ham & Pineapple Tortilla Pizzas

Servings:2
Cooking Time: 15 Minutes
Ingredients:
- 2 tortillas
- 8 ham slices
- 8 mozzarella cheese slices
- 8 thin pineapple slices
- 2 tbsp tomato sauce
- 1 tsp dried parsley

Directions:
1. Preheat Breville on Pizza function to 330 F. Spread the tomato sauce onto the tortillas. Arrange 4 ham slices on each tortilla. Top with pineapple and mozzarella slices and sprinkle with parsley. Place in the oven and press Start. Cook for 10 minutes and serve.

9. Chicken Nuggets

Servings: 6
Cooking Time: 10 Minutes

Ingredients:
- 2 large chicken breasts, cut into 1-inch cubes
- 1 cup breadcrumbs
- 1/3 tablespoon Parmesan cheese, shredded
- 1 teaspoon onion powder
- ¼ teaspoon smoked paprika
- Salt and ground black pepper, as required

Directions:
1. In a large resealable bag, add all the ingredients.
2. Seal the bag and shake well to coat completely.
3. Press "Power Button" of Air Fry Oven and turn the dial to select the "Air Fry" mode.
4. Press the Time button and again turn the dial to set the cooking time to 10 minutes.
5. Now push the Temp button and rotate the dial to set the temperature at 400 degrees F.
6. Press "Start/Pause" button to start.
7. When the unit beeps to show that it is preheated, open the lid.
8. Arrange the nuggets in "Air Fry Basket" and insert in the oven.
9. Serve warm.
- **Nutrition Info:** Calories 218 Total Fat 6.6 g Saturated Fat 1.8 g Cholesterol 67 mg Sodium 229 mg Total Carbs 13.3 g Fiber 0.9 g Sugar 1.3 g Protein 24.4 g

10. Baked Root Vegetables

Servings: 6
Cooking Time: 30 Minutes
Ingredients:
- 1 lb beetroot, cubed
- 3 tsp paprika
- 1/2 lb carrots, cut into chunks
- 1 lb sweet potato, cubed
- 2 tsp olive oil

Directions:
1. Fit the Cuisinart oven with the rack in position
2. Add all ingredients in a large mixing bowl and toss well.
3. Transfer root mixture onto a baking pan.
4. Set to bake at 350 F for 35 minutes. After 5 minutes place the baking pan in the preheated oven.
5. Serve and enjoy.
- **Nutrition Info:** Calories 133 Fat 2 g Carbohydrates 27.5 g Sugar 12.9 g Protein 3.3 g Cholesterol 0 mg

11. Buffalo Quesadillas

Servings: 8
Cooking Time: 5 Minutes
Ingredients:
- Nonstick cooking spray
- 2 cups chicken, cooked & chopped fine
- ½ cup Buffalo wing sauce
- 2 cups Monterey Jack cheese, grated
- ½ cup green onions, sliced thin

- 8 flour tortillas, 8-inch diameter
- ¼ cup blue cheese dressing

Directions:
1. Lightly spray the baking pan with cooking spray.
2. In a medium bowl, add chicken and wing sauce and toss to coat.
3. Place tortillas, one at a time on work surface. Spread ¼ of the chicken mixture over tortilla and sprinkle with cheese and onion. Top with a second tortilla and place on the baking pan.
4. Set oven to broil on 400°F for 8 minutes. After 5 minutes place baking pan in position 2. Cook quesadillas 2-3 minutes per side until toasted and cheese has melted. Repeat with remaining ingredients.
5. Cut quesadillas in wedges and serve with blue cheese dressing or other dipping sauce.
- **Nutrition Info:** Calories 376, Total Fat 20g, Saturated Fat 8g, Total Carbs 27g, Net Carbs 26g, Protein 22g, Sugar 2g, Fiber 2g, Sodium 685mg, Potassium 201mg, Phosphorus 301mg

12. Grandma's Apple Cinnamon Chips

Servings: 2
Cooking Time: 25 Minutes
Ingredients:
- 1 tsp sugar
- 1 tsp salt
- 1 whole apple, sliced
- ½ tsp cinnamon
- Confectioners' sugar for serving

Directions:
1. Preheat your Cuisinart to 400 F on Bake function. In a bowl, mix cinnamon, salt, and sugar. Add in the apple slices and toss to coat. Place the prepared apple slices in the greased air fryer basket and fit in the cooking tray. Cook for 10 minutes, flipping once. Dust with sugar and serve.

13. Parsley Mushroom Pilaf

Servings:4
Cooking Time: 35 Minutes
Ingredients:
- 2 tbsp olive oil
- 2 cups heated vegetable stock
- 1 cups long-grain rice
- 1 onion, chopped
- 2 garlic cloves, minced
- 2 cups cremini mushrooms, chopped
- Salt and black pepper to taste
- 1 tbsp fresh parsley, chopped

Directions:
1. Preheat Breville on AirFry function to 400 F. Heat olive oil in a frying pan over medium heat. and sauté mushrooms, onion, and garlic for 5 minutes until tender. Stir in rice for 1-2 minutes.
2. Pour in the vegetable stock. Season with salt and pepper. Transfer to a baking dish and

place in your Breville oven. Press Start and cook for 20 minutes. Serve sprinkled with chopped parsley.

14. Sunday Calamari Rings

Servings:4
Cooking Time: 20 Minutes
Ingredients:
- 1 lb calamari (squid), cut in rings
- ¼ cup flour
- 2 large beaten eggs
- 1 cup breadcrumbs

Directions:
1. Coat the calamari rings with the flour and dip them in the eggs. Then, roll in the breadcrumbs. Refrigerate for 2 hours. Line them in the frying basket and spray with cooking spray.
2. Select AirFry function, adjust the temperature to 380 F, and press Start. Cook for 14 minutes. Serve with garlic mayo and lemon wedges.

15. Buttered Corn

Servings: 2
Cooking Time: 20 Minutes
Ingredients:
- 2 corn on the cob
- Salt and freshly ground black pepper, as needed
- 2 tablespoons butter, softened and divided

Directions:
1. Sprinkle the cobs evenly with salt and black pepper.
2. Then, rub with 1 tablespoon of butter.
3. With 1 piece of foil, wrap each cob.
4. Press "Power Button" of Air Fry Oven and turn the dial to select the "Air Fry" mode.
5. Press the Time button and again turn the dial to set the cooking time to 20 minutes.
6. Now push the Temp button and rotate the dial to set the temperature at 320 degrees F.
7. Press "Start/Pause" button to start.
8. When the unit beeps to show that it is preheated, open the lid.
9. Arrange the cobs in "Air Fry Basket" and insert in the oven.
10. Serve warm.
- **Nutrition Info:** Calories 186 Total Fat 12.2 g Saturated Fat 7.4 g Cholesterol 31 mg Sodium 163 mg Total Carbs 20.1 g Fiber 2.5 g Sugar 3.2g Protein 2.9 g

16. Baked Potatoes Eggplant

Servings: 4
Cooking Time: 40 Minutes
Ingredients:
- 2 medium eggplants, cut into pieces
- 1 tbsp lemon juice
- 1 lb potatoes, cut into cubes
- 1/4 cup olive oil
- Pepper
- Salt

Directions:
1. Fit the Cuisinart oven with the rack in position
2. Add eggplant, potatoes, oil, pepper, and salt in a baking dish and toss well.
3. Set to bake at 400 F for 45 minutes. After 5 minutes place the baking dish in the preheated oven.
4. Drizzle with lemon juice and serve.
- **Nutrition Info:** Calories 244 Fat 13.2 g Carbohydrates 31.4 g Sugar 8.3 g Protein 4.2 g Cholesterol 0 mg

17. Garlic Herb Tomatoes

Servings: 4
Cooking Time: 45 Minutes
Ingredients:
- 10 medium-sized tomatoes
- 10 garlic cloves
- Bread crumbs
- Thyme
- Sage
- Oregano

Directions:
1. Start by finely chopping garlic and herbs.
2. Cut tomatoes in half and place cut-side up on a baking sheet lined with parchment paper.
3. Pour garlic and herb mixture over tomatoes.
4. Roast at 350°F for 30 minutes in toaster oven.
5. Top with bread crumbs and roast another 15 minutes.
- **Nutrition Info:** Calories: 103, Sodium: 68 mg, Dietary Fiber: 5.4 g, Total Fat: 1.3 g, Total Carbs: 21.4 g, Protein: 4.4 g.

18. Pineapple Pork Ribs

Servings: 4
Cooking Time: 30 Minutes
Ingredients:
- 2 lb cut spareribs
- 7 oz salad dressing
- 1 (5-oz) can pineapple juice
- 2 cups water
- Salt and black pepper to taste

Directions:
1. Preheat your Cuisinart to 390 F on Bake function. Sprinkle the ribs with salt and pepper and place them in a greased baking dish. Cook for 15 minutes. Prepare the sauce by combining the salad dressing and the pineapple juice. Serve the ribs drizzled with the sauce.

19. Ham Rolls With Vegetables & Walnuts

Servings: 4
Cooking Time: 15 Minutes
Ingredients:
- 8 ham slices
- 4 carrots, chopped
- 4 slices ham
- 2 oz walnuts, finely chopped
- 1 zucchini
- 1 clove garlic
- 1 tbsp olive oil
- 1 tbsp ginger powder
- ¼ cup basil leaves, finely chopped
- Salt and black pepper to taste

Directions:
1. Heat the olive oil in a pan over medium heat and add the zucchini, carrots, garlic, ginger and salt; cook for 5 minutes. Add the basil and walnuts, and keep stirring.
2. Divide the mixture between the ham slices. Then fold one side above the filling and roll in. Cook the rolls in the preheated Cuisinart for 8 minutes at 300 F on Bake function.

20. Air Fryer Corn

Servings: 2
Cooking Time: 10 Minutes
Ingredients:
- 2 fresh ears of corn, remove husks, wash, and pat dry
- 1 tbsp fresh lemon juice
- 2 tsp oil
- Pepper
- Salt

Directions:
1. Fit the Cuisinart oven with the rack in position 2.
2. Cut the corn to fit in the air fryer basket.
3. Drizzle oil over the corn. Season with pepper and salt.
4. Place corn in the air fryer basket then places an air fryer basket in the baking pan.
5. Place a baking pan on the oven rack. Set to air fry at 400 F for 10 minutes.
6. Serve and enjoy.
7. Drizzle lemon juice over corn and serve.
- **Nutrition Info:** Calories 122 Fat 5.6 g Carbohydrates 18.2 g Sugar 4.2 g Protein 3.1 g Cholesterol 0 mg

21. Blistered Shishito Peppers With Lime Juice

Servings:3
Cooking Time: 9 Minutes
Ingredients:
- ½ pound (227 g) shishito peppers, rinsed
- Cooking spray
- Sauce:
- 1 tablespoon tamari or shoyu
- 2 teaspoons fresh lime juice
- 2 large garlic cloves, minced

Directions:
1. Spritz the air fryer basket with cooking spray.
2. Place the shishito peppers in the basket and spritz them with cooking spray.
3. Put the air fryer basket on the baking pan and slide into Rack Position 2, select Roast,

set temperature to 392ºF (200ºC), and set time to 9 minutes.

4. Meanwhile, whisk together all the ingredients for the sauce in a large bowl. Set aside.
5. After 3 minutes, remove from the oven. Flip the peppers and spritz them with cooking spray. Return to the oven and continue cooking.
6. After another 3 minutes, remove from the oven. Flip the peppers and spray with cooking spray. Return to the oven and continue roasting for 3 minutes more, or until the peppers are blistered and nicely browned.
7. When cooking is complete, remove the peppers from the oven to the bowl of sauce. Toss to coat well and serve immediately.

22. Savory Cod Fingers

Servings:3
Cooking Time: 25 Minutes
Ingredients:
- 2 cups flour
- 1 tsp seafood seasoning
- 2 whole eggs, beaten
- 1 cup cornmeal
- 1 pound cod fillets, cut into fingers
- 2 tbsp milk
- 2 eggs, beaten
- 1 cup breadcrumbs

Directions:
1. Preheat Breville on Air Fryer function to 400 F. In a bowl, mix beaten eggs with milk. In a separate bowl, mix flour, cornmeal, and seafood seasoning. In a third bowl, pour the breadcrumbs.
2. Dip cod fingers in the flour mixture, followed by a dip in the egg mixture and finally coat with breadcrumbs. Place the fingers in the frying basket and Press Start. AirFry for 10 minutes.

23. Cheesy Squash Casserole

Servings: 6
Cooking Time: 30 Minutes
Ingredients:
- 2 lbs yellow summer squash, cut into chunks
- 1/2 cup liquid egg substitute
- 3/4 cup cheddar cheese, shredded
- 1/4 cup mayonnaise
- 1/4 tsp salt

Directions:
1. Fit the Cuisinart oven with the rack in position
2. Add squash in a saucepan then pour enough water in a saucepan to cover the squash. Bring to boil.
3. Turn heat to medium and cook for 10 minutes or until tender. Drain well.

4. In a large mixing bowl, combine together squash, egg substitute, mayonnaise, 1/2 cup cheese, and salt.
5. Transfer squash mixture into a greased baking dish.
6. Set to bake at 375 F for 35 minutes. After 5 minutes place the baking dish in the preheated oven.
7. Sprinkle remaining cheese on top.
8. Serve and enjoy.
- **Nutrition Info:** Calories 130 Fat 8.2 g Carbohydrates 7.7 g Sugar 3.5 g Protein 8 g Cholesterol 18 mg

24. Garlic & Olive Oil Spring Vegetables

Servings: 4
Cooking Time: 20 Minutes
Ingredients:
- 1 pound assorted spring vegetables (such as carrots, asparagus, radishes, spring onions, or sugar snap peas)
- 4 unpeeled garlic cloves
- 2 tablespoons olive oil
- Salt and pepper to taste

Directions:
1. Start by preheating toaster oven to 450°F.
2. Combine vegetables, garlic, oil, salt, and pepper in a bowl and toss.
3. Roast for 20 minutes or until vegetables start to brown.
- **Nutrition Info:** Calories: 105, Sodium: 255 mg, Dietary Fiber: 4.4 g, Total Fat: 7.3 g, Total Carbs: 9.1 g, Protein: 1.8 g.

25. Mixed Veggie Bites

Servings: 5
Cooking Time: 10 Minutes
Ingredients:
- ¾ lb. fresh spinach, blanched, drained and chopped
- ¼ of onion, chopped
- ½ of carrot, peeled and chopped
- 1 garlic clove, minced
- 1 American cheese slice, cut into tiny pieces
- 1 bread slice, toasted and processed into breadcrumbs
- ½ tablespoon corn flour
- ½ teaspoon red chili flakes
- Salt, as required

Directions:
1. In a bowl, add all the ingredients except breadcrumbs and mix until well combined.
2. Add the breadcrumbs and gently stir to combine.
3. Make 10 equal-sized balls from the mixture.
4. Press "Power Button" of Air Fry Oven and turn the dial to select the "Air Fry" mode.
5. Press the Time button and again turn the dial to set the cooking time to 10 minutes.
6. Now push the Temp button and rotate the dial to set the temperature at 355 degrees F.
7. Press "Start/Pause" button to start.

8. When the unit beeps to show that it is preheated, open the lid.
9. Arrange the veggie balls in "Air Fry Basket" and insert in the oven.
10. Serve warm.
- **Nutrition Info:** Calories 43 Total Fat 1.4 g Saturated Fat 0.7 g Cholesterol 3 mg Sodium 155 mg Total Carbs 5.6 g Fiber 1.9 g Sugar 1.2 g Protein 3.1 g

26. Air Fried Mac & Cheese

Servings: 1
Cooking Time: 15 Minutes
Ingredients:
- 1 cup cooked macaroni
- 1 cup grated cheddar cheese
- ½ cup warm milk
- 1 tbsp Parmesan cheese
- Salt and black pepper to taste

Directions:
1. Preheat Cuisinart on Air Fry function to 350 F. Add the macaroni to Air Fryer baking pan. Stir in the cheddar cheese and milk. Season with salt and pepper. Place the dish in the toaster oven and cook for 10 minutes. Sprinkle with Parmesan cheese and serve.

27. Feta Lime Corn

Servings: 2
Cooking Time: 20 Minutes
Ingredients:
- 2 ears of corn
- Juice of 2 small limes
- 2 tsp paprika
- 4 oz feta cheese, grated

Directions:
1. Preheat Cuisinart on Air Fry function to 370 F. Peel the corn and remove the silk. Place the corn in the baking pan and cook for 15 minutes. Squeeze the juice of 1 lime on top of each ear of corn. Top with feta cheese and serve.

28. Homemade Cheddar Biscuits

Servings: 8
Cooking Time: 35 Minutes
Ingredients:
- ½ cup + 1 tbsp butter
- 2 tbsp sugar
- 3 cups flour
- 1 ⅓ cups buttermilk
- ½ cup cheddar cheese, grated

Directions:
1. Preheat Cuisinart on Bake function to 380 F. Lay a parchment paper on a baking plate. In a bowl, mix sugar, flour, ½ cup of butter, half of the cheddar cheese, and buttermilk to form a batter. Make 8 balls from the batter and roll in flour.
2. Place the balls in your Air Fryer baking tray and flatten into biscuit shapes. Sprinkle the remaining cheddar cheese and remaining

butter on top. Cook for 30 minutes, tossing every 10 minutes. Serve.

29. Creamy Fennel(2)

Servings: 4
Cooking Time: 8 Minutes
Ingredients:
- 2 big fennel bulbs; sliced
- ½ cup coconut cream
- 2 tbsp. butter; melted
- Salt and black pepper to taste.

Directions:
1. In a pan that fits the air fryer, combine all the ingredients, toss, introduce in the machine and cook at 370°F for 12 minutes
2. Divide between plates and serve as a side dish.
- **Nutrition Info:** Calories: 151; Fat: 3g; Fiber: 2g; Carbs: 4g; Protein: 6g

30. Sausage Mushroom Caps(2)

Servings: 2
Cooking Time: 20 Minutes
Ingredients:
- ½ lb. Italian sausage
- 6 large Portobello mushroom caps
- ¼ cup grated Parmesan cheese.
- ¼ cup chopped onion
- 2 tbsp. blanched finely ground almond flour
- 1 tsp. minced fresh garlic

Directions:
1. Use a spoon to hollow out each mushroom cap, reserving scrapings.
2. In a medium skillet over medium heat, brown the sausage about 10 minutes or until fully cooked and no pink remains. Drain and then add reserved mushroom scrapings, onion, almond flour, Parmesan and garlic.
3. Gently fold ingredients together and continue cooking an additional minute, then remove from heat
4. Evenly spoon the mixture into mushroom caps and place the caps into a 6-inch round pan. Place pan into the air fryer basket
5. Adjust the temperature to 375 Degrees F and set the timer for 8 minutes. When finished cooking, the tops will be browned and bubbling. Serve warm.
- **Nutrition Info:** Calories: 404; Protein: 24.3g; Fiber: 4.5g; Fat: 25.8g; Carbs: 18.2g

31. Winter Vegetables With Herbs

Servings: 2
Cooking Time: 20 Minutes
Ingredients:
- 1/2-pound broccoli florets
- 1 celery root, peeled and cut into 1-inch pieces
- 1 onion, cut into wedges
- 2 tablespoons unsalted butter, melted
- 1/2 cup chicken broth

- 1/4 cup tomato sauce
- 1 teaspoon parsley
- 1 teaspoon rosemary
- 1 teaspoon thyme

Directions:
1. Start by preheating your Air Fryer to 380 degrees F. Place all ingredients in a lightly greased casserole dish. Stir to combine well.
2. Bake in the preheated Air Fryer for 10 minutes. Gently stir the vegetables with a large spoon and cook for 5 minutes more.
3. Serve in individual bowls with a few drizzles of lemon juice.
- **Nutrition Info:** 141 Calories; 13g Fat; 1g Carbs; 5g Protein; 9g Sugars; 6g Fiber

32. Garlic And Parmesan Asparagus

Servings: 4
Cooking Time: 8 Minutes
Ingredients:
- 1 cup water
- 3 garlic cloves, peeled and minced
- 1 bunch asparagus, trimmed
- 3 tablespoons Parmesan cheese, grated
- 3 tablespoons butter

Directions:
1. Place the water in the Instant Pot. Place the asparagus in aluminum foil, add the garlic and butter and seal the edges of the leaf.
2. Place in the pan, cover and cook for 8 minutes in the Manual setting. Relieve the pressure, arrange the asparagus on the plates, sprinkle with cheese and serve.
- **Nutrition Info:** Calories: 70, Fats: 5.2, Fiber: 1.8, Carbohydrate: 3.8, Proteins: 4

33. Baked Italian Vegetables

Servings: 6
Cooking Time: 30 Minutes
Ingredients:
- 1 eggplant, sliced
- 1 onion, sliced
- 1 potato, peel & cut into chunks
- 1 bell pepper, cut into strips
- 2 zucchini, sliced
- 2 tomatoes, quartered
- 5 fresh basil leaves, sliced
- 2 tsp Italian seasoning
- 2 tbsp olive oil
- Pepper
- Salt

Directions:
1. Fit the Cuisinart oven with the rack in position
2. Add all ingredients except basil leaves into the mixing bowl and toss well.
3. Transfer vegetable mixture on a prepared baking pan.
4. Set to bake at 400 F for 35 minutes. After 5 minutes place the baking dish in the preheated oven.
5. Garnish with basil leaves and serve.

- **Nutrition Info:** Calories 117 Fat 5.6 g Carbohydrates 16.6 g Sugar 6.6 g Protein 2.9 g Cholesterol 1 mg

34. Coriander Artichokes(1)

Servings: 4
Cooking Time: 20 Minutes
Ingredients:
- 12 oz. artichoke hearts
- 1 tbsp. lemon juice
- 1 tsp. coriander, ground
- ½ tsp. cumin seeds
- ½ tsp. olive oil
- Salt and black pepper to taste.

Directions:
1. In a pan that fits your air fryer, mix all the ingredients, toss, introduce the pan in the fryer and cook at 370°F for 15 minutes
2. Divide the mix between plates and serve as a side dish.
- **Nutrition Info:** Calories: 200; Fat: 7g; Fiber: 2g; Carbs: 5g; Protein: 8g

35. Ranch Potatoes

Servings: 6
Cooking Time: 20 Minutes
Ingredients:
- 1 1/2 lbs baby potatoes, cut in half
- 1/2 tsp paprika
- 1/2 tsp onion powder
- 1/2 tsp dill
- 1/2 tsp chives
- 1/2 tsp parsley
- 1/2 tsp garlic powder
- 2 tbsp olive oil
- 1/2 tsp salt

Directions:
1. Fit the Cuisinart oven with the rack in position 2.
2. Add baby potatoes and remaining ingredients into the mixing bowl and toss until well coated.
3. Transfer baby potatoes in air fryer basket then place air fryer basket in baking pan.
4. Place a baking pan on the oven rack. Set to air fry at 400 F for 20 minutes.
5. Serve and enjoy.
- **Nutrition Info:** Calories 108 Fat 4.8 g Carbohydrates 14.6 g Sugar 0.2 g Protein 3 g Cholesterol 0 mg

36. Sweet Coconut Shrimp

Servings:4
Cooking Time: 25 Minutes
Ingredients:
- 1 lb jumbo shrimp, peeled and deveined
- ¾ cup shredded coconut
- 1 tbsp maple syrup
- ½ cup breadcrumbs
- ⅓ cup cornstarch
- ½ cup milk

Directions:

1. Pour the cornstarch in a zipper bag and add in the shrimp. Seal the bag and shake vigorously to coat. In a bowl, mix the syrup with milk. In a separate bowl, combine the breadcrumbs and coconut. Open the zipper bag and remove the shrimp while shaking off excess starch.
2. Dip shrimp in the milk mixture and then in the crumbs, pressing loosely to trap enough crumbs and coconut. Place the coated shrimp in the basket without overcrowding. Select AirFry function, adjust the temperature to 360 F, and press Start. Cook for 12 minutes until crispy.

37. Cheesy Garlic Biscuits

Servings: 4
Cooking Time: 20 Minutes
Ingredients:
- 1 large egg.
- 1 scallion, sliced
- ¼ cup unsalted butter; melted and divided
- ½ cup shredded sharp Cheddar cheese.
- ⅓ cup coconut flour
- ½ tsp. baking powder.
- ½ tsp. garlic powder.

Directions:
1. Take a large bowl, mix coconut flour, baking powder and garlic powder.
2. Stir in egg, half of the melted butter, Cheddar cheese and scallions. Pour the mixture into a 6-inch round baking pan. Place into the air fryer basket
3. Adjust the temperature to 320 Degrees F and set the timer for 12 minutes
4. To serve, remove from pan and allow to fully cool. Slice into four pieces and pour remaining melted butter over each.
- **Nutrition Info:** Calories: 218; Protein: 7.2g; Fiber: 3.4g; Fat: 16.9g; Carbs: 6.8g

38. Baked Garlic Mushrooms

Servings: 2
Cooking Time: 10 Minutes
Ingredients:
- 1 lb button mushrooms, clean and stems removed
- 2 tbsp olive oil
- 2 tbsp fresh chives, sliced
- 3 garlic cloves, chopped
- 1/2 tsp salt

Directions:
1. Fit the Cuisinart oven with the rack in position
2. Add mushrooms, chives, garlic, olive oil, and salt into the zip-lock bag and shake well.
3. Place mushrooms in baking pan.
4. Set to bake at 400 F for 15 minutes. After 5 minutes place the baking pan in the preheated oven.
5. Serve and enjoy.

- **Nutrition Info:** Calories 176 Fat 14.7 g Carbohydrates 9.1 g Sugar 4 g Protein 7.5 g Cholesterol 0 mg

39. Savory Curly Potatoes

Servings: 2
Cooking Time: 20 Minutes
Ingredients:
- 2 potatoes, spiralized
- 1 tbsp extra-virgin olive oil
- Salt and black pepper to taste
- 1 tsp paprika

Directions:
1. Preheat Cuisinart on Air Fry function to 350 F. Place the potatoes in a bowl and coat with oil. Transfer them to the cooking basket and fit in the baking tray. Cook for 15 minutes, shaking once. Sprinkle with salt, pepper, and paprika and to serve.

40. Wonton Poppers

Servings: 10
Cooking Time: 10 Minutes
Ingredients:
- Nonstick cooking spray
- 1 package refrigerated square wonton wrappers
- 1 8-ounce package cream cheese, softened
- 3 jalapenos, seeds and ribs removed, finely chopped
- 1/2 cup shredded cheddar cheese

Directions:
1. Place baking pan in position 2 of the oven. Lightly spray fryer basket with cooking spray.
2. In a large bowl, combine all ingredients except the wrappers until combined.
3. Lay wrappers in a single layer on a baking sheet. Spoon a teaspoon of filling in the center. Moisten the edges with water and fold wrappers over filling, pinching edges to seal. Place in a single layer in the basket.
4. Place the basket in the oven and set to air fry on 375°F for 10 minutes. Cook until golden brown and crisp, turning over halfway through cooking time. Repeat with remaining ingredients. Serve immediately.
- **Nutrition Info:** Calories 287, Total Fat 11g, Saturated Fat 6g, Total Carbs 38g, Net Carbs 37g, Protein 9g, Sugar 1g, Fiber 1g, Sodium 485mg, Potassium 98mg, Phosphorus 104mg

41. Cheese Biscuits

Servings:6
Cooking Time: 35 Minutes
Ingredients:
- ½ cup + 1 tbsp butter
- 2 tbsp sugar
- 3 cups flour
- 1 ⅓ cups buttermilk
- ½ cup cheddar cheese, grated

Directions:

1. Preheat Breville on AirFry function to 380 F. Lay a parchment paper on a baking plate. In a bowl, mix sugar, flour, ½ cup butter, cheese, and buttermilk to form a batter. Make balls from the batter and roll in the flour. Place the balls in the baking plate and flatten into biscuit shapes. Sprinkle with cheese and the remaining butter. Place in the oven and press Start. Cook for 30 minutes, tossing every 10 minutes. Serve chilled.

42. Bread Sticks

Servings: 6
Cooking Time: 6 Minutes
Ingredients:

- 1 egg 1/8 teaspoon ground cinnamon
- Pinch of ground nutmeg Pinch of ground cloves
- Salt, to taste
- 2 bread slices
- 1 tablespoon butter, softened
- Nonstick cooking spray
- 1 tablespoon icing sugar

Directions:

1. In a bowl, add the eggs, cinnamon, nutmeg, cloves and salt and beat until well combined.
2. Spread the butter over both sides of the slices evenly.
3. Cut each bread slice into strips.
4. Dip bread strips into egg mixture evenly.
5. Press "Power Button" of Air Fry Oven and turn the dial to select the "Air Fry" mode.
6. Press the Time button and again turn the dial to set the cooking time to 6 minutes.
7. Now push the Temp button and rotate the dial to set the temperature at 355 degrees F.
8. Press "Start/Pause" button to start.
9. When the unit beeps to show that it is preheated, open the lid.
10. Arrange the breadsticks in "Air Fry Basket" and insert in the oven.
11. After 2 minutes of cooking, spray the both sides of the bread strips with cooking spray.
12. Serve immediately with the topping of icing sugar.
- **Nutrition Info:** Calories 41 Total Fat 2.8 g Saturated Fat 1.5 g Cholesterol 32 mg Sodium 72 mg Total Carbs 3 g Fiber 0.1 g Sugar 1.5 g Protein 1.2 g

43. Healthy Asparagus Potatoes

Servings: 4
Cooking Time: 35 Minutes
Ingredients:

- 9 oz asparagus, cut into 2-inch pieces
- 2 lbs potatoes, cut into quarters
- 1/4 cup balsamic vinegar
- 2 tbsp olive oil

Directions:

1. Fit the Cuisinart oven with the rack in position

2. In a large bowl, add potatoes, balsamic vinegar, olive oil, and salt and toss well.
3. Spread potatoes in baking pan.
4. Set to bake at 390 F for 25 minutes. After 5 minutes place the baking pan in the preheated oven.
5. Add asparagus and stir well and bake for 15 minutes more.
6. Season with pepper and salt.
7. Serve and enjoy.
- **Nutrition Info:** Calories 232 Fat 7.3 g Carbohydrates 38.3 g Sugar 3.9 g Protein 5.2 g Cholesterol 0 mg

44. Puffed Asparagus Spears

Servings: 10
Cooking Time: 10 Minutes
Ingredients:

- Nonstick cooking spray
- 3 oz. prosciutto, sliced thin & cut in 30 long strips
- 30 asparagus spears, trimmed
- 10 (14 x 9-inch) sheets phyllo dough, thawed

Directions:

1. Place baking pan in position 2 of the oven.
2. Wrap each asparagus spear with a piece of prosciutto, like a barber pole.
3. One at a time, place a sheet of phyllo on a work surface and cut into 3 4 1/2x9-inch rectangles.
4. Place an asparagus spear across a short end and roll up. Place in a single layer in the fryer basket. Spray with cooking spray.
5. Place the basket in the oven and set to air fry on 450°F for 10 minutes. Cook until phyllo is crisp and golden, about 8-10 minutes, turning over halfway through cooking time. Repeat with remaining ingredients. Serve warm.
- **Nutrition Info:** Calories 74, Total Fat 2g, Saturated Fat 0g, Total Carbs 11g, Net Carbs 10g, Protein 3g, Sugar 0g, Fiber 1g, Sodium 189mg, Potassium 60mg, Phosphorus 33mg

45. Creamy Eggplant Cakes

Servings: 4
Cooking Time: 20 Minutes
Ingredients:

- 1 ½ cups flour
- 1 tsp cinnamon
- 3 eggs
- 2 tsp baking powder
- 2 tbsp sugar
- 1 cup milk
- 2 tbsp butter, melted
- 1 tbsp yogurt
- ½ cup shredded eggplant
- Pinch of salt
- 2 tbsp cream cheese

Directions:

1. Preheat Cuisinart on Air Fry function to 350 F. In a bowl, whisk the eggs along with the

sugar, salt, cinnamon, cream cheese, flour, and baking powder. In another bowl, combine all of the liquid ingredients. Gently combine the dry and liquid mixtures; stir in eggplant.

2. Line the muffin tins and pour the batter inside; cook for 12 minutes. Check with a toothpick: you may need to cook them for an additional 2 to 3 minutes. Serve chilled.

46. Salty Carrot Chips

Servings:2
Cooking Time: 20 Minutes
Ingredients:
- 3 large carrots, washed and peeled
- Salt to taste

Directions:
1. Using a mandolin slicer, cut the carrots very thinly heightwise. Season with salt to taste. Place in the frying basket and spray them lightly with cooking spray. Select AirFry function, adjust the temperature to 380 F, and press Start. Cook for 14-16 minutes until crispy.

47. Healthy Green Beans

Servings: 2
Cooking Time: 10 Minutes
Ingredients:
- 8 oz green beans, trimmed and cut in half
- 1 tbsp tamari
- 1 tsp toasted sesame oil

Directions:
1. Fit the Cuisinart oven with the rack in position 2.
2. Add all ingredients into the large bowl and toss well.
3. Transfer green beans in the air fryer basket then place an air fryer basket in the baking pan.
4. Place a baking pan on the oven rack. Set to air fry at 400 F for 10 minutes.
5. Serve and enjoy.
- **Nutrition Info:** Calories 61 Fat 2.4 g Carbohydrates 8.6 g Sugar 1.7 g Protein 3 g Cholesterol 0 mg

48. Party Chicken Wings

Servings: 3
Cooking Time: 20 Minutes
Ingredients:
- 15 chicken wings
- Salt and black pepper to taste
- ⅓ cup chili sauce
- ⅓ cup butter
- ½ tbsp vinegar

Directions:
1. Preheat Cuisinart on Air Fry function to 360 F. Season the wings with salt and pepper. Add them to the greased basket and fit in the baking tray. Cook for 15 minutes. Toss every 5 minutes. Once ready, remove them to a bowl.

2. Melt the butter in a saucepan over low heat. Add in the vinegar and hot sauce. Stir and cook for a minute. Turn the heat off. Pour the sauce over the chicken. Toss to coat thoroughly. Transfer the chicken to a serving platter. Serve with a side of celery strips and blue cheese dressing.

49. Ham And Cheese Grilled Sandwich

Servings: 2
Cooking Time: 15 Minutes
Ingredients:
- 4 slices bread
- ¼ cup butter
- 2 slices ham
- 2 slices cheese

Directions:
1. Preheat Cuisinart on Air Fry function to 360 F. Place 2 bread slices on a flat surface. Spread butter on the exposed surfaces. Lay cheese and ham on two of the slices. Cover with the other 2 slices to form sandwiches. Place the sandwiches in the cooking basket and cook for 5 minutes on Bake function. For additional crispiness, set on Toast function for 2 minutes.

50. Butterbeans With Feta & Bacon

Servings:2
Cooking Time: 20 Minutes
Ingredients:
- 1 (14 oz) can butter beans
- 1 tbsp fresh chives, chopped
- ½ cup feta cheese, crumbled
- Black pepper to taste
- 1 tsp olive oil
- 2 oz bacon, sliced

Directions:
1. Preheat Breville on AirFry function to 340 F. Blitz beans, oil, and pepper in a small blender. Arrange bacon slices on the frying basket.
2. Top with chives and place in the oven. Press Start and cook for 12 minutes. Add feta to the bean mixture and stir. Serve bacon with the dip.

51. Chickpeas With Rosemary & Sage

Servings: 4
Cooking Time: 20 Minutes
Ingredients:
- 2 (14.5-ounce) cans chickpeas, rinsed
- 2 tbsp olive oil
- 1 tsp dried rosemary
- ½ tsp dried thyme
- ¼ tsp dried sage
- ¼ tsp salt

Directions:
1. In a bowl, mix together chickpeas, oil, rosemary, thyme, sage, and salt. Transfer them to the Cuisinart Air Fryer baking dish and spread in an even layer. Cook for 15

minutes at 380 F on Bake function, shaking once halfway through cooking. Serve.

52. Holiday Pumpkin Wedges

Servings: 3
Cooking Time: 30 Minutes
Ingredients:
- ½ pumpkin, washed and cut into wedges
- 1 tbsp paprika
- 1 whole lime, squeezed
- 1 cup paleo dressing
- 1 tbsp balsamic vinegar
- Salt and black pepper to taste
- 1 tsp turmeric

Directions:
1. Preheat Cuisinart on Air Fry function to 360 F. Place the pumpkin wedges in your Air Fryer baking tray and cook for 20 minutes. In a bowl, mix lime juice, vinegar, turmeric, salt, pepper and paprika to form a marinade. Pour the marinade over pumpkin and cook for 5 more minutes.

53. Bbq Chicken Wings

Servings: 4
Cooking Time: 19 Minutes
Ingredients:
- 2 lbs. chicken wings
- 1 teaspoon olive oil
- 1 teaspoon smoked paprika
- 1 teaspoon garlic powder
- Salt and ground black pepper, as required
- ¼ cup BBQ sauce

Directions:
1. In a large bowl combine chicken wings, smoked paprika, garlic powder, oil, salt, and pepper and mix well.
2. Press "Power Button" of Air Fry Oven and turn the dial to select the "Air Fry" mode.
3. Press the Time button and again turn the dial to set the cooking time to 19 minutes.
4. Now push the Temp button and rotate the dial to set the temperature at 360 degrees F.
5. Press "Start/Pause" button to start.
6. When the unit beeps to show that it is preheated, open the lid.
7. Arrange the chicken wings in "Air Fry Basket" and insert in the oven.
8. After 12 minutes of cooking, flip the wings and coat with barbecue sauce evenly.
9. Serve immediately.
- **Nutrition Info:** Calories 468 Total Fat 18.1 g Saturated Fat 4.8 g Cholesterol 202mg Sodium 409 mg Total Carbs 6.5 g Fiber 0.4 g Sugar 4.3 g Protein 65.8 g

54. Ham & Mozzarella Eggplant Boats

Servings:2
Cooking Time: 20 Minutes
Ingredients:
- 1 eggplant
- 4 ham slices, chopped
- 1 cup shredded mozzarella cheese, divided
- 1 tsp dried parsley
- Salt and black pepper to taste

Directions:
1. Preheat Breville on AirFry function to 330 F. Peel the eggplant and cut it in half, lengthwise; scoop some of the flesh out. Season with salt and pepper. Divide half of mozzarella cheese between the eggplant halves and top with the ham. Sprinkle with the remaining mozzarella cheese and cook for 12 minutes until nice and golden on top. Serve topped with parsley.

55. Baked Eggplant Pepper & Mushrooms

Servings: 4
Cooking Time: 20 Minutes
Ingredients:
- 2 eggplants
- 2 cups mushrooms
- 1/4 tsp black pepper
- 4 bell peppers
- 2 tbsp olive oil
- 1 tsp salt

Directions:
1. Fit the Cuisinart oven with the rack in position
2. Cut all vegetables into the small bite-sized pieces and place in a baking dish.
3. Drizzle vegetables with olive oil and season with pepper and salt.
4. Set to bake at 390 F for 25 minutes. After 5 minutes place the baking dish in the preheated oven.
5. Serve and enjoy.
- **Nutrition Info:** Calories 87 Fat 4 g Carbohydrates 13.2 g Sugar 7.4 g Protein 2.5 g Cholesterol 0 mg

56. Baked Lemon Broccoli

Servings: 4
Cooking Time: 20 Minutes
Ingredients:
- 1 1/2 lbs broccoli florets
- 3 tbsp slivered almonds, toasted
- 2 garlic cloves, sliced
- 3 tbsp olive oil
- 1 tbsp fresh lemon juice

Directions:
1. Fit the Cuisinart oven with the rack in position
2. Add broccoli, pepper, salt, garlic, and oil in a large bowl and toss well.
3. Spread broccoli in baking dish.
4. Set to bake at 425 F for 25 minutes. After 5 minutes place the baking dish in the preheated oven.
5. Add lemon juice and almonds over broccoli and toss well.
6. Serve and enjoy.
- **Nutrition Info:** Calories 177 Fat 13.3 g Carbohydrates 12.8 g Sugar 3.2 g Protein 5.8 g Cholesterol 0 mg

57. Sweet Pickle Chips With Buttermilk

Servings: 3
Cooking Time: 20 Minutes
Ingredients:
- 36 sweet pickle chips
- 1 cup buttermilk
- 3 tbsp smoked paprika
- 2 cups flour
- ¼ cup cornmeal
- Salt and black pepper to taste

Directions:
1. Preheat Cuisinart on Air Fryer function to 400 F. In a bowl, mix flour, paprika, pepper, salt, cornmeal, and powder. Place pickles in buttermilk and set aside for 5 minutes. Dip the pickles in the spice mixture and place them in the greased air fryer basket. Fit in the baking tray and cook for 10 minutes. Serve warm.

58. Herbed Radish Sauté(1)

Servings: 4
Cooking Time: 20 Minutes
Ingredients:
- 2 bunches red radishes; halved
- 2 tbsp. parsley; chopped.
- 2 tbsp. balsamic vinegar
- 1 tbsp. olive oil
- Salt and black pepper to taste.

Directions:
1. Take a bowl and mix the radishes with the remaining ingredients except the parsley, toss and put them in your air fryer's basket.
2. Cook at 400°F for 15 minutes, divide between plates, sprinkle the parsley on top and serve as a side dish
- **Nutrition Info:** Calories: 180; Fat: 4g; Fiber: 2g; Carbs: 3g; Protein: 5g

59. Weekend Chicken Wings

Servings:3
Cooking Time: 20 Minutes
Ingredients:
- 15 chicken wings
- ⅓ cup chili sauce
- ⅓ cup butter
- ½ tbsp vinegar

Directions:
1. Preheat Breville on AirFry function to 360 F. Season the wings with pepper and salt. Add them to the toaster oven. Press Start and cook for 15 minutes. Once ready, remove them to a bowl.
2. Melt the butter in a saucepan over low heat. Add in the vinegar and hot sauce. Stir and cook for 2-3 minutes. Turn the heat off. Pour the sauce over the chicken and toss to coat. Transfer the chicken to a serving platter. Serve with a side of celery strips and blue cheese dressing.

60. Tasty Hassel Back Potatoes

Servings: 4
Cooking Time: 30 Minutes
Ingredients:
- 4 potatoes, peel & cut potato across the potato to make 1/8-inch slices
- 1/4 cup parmesan cheese, shredded
- 1 tbsp olive oil

Directions:
1. Fit the Cuisinart oven with the rack in position 2.
2. Brush potatoes with olive oil.
3. Place potatoes in the air fryer basket then place an air fryer basket in the baking pan.
4. Place a baking pan on the oven rack. Set to air fry at 350 F for 30 minutes.
5. Sprinkle cheese on top of potatoes and serve.
- **Nutrition Info:** Calories 195 Fat 4.9 g Carbohydrates 33.7 g Sugar 2.5 g Protein 5.4 g Cholesterol 4 mg

61. Pineapple & Mozzarella Tortillas

Servings: 2
Cooking Time: 15 Minutes
Ingredients:
- 2 tortillas
- 8 ham slices
- 8 mozzarella slices
- 8 thin pineapple slices
- 2 tbsp tomato sauce
- ½ tsp dried parsley

Directions:
1. Preheat Cuisinart on Air Fry function to 330 F. Spread the tomato sauce onto the tortillas. Arrange 4 ham slices on each tortilla. Top the ham with the pineapple and sprinkle with mozzarella and parsley. Cook for 10 minutes and enjoy.

62. Pineapple Spareribs

Servings:4
Cooking Time: 35 Minutes
Ingredients:
- 2 lb cut spareribs
- 7 oz salad dressing
- 1 (5-oz) can pineapple juice
- 2 cups water
- 1 tsp garlic powder
- Salt and black pepper

Directions:
1. Sprinkle the ribs with garlic powder, salt, and pepper. Arrange them on the frying basket. sprinkle with garlic salt. Select AirFry function, adjust the temperature to 400 F, and press Start. Cook for 20-25 minutes until golden brown. Prepare the sauce by combining the salad dressing and the pineapple juice. Serve the ribs drizzled with the sauce.

63. Baked Honey Carrots

Servings: 4
Cooking Time: 25 Minutes
Ingredients:
- 1 lb baby carrots
- 2 tbsp butter, melted
- 3 tbsp honey
- 2 tsp fresh parsley, chopped
- 1 tbsp Dijon mustard
- Pepper
- Salt

Directions:
1. Fit the Cuisinart oven with the rack in position
2. In a large bowl, toss carrots with Dijon mustard, honey, butter, pepper, and salt.
3. Transfer carrots in a baking dish and spread evenly.
4. Set to bake at 400 F for 30 minutes. After 5 minutes place the baking dish in the preheated oven.
5. Serve and enjoy.
- **Nutrition Info:** Calories 141 Fat 6.1 g Carbohydrates 22.6 g Sugar 18.4 g Protein 1 g Cholesterol 15 mg

64. Classic Cauliflower Hash Browns

Servings: 2
Cooking Time: 20 Minutes
Ingredients:
- 2/3 pound cauliflower, peeled and grated
- 2 eggs, whisked
- 1/4 cup scallions, chopped
- 1 teaspoon fresh garlic, minced
- Sea salt and ground black pepper, to taste
- 1/4 teaspoon ground allspice
- 1/2 teaspoon cinnamon
- 1 tablespoon peanut oil

Directions:
1. Boil cauliflower over medium-low heat until fork-tender, 5 to 7 minutes Drain the water; pat cauliflower dry with a kitchen towel.
2. Now, add the remaining ingredients; stir to combine well.
3. Cook in the preheated Air Fryer at 395 degrees F for 20 minutes. Shake the basket once or twice. Serve with low-carb tomato sauce.
- **Nutrition Info:** 157 Calories; 12g Fat; 3g Carbs; 8g Protein; 6g Sugars; 6g Fiber

65. Bacon & Potato Salad With Mayonnaise

Servings: 6
Cooking Time: 10 Minutes
Ingredients:
- 4 lb boiled and cubed potatoes
- 15 bacon slices, chopped
- 2 cups shredded cheddar cheese
- 15 oz sour cream
- 2 tbsp mayonnaise
- 1 tsp salt
- 1 tsp pepper
- 1 tsp dried herbs, any

Directions:
1. Preheat Cuisinart on Air Fry function to 350 F. Combine the potatoes, bacon, salt, pepper, and herbs in a large bowl. Transfer to the Cuisinart baking pan. Cook for about 7 minutes. Remove and stir in sour cream and mayonnaise and serve.

66. Air Fried Eggplant Cubes

Servings: 2
Cooking Time: 12 Minutes
Ingredients:
- 1 eggplant, cut into cubes
- 1/4 tsp oregano
- 1 tbsp olive oil
- 1/2 tsp garlic powder

Directions:
1. Fit the Cuisinart oven with the rack in position 2.
2. Add all ingredients into the large bowl and toss well.
3. Transfer eggplant into in air fryer basket then places the air fryer basket in the baking pan.
4. Place a baking pan on the oven rack. Set to air fry at 390 F for 12 minutes.
5. Serve and enjoy.
- **Nutrition Info:** Calories 120 Fat 7.4 g Carbohydrates 14.1 g Sugar 7.1 g Protein 2.4 g Cholesterol 0 mg

67. Paprika Potatoes

Servings: 4
Cooking Time: 30 Minutes
Ingredients:
- 1 lb baby potatoes, quartered
- 1/4 tsp rosemary, crushed
- 1/2 tsp thyme
- 2 tbsp paprika
- 2 tbsp coconut oil, melted
- 1 tbsp olive oil
- Pepper
- Salt

Directions:
1. Fit the Cuisinart oven with the rack in position
2. Place potatoes in a baking dish and sprinkle with paprika, rosemary, thyme, pepper, and salt.
3. Drizzle with oil and melted coconut oil.
4. Set to bake at 425 F for 35 minutes. After 5 minutes place the baking dish in the preheated oven.
5. Serve and enjoy.
- **Nutrition Info:** Calories 165 Fat 10.9 g Carbohydrates 16.2 g Sugar 0.4 g Protein 3.4 g Cholesterol 0 mg

68. Jalapeno Bread

Servings: 10

Cooking Time: 50 Minutes

Ingredients:

- 3 cups all-purpose flour
- 8 oz cheddar cheese, shredded
- 1/2 tsp ground white pepper
- 1 1/2 tbsp baking powder
- 1/4 cup butter, melted
- 1 1/2 cups buttermilk
- 3 jalapeno peppers, chopped
- 2 tbsp sugar
- 1 1/4 tsp salt

Directions:

1. Fit the Cuisinart oven with the rack in position
2. In a mixing bowl, mix flour, baking powder, sugar, white pepper, and salt.
3. Add jalapenos and cheese and stir to combine.
4. Whisk butter and buttermilk together and add to the flour mixture. Stir until just combined.
5. Pour batter into the greased 9*5-inch loaf pan.
6. Set to bake at 375 F for 55 minutes. After 5 minutes place the loaf pan in the preheated oven.
7. Slice and serve.
- **Nutrition Info:** Calories 297 Fat 12.9 g Carbohydrates 34.5 g Sugar 4.5 g Protein 10.9 g Cholesterol 37 mg

BREAKFAST RECIPES

69. Strawberry Cheesecake Pastries

Servings: 6
Cooking Time: 20 Minutes
Ingredients:
- 1 sheet puff pastry, thawed
- ¼ cup cream cheese, soft
- 1 tbsp. strawberry jam
- 1 ½ cups strawberries, sliced
- 1 egg
- 1 tbsp. water
- 6 tsp powdered sugar, sifted

Directions:
1. Line the baking pan with parchment paper.
2. Lay the puff pastry on a cutting board and cut into 6 rectangles. Transfer to prepared pan, placing them 1-inch apart.
3. Lightly score the pastry, creating a ½-inch border, do not cut all the way through. Use a fork to prick the center.
4. In a small bowl, combine cream cheese and jam until thoroughly combined. Spoon mixture evenly into centers of the pastry and spread it within the scored area.
5. Top pastries with sliced berries.
6. In a small bowl, whisk together egg and water. Brush edges of pastry with the egg wash.
7. Set to bake at 350°F for 20 minutes. After 5 minutes, place the baking pan in position 1 and bake pastries until golden brown and puffed.
8. Remove from oven and let cool. Dust with powdered sugar before serving.
- **Nutrition Info:** Calories 205, Total Fat 13g, Saturated Fat 4g, Total Carbs 19g, Net Carbs 18g, Protein 3g, Sugar 6g, Fiber 1g, Sodium 107mg, Potassium 97mg, Phosphorus 50mg

70. Mini Brown Rice Quiches

Servings:6
Cooking Time: 14 Minutes
Ingredients:
- 4 ounces (113 g) diced green chilies
- 3 cups cooked brown rice
- 1 cup shredded reduced-fat Cheddar cheese, divided
- ½ cup egg whites
- $^1/_3$ cup fat-free milk
- ¼ cup diced pimiento
- ½ teaspoon cumin
- 1 small eggplant, cubed
- 1 bunch fresh cilantro, finely chopped
- Cooking spray

Directions:
1. Spritz a 12-cup muffin pan with cooking spray.
2. In a large bowl, stir together all the ingredients, except for ½ cup of the cheese.
3. Scoop the mixture evenly into the muffin cups and sprinkle the remaining ½ cup of the cheese on top.
4. Put the muffin pan into Rack Position 1, select Convection Bake, set temperature to 400ºF (205ºC) and set time to 14 minutes.
5. When cooking is complete, remove from the oven and check the quiches. They should be set.
6. Carefully transfer the quiches to a platter and serve immediately.

71. Nutmeg Potato Gratin

Servings: 5
Cooking Time: 45 Minutes
Ingredients:
- 5 large potatoes
- ½ cup sour cream
- ½ cup grated cheese
- ½ cup milk
- ½ tsp nutmeg
- Salt and black pepper to taste

Directions:
1. Preheat Cuisinart on Bake function to 375 F, peel and slice the potatoes. In a bowl, combine the sour cream, milk, pepper, salt, and nutmeg. Add in the potato slices and stir to coat them well.
2. Transfer the mixture to an ovenproof casserole. Cook for 15 minutes on Bake function, then sprinkle the cheese on top and cook for 10 minutes. Allow to sit for 10 minutes before serving.

72. Bacon Bread Egg Casserole

Servings: 4
Cooking Time: 20 Minutes
Ingredients:
- 6 eggs
- 1 cup cheddar cheese, shredded
- 1/2 tsp garlic, minced
- 3 tbsp milk
- 2 tbsp green onion, chopped
- 1/3 bell pepper, diced
- 2 bread slices, cubed
- 5 bacon slices, diced
- Pepper
- Salt

Directions:
1. Fit the Cuisinart oven with the rack in position
2. Add all ingredients into the large bowl and stir until well combined.
3. Pour into the greased baking dish.
4. Set to bake at 350 F for 25 minutes. After 5 minutes place the baking dish in the preheated oven.
5. Serve and enjoy.
- **Nutrition Info:** Calories 231 Fat 26.3 g Carbohydrates 5.2 g Sugar 1.9 g Protein 25 g Cholesterol 302 mg

73. Cherry Cinnamon Almond Breakfast Scones

Servings:x
Cooking Time:x
Ingredients:
- 2 cups all-purpose flour
- ½ cup chopped almonds
- ¾ cup milk
- ½ tsp cinnamon
- 2 tsp baking powder
- 3 Tbsp brown sugar
- Pinch of salt
- ½ cup cold butter
- 1½ cups dried cherries
- Zest of one lemon
- 2 Tbsp turbinado sugar

Directions:
1. Preheat oven to 375°F.
2. Combine flour, baking powder, brown sugar and salt.
3. Add cold butter, cut into small pieces, and pinch until dough becomes crumbly.
4. Add dried cherries, zest and chopped almonds to combine.
5. Add the milk and mix dough gently. Do not overwork.
6. Grease Breville smart oven and spread dough uniformly.
7. Combine cinnamon and turbinado sugar and sprinkle on top.
8. Bake for about 25 minutes or until scone is cooked through.

74. Veggies Breakfast Salad

Servings: 4
Cooking Time: 15 Minutes
Ingredients:
- 2 tablespoons olive oil
- 1 cup cherry tomatoes, halved
- 1 zucchini, cubed
- 1 eggplant, cubed
- 1 red onion, chopped
- 1 fennel bulb, shredded
- 1 cup cheddar, shredded
- 2 tablespoons chives, chopped
- Salt and black pepper to the taste
- 8 eggs, whisked

Directions:
1. Add the oil to your air fryer, heat it up at 350 degrees F, add the onion and fennel and cook for 2 minutes.
2. Add the tomatoes and the other ingredients except the cheese and toss.
3. Sprinkle the cheese on top, cook the mix for 13 minutes more, divide into bowls and serve for breakfast.
- **Nutrition Info:** calories 221, fat 8, fiber 3, carbs 4, protein 8

75. Italian Sandwich

Servings:1
Cooking Time: 7 Minutes

Ingredients:
- 2 bread slices
- 4 tomato slices
- 4 mozzarella cheese slices
- 1 tbsp olive oil
- 1 tbsp fresh basil, chopped
- Salt and black pepper to taste

Directions:
1. Preheat Breville on Toast function to 350 F. Place the bread slices in the toaster oven and toast for 5 minutes. Arrange two tomato slices on each bread slice. Season with salt and pepper.
2. Top each slice with 2 mozzarella slices. Return to the oven and cook for 1 more minute. Drizzle the caprese toasts with olive oil and top with chopped basil.

76. Broccoli Asparagus Frittata

Servings: 6
Cooking Time: 20 Minutes
Ingredients:
- 6 eggs
- 1/2 cup onion, diced & sautéed
- 1 cup asparagus, chopped & sautéed
- 1 cup broccoli, chopped & sautéed
- 3 bacon slices, cooked & chopped
- 1/3 cup parmesan cheese, grated
- 1/2 cup milk
- 1/2 tsp pepper
- 1 tsp salt

Directions:
1. Fit the Cuisinart oven with the rack in position
2. In a mixing bowl, whisk eggs with milk, cheese, pepper, and salt.
3. Add onion, asparagus, broccoli, and bacon and stir well.
4. Pour egg mixture into the greased baking dish.
5. Set to bake at 350 F for 25 minutes. After 5 minutes place the baking dish in the preheated oven.
6. Serve and enjoy.
- **Nutrition Info:** Calories 154 Fat 9.9 g Carbohydrates 4.6 g Sugar 2.4 g Protein 12.4 g Cholesterol 179 mg

77. Zucchini Omelet

Servings: 2
Cooking Time: 14 Minutes
Ingredients:
- 1 teaspoon butter
- 1 zucchini, julienned
- 4 eggs
- ¼ teaspoon fresh basil, chopped
- ¼ teaspoon red pepper flakes, crushed
- Salt and ground black pepper, as required

Directions:
1. In a skillet, melt the butter over medium heat and cook the zucchini for about 3-4 minutes.

2. Remove from the heat and set aside to cool slightly.
3. Meanwhile, in a bowl, mix together the eggs, basil, red pepper flakes, salt, and black pepper.
4. Add the cooked zucchini and gently, stir to combine.
5. Place the zucchini mixture into a small baking pan.
6. Press "Power Button" of Air Fry Oven and turn the dial to select the "Air Fry" mode.
7. Press the Time button and again turn the dial to set the cooking time to 10 minutes.
8. Now push the Temp button and rotate the dial to set the temperature at 355 degrees F.
9. Press "Start/Pause" button to start.
10. When the unit beeps to show that it is preheated, open the lid.
11. Arrange pan over the "Wire Rack" and insert in the oven.
12. Cut the omelet into 2 portions and serve hot.
- **Nutrition Info:** Calories 159 Total Fat 10.9 g Saturated Fat 4 g Cholesterol 332 mg Sodium 224 mg Total Carbs 4.1 g Fiber 1.1 g Sugar 2.4 g Protein 12.3 g

78. Cheesy Spring Chicken Wraps

Servings:12
Cooking Time: 5 Minutes
Ingredients:
- 2 large-sized chicken breasts, cooked and shredded
- 2 spring onions, chopped
- 10 ounces (284 g) Ricotta cheese
- 1 tablespoon rice vinegar
- 1 tablespoon molasses
- 1 teaspoon grated fresh ginger
- ¼ cup soy sauce
- $^1/_3$ teaspoon sea salt
- ¼ teaspoon ground black pepper, or more to taste
- 48 wonton wrappers
- Cooking spray

Directions:
1. Spritz the air fryer basket with cooking spray.
2. Combine all the ingredients, except for the wrappers in a large bowl. Toss to mix well.
3. Unfold the wrappers on a clean work surface, then divide and spoon the mixture in the middle of the wrappers.
4. Dab a little water on the edges of the wrappers, then fold the edge close to you over the filling. Tuck the edge under the filling and roll up to seal.
5. Arrange the wraps in the pan.
6. Put the air fryer basket on the baking pan and slide into Rack Position 2, select Air Fry, set temperature to 375ºF (190ºC) and set time to 5 minutes.
7. Flip the wraps halfway through the cooking time.

8. When cooking is complete, the wraps should be lightly browned.
9. Serve immediately.

79. Cauliflower Hash Brown

Servings: 4
Cooking Time: 10 Minutes
Ingredients:
- 2 cups cauliflower, finely grated, soaked and drained
- 2 tablespoons xanthan gum
- Salt, to taste
- Pepper powder, to taste
- 2 teaspoons chili flakes
- 1 teaspoon garlic
- 1 teaspoon onion powder
- 2 teaspoons vegetable oil

Directions:
1. Preheat the Air fryer to 300-degree F and grease an Air fryer basket with oil.
2. Heat vegetable oil in a nonstick pan and add cauliflower.
3. Sauté for about 4 minutes and dish out the cauliflower in a plate.
4. Mix the cauliflower with xanthum gum, salt, chili flakes, garlic and onion powder.
5. Mix well and refrigerate the hash for about 20 minutes.
6. Place the hash in the Air fryer basket and cook for about 10 minutes.
7. Flip the hash after cooking halfway through and dish out to serve warm.
- **Nutrition Info:** Calories: 291, Fat: 2.8g, Carbs: 6.5g, Sugar: 4.5g, Protein: 6.6g, Sodium: 62mg

80. Delicious Broccoli Quiche

Servings: 8
Cooking Time: 45 Minutes
Ingredients:
- 2 eggs
- 2 1/2 cups broccoli, cooked & chopped
- 8 oz cheddar cheese, shredded
- 1/2 cup onion, chopped
- 1 1/2 cups milk
- 1 tsp baking powder
- 1 cup flour
- 1 tsp salt

Directions:
1. Fit the Cuisinart oven with the rack in position
2. In a large bowl, mix flour, baking powder, and salt and set aside.
3. In a separate bowl, whisk eggs. Add onion and stir well.
4. Pour egg mixture into the flour mixture and stir to combine.
5. Stir in broccoli and cheese.
6. Pour egg mixture into the greased 9-inch pie dish.
7. Set to bake at 350 F for 50 minutes. After 5 minutes place the pie dish in the preheated oven.

8. Serve and enjoy.
- **Nutrition Info:** Calories 223 Fat 11.7 g Carbohydrates 17.5 g Sugar 3.1 g Protein 12.4 g Cholesterol 74 mg

81. Avocado And Slaw Tacos

Servings:4
Cooking Time: 6 Minutes
Ingredients:
- ¼ cup all-purpose flour
- ¼ teaspoon salt, plus more as needed
- ¼ teaspoon ground black pepper
- 2 large egg whites
- 1¼ cups panko bread crumbs
- 2 tablespoons olive oil
- 2 avocados, peeled and halved, cut into ½-inch-thick slices
- ½ small red cabbage, thinly sliced
- 1 deseeded jalapeño, thinly sliced
- 2 green onions, thinly sliced
- ½ cup cilantro leaves
- ¼ cup mayonnaise
- Juice and zest of 1 lime
- 4 corn tortillas, warmed
- ½ cup sour cream
- Cooking spray

Directions:
1. Spritz the air fryer basket with cooking spray.
2. Pour the flour in a large bowl and sprinkle with salt and black pepper, then stir to mix well.
3. Whisk the egg whites in a separate bowl. Combine the panko with olive oil on a shallow dish.
4. Dredge the avocado slices in the bowl of flour, then into the egg to coat. Shake the excess off, then roll the slices over the panko.
5. Arrange the avocado slices in a single layer in the pan and spritz the cooking spray.
6. Put the air fryer basket on the baking pan and slide into Rack Position 2, select Air Fry, set temperature to 400ºF (205ºC) and set time to 6 minutes.
7. Flip the slices halfway through with tongs.
8. When cooking is complete, the avocado slices should be tender and lightly browned.
9. Combine the cabbage, jalapeño, onions, cilantro leaves, mayo, lime juice and zest, and a touch of salt in a separate large bowl. Toss to mix well.
10. Unfold the tortillas on a clean work surface, then spread with cabbage slaw and air fried avocados. Top with sour cream and serve.

82. Berry Breakfast Oatmeal

Servings: 4
Cooking Time: 20 Minutes
Ingredients:
- 1 egg
- 2 cups old fashioned oats

- 1 cup blueberries
- 1/4 cup maple syrup
- 1 1/2 cups milk
- 1/2 cup blackberries
- 1/2 cup strawberries, sliced
- 1 1/2 tsp baking powder
- 1/2 tsp salt

Directions:
1. Fit the Cuisinart oven with the rack in position
2. In a bowl, mix together oats, salt, and baking powder.
3. Add vanilla, egg, maple syrup, and milk and stir well. Add berries and fold well.
4. Pour mixture into the greased baking dish.
5. Set to bake at 375 F for 25 minutes. After 5 minutes place the baking dish in the preheated oven.
6. Serve and enjoy.
- **Nutrition Info:** Calories 461 Fat 8.4 g Carbohydrates 80.7 g Sugar 23.4 g Protein 15 g Cholesterol 48 mg

83. Choco Chip Banana Bread

Servings: 10
Cooking Time: 50 Minutes
Ingredients:
- 2 eggs
- 3 ripe bananas
- 1 tsp vanilla
- 1 cup granulated sugar
- 1/2 cup sour cream
- 1/2 cup butter, melted
- 1/2 cup chocolate chips
- 1 1/2 cups all-purpose flour
- 1 tsp baking soda
- 1 tsp salt

Directions:
1. Fit the Cuisinart oven with the rack in position
2. In a large bowl, add bananas and mash using a fork until smooth.
3. Stir in sour cream and melted butter.
4. Add eggs, vanilla, sugar, and salt and stir well.
5. Add flour, baking soda, and salt and stir until just combined.
6. Add chocolate chips and stir well.
7. Pour batter into the greased 9*8-inch loaf pan.
8. Set to bake at 350 F for 55 minutes, after 5 minutes, place the loaf pan in the oven.
9. Slice and serve.
- **Nutrition Info:** Calories 339 Fat 15.3 g Carbohydrates 48 g Sugar 28.9 g Protein 4.5 g Cholesterol 64 mg

84. Apple Cinnamon Oat Muffins

Servings: 12
Cooking Time: 15 Minutes
Ingredients:
- 1 egg

- 1 apple, peel & dice
- 1 tsp cinnamon
- 1/2 cup milk
- 2 bananas, mashed
- 2 cups rolled oats
- 1 tsp baking powder
- Pinch of salt

Directions:
1. Fit the Cuisinart oven with the rack in position
2. Line the muffin tray with cupcake liners and set aside.
3. In a mixing bowl, whisk the egg with cinnamon, baking powder, milk, oats, bananas, and salt.
4. Add apple and stir well.
5. Pour mixture into the prepared muffin tray.
6. Set to bake at 375 F for 20 minutes. After 5 minutes place the muffin tray in the preheated oven.
7. Serve and enjoy.
- **Nutrition Info:** Calories 90 Fat 1.6 g Carbohydrates 17.2 g Sugar 5 g Protein 2.9 g Cholesterol 14 mg

85. Cabbage And Pork Gyoza

Servings: 48 Gyozas
Cooking Time: 10 Minutes
Ingredients:
- 1 pound (454 g) ground pork
- 1 head Napa cabbage (about 1 pound / 454 g), sliced thinly and minced
- ½ cup minced scallions
- 1 teaspoon minced fresh chives
- 1 teaspoon soy sauce
- 1 teaspoon minced fresh ginger
- 1 tablespoon minced garlic
- 1 teaspoon granulated sugar
- 2 teaspoons kosher salt
- 48 to 50 wonton or dumpling wrappers
- Cooking spray

Directions:
1. Spritz the air fryer basket with cooking spray. Set aside.
2. Make the filling: Combine all the ingredients, except for the wrappers in a large bowl. Stir to mix well.
3. Unfold a wrapper on a clean work surface, then dab the edges with a little water. Scoop up 2 teaspoons of the filling mixture in the center.
4. Make the gyoza: Fold the wrapper over to filling and press the edges to seal. Pleat the edges if desired. Repeat with remaining wrappers and fillings.
5. Arrange the gyozas in the pan and spritz with cooking spray.
6. Put the air fryer basket on the baking pan and slide into Rack Position 2, select Air Fry, set temperature to 360ºF (182ºC) and set time to 10 minutes.
7. Flip the gyozas halfway through the cooking time.

8. When cooked, the gyozas will be golden brown.
9. Serve immediately.

86. Crispy Ham Egg Cups

Servings: 2
Cooking Time: 30 Minutes
Ingredients:
- 4 large eggs.
- 4: 1-oz. slices deli ham
- ½ cup shredded medium Cheddar cheese.
- ¼ cup diced green bell pepper.
- 2 tbsp. diced red bell pepper.
- 2 tbsp. diced white onion.
- 2 tbsp. full-fat sour cream.

Directions:
1. Place one slice of ham on the bottom of four baking cups.
2. Take a large bowl, whisk eggs with sour cream. Stir in green pepper, red pepper and onion
3. Pour the egg mixture into ham-lined baking cups. Top with Cheddar. Place cups into the air fryer basket. Adjust the temperature to 320 Degrees F and set the timer for 12 minutes or until the tops are browned. Serve warm.
- **Nutrition Info:** Calories: 382; Protein: 29.4g; Fiber: 1.4g; Fat: 23.6g; Carbs: 6.0g

87. Protein Packed Breakfast Casserole

Servings: 8
Cooking Time: 40 Minutes
Ingredients:
- 12 eggs
- 2 cups cooked chicken, diced
- 1/2 cup cheddar cheese, shredded
- 1 tsp garlic powder
- 1 cup milk
- 1/4 cup onion, diced
- 1 green bell pepper, cubed
- 1 red bell pepper, cubed
- 2 medium potatoes, cubed
- 1/4 tsp pepper
- 1 tsp salt

Directions:
1. Fit the Cuisinart oven with the rack in position
2. Spray 9*13-inch baking pan with cooking spray and set aside.
3. Add bell peppers, potatoes, and cooked chicken into the prepared baking pan and spread evenly.
4. In a large bowl, whisk eggs with milk, garlic powder, pepper, and salt.
5. Pour egg mixture over vegetables and sprinkle with cheese and onion.
6. Set to bake at 350 F for 45 minutes. After 5 minutes place the baking pan in the preheated oven.
7. Serve and enjoy.

- **Nutrition Info:** Calories 240 Fat 10.7 g Carbohydrates 13.4 g Sugar 4.3 g Protein 22.5 g Cholesterol 282 mg

88. Simply Bacon

Servings: 1 Person
Cooking Time: 10 Minutes
Ingredients:
- 4 pieces of bacon

Directions:
1. Place the bacon strips on the instant vortex air fryer.
2. Cook for 10 minutes
3. at 200 degrees Celsius.
4. Check when it browns and shows to be ready. Serve.
- **Nutrition Info:** Calories 165, Fat 13g, Proteins 12 g, Carbs 0g

89. Banana Coconut Muffins

Servings: 12
Cooking Time: 15 Minutes
Ingredients:
- 1 egg
- 3 ripe bananas, mashed
- 1/2 cup shredded coconut
- 2 cups all-purpose flour
- 2 tsp baking powder
- 1/2 tsp baking soda
- 1 cup of sugar
- 1 tsp vanilla
- 1/2 cup milk
- 1/2 cup applesauce
- 1/2 tsp salt

Directions:
1. Fit the Cuisinart oven with the rack in position
2. Line a 12-cup muffin tray with cupcake liners and set aside.
3. In a mixing bowl, whisk the egg with vanilla, milk, applesauce, and salt until well combined.
4. Add baking powder, baking soda, and sugar and mix well.
5. Add flour and mix until just combined.
6. Add shredded coconut and stir well.
7. Pour mixture into the prepared muffin tray.
8. Set to bake at 350 F for 20 minutes. After 5 minutes place the muffin tray in the preheated oven.
9. Serve and enjoy.
- **Nutrition Info:** Calories 193 Fat 2 g Carbohydrates 41.9 g Sugar 22.1 g Protein 3.4 g Cholesterol 14 mg

90. Spinach & Kale Balsamic Chicken

Servings: 1
Cooking Time: 20 Minutes
Ingredients:
- ½ cup baby spinach leaves
- ½ cup shredded romaine
- 3 large kale leaves, chopped
- 4 oz chicken breasts, cut into cubes
- 3 tbsp olive oil, divided
- 1 tsp balsamic vinegar
- 1 garlic clove, minced
- Salt and black pepper to taste

Directions:
1. Place the chicken, 1 tbsp of olive oil, and garlic in a bowl. Season with salt and pepper and toss to combine. Put on a lined Air Fryer pan and cook for 14 minutes at 390 F on Bake function.
2. Place the greens in a large bowl. Add the remaining olive oil and balsamic vinegar. Season with salt and pepper and toss to combine. Top with the chicken and serve.

91. Cinnamon-orange Toast

Servings: 6
Cooking Time: 15 Minutes
Ingredients:
- 12 slices bread
- ½ cup sugar
- 1 stick butter
- 1½ tbsp vanilla extract
- 1½ tbsp cinnamon
- 2 oranges, zested

Directions:
1. Mix butter, sugar, and vanilla extract and microwave for 30 seconds until everything melts. Add in orange zest. Pour the mixture over bread slices. Lay the bread slices in your Cuisinart Air Fryer pan and cook for 5 minutes at 400 F on Toast function. Serve with berry sauce.

92. Egg English Muffin With Bacon

Servings:1
Cooking Time: 10 Minutes
Ingredients:
- 1 egg
- 1 English muffin
- 2 slices of bacon
- Salt and black pepper to taste

Directions:
1. Preheat Breville on Bake function to 395 F. Crack the egg into a ramekin. Place the muffin, egg and bacon in the oven. Cook for 9 minutes. Let cool slightly so you can assemble the sandwich.
2. Cut the muffin in half. Place the egg on one half and season with salt and pepper. Arrange the bacon on top. Top with the other muffin half.

93. Zucchini Breakfast Bread

Servings: 10
Cooking Time: 50 Minutes
Ingredients:
- 2 eggs
- 1 1/2 cups zucchini, grated
- 1 tsp vanilla extract
- 1/4 cup yogurt

- 1/2 tsp baking powder
- 1 1/2 cups whole wheat flour
- 1/2 cup applesauce
- 1/4 cup coconut sugar
- 1 tsp ground cinnamon
- 1/2 tsp baking soda
- 1/2 cup apple, grated
- 1/4 tsp sea salt

Directions:
1. Fit the Cuisinart oven with the rack in position
2. In a bowl, mix all dry ingredients.
3. In another bowl, whisk eggs, coconut sugar, vanilla, yogurt, and applesauce.
4. Add dry ingredients mixture into the wet mixture and stir until well combined.
5. Add apples and zucchini and stir well.
6. Pour batter into the 9*5-inch greased loaf pan.
7. Set to bake at 350 F for 55 minutes, after 5 minutes, place the loaf pan in the oven.
8. Slice and serve.
- **Nutrition Info:** Calories 103 Fat 1.2 g Carbohydrates 19.1 g Sugar 3.3 g Protein 3.7 g Cholesterol 33 mg

94. Feta & Spinach Omelet With Mushrooms

Servings:2
Cooking Time: 10 Minutes
Ingredients:
- 4 eggs, lightly beaten
- 2 tbsp heavy cream
- 2 cups spinach, chopped
- 1 cup mushrooms, chopped
- 3 oz feta cheese, crumbled
- A handful of fresh parsley, chopped
- Salt and black pepper to taste

Directions:
1. In a bowl, whisk eggs and stir in spinach, mushrooms, feta, parsley, salt, and pepper. Pour into a greased baking pan and cook in the Breville oven for 12-14 minutes at 350 F on Bake function..

95. Chicken Breakfast Sausages

Servings: 8 Patties
Cooking Time: 10 Minutes
Ingredients:
- 1 Granny Smith apple, peeled and finely chopped
- 2 tablespoons apple juice
- 2 garlic cloves, minced
- 1 egg white
- $^1/_3$ cup minced onion
- 3 tablespoons ground almonds
- ⅛ teaspoon freshly ground black pepper
- 1 pound (454 g) ground chicken breast

Directions:
1. Combine all the ingredients except the chicken in a medium mixing bowl and stir well.

2. Add the chicken breast to the apple mixture and mix with your hands until well incorporated.
3. Divide the mixture into 8 equal portions and shape into patties. Arrange the patties in the air fryer basket.
4. Put the air fryer basket on the baking pan and slide into Rack Position 2, select Air Fry, set temperature to 330ºF (166ºC) and set time to 10 minutes.
5. When done, a meat thermometer inserted in the center of the chicken should reach at least 165ºF (74ºC).
6. Remove from the oven to a plate. Let the chicken cool for 5 minutes and serve warm.

96. Walnuts And Mango Oatmeal

Servings: 4
Cooking Time: 20 Minutes
Ingredients:
- 2 cups almond milk
- ½ cup walnuts, chopped
- 1 teaspoon vanilla extract
- 1 cup mango, peeled and cubed
- 3 tablespoons sugar
- ½ cup steel cut oats

Directions:
1. In your air fryer, combine the almond milk with the oats and the other ingredients, toss and cook at 360 degrees F for 20 minutes.
2. Divide the mix into bowls and serve for breakfast.
- **Nutrition Info:** calories 141, fat 4, fiber 7, carbs 8, protein 5

97. Sweet Breakfast Casserole

Servings: 4
Cooking Time: 30 Minutes
Ingredients:
- 3 tablespoons brown sugar
- 4 tablespoons margarine
- 2 tablespoons white sugar
- 1/2 tsp. cinnamon powder
- 1/2 cup flour
- For the casserole:
- 2 eggs
- 2 tablespoons white sugar
- 2 and 1/2 cups white flour
- 1 tsp. baking soda
- 1 tsp. baking powder
- 2 eggs
- 1/2 cup milk
- 2 cups margarine milk
- 4 tablespoons margarine
- Zest from 1 lemon, grated
- 1 and 2/3 cup blueberries

Directions:
1. In a bowl, mix eggs with 2 tablespoons white sugar, 2 and 1/2 cups white flour, baking powder, baking soda, 2 eggs, milk, margarine milk, 4 tablespoons margarine,

lemon zest and blueberries, stir and pour into a pan that fits your air fryer.
2. In another bowls, mix 3 tablespoons brown sugar with 2 tablespoons white sugar, 4 tablespoons margarine, 1/2 cup flour and cinnamon, stir until you obtain a crumble and spread over blueberries mix.
3. Place in preheated air fryer and bake at 300 °F for 30 minutes.
4. Divide among plates and serve for breakfast.
- **Nutrition Info:** Calories 101 Fat 9.4 g Carbohydrates 0.3 g Sugar 0.2 g Protein 7 g Cholesterol 21 mg

98. Ricotta & Chorizo Corn Frittata

Servings:2
Cooking Time: 12 Minutes
Ingredients:
- 4 eggs, beaten
- 1 large potato, boiled and cubed
- ½ cup frozen corn
- ½ cup ricotta cheese, crumbled
- 1 tbsp chopped parsley
- ½ chorizo, sliced
- 1 tbsp olive oil
- Salt and black pepper to taste

Directions:
1. Preheat Breville on Bake function to 330 F. Cook the chorizo in a greased skillet over medium heat for 3 minutes; transfer to a baking dish. Mix the eggs, salt, and pepper in a bowl. Stir in the remaining ingredients. Pour the mixture over the chorizo and press Start. Cook for 25 minutes.

99. Fennel And Eggs Mix

Servings: 4
Cooking Time: 20 Minutes
Ingredients:
- 1 tablespoon avocado oil
- 1 yellow onion, chopped
- ½ teaspoon cumin, ground
- 1 teaspoon rosemary, dried
- 8 eggs, whisked
- 1 fennel bulb, shredded
- 1 tablespoon chives, chopped
- Salt and black pepper to the taste

Directions:
1. In a bowl, combine the onion with the eggs, fennel and the other ingredients except the oil and whisk.
2. Heat up your air fryer with the oil at 360 degrees F, add the oil, add the fennel mix, cover, cook for 20 minutes, divide between plates and serve for breakfast.
- **Nutrition Info:** calories 220, fat 11, fiber 3, carbs 4, protein 6

100. Hash Browns

Servings: 3
Cooking Time: 18 Minutes
Ingredients:

- 1 tsp flour
- 1 ½ pound potatoes peeled
- ½ shallot
- ½ tsp Cajun seasoning
- 1 egg white
- ½ tsp black pepper
- 1 tsp coconut oil

Directions:
1. Keep the peeled potatoes in a bowl of water and mix them with Cajun seasoning as well as flour. Grate the potatoes and pour some cold water with a little salt to reduce the starch content. Set this mixture aside.
2. Grate the shallot and set it aside, strain your potatoes using a fine strainer or cheesecloth. Ensure all the water has been strained out of the potatoes.
3. Mix the ingredients in a bowl except the potatoes and ensure that they are well combined. Add the potatoes and mix them thoroughly. Form several patties.
4. Place your instant air fryer at 400 degrees Fahrenheit. Once the fryer indicates add food, add the patties on the pan. Flip every time the panel indicates turn food.
5. Serve while hot.
- **Nutrition Info:** Calories 145 Fat 9g, Carbohydrates 15g, Proteins 1g, Sodium: 1990 Mg.

101. Avocado Oil Gluten Free Banana Bread Recipe

Servings:x
Cooking Time:x
Ingredients:
- 1/2 cup Granulated Sugar
- 1 cup Mashed Banana
- 1/2 cup Light Brown Sugar
- 1/3 cup Avocado Oil, (or canola oil)
- 2 cups All-Purpose Gluten Free Flour, (see notes)
- 3/4 teaspoon Xanthan Gum, (omit if your flour blend contains it)
- 1 teaspoon Baking Powder
- 1/2 teaspoon Baking Soda
- 1/2 teaspoon Fine Sea Salt
- 2 large Eggs, room temperature
- 2/3 cup Milk, (dairy free or regular milk), room temperature
- 1 teaspoon Pure Vanilla Extract

Directions:
1. Preheat oven to 350°F and spray a 9x9 inch square pan with non-stick spray and line with parchment paper.
2. In a large bowl, whisk together the flour, xanthan gum, baking powder, baking soda, salt, and granulated sugar.
3. In a separate bowl, whisk together the mashed banana, brown sugar, oil, eggs, milk, and vanilla extract. Pour the wet ingredients into the dry ingredients and stir to combine.

4. Pour the batter into the prepared pan and bake at 350°F for 25-30 minutes or until a toothpick or cake tester comes out clean or with a few moist crumbs attached. Cooking time will vary depending on your oven - mine took 29 minutes.
5. Cool the bread in the pan on a cooling rack. Cut into 16 pieces and serve slightly warm or room temperature.
6. To store, wrap tightly in foil or store slices in an air-tight container. It will stay fresh up to 3 days. This bread also freezes well. To freeze, slice into individual pieces and freeze in a freezer bag.

102.Baked Apple Breakfast Oats

Servings: 1
Cooking Time: 15 Minutes
Ingredients:
- 1/3 cup vanilla Greek yogurt
- 1/3 cup rolled oats
- 1 apple
- 1 tablespoon peanut butter

Directions:
1. Preheat toaster oven to 400°F and set it on the warm setting.
2. Cut apples into chunks approximately 1/2-inch-thick.
3. Place apples in an oven-safe dish with some space between each chunk and sprinkle with cinnamon.
4. Bake in the oven for 12 minutes.
5. Combine yogurt and oats in a bowl.
6. Remove the apples from the oven and combine with the yogurt.
7. Top with peanut butter for a delicious and high-protein breakfast.
- **Nutrition Info:** Calories: 350, Sodium: 134 mg, Dietary Fiber: 8.1 g, Total Fat: 11.2 g, Total Carbs: 52.5 g, Protein: 12.7 g.

103.Crustless Broccoli Quiche

Servings:4
Cooking Time: 10 Minutes
Ingredients:
- 1 cup broccoli florets
- ¾ cup chopped roasted red peppers
- 1¼ cups grated Fontina cheese
- 6 eggs
- ¾ cup heavy cream
- ½ teaspoon salt
- Freshly ground black pepper, to taste
- Cooking spray

Directions:
1. Spritz the baking pan with cooking spray
2. Add the broccoli florets and roasted red peppers to the pan and scatter the grated Fontina cheese on top.
3. In a bowl, beat together the eggs and heavy cream. Sprinkle with salt and pepper. Pour the egg mixture over the top of the cheese. Wrap the pan in foil.

4. Put the air fryer basket on the baking pan and slide into Rack Position 2, select Air Fry, set temperature to 325ºF (163ºC) and set time to 10 minutes.
5. After 8 minutes, remove the pan from the oven. Remove the foil. Return to the oven and continue to cook for another 2 minutes.
6. When cooked, the quiche should be golden brown.
7. Rest for 5 minutes before cutting into wedges and serve warm.

104.Breakfast Pockets

Servings: 4
Cooking Time: 30 Minutes
Ingredients:
- 2 sheets: 17.25 oz almond flour puff pastry, cut into 4 equal sized pieces
- 1 package: 6 oz.ground breakfast sausage, crumbled
- 2 eggs, lightly beaten
- 1 cup cheddar cheese, shredded
- 1 teaspoon kosher salt
- ½ teaspoon ground black pepper
- 2 tablespoons canola oil

Directions:
1. Preheat the Air fryer to 375-degree F and grease the Air fryer basket.
2. Arrange the sausages in the basket and roast for about 15 minutes.
3. Place the eggs into the basket and cook for about 5 minutes.
4. Season with salt and black pepper and divide the egg sausages mixture over the 4 puff pastry rectangles.
5. Top with shredded cheddar cheese and drizzle with canola oil.
6. Place 1 egg pocket in the basket and cook for 6 minutes at 400-degree F.
7. Remove from the Air fryer and repeat with the remaining pockets.
8. Serve warm and enjoy.
- **Nutrition Info:** Calories: 197, Fats: 15.4g, Carbs: 8.5g, Sugar: 1.1g, Proteins: 7.9g, Sodium: 203mg

105.Chives Salmon And Shrimp Bowls

Servings: 4
Cooking Time: 12 Minutes
Ingredients:
- 1 pound shrimp, peeled and deveined
- ½ pound salmon fillets, boneless and cubed
- 2 spring onions, chopped
- 2 teaspoons olive oil
- 1 cup baby kale
- Salt and black pepper to the taste
- 1 tablespoon chives, chopped

Directions:
1. Preheat the air fryer with the oil at 330 degrees F, add the shrimp, salmon and the other ingredients, toss gently and cook for 12 minutes.
2. Divide everything into bowls and serve.

- **Nutrition Info:** calories 244, fat 11, fiber 4, carbs 5, protein 7

106.Almond & Berry Oat Bars

Servings:6
Cooking Time: 35 Minutes + Cooling Time
Ingredients:
- 3 cups rolled oats
- ½ cup ground almonds
- ½ cup flour
- 1 tsp baking powder
- 1 tsp ground cinnamon
- 3 eggs, lightly beaten
- ½ cup canola oil
- ⅓ cup milk
- 2 tsp vanilla extract
- 2 cups mixed berries

Directions:
1. Spray a baking pan with cooking spray. In a bowl, add oats, almonds, flour, baking powder, and cinnamon in a bowl and stir well. In another bowl, whisk eggs, oil, milk, and vanilla.
2. Stir wet ingredients into oat mixture. Fold in the berries. Pour the mixture in the pan and place in the Breville. Cook for 25 minutes at 330 F on Bake function. Let cool before slicing into bars.

107.Ham And Cheese Bagel Sandwiches

Servings: 2
Cooking Time: 5 Minutes
Ingredients:
- 2 bagels
- 4 teaspoons honey mustard
- 4 slices cooked honey ham
- 4 slices Swiss cheese

Directions:
1. Start by preheating toaster oven to 400°F.
2. Spread honey mustard on each half of the bagel.
3. Add ham and cheese and close the bagel.
4. Bake the sandwich until the cheese is fully melted, approximately 5 minutes.
- **Nutrition Info:** Calories: 588, Sodium: 1450 mg, Dietary Fiber: 2.3 g, Total Fat: 20.1 g, Total Carbs: 62.9 g, Protein: 38.4 g.

108.Ham Egg Muffins

Servings: 12
Cooking Time: 20 Minutes
Ingredients:
- 12 eggs
- 2 cups ham, diced
- 1 3/4 cup cheddar cheese, shredded
- 1/2 pepper
- 1/2 tsp salt

Directions:
1. Fit the Cuisinart oven with the rack in position
2. Spray 12-cups muffin tin with cooking spray and set aside.
3. In a bowl, whisk eggs with pepper and salt.
4. Stir in cheddar cheese and ham.
5. Pour egg mixture into prepared muffin tin.
6. Set to bake at 375 F for 25 minutes, after 5 minutes, place the muffin tin in the oven.
7. Serve and enjoy.
- **Nutrition Info:** Calories 166 Fat 11.8 g Carbohydrates 1.5 g Sugar 0.4 g Protein 13.4 g Cholesterol 194 mg

109.Buttery Orange Toasts

Servings:6
Cooking Time: 15 Minutes
Ingredients:
- 12 bread slices
- ½ cup sugar
- 1 stick butter
- 1 ½ tbsp vanilla extract
- 1 ½ tbsp cinnamon
- 2 oranges, zested

Directions:
1. Mix butter, sugar, and vanilla extract and microwave the mixture for 30 seconds until it melts. Add in orange zest. Spread the mixture onto bread slices. Lay the bread slices on the cooking basket and cook in the Breville oven for 5 minutes at 400 F on Toast function. Serve warm.

110.Yogurt & Cream Cheese Zucchini Cakes

Servings: 4
Cooking Time: 20 Minutes
Ingredients:
- 1 ½ cups flour
- 1 tsp cinnamon
- 3 eggs
- 2 tsp baking powder
- 2 tbsp sugar
- 1 cup milk
- 2 tbsp butter, melted
- 1 tbsp yogurt
- ½ cup shredded zucchini
- 2 tbsp cream cheese

Directions:
1. In a bowl, whisk the eggs along with the sugar, salt, cinnamon, cream cheese, flour, and baking powder. In another bowl, combine all of the liquid ingredients. Gently combine the dry and liquid mixtures. Stir in zucchini.
2. Line muffin tins with baking paper, and pour the batter inside them. Arrange on the Air Fryer tray and cook for 15-18 minutes on Bake function at 380 F. Serve chilled.

111.Amazing Strawberry Pancake

Servings:4
Cooking Time: 30 Minutes
Ingredients:
- 3 eggs, beaten
- 2 tbsp unsalted butter

- ½ cup flour
- 2 tbsp sugar, powdered
- ½ cup milk
- 1 ½ cups fresh strawberries, sliced

Directions:
1. Preheat Breville to 330 F on Bake function. Add butter to a pan and melt over low heat. In a bowl, mix flour, milk, eggs, and vanilla. Add the mixture to the pan with melted butter.
2. Place the pan in the Breville oven and press Start. Cook for 14-16 minutes until the pancake is fluffy and golden brown. Drizzle powdered sugar and toss sliced strawberries on top.

112.Olives, Kale, And Pecorino Baked Eggs

Servings:2
Cooking Time: 11 Minutes
Ingredients:
- 1 cup roughly chopped kale leaves, stems and center ribs removed
- ¼ cup grated pecorino cheese
- ¼ cup olive oil
- 1 garlic clove, peeled
- 3 tablespoons whole almonds
- Kosher salt and freshly ground black pepper, to taste
- 4 large eggs
- 2 tablespoons heavy cream
- 3 tablespoons chopped pitted mixed olives

Directions:
1. Place the kale, pecorino, olive oil, garlic, almonds, salt, and pepper in a small blender and blitz until well incorporated.
2. One at a time, crack the eggs in the baking pan. Drizzle the kale pesto on top of the egg whites. Top the yolks with the cream and swirl together the yolks and the pesto.
3. Slide the baking pan into Rack Position 1, select Convection Bake, set temperature to 300ºF (150ºC) and set time to 11 minutes.
4. When cooked, the top should begin to brown and the eggs should be set.
5. Allow the eggs to cool for 5 minutes. Scatter the olives on top and serve warm.

113.Paprika Baked Eggs

Servings:6
Cooking Time: 10 Minutes
Ingredients:
- 6 large eggs
- 1 tsp paprika

Directions:
1. Preheat Breville fryer to 300 F. Lay the eggs in the basket and press Start. Cook for 8 minutes on Bake function. Using tongs, dip the eggs in a bowl with icy water. Let sit for 5 minutes before peeling. Slice, sprinkle with paprika, and serve.

114.Whole30 Creamy Mushroom Smothered Pork Chops

Servings:4
Cooking Time: 18 Minutes
Ingredients:
- 2 cloves garlic
- 4 boneless pork chops
- ½ tsp ground black pepper
- 1 ½ tsp kosher salt
- 1 tsp finely chopped rosemary leaves
- 2 tsp extra virgin oil
- 8 ounces mushrooms
- 1 cup unsweetened milk

Directions:
1. Season the 4 boneless porkchops with ½ tsp black pepper and 1 tsp kosher salt
2. Finely chop 2 cloves garlic, 1 tsp fresh rosemary leaves and thinly slice 8-ounce mushrooms.
3. Heat 2 tsp oil in a pan and add the pork chops while working in batches and cook them until they are golden brown. Once done transfer them into a plate.
4. Add the mushrooms and kosher salt and put them in a baking tray. Put your appliance on bake mode and put the chicken inside the baking tray. Allow it to cook until it is golden brown. Add the mushrooms and cook them until all of them have browned well.
5. Add mushrooms and ½ tsp of kosher salt and cook for 5 more minutes
6. add garlic and rosemary and allow it to add fragrance. Cook until you love your pork chops.
- **Nutrition Info:** Calories 473.1 Fat 33.1g, Carbs 4.8 g, Fiber 0.5g, Proteins 39.0g, Sodium: 679.4mg

115.Garlic And Cheese Bread Rolls

Servings: 2
Cooking Time: 5 Minutes
Ingredients:
- 8 tablespoons of grated cheese
- 6 tsp.s of melted margarine
- Garlic bread spice mix
- 2 bread rolls

Directions:
1. Slice the bread rolls from top in a crisscross pattern but not cut through at the bottom.
2. Put all the cheese into the slits and brush the tops of the bread rolls with melted margarine. Sprinkle the garlic mix on the rolls.
3. Heat the air fryer to 350°F. Place the rolls into the basket and cook until cheese is melted for about 5 minutes.
- **Nutrition Info:** Calories 113 Fat 8.2 g Carbohydrates 0.3 g Sugar 0.2 g Protein 5.4 g Cholesterol 18 mg

116.Spinach And Ricotta Pockets

Servings: 8 Pockets
Cooking Time: 10 Minutes
Ingredients:
- 2 large eggs, divided
- 1 tablespoon water
- 1 cup baby spinach, roughly chopped
- ¼ cup sun-dried tomatoes, finely chopped
- 1 cup ricotta cheese
- 1 cup basil, chopped
- ¼ teaspoon red pepper flakes
- ¼ teaspoon kosher salt
- 2 refrigerated rolled pie crusts
- 2 tablespoons sesame seeds

Directions:
1. Spritz the air fryer basket with cooking spray.
2. Whisk an egg with water in a small bowl.
3. Combine the spinach, tomatoes, the other egg, ricotta cheese, basil, red pepper flakes, and salt in a large bowl. Whisk to mix well.
4. Unfold the pie crusts on a clean work surface and slice each crust into 4 wedges. Scoop up 3 tablespoons of the spinach mixture on each crust and leave ½ inch space from edges.
5. Fold the crust wedges in half to wrap the filling and press the edges with a fork to seal.
6. Arrange the wraps in the pan and spritz with cooking spray. Sprinkle with sesame seeds.
7. Put the air fryer basket on the baking pan and slide into Rack Position 2, select Air Fry, set temperature to 380ºF (193ºC) and set time to 10 minutes.
8. Flip the wraps halfway through the cooking time.
9. When cooked, the wraps will be crispy and golden.
10. Serve immediately.

117.Cinnamon Sweet Potato Chips

Servings: 6 To 8 Slices
Cooking Time: 8 Minutes
Ingredients:
- 1 small sweet potato, cut into ⅜ inch-thick slices
- 2 tablespoons olive oil
- 1 to 2 teaspoon ground cinnamon

Directions:
1. Add the sweet potato slices and olive oil in a bowl and toss to coat. Fold in the cinnamon and stir to combine.
2. Lay the sweet potato slices in a single layer in the air fryer basket.
3. Put the air fryer basket on the baking pan and slide into Rack Position 2, select Air Fry, set temperature to 390ºF (199ºC), and set time to 8 minutes.
4. Stir the potato slices halfway through the cooking time.

5. When cooking is complete, the chips should be crisp. Remove the pan from the oven. Allow to cool for 5 minutes before serving.

118.Middle Eastern Shakshuka With Smoked Paprika

Servings:x
Cooking Time:x
Ingredients:
- 2 Tbsp olive oil
- ½ yellow onion, diced
- 1 small serrano or jalapeno chili, seeds removed, diced
- 1 tsp cumin
- 1 tsp paprika
- ½ tsp smoked paprika
- ¼ tsp coriander
- 2 eggs
- 1 can chopped tomatoes
- ½ green pepper, diced
- Salt and pepper, to taste
- Chopped parsley or cilantro

Directions:
1. Preheat Breville smart oven over medium heat.
2. Heat olive oil and saute onion until softened.
3. Add tomatoes, green pepper and chili. Cook for 4-5 minutes.
4. Add seasonings and cook for several minutes until liquid slightly reduces.
5. Make two indentations in mixture and crack eggs into them. Cover and
6. cook until eggs are done.
7. Sprinkle with salt, pepper, parsley and cilantro and serve while bubbly and hot.

119.Bacon And Hot Dogs Omelet

Servings: 2
Cooking Time: 10 Minutes
Ingredients:
- 4 eggs
- 1 bacon slice, chopped
- 2 hot dogs, chopped
- 2 small onions, chopped
- 2 tablespoons milk
- Salt and black pepper, to taste

Directions:
1. Preheat the Air fryer to 325 ºF and grease an Air Fryer pan.
2. Whisk together eggs and stir in the remaining ingredients.
3. Stir well to combine and place in the Air fryer.
4. Cook for about 10 minutes and serve hot.
- **Nutrition Info:** Calories: 418 Cal Total Fat: 31.5 g Saturated Fat: 0 g Cholesterol: 0 mg Sodium: 1000 mg Total Carbs: 9.7 g Fiber: 0 g Sugar: 5.6 g Protein: 23.4 g

120.Apple Butter Pancake

Servings:x
Cooking Time:x
Ingredients:
- 1 tsp cinnamon

- ½ tsp ginger
- 3 large eggs, room temperature
- ¾ cup whole milk
- ¾ cup all-purpose flour
- 1 tsp almond extract
- ¼ tsp salt
- 2 Granny Smith apples, peeled, cored and sliced
- 1 Tbsp sugar
- 4 Tbsp butter, divided
- 2 tsp light brown sugar

Directions:
1. Preheat oven to 400°F.
2. Whisk together eggs, milk, flour, extract and salt.
3. Place sliced apples in a bowl with sugar, cinnamon and ginger.
4. Melt 2 Tbsp butter in heated Breville smart oven.
5. Sprinkle brown sugar inside pot.
6. Add apples and cook until apples have softened. Transfer to plate.
7. Wipe out Breville smart oven and melt remaining 2 Tbsp butter.
8. When pot is very hot, add apples and pour batter. Bake for about 13-15 minutes.

121.Milky Semolina Cutlets

Servings: 2
Cooking Time: 15 | Minutes
Ingredients:
- 3 tablespoons of vegetable oil
- 1 cup of semolina
- 12 ounces of mixed vegetables (any of your choice), diced
- 2 & 1/2 pounds of milk
- 1/2tsp. salt
- 1/2 tsp. black pepper, ground

Directions:
1. Pour the milk into a sauce pan and heat. Add the mixed vegetables and allow it to cook until they are soft for about 3 minutes.
2. Add the pepper and salt and then the semolina. Cook until the mixture thicken; this will take about 10 minutes.
3. Grease a flat plate with oil; spread the semolina mixture on it. Refrigerate for about 4 hours until it is firm.
4. Heat the air fryer to 350°F.
5. Remove from the refrigerator and cut into flat round shapes. Brush the cutlets with oil and place them into the air fryer.
6. Cook for 10 minutes. Serve while hot with any sauce of your choice.
- **Nutrition Info:** Calories 117 Fat 8.4 g Carbohydrates 0.2 g Sugar 0.2 g Protein 5 g Cholesterol 18 mg

122.Zucchini Squash Pita Sandwiches Recipe

Servings:x
Cooking Time:x
Ingredients:
- 1 small Zucchini Squash, (5-6 ounces)

- Salt and Pepper, to taste
- 2 Whole Wheat Pitas
- 1/2 cup Hummus
- 1 1/2 cups Fresh Spinach, (2 handfuls)
- 1/2 cup Diced Red Bell Pepper, (about half a large pepper)
- 1/2 cup Chopped Red Onion, (about 1/4 a large onion)
- 2 teaspoons Olive Oil
- 1/4 teaspoon Dried Oregano
- 1/4 teaspoon Dried Thyme
- 1/4 teaspoon Garlic Powder
- 2 tablespoons Crumbled Feta Cheese, (about 1 ounce)

Directions:
1. Adjust the cooking rack to the lowest placement and preheat toaster oven to 425°F on the BAKE setting.
2. While the oven preheats, quarter the zucchini lengthwise and then cut into 1/2-inch thick pieces. Cut the bell pepper and onion into 1-inch thick pieces.
3. Add the vegetables to a roasting pan. Drizzle with oil and sprinkle over the oregano, garlic powder, and salt and pepper, to taste. Toss to combine.
4. Roast vegetables for 10 minutes. Carefully remove the pan and stir. Return pan to oven and continue cooking until the vegetables have softened and started to brown, about 5 minutes more. Remove from the toaster oven and set aside.
5. Reduce the temperature to 375°F and warm the pitas by placing them directly on the cooking rack for 1 to 2 minutes.
6. Spread warm pitas with hummus. Layer with spinach, roasted vegetables, and crumbled feta.

123.Tomato, Basil & Mozzarella Breakfast

Servings: 1
Cooking Time: 10 Minutes
Ingredients:
- 2 slices of bread
- 4 tomato slices
- 4 mozzarella slices
- 1 tbsp olive oil
- 1 tbsp chopped basil
- Salt and black pepper to taste

Directions:
1. Preheat Cuisinart on Toast function to 350 F. Place the bread slices in the toaster oven and toast for 5 minutes. Arrange two tomato slices on each bread slice. Season with salt and pepper.

124.Flavorful Zucchini Frittata

Servings: 4
Cooking Time: 25 Minutes
Ingredients:
- 6 eggs
- 2 cups zucchini, grated & squeeze out excess liquid
- 1 cup cheddar cheese, shredded
- 1 cup ham, chopped

- 1/4 cup heavy cream
- 2 tbsp butter
- 1/4 tsp pepper
- 1 tsp salt

Directions:
1. Fit the Cuisinart oven with the rack in position
2. Melt butter in a pan over medium heat.
3. Add zucchini in the pan and sauté until tender. Remove pan from heat.
4. In a bowl, whisk eggs and cream. Stir in zucchini, cheese, ham, pepper, and salt.
5. Pour mixture into the greased baking dish.
6. Set to bake at 325 F for 30 minutes. After 5 minutes place the baking dish in the preheated oven.
7. Serve and enjoy.
- **Nutrition Info:** Calories 349 Fat 27.5 g Carbohydrates 4.3 g Sugar 1.7 g Protein 21.8 gCholesterol 320 mg

125.Healthy Baked Oatmeal

Servings: 6
Cooking Time: 20 Minutes
Ingredients:
- 1 egg
- 1/3 cup dried cranberries
- 1 tsp vanilla
- 1 1/2 tsp cinnamon
- 2 tbsp butter, melted
- 1/2 cup applesauce
- 1 1/2 cups milk
- 1 tsp baking powder
- 1/3 cup light brown sugar
- 2 cups old fashioned oats
- 1/4 tsp salt

Directions:
1. Fit the Cuisinart oven with the rack in position
2. Grease 8*8-inch baking dish and set aside.
3. In a bowl, mix egg, vanilla, butter, applesauce, baking powder, cinnamon, brown sugar, oats, and salt.
4. Add milk and stir well.
5. Add cranberries and fold well.
6. Pour mixture into the prepared baking dish.
7. Set to bake at 350 F for 25 minutes. After 5 minutes place the baking dish in the preheated oven.
8. Serve and enjoy.
- **Nutrition Info:** Calories 330 Fat 9.3 g Carbohydrates 50.6 g Sugar 14.4 g Protein 9.7 g Cholesterol 42 mg

126.Banana Cake With Peanut Butter

Servings:2
Cooking Time: 35 Minutes
Ingredients:
- 1 cup + 1 tbsp flour
- 1 tsp baking powder
- ⅓ cup sugar
- 2 bananas, mashed
- ¼ cup vegetable oil
- 1 egg, beaten

- 1 tsp vanilla extract
- ¾ cup chopped walnuts
- ¼ tsp salt
- 2 tbsp peanut butter
- 2 tbsp sour cream

Directions:
1. Preheat Breville on AirFry function to 330 F. In a bowl, combine flour, salt, and baking powder In another bowl, combine bananas, oil, egg, peanut butter, vanilla, sugar, and sour cream.
2. Gently mix the both mixtures. Stir in the chopped walnuts. Pour the batter into a greased baking dish and press Start. Cook for 25 minutes. Serve chilled.

127.Cinnamon & Vanilla Toast

Servings:6
Cooking Time: 10 Minutes
Ingredients:
- 12 bread slices
- ½ cup sugar
- 1 ½ tsp cinnamon
- 1 stick of butter, softened
- 1 tsp vanilla extract

Directions:
1. Preheat Breville on Toast function to 300 F. Combine all ingredients, except the bread, in a bowl. Spread the buttery cinnamon mixture onto the bread slices. Place the bread slices in the oven and press Start. Cook for 8 minutes. Serve.

128.Golden Cod Tacos With Salsa

Servings:4
Cooking Time: 15 Minutes
Ingredients:
- 2 eggs
- 1¼ cups Mexican beer
- 1½ cups coconut flour
- 1½ cups almond flour
- ½ tablespoon chili powder
- 1 tablespoon cumin
- Salt, to taste
- 1 pound (454 g) cod fillet, slice into large pieces
- 4 toasted corn tortillas
- 4 large lettuce leaves, chopped
- ¼ cup salsa
- Cooking spray

Directions:
1. Spritz the air fryer basket with cooking spray.
2. Break the eggs in a bowl, then pour in the beer. Whisk to combine well.
3. Combine the coconut flour, almond flour, chili powder, cumin, and salt in a separate bowl. Stir to mix well.
4. Dunk the cod pieces in the egg mixture, then shake the excess off and dredge into the flour mixture to coat well. Arrange the cod in the pan.
5. Put the air fryer basket on the baking pan and slide into Rack Position 2, select Air Fry,

set temperature to 375ºF (190ºC) and set time to 15 minutes.

6. Flip the cod halfway through the cooking time.
7. When cooking is complete, the cod should be golden brown.
8. Unwrap the toasted tortillas on a large plate, then divide the cod and lettuce leaves on top. Baste with salsa and wrap to serve.

129.Rice, Shrimp, And Spinach Frittata

Servings:4
Cooking Time: 16 Minutes
Ingredients:
- 4 eggs
- Pinch salt
- ½ cup cooked rice
- ½ cup chopped cooked shrimp
- ½ cup baby spinach
- ½ cup grated Monterey Jack cheese
- Nonstick cooking spray

Directions:
1. Spritz the baking pan with nonstick cooking spray.
2. Whisk the eggs and salt in a small bowl until frothy.
3. Place the cooked rice, shrimp, and baby spinach in the baking pan. Pour in the whisked eggs and scatter the cheese on top.
4. Slide the baking pan into Rack Position 1, select Convection Bake, set temperature to 320ºF (160ºC) and set time to 16 minutes.
5. When cooking is complete, the frittata should be golden and puffy.
6. Let the frittata cool for 5 minutes before slicing to serve.

130.Mushroom Leek Frittata

Servings: 4
Cooking Time: 32 Minutes
Ingredients:
- 6 eggs
- 6 oz mushrooms, sliced 1 cup leeks, sliced
- Salt

Directions:
1. Preheat the air fryer to 325 F.
2. Spray air fryer baking dish with cooking spray and set aside.
3. Heat another pan over medium heat. Spray pan with cooking spray.
4. Add mushrooms, leeks, and salt in a pan sauté for 6 minutes.
5. Break eggs in a bowl and whisk well.
6. Transfer sautéed mushroom and leek mixture into the prepared baking dish.
7. Pour egg over mushroom mixture.
8. Place dish in the air fryer and cook for 32 minutes.
9. Serve and enjoy.
- **Nutrition Info:** Calories 116 Fat 7 g Carbohydrates 5.1 g Sugar 2.1 g Protein 10 g Cholesterol 245 mg

131.Chicken & Zucchini Omelet

Servings: 6

Cooking Time: 35 Minutes
Ingredients:
- 8 eggs
- ½ cup milk
- Salt and ground black pepper, as required
- 1 cup cooked chicken, chopped
- 1 cup Cheddar cheese, shredded
- ½ cup fresh chives, chopped
- ¾ cup zucchini, chopped

Directions:
1. In a bowl, add the eggs, milk, salt and black pepper and beat well.
2. Add the remaining ingredients and stir to combine.
3. Place the mixture into a greased baking pan.
4. Press "Power Button" of Air Fry Oven and turn the dial to select the "Air Bake" mode.
5. Press the Time button and again turn the dial to set the cooking time to 35 minutes.
6. Now push the Temp button and rotate the dial to set the temperature at 315 degrees F.
7. Press "Start/Pause" button to start.
8. When the unit beeps to show that it is preheated, open the lid.
9. Arrange pan over the "Wire Rack" and insert in the oven.
10. Cut into equal-sized wedges and serve hot.
- **Nutrition Info:** Calories 209 Total Fat 13.3 g Saturated Fat 6.3 g Cholesterol 258 mg Sodium 252 mg Total Carbs 2.3 g Fiber 0.3 g Sugar 1.8 g Protein 9.8 g

132.Spinach And Bacon Roll-ups

Servings:4
Cooking Time: 8 To 9 Minutes
Ingredients:
- 4 flour tortillas (6- or 7-inch size)
- 4 slices Swiss cheese
- 1 cup baby spinach leaves
- 4 slices turkey bacon
- Special Equipment:
- 4 toothpicks, soak in water for at least 30 minutes

Directions:
1. On a clean work surface, top each tortilla with one slice of cheese and ¼ cup of spinach, then tightly roll them up.
2. Wrap each tortilla with a strip of turkey bacon and secure with a toothpick.
3. Arrange the roll-ups in the air fryer basket, leaving space between each roll-up.
4. Put the air fryer basket on the baking pan and slide into Rack Position 2, select Air Fry, set temperature to 390ºF (199ºC), and set time to 8 minutes.
5. After 4 minutes, remove the pan from the oven. Flip the roll-ups with tongs and rearrange them for more even cooking. Return to the oven and continue cooking for another 4 minutes.
6. When cooking is complete, the bacon should be crisp. If necessary, continue cooking for 1 minute more. Remove the pan from the oven. Rest for 5 minutes and remove the toothpicks before serving.

133.Cheesy Breakfast Casserole

Servings:4
Cooking Time: 16 Minutes
Ingredients:
- 6 slices bacon
- 6 eggs
- Salt and pepper, to taste
- Cooking spray
- ½ cup chopped green bell pepper
- ½ cup chopped onion
- ¾ cup shredded Cheddar cheese

Directions:
1. Place the bacon in a skillet over medium-high heat and cook each side for about 4 minutes until evenly crisp. Remove from the heat to a paper towel-lined plate to drain. Crumble it into small pieces and set aside.
2. Whisk the eggs with the salt and pepper in a medium bowl.
3. Spritz the baking pan with cooking spray.
4. Place the whisked eggs, crumbled bacon, green bell pepper, and onion in the prepared pan.
5. Slide the baking pan into Rack Position 1, select Convection Bake, set temperature to 400ºF (205ºC) and set time to 8 minutes.
6. After 6 minutes, remove the pan from the oven. Scatter the Cheddar cheese all over. Return the pan to the oven and continue to cook for another 2 minutes.
7. When cooking is complete, let sit for 5 minutes and serve on plates.

134.Basil Dill Egg Muffins

Servings: 6
Cooking Time: 20 Minutes
Ingredients:
- 6 eggs
- 1 tbsp chives, chopped
- 1 tbsp fresh basil, chopped
- 1 tbsp fresh cilantro, chopped
- 1/4 cup mozzarella cheese, grated
- 1 tbsp fresh dill, chopped
- 1 tbsp fresh parsley, chopped
- Pepper
- Salt

Directions:
1. Fit the Cuisinart oven with the rack in position
2. Spray 6-cups muffin tin with cooking spray and set aside.
3. In a bowl, whisk eggs with pepper and salt.
4. Add remaining ingredients and stir well.
5. Pour egg mixture into the prepared muffin tin.
6. Set to bake at 350 F for 25 minutes. After 5 minutes place muffin tin in the preheated oven.
7. Serve and enjoy.

- **Nutrition Info:** Calories 68 Fat 4.6 g Carbohydrates 0.8 g Sugar 0.4 g Protein 6 g Cholesterol 164 mg

135.Wheat &seed Bread

Servings: 4
Cooking Time: 18 Minutes
Ingredients:
- 31/2 ounces of flour
- 1 tsp. of yeast
- 1 tsp. of salt
- 3 &1/2 ounces of wheat flour ¼ cup of pumpkin seeds

Directions:
1. Mix the wheat flour, yeast, salt, seeds and the plain flour together in a large bowl. Stir in ¾ cup of lukewarm water and keep stirring until dough becomes soft.
2. Knead for another 5 minutes until the dough becomes elastic and smooth. Mold into a ball and cover with a plastic bag. Set aside for 30 minutes for it to rise.
3. Heat your air fryer to 392°F.
4. Transfer the dough into a small pizza pan and place in the air fryer. Bake for 18 minutes until golden. Remove and place on a wire rack to cool.
- **Nutrition Info:** Calories 116 Fat 9.4 g Carbohydrates 0.3 g Sugar 0.2 g Protein 6 g Cholesterol 21 mg

136.Breakfast Blueberry Cobbler

Servings:4
Cooking Time: 15 Minutes
Ingredients:
- ¾ teaspoon baking powder
- $^1/_3$ cup whole-wheat pastry flour
- Dash sea salt
- $^1/_3$ cup unsweetened nondairy milk
- 2 tablespoons maple syrup
- ½ teaspoon vanilla
- Cooking spray
- ½ cup blueberries
- ¼ cup granola
- Nondairy yogurt, for topping (optional)

Directions:
1. Spritz the baking pan with cooking spray.
2. Mix together the baking powder, flour, and salt in a medium bowl. Add the milk, maple syrup, and vanilla and whisk to combine.
3. Scrape the mixture into the prepared pan. Scatter the blueberries and granola on top.
4. Slide the baking pan into Rack Position 1, select Convection Bake, set temperature to 347ºF (175ºC) and set time to 15 minutes.
5. When done, the top should begin to brown and a knife inserted in the center should come out clean.
6. Let the cobbler cool for 5 minutes and serve with a drizzle of nondairy yogurt.

LUNCH RECIPES

137.Greek Lamb Meatballs

Servings: 12
Cooking Time: 12 Minutes
Ingredients:

- 1 pound ground lamb
- ½ cup breadcrumbs
- ¼ cup milk
- 2 egg yolks
- 1 teaspoon ground coriander
- 1 teaspoon ground cumin
- 3 garlic cloves, minced
- 1 teaspoon dried oregano
- ½ teaspoon salt
- ½ teaspoon black pepper
- 1 lemon, juiced and zested
- ¼ cup fresh parsley, chopped
- ½ cup crumbled feta cheese
- Olive oil, for shaping
- Tzatziki, for dipping

Directions:

1. Combine all ingredients except olive oil in a large mixing bowl and mix until fully incorporated.
2. Form 12 meatballs, about 2 ounces each. Use olive oil on your hands so they don't stick to the meatballs. Set aside.
3. Select the Broil function on the COSORI Air Fryer Toaster Oven, set time to 12 minutes, then press Start/Cancel to preheat.
4. Place the meatballs on the food tray, then insert the tray at top position in the preheated air fryer toaster oven. Press Start/Cancel.
5. Take out the meatballs when done and serve with a side of tzatziki.
- **Nutrition Info:** Calories: 129 kcal Total Fat: 6.4 g Saturated Fat: 0 g Cholesterol: 0 mg Sodium: 0 mg Total Carbs: 4.9 g Fiber: 0 g Sugar: 0 g Protein: 12.9 g

138.Chicken Parmesan

Servings: 4
Cooking Time: 10 Minutes
Ingredients:

- 2 (6-oz.boneless, skinless chicken breasts
- 1 oz. pork rinds, crushed
- ½ cup grated Parmesan cheese, divided.
- 1 cup low-carb, no-sugar-added pasta sauce.
- 1 cup shredded mozzarella cheese, divided.
- 4 tbsp. full-fat mayonnaise, divided.
- ½ tsp. garlic powder.
- ¼ tsp. dried oregano.
- ½ tsp. dried parsley.

Directions:

1. Slice each chicken breast in half lengthwise and lb. out to 3/4-inch thickness. Sprinkle with garlic powder, oregano and parsley
2. Spread 1 tbsp. mayonnaise on top of each piece of chicken, then sprinkle ¼ cup mozzarella on each piece.

3. In a small bowl, mix the crushed pork rinds and Parmesan. Sprinkle the mixture on top of mozzarella
4. Pour sauce into 6-inch round baking pan and place chicken on top. Place pan into the air fryer basket. Adjust the temperature to 320 Degrees F and set the timer for 25 minutes
5. Cheese will be browned and internal temperature of the chicken will be at least 165 Degrees F when fully cooked. Serve warm.
- **Nutrition Info:** Calories: 393; Protein: 32g; Fiber: 1g; Fat: 28g; Carbs: 8g

139.Maple Chicken Thighs

Servings: 4
Cooking Time: 30 Minutes
Ingredients:

- 4 large chicken thighs, bone-in
- 2 tablespoons French mustard
- 2 tablespoons Dijon mustard
- 1 clove minced garlic
- 1/2 teaspoon dried marjoram
- 2 tablespoons maple syrup

Directions:

1. Mix chicken with everything in a bowl and coat it well.
2. Place the chicken along with its marinade in the baking pan.
3. Press "Power Button" of Air Fry Oven and turn the dial to select the "Bake" mode.
4. Press the Time button and again turn the dial to set the cooking time to 30 minutes.
5. Now push the Temp button and rotate the dial to set the temperature at 370 degrees F.
6. Once preheated, place the baking pan inside and close its lid.
7. Serve warm.
- **Nutrition Info:** Calories 301 Total Fat 15.8 g Saturated Fat 2.7 g Cholesterol 75 mg Sodium 189 mg Total Carbs 31.7 g Fiber 0.3 g Sugar 0.1 g Protein 28.2 g

140.Air Fryer Beef Steak

Servings: 4
Cooking Time: 15 Minutes
Ingredients:

- 1 tbsp. Olive oil
- Pepper and salt
- 2 pounds of ribeye steak

Directions:

1. Preparing the ingredients. Season meat on both sides with pepper and salt.
2. Rub all sides of meat with olive oil.
3. Preheat instant crisp air fryer to 356 degrees and spritz with olive oil.
4. Air frying. Close air fryer lid. Set temperature to 356°f, and set time to 7 minutes. Cook steak 7 minutes. Flip and cook an additional 6 minutes.

5. Let meat sit 2-5 minutes to rest. Slice and serve with salad.
- **Nutrition Info:** Calories: 233; Fat: 19g; Protein:16g; Sugar:0g

141.Parmigiano Reggiano And Prosciutto Toasts With Balsamic Glaze

Servings: 8
Cooking Time: 15 Minutes
Ingredients:
- 3 ounces thinly sliced prosciutto, cut crosswise into 1/4-inch-wide strips
- 1 (3-ounce) piece Parmigiano Reggiano cheese
- 1/2 cup balsamic vinegar
- 1 medium red onion, thinly sliced
- 1 loaf ciabatta, cut into 3/4-inch-thick slices
- 1 tablespoon extra-virgin olive oil
- 1 clove garlic
- Black pepper to taste

Directions:
1. Preheat toaster oven to 350°F.
2. Place onion in a bowl of cold water and let sit for 10 minutes.
3. Bring vinegar to a boil, then reduce heat and simmer for 5 minutes.
4. Remove from heat completely and set aside to allow the vinegar to thicken.
5. Drain the onion.
6. Brush the tops of each bun with oil, rub with garlic, and sprinkle with pepper.
7. Use a vegetable peeler to make large curls of Parmigiano Reggiano cheese and place them on the bun.
8. Bake for 15 minutes or until the bread just starts to crisp.
9. Sprinkle prosciutto and onions on top, then drizzle vinegar and serve.
- **Nutrition Info:** Calories: 154, Sodium: 432 mg, Dietary Fiber: 1.0 g, Total Fat: 5.6 g, Total Carbs: 17.3 g, Protein: 8.1 g.

142.Easy Turkey Breasts With Basil

Servings: 4
Cooking Time: 10 Minutes
Ingredients:
- 2 tablespoons olive oil
- 2 pounds turkey breasts, bone-in skin-on
- Coarse sea salt and ground black pepper, to taste
- 1 teaspoon fresh basil leaves, chopped
- 2 tablespoons lemon zest, grated

Directions:
1. Rub olive oil on all sides of the turkey breasts; sprinkle with salt, pepper, basil, and lemon zest.
2. Place the turkey breasts skin side up on a parchment-lined cooking basket.
3. Cook in the preheated Air Fryer at 330 degrees F for 30 minutes. Now, turn them over and cook an additional 28 minutes.
4. Serve with lemon wedges, if desired.

- **Nutrition Info:** 416 Calories; 26g Fat; 0g Carbs; 49g Protein; 0g Sugars; 2g Fiber

143.Garlic Chicken Potatoes

Servings: 4
Cooking Time: 30 Minutes
Ingredients:
- 2 lbs. red potatoes, quartered
- 3 tablespoons olive oil
- 1/2 teaspoon cumin seeds
- Salt and black pepper, to taste
- 4 garlic cloves, chopped
- 2 tablespoons brown sugar
- 1 lemon (1/2 juiced and 1/2 cut into wedges)
- Pinch of red pepper flakes
- 4 skinless, boneless chicken breasts
- 2 tablespoons cilantro, chopped

Directions:
1. Place the chicken, lemon, garlic, and potatoes in a baking pan.
2. Toss the spices, herbs, oil, and sugar in a bowl.
3. Add this mixture to the chicken and veggies then toss well to coat.
4. Press "Power Button" of Air Fry Oven and turn the dial to select the "Bake" mode.
5. Press the Time button and again turn the dial to set the cooking time to 30 minutes.
6. Now push the Temp button and rotate the dial to set the temperature at 400 degrees F.
7. Once preheated, place the baking pan inside and close its lid.
8. Serve warm.
- **Nutrition Info:** Calories 545 Total Fat 36.4 g Saturated Fat 10.1 g Cholesterol 200 mg Sodium 272 mg Total Carbs 40.7 g Fiber 0.2 g Sugar 0.1 g Protein 42.5 g

144.Chicken & Rice Casserole

Servings: 6
Cooking Time: 40 Minutes
Ingredients:
- 2 lbs. bone-in chicken thighs
- Salt and black pepper
- 1 teaspoon olive oil
- 5 cloves garlic, chopped
- 2 large onions, chopped
- 2 large red bell peppers, chopped
- 1 tablespoon sweet Hungarian paprika
- 1 teaspoon hot Hungarian paprika
- 2 tablespoons tomato paste
- 2 cups chicken broth
- 3 cups brown rice, thawed
- 2 tablespoons parsley, chopped
- 6 tablespoons sour cream

Directions:
1. Mix broth, tomato paste, and all the spices in a bowl.
2. Add chicken and mix well to coat.
3. Spread the rice in a casserole dish and add chicken along with its marinade.

4. Top the casserole with the rest of the Ingredients:.
5. Press "Power Button" of Air Fry Oven and turn the dial to select the "Bake" mode.
6. Press the Time button and again turn the dial to set the cooking time to 40 minutes.
7. Now push the Temp button and rotate the dial to set the temperature at 350 degrees F.
8. Once preheated, place the baking pan inside and close its lid.
9. Serve warm.
- **Nutrition Info:** Calories 440 Total Fat 7.9 g Saturated Fat 1.8 g Cholesterol 5 mg Sodium 581 mg Total Carbs 21.8 g Sugar 7.1 g Fiber 2.6 g Protein 37.2 g

145.Sweet Potato Chips

Servings: 2
Cooking Time: 40 Minutes
Ingredients:
- 2 sweet potatoes
- Salt and pepper to taste
- Olive oil
- Cinnamon

Directions:
1. Start by preheating toaster oven to 400°F.
2. Cut off each end of potato and discard.
3. Cut potatoes into 1/2-inch slices.
4. Brush a pan with olive oil and lay potato slices flat on the pan.
5. Bake for 20 minutes, then flip and bake for another 20.
- **Nutrition Info:** Calories: 139, Sodium: 29 mg, Dietary Fiber: 8.2 g, Total Fat: 0.5 g, Total Carbs: 34.1 g, Protein: 1.9 g.

146.Coconut Shrimp With Dip

Servings: 4
Cooking Time: 9 Minutes
Ingredients:
- 1 lb large raw shrimp peeled and deveined with tail on
- 2 eggs beaten
- ¼ cup Panko Breadcrumbs
- 1 tsp salt
- ¼ tsp black pepper
- ½ cup All-Purpose Flour
- ½ cup unsweetened shredded coconut
- Oil for spraying

Directions:
1. Clean and dry the shrimp. Set it aside.
2. Take 3 bowls. Put flour in the first bowl. Beat eggs in the second bowl. Mix coconut, breadcrumbs, salt, and black pepper in the third bowl.
3. Select the Air Fry option and adjust the temperature to 390°F. Push start and preheating will start.
4. Dip each shrimp in flour followed by the egg and then coconut mixture, ensuring shrimp is covered on all sides during each dip.
5. Once the preheating is done, place shrimp in a single layer on greased tray in the

basket of the Instant Pot Duo Crisp Air Fryer.
6. Spray the shrimp with oil lightly, and then close the Air Fryer basket lid. Cook for around 4 minutes.
7. After 4 minutes
8. open the Air Fryer basket lid and flip the shrimp over. Respray the shrimp with oil, close the Air Fryer basket lid, and cook for five more minutes.
9. Remove shrimp from the basket and serve with Thai Sweet Chili Sauce.
- **Nutrition Info:** Calories 279, Total Fat 11g, Total Carbs 17g, Protein 28g

147.Parmesan Chicken Meatballs

Servings: 4
Cooking Time: 12 Minutes
Ingredients:
- 1-lb. ground chicken
- 1 large egg, beaten
- ½ cup Parmesan cheese, grated
- ½ cup pork rinds, ground
- 1 teaspoon garlic powder
- 1 teaspoon paprika
- 1 teaspoon kosher salt
- ½ teaspoon pepper
- Crust:
- ½ cup pork rinds, ground

Directions:
1. Toss all the meatball Ingredients: in a bowl and mix well.
2. Make small meatballs out this mixture and roll them in the pork rinds.
3. Place the coated meatballs in the air fryer basket.
4. Press "Power Button" of Air Fry Oven and turn the dial to select the "Bake" mode.
5. Press the Time button and again turn the dial to set the cooking time to 12 minutes.
6. Now push the Temp button and rotate the dial to set the temperature at 400 degrees F.
7. Once preheated, place the air fryer basket inside and close its lid.
8. Serve warm.
- **Nutrition Info:** Calories 529 Total Fat 17 g Saturated Fat 3 g Cholesterol 65 mg Sodium 391 mg Total Carbs 55 g Fiber 6 g Sugar 8 g Protein 41g

148.Herbed Radish Sauté(3)

Servings: 4
Cooking Time: 12 Minutes
Ingredients:
- 2 bunches red radishes; halved
- 2 tbsp. parsley; chopped.
- 2 tbsp. balsamic vinegar
- 1 tbsp. olive oil
- Salt and black pepper to taste.

Directions:
1. Take a bowl and mix the radishes with the remaining ingredients except the parsley, toss and put them in your air fryer's basket.

2. Cook at 400°F for 15 minutes, divide between plates, sprinkle the parsley on top and serve as a side dish
- **Nutrition Info:** Calories: 180; Fat: 4g; Fiber: 2g; Carbs: 3g; Protein: 5g

149.Chicken Legs With Dilled Brussels Sprouts

Servings: 2
Cooking Time: 10 Minutes
Ingredients:
- 2 chicken legs
- 1/2 teaspoon paprika
- 1/2 teaspoon kosher salt
- 1/2 teaspoon black pepper
- 1/2 pound Brussels sprouts
- 1 teaspoon dill, fresh or dried

Directions:
1. Start by preheating your Air Fryer to 370 degrees F.
2. Now, season your chicken with paprika, salt, and pepper. Transfer the chicken legs to the cooking basket. Cook for 10 minutes.
3. Flip the chicken legs and cook an additional 10 minutes. Reserve.
4. Add the Brussels sprouts to the cooking basket; sprinkle with dill. Cook at 380 degrees F for 15 minutes, shaking the basket halfway through.
5. Serve with the reserved chicken legs.
- **Nutrition Info:** 365 Calories; 21g Fat; 3g Carbs; 36g Protein; 2g Sugars; 3g Fiber

150.Creamy Green Beans And Tomatoes

Servings: 4
Cooking Time: 20 Minutes
Ingredients:
- 1 pound green beans, trimmed and halved
- ½ pound cherry tomatoes, halved
- 2 tablespoons olive oil
- 1 teaspoon oregano, dried
- 1 teaspoon basil, dried
- Salt and black pepper to the taste
- 1 cup heavy cream
- ½ tablespoon cilantro, chopped

Directions:
1. In your air fryer's pan, combine the green beans with the tomatoes and the other Ingredients:, toss and cook at 360 degrees F for 20 minutes.
2. Divide the mix between plates and serve.
- **Nutrition Info:** Calories 174, fat 5, fiber 7, carbs 11, protein 4

151.Carrot And Beef Cocktail Balls

Servings: 10
Cooking Time: 20 Minutes
Ingredients:
- 1-pound ground beef
- 2 carrots
- 1 red onion, peeled and chopped
- 2 cloves garlic

- 1/2 teaspoon dried rosemary, crushed
- 1/2 teaspoon dried basil
- 1 teaspoon dried oregano
- 1 egg
- 3/4 cup breadcrumbs
- 1/2 teaspoon salt
- 1/2 teaspoon black pepper, or to taste
- 1 cup plain flour

Directions:
1. Preparing the ingredients. Place ground beef in a large bowl.
2. In a food processor, pulse the carrot, onion and garlic; transfer the vegetable mixture to a large-sized bowl.
3. Then, add the rosemary, basil, oregano, egg, breadcrumbs, salt, and black pepper.
4. Shape the mixture into even balls; refrigerate for about 30 minutes.
5. Roll the balls into the flour.
6. Air frying. Close air fryer lid.
7. Then, air-fry the balls at 350 degrees f for about 20 minutes, turning occasionally; work with batches. Serve with toothpicks.
- **Nutrition Info:** Calories 284 Total fat 7.9 g Saturated fat 1.4 g Cholesterol 36 mg Sodium 704 mg Total carbs 46 g Fiber 3.6 g Sugar 5.5 g Protein 17.9 g

152.Lamb Gyro

Servings: 4
Cooking Time: 25 Minutes
Ingredients:
- 1 pound ground lamb
- ¼ red onion, minced
- ¼ cup mint, minced
- ¼ cup parsley, minced
- 2 cloves garlic, minced
- ½ teaspoon salt
- ⅛ teaspoon rosemary
- ½ teaspoon black pepper
- 4 slices pita bread
- ¾ cup hummus
- 1 cup romaine lettuce, shredded
- ½ onion sliced
- 1 Roma tomato, diced
- ½ cucumber, skinned and thinly sliced
- 12 mint leaves, minced
- Tzatziki sauce, to taste

Directions:
1. Mix ground lamb, red onion, mint, parsley, garlic, salt, rosemary, and black pepper until fully incorporated.
2. Select the Broil function on the COSORI Air Fryer Toaster Oven, set time to 25 minutes and temperature to 450°F, then press Start/Cancel to preheat.
3. Line the food tray with parchment paper and place ground lamb on top, shaping it into a patty 1-inch-thick and 6 inches in diameter.

4. Insert the food tray at top position in the preheated air fryer toaster oven, then press Start/Cancel.
5. Remove when done and cut into thin slices.
6. Assemble each gyro starting with pita bread, then hummus, lamb meat, lettuce, onion, tomato, cucumber, and mint leaves, then drizzle with tzatziki.
7. Serve immediately.
- **Nutrition Info:** Calories: 409 kcal Total Fat: 14.6 g Saturated Fat: 0 g Cholesterol: 0 mg Sodium: 0 mg Total Carbs: 29.9 g Fiber: 0 g Sugar: 0 g Protein: 39.4 g

153.Air Fryer Fish

Servings: 4
Cooking Time: 17 Minutes
Ingredients:
- 4-6 Whiting Fish fillets cut in half
- Oil to mist
- Fish Seasoning
- ¾ cup very fine cornmeal
- ¼ cup flour
- 2 tsp old bay
- 1 ½ tsp salt
- 1 tsp paprika
- ½ tsp garlic powder
- ½ tsp black pepper

Directions:
1. Put the Ingredients: for fish seasoning in a Ziplock bag and shake it well. Set aside.
2. Rinse and pat dry the fish fillets with paper towels. Make sure that they still are damp.
3. Place the fish fillets in a ziplock bag and shake until they are completely covered with seasoning.
4. Place the fillets on a baking rack to let any excess flour to fall off.
5. Grease the bottom of the Instant Pot Duo Crisp Air Fryer basket tray and place the fillets on the tray. Close the lid, select the Air Fry option and cook filets on 400°F for 10 minutes.
6. Open the Air Fryer lid and spray the fish with oil on the side facing up before flipping it over, ensure that the fish is fully coated. Flip and cook another side of the fish for 7 minutes. Remove the fish and serve.
- **Nutrition Info:** Calories 193, Total Fat 1g, Total Carbs 27g, Protein 19g

154.Cheese-stuffed Meatballs

Servings: 4
Cooking Time: 10 Minutes
Ingredients:
- ⅓ cup soft bread crumbs
- 3 tablespoons milk
- 1 tablespoon ketchup
- 1 egg
- ½ teaspoon dried marjoram
- Pinch salt
- Freshly ground black pepper

- 1-pound 95 percent lean ground beef
- 20 ½-inch cubes of cheese
- Olive oil for misting

Directions:
1. Preparing the ingredients. In a large bowl, combine the bread crumbs, milk, ketchup, egg, marjoram, salt, and pepper, and mix well. Add the ground beef and mix gently but thoroughly with your hands. Form the mixture into 20 meatballs. Shape each meatball around a cheese cube. Mist the meatballs with olive oil and put into the instant crisp air fryer basket.
2. Air frying. Close air fryer lid. Bake for 10 to 13 minutes or until the meatballs register 165°f on a meat thermometer.
- **Nutrition Info:** Calories: 393; Fat: 17g; Protein:50g; Fiber:0g

155.Sweet Potato And Parsnip Spiralized Latkes

Servings: 12
Cooking Time: 20 Minutes
Ingredients:
- 1 medium sweet potato
- 1 large parsnip
- 4 cups water
- 1 egg + 1 egg white
- 2 scallions
- 1/2 teaspoon garlic powder
- 1/2 teaspoon sea salt
- 1/2 teaspoon ground pepper

Directions:
1. Start by spiralizing the sweet potato and parsnip and chopping the scallions, reserving only the green parts.
2. Preheat toaster oven to 425°F.
3. Bring 4 cups of water to a boil. Place all of your noodles in a colander and pour the boiling water over the top, draining well.
4. Let the noodles cool, then grab handfuls and place them in a paper towel; squeeze to remove as much liquid as possible.
5. In a large bowl, beat egg and egg white together. Add noodles, scallions, garlic powder, salt, and pepper, mix well.
6. Prepare a baking sheet; scoop out 1/4 cup of mixture at a time and place on sheet.
7. Slightly press down each scoop with your hands, then bake for 20 minutes, flipping halfway through.
- **Nutrition Info:** Calories: 24, Sodium: 91 mg, Dietary Fiber: 1.0 g, Total Fat: 0.4 g, Total Carbs: 4.3 g, Protein: 0.9 g.

156.Chicken Breasts With Chimichurri

Servings: 1
Cooking Time: 35 Minutes
Ingredients:
- 1 chicken breast, bone-in, skin-on
- Chimichurri
- ½ bunch fresh cilantro

- 1/4 bunch fresh parsley
- ½ shallot, peeled, cut in quarters
- ½ tablespoon paprika ground
- ½ tablespoon chili powder
- ½ tablespoon fennel ground
- ½ teaspoon black pepper, ground
- ½ teaspoon onion powder
- 1 teaspoon salt
- ½ teaspoon garlic powder
- ½ teaspoon cumin ground
- ½ tablespoon canola oil
- Chimichurri
- 2 tablespoons olive oil
- 4 garlic cloves, peeled
- Zest and juice of 1 lemon
- 1 teaspoon kosher salt

Directions:
1. Preheat the Air fryer to 300 degree F and grease an Air fryer basket.
2. Combine all the spices in a suitable bowl and season the chicken with it.
3. Sprinkle with canola oil and arrange the chicken in the Air fryer basket.
4. Cook for about 35 minutes and dish out in a platter.
5. Put all the ingredients in the blender and blend until smooth.
6. Serve the chicken with chimichurri sauce.
- **Nutrition Info:** Calories: 140, Fats: 7.9g, Carbohydrates: 1.8g, Sugar: 7.1g, Proteins: 7.2g, Sodium: 581mg

157. Turkey And Almonds

Servings: 2
Cooking Time: 10 Minutes
Ingredients:
- 1 big turkey breast, skinless; boneless and halved
- 2 shallots; chopped
- 1/3 cup almonds; chopped
- 1 tbsp. sweet paprika
- 2 tbsp. olive oil
- Salt and black pepper to taste.

Directions:
1. In a pan that fits the air fryer, combine the turkey with all the other ingredients, toss.
2. Put the pan in the machine and cook at 370°F for 25 minutes
3. Divide everything between plates and serve.
- **Nutrition Info:** Calories: 274; Fat: 12g; Fiber: 3g; Carbs: 5g; Protein: 14g

158. Balsamic Roasted Chicken

Servings: 4
Cooking Time: 1 Hour
Ingredients:
- 1/2 cup balsamic vinegar
- 1/4 cup Dijon mustard
- 1/3 cup olive oil
- Juice and zest from 1 lemon
- 3 minced garlic cloves
- 1 teaspoon salt

- 1 teaspoon pepper
- 4 bone-in, skin-on chicken thighs
- 4 bone-in, skin-on chicken drumsticks
- 1 tablespoon chopped parsley

Directions:
1. Mix vinegar, lemon juice, mustard, olive oil, garlic, salt, and pepper in a bowl, then pour into a sauce pan.
2. Roll chicken pieces in the pan, then cover and marinate for at least 2 hours, but up to 24 hours.
3. Preheat the toaster oven to 400°F and place the chicken on a fresh baking sheet, reserving the marinade for later.
4. Roast the chicken for 50 minutes.
5. Remove the chicken and cover it with foil to keep it warm. Place the marinade in the toaster oven for about 5 minutes until it simmers down and begins to thicken.
6. Pour marinade over chicken and sprinkle with parsley and lemon zest.
- **Nutrition Info:** Calories: 1537, Sodium: 1383 mg, Dietary Fiber: 0.8 g, Total Fat: 70.5 g, Total Carbs: 2.4 g, Protein: 210.4 g.

159. Chicken Wings With Prawn Paste

Servings: 6
Cooking Time: 8 Minutes
Ingredients:
- Corn flour, as required
- 2 pounds mid-joint chicken wings
- 2 tablespoons prawn paste
- 4 tablespoons olive oil
- 1½ teaspoons sugar
- 2 teaspoons sesame oil
- 1 teaspoon Shaoxing wine
- 2 teaspoons fresh ginger juice

Directions:
1. Preheat the Air fryer to 360 degree F and grease an Air fryer basket.
2. Mix all the ingredients in a bowl except wings and corn flour.
3. Rub the chicken wings generously with marinade and refrigerate overnight.
4. Coat the chicken wings evenly with corn flour and keep aside.
5. Set the Air fryer to 390 degree F and arrange the chicken wings in the Air fryer basket.
6. Cook for about 8 minutes and dish out to serve hot.
- **Nutrition Info:** Calories: 416, Fat: 31.5g, Carbohydrates: 11.2g, Sugar: 1.6g, Protein: 24.4g, Sodium: 661mg

160. Simple Lamb Bbq With Herbed Salt

Servings: 8
Cooking Time: 1 Hour 20 Minutes
Ingredients:
- 2 ½ tablespoons herb salt
- 2 tablespoons olive oil
- 4 pounds boneless leg of lamb, cut into 2-inch chunks

Directions:
1. Preheat the air fryer to 390 ºF.
2. Place the grill pan accessory in the air fryer.
3. Season the meat with the herb salt and brush with olive oil.
4. Grill the meat for 20 minutes per batch.
5. Make sure to flip the meat every 10 minutes for even cooking.
- **Nutrition Info:** Calories: 347 kcal Total Fat: 17.8 g Saturated Fat: 0 g Cholesterol: 0 mg Sodium: 0 mg Total Carbs: 0 g Fiber: 0 g Sugar: 0 g Protein: 46.6 g

161.Delightful Turkey Wings

Servings: 4
Cooking Time: 26 Minutes
Ingredients:
- 2 pounds turkey wings
- 4 tablespoons chicken rub
- 3 tablespoons olive oil

Directions:
1. Preheat the Air fryer to 380 degree F and grease an Air fryer basket.
2. Mix the turkey wings, chicken rub, and olive oil in a bowl until well combined.
3. Arrange the turkey wings into the Air fryer basket and cook for about 26 minutes, flipping once in between.
4. Dish out the turkey wings in a platter and serve hot.
- **Nutrition Info:** Calories: 204, Fat: 15.5g, Carbohydrates: 3g, Sugar: 0g, Protein: 12g, Sodium: 465mg

162.Vegetarian Philly Sandwich

Servings: 2
Cooking Time: 20 Minutes
Ingredients:
- 2 tablespoons olive oil
- 8 ounces sliced portabello mushrooms
- 1 vidalia onion, thinly sliced
- 1 green bell pepper, thinly sliced
- 1 red bell pepper, thinly sliced
- Salt and pepper
- 4 slices 2% provolone cheese
- 4 rolls

Directions:
1. Preheat toaster oven to 475°F.
2. Heat the oil in a medium sauce pan over medium heat.
3. Sauté mushrooms about 5 minutes, then add the onions and peppers and sauté another 10 minutes.
4. Slice rolls lengthwise and divide the vegetables into each roll.
5. Add the cheese and toast until the rolls start to brown and the cheese melts.
- **Nutrition Info:** Calories: 645, Sodium: 916 mg, Dietary Fiber: 7.2 g, Total Fat: 33.3 g, Total Carbs: 61.8 g, Protein: 27.1 g.

163.Onion Omelet

Servings: 2

Cooking Time: 15 Minutes
Ingredients:
- 4 eggs
- ¼ teaspoon low-sodium soy sauce
- Ground black pepper, as required
- 1 teaspoon butter
- 1 medium yellow onion, sliced
- ¼ cup Cheddar cheese, grated

Directions:
1. In a skillet, melt the butter over medium heat and cook the onion and cook for about 8-10 minutes.
2. Remove from the heat and set aside to cool slightly.
3. Meanwhile, in a bowl, add the eggs, soy sauce and black pepper and beat well.
4. Add the cooked onion and gently, stir to combine.
5. Place the zucchini mixture into a small baking pan.
6. Press "Power Button" of Air Fry Oven and turn the dial to select the "Air Fry" mode.
7. Press the Time button and again turn the dial to set the cooking time to 5 minutes.
8. Now push the Temp button and rotate the dial to set the temperature at 355 degrees F.
9. Press "Start/Pause" button to start.
10. When the unit beeps to show that it is preheated, open the lid.
11. Arrange pan over the "Wire Rack" and insert in the oven.
12. Cut the omelet into 2 portions and serve hot.
- **Nutrition Info:** Calories: 222 Cal Total Fat: 15.4 g Saturated Fat: 6.9 g Cholesterol: 347 mg Sodium: 264 mg Total Carbs: 6.1 g Fiber: 1.2 g Sugar: 3.1 g Protein: 15.3 g

164.Buttery Artichokes

Servings: 4
Cooking Time: 20 Minutes
Ingredients:
- 4 artichokes, trimmed and halved
- 3 garlic cloves, minced
- 1 tablespoon olive oil
- Salt and black pepper to the taste
- 4 tablespoons butter, melted
- ¼ teaspoon cumin, ground
- 1 tablespoon lemon zest, grated

Directions:
1. In a bowl, combine the artichokes with the oil, garlic and the other Ingredients:, toss well and transfer them to the air fryer's basket.
2. Cook for 20 minutes at 370 degrees F, divide between plates and serve as a side dish.
- **Nutrition Info:** Calories 214, fat 5, fiber 8, carbs 12, protein 5

165.Herbed Duck Legs

Servings: 2
Cooking Time: 30 Minutes
Ingredients:

- ½ tablespoon fresh thyme, chopped
- ½ tablespoon fresh parsley, chopped
- 2 duck legs
- 1 garlic clove, minced
- 1 teaspoon five spice powder
- Salt and black pepper, as required

Directions:
1. Preheat the Air fryer to 340 degree F and grease an Air fryer basket.
2. Mix the garlic, herbs, five spice powder, salt, and black pepper in a bowl.
3. Rub the duck legs with garlic mixture generously and arrange into the Air fryer basket.
4. Cook for about 25 minutes and set the Air fryer to 390 degree F.
5. Cook for 5 more minutes and dish out to serve hot.
- **Nutrition Info:** Calories: 138, Fat: 4.5g, Carbohydrates: 1g, Sugar: 0g, Protein: 25g, Sodium: 82mg

166. Turkey Legs

Servings: 2
Cooking Time: 40 Minutes
Ingredients:
- 2 large turkey legs
- 1 1/2 tsp smoked paprika
- 1 tsp brown sugar
- 1 tsp season salt
- ½ tsp garlic powder
- oil for spraying avocado, canola, etc.

Directions:
1. Mix the smoked paprika, brown sugar, seasoned salt, garlic powder thoroughly.
2. Wash and pat dry the turkey legs.
3. Rub the made seasoning mixture all over the turkey legs making sure to get under the skin also.
4. While preparing for cooking, select the Air Fry option. Press start to begin preheating.
5. Once the preheating temperature is reached, place the turkey legs on the tray in the Instant Pot Duo Crisp Air Fryer basket. Lightly spray them with oil.
6. Air Fry the turkey legs on 400°F for 20 minutes. Then, open the Air Fryer lid and flip the turkey legs and lightly spray with oil. Close the Instant Pot Duo Crisp Air Fryer lid and cook for 20 more minutes.
7. Remove and Enjoy.
- **Nutrition Info:** Calories 958, Total Fat 46g, Total Carbs 3g, Protein 133g

167. Squash And Zucchini Mini Pizza

Servings: 4
Cooking Time: 15 Minutes
Ingredients:
- 1 pizza crust
- 1/2 cup parmesan cheese
- 4 tablespoons oregano
- 1 zucchini

- 1 yellow summer squash
- Olive oil
- Salt and pepper

Directions:
1. Start by preheating toaster oven to 350°F.
2. If you are using homemade crust, roll out 8 mini portions; if crust is store-bought, use a cookie cutter to cut out the portions.
3. Sprinkle parmesan and oregano equally on each piece. Layer the zucchini and squash in a circle – one on top of the other – around the entire circle.
4. Brush with olive oil and sprinkle salt and pepper to taste.
5. Bake for 15 minutes and serve.
- **Nutrition Info:** Calories: 151, Sodium: 327 mg, Dietary Fiber: 3.1 g, Total Fat: 8.6 g, Total Carbs: 10.3 g, Protein: 11.4 g.

168. Crisp Chicken Casserole

Servings: 4
Cooking Time: 15 Minutes
Ingredients:
- 3 cup chicken, shredded
- 12 oz bag egg noodles
- 1/2 large onion
- 1/2 cup chopped carrots
- 1/4 cup frozen peas
- 1/4 cup frozen broccoli pieces
- 2 stalks celery chopped
- 5 cup chicken broth
- 1 tsp garlic powder
- salt and pepper to taste
- 1 cup cheddar cheese, shredded
- 1 package French's onions
- 1/4 cup sour cream
- 1 can cream of chicken and mushroom soup

Directions:
1. Place the chicken, vegetables, garlic powder, salt and pepper, and broth and stir. Then place it into the Instant Pot Duo Crisp Air Fryer Basket.
2. Press or lightly stir the egg noodles into the mix until damp/wet.
3. Select the option Air Fryer and cook for 4 minutes.
4. Stir in the sour cream, can of soup, cheese, and 1/3 of the French's onions.
5. Top with the remaining French's onions and close the Air Fryer lid and cook for about 10 more minutes.
- **Nutrition Info:** Calories 301, Total Fat 17g, Total Carbs 17g, Protein 20g

169. Tomato Frittata

Servings: 2
Cooking Time: 30 Minutes
Ingredients:
- 4 eggs
- ¼ cup onion, chopped
- ½ cup tomatoes, chopped
- ½ cup milk

- 1 cup Gouda cheese, shredded
- Salt, as required

Directions:
1. In a small baking pan, add all the ingredients and mix well.
2. Press "Power Button" of Air Fry Oven and turn the dial to select the "Air Fry" mode.
3. Press the Time button and again turn the dial to set the cooking time to 30 minutes.
4. Now push the Temp button and rotate the dial to set the temperature at 340 degrees F.
5. Press "Start/Pause" button to start.
6. When the unit beeps to show that it is preheated, open the lid.
7. Arrange the baking pan over the "Wire Rack" and insert in the oven.
8. Cut into 2 wedges and serve.
- **Nutrition Info:** Calories: 247 Cal Total Fat: 16.1 g Saturated Fat: 7.5 g Cholesterol: 332 mg Sodium: 417 mg Total Carbs: 7.30 g Fiber: 0.9 g Sugar: 5.2 g Protein: 18.6 g

170.Fried Chicken Tacos

Servings: 4
Cooking Time: 10 Minutes
Ingredients:
- Chicken
- 1 lb. chicken tenders or breast chopped into 2-inch pieces
- 1 tsp garlic powder
- ½ tsp onion powder
- 1 large egg
- 1 ½ tsp salt
- 1 tsp paprika
- 3 Tbsp buttermilk
- ¾ cup All-purpose flour
- 3 Tbsp corn starch
- ½ tsp black pepper
- ½ tsp cayenne pepper
- oil for spraying
- Coleslaw
- ¼ tsp red pepper flakes
- 2 cups coleslaw mix
- 1 Tbsp brown sugar
- ½ tsp salt
- 2 Tbsp apple cider vinegar
- 1 Tbsp water
- Spicy Mayo
- ½ tsp salt
- ¼ cup mayonnaise
- 1 tsp garlic powder
- 2 Tbsp hot sauce
- 1 Tbsp buttermilk
- Tortilla wrappers

Directions:
1. Take a large bowl and mix together coleslaw mix, water, brown sugar, salt, apple cider vinegar, and red pepper flakes. Set aside.
2. Take another small bowl and combine mayonnaise, hot sauce, buttermilk, garlic powder, and salt. Set this mixture aside.

3. Select the Instant Pot Duo Crisp Air Fryer option, adjust the temperature to 360°F and push start. Preheating will start.
4. Create a clear station by placing two large flat pans side by side. Whisk together egg and buttermilk with salt and pepper in one of them. In the second, whisk flour, corn starch, black pepper, garlic powder, onion powder, salt, paprika, and cayenne pepper.
5. Cut the chicken tenders into 1-inch pieces. Season all pieces with a little salt and pepper.
6. Once the Instant Pot Duo Crisp Air Fryer is preheated, remove the tray and lightly spray it with oil. Coat your chicken with egg mixture while shaking off any excess egg, followed by the flour mixture, and place it on the tray and tray in the basket, making sure your chicken pieces don't overlap.
7. Close the Air Fryer lid, and cook on 360°F for 10 minutes
8. while flipping and spraying halfway through cooking.
9. Once the chicken is done, remove and place chicken into warmed tortilla shells. Top with coleslaw and spicy mayonnaise.
- **Nutrition Info:** Calories 375, Total Fat 15g, Total Carbs 31g, Protein 29g

171.Green Bean Casserole(2)

Servings: 4
Cooking Time: 12 Minutes
Ingredients:
- 1 lb. fresh green beans, edges trimmed
- ½ oz. pork rinds, finely ground
- 1 oz. full-fat cream cheese
- ½ cup heavy whipping cream.
- ¼ cup diced yellow onion
- ½ cup chopped white mushrooms
- ½ cup chicken broth
- 4 tbsp. unsalted butter.
- ¼ tsp. xanthan gum

Directions:
1. In a medium skillet over medium heat, melt the butter. Sauté the onion and mushrooms until they become soft and fragrant, about 3–5 minutes.
2. Add the heavy whipping cream, cream cheese and broth to the pan. Whisk until smooth. Bring to a boil and then reduce to a simmer. Sprinkle the xanthan gum into the pan and remove from heat
3. Chop the green beans into 2-inch pieces and place into a 4-cup round baking dish. Pour the sauce mixture over them and stir until coated. Top the dish with ground pork rinds. Place into the air fryer basket
4. Adjust the temperature to 320 Degrees F and set the timer for 15 minutes. Top will be golden and green beans fork tender when fully cooked. Serve warm.
- **Nutrition Info:** Calories: 267; Protein: 6g; Fiber: 2g; Fat: 24g; Carbs: 7g

172. Pecan Crunch Catfish And Asparagus

Servings: 4
Cooking Time: 12 Minutes
Ingredients:
- 1 cup whole wheat panko breadcrumbs
- 1/4 cup chopped pecans
- 3 teaspoons chopped fresh thyme
- 1-1/2 tablespoons extra-virgin olive oil, plus more for the pan
- Salt and pepper to taste
- 1-1/4 pounds asparagus
- 1 tablespoon honey
- 4 (5- to 6-ounce each) catfish filets

Directions:
1. Start by preheating toaster oven to 425°F.
2. Combine breadcrumbs, pecans, 2 teaspoons thyme, 1 tablespoon oil, salt, pepper and 2 tablespoons water.
3. In another bowl combine asparagus, the rest of the thyme, honey, salt, and pepper.
4. Spread the asparagus in a flat layer on a baking sheet. Sprinkle a quarter of the breadcrumb mixture over the asparagus.
5. Lay the catfish over the asparagus and press the rest of the breadcrumb mixture into each piece. Roast for 12 minutes.
- **Nutrition Info:** Calories: 531, Sodium: 291 mg, Dietary Fiber: 6.1 g, Total Fat: 30.4 g, Total Carbs: 31.9 g, Protein: 34.8 g.

173. Air Fried Sausages

Servings: 6
Cooking Time: 13 Minutes
Ingredients:
- 6 sausage
- olive oil spray

Directions:
1. Pour 5 cup of water into Instant Pot Duo Crisp Air Fryer. Place air fryer basket inside the pot, spray inside with nonstick spray and put sausage links inside.
2. Close the Air Fryer lid and steam for about 5 minutes.
3. Remove the lid once done. Spray links with olive oil and close air crisp lid.
4. Set to air crisp at 400°F for 8 min flipping halfway through so both sides get browned.
- **Nutrition Info:** Calories 267, Total Fat 23g, Total Carbs 2g, Protein 13g

174. Rosemary Lemon Chicken

Servings: 8
Cooking Time: 45 Minutes
Ingredients:
- 4-lb. chicken, cut into pieces
- Salt and black pepper, to taste
- Flour for dredging 3 tablespoons olive oil
- 1 large onion, sliced
- Peel of ½ lemon
- 2 large garlic cloves, minced
- 1 1/2 teaspoons rosemary leaves
- 1 tablespoon honey
- 1/4 cup lemon juice
- 1 cup chicken broth

Directions:
1. Dredges the chicken through the flour then place in the baking pan.
2. Whisk broth with the rest of the Ingredients: in a bowl.
3. Pour this mixture over the dredged chicken in the pan.
4. Press "Power Button" of Air Fry Oven and turn the dial to select the "Bake" mode.
5. Press the Time button and again turn the dial to set the cooking time to 45 minutes.
6. Now push the Temp button and rotate the dial to set the temperature at 400 degrees F.
7. Once preheated, place the baking pan inside and close its lid.
8. Baste the chicken with its sauce every 15 minutes.
9. Serve warm.
- **Nutrition Info:** Calories 405 Total Fat 22.7 g Saturated Fat 6.1 g Cholesterol 4 mg Sodium 227 mg Total Carbs 26.1 g Fiber 1.4 g Sugar 0.9 g Protein 45.2 g

175. Dijon And Swiss Croque Monsieur

Servings: 2
Cooking Time: 13 Minutes
Ingredients:
- 4 slices white bread
- 2 tablespoons unsalted butter
- 1 tablespoon all-purpose flour
- 1/2 cup whole milk
- 3/4 cups shredded Swiss cheese
- 1/4 teaspoon freshly ground black pepper
- 1/8 teaspoon salt
- 1 tablespoon Dijon mustard
- 4 slices ham

Directions:
1. Start by cutting crusts off bread and placing them on a pan lined with parchment paper.
2. Melt 1 tablespoon of butter in a sauce pan, then dab the top sides of each piece of bread with butter.
3. Toast bread inoven for 3-5 minutes until each piece is golden brown.
4. Melt the second tablespoon of butter in the sauce pan and add the flour, mix together until they form a paste.
5. Add the milk and continue to mix until the sauce begins to thicken.
6. Remove from heat and mix in 1 tablespoon of Swiss cheese, salt, and pepper; continue stirring until cheese is melted.
7. Flip the bread over in the pan so the untoasted side is facing up.
8. Set two slices aside and spread Dijon on the other two slices.
9. Add ham and sprinkle 1/4 cup Swiss over each piece.
10. Broil for about 3 minutes.
11. Top the sandwiches off with the other slices of bread, soft-side down.

12. Top with sauce and sprinkle with remaining Swiss. Toast for another 5 minutes or until the cheese is golden brown.
13. Serve immediately.
- **Nutrition Info:** Calories: 452, Sodium: 1273 mg, Dietary Fiber: 1.6 g, Total Fat: 30.5 g, Total Carbs: 19.8 g, Protein: 24.4 g.

176.Oregano Chicken Breast

Servings: 6
Cooking Time: 25 Minutes
Ingredients:
- 2 lbs. chicken breasts, minced
- 1 tablespoon avocado oil
- 1 teaspoon smoked paprika
- 1 teaspoon garlic powder
- 1 teaspoon oregano
- 1/2 teaspoon salt
- Black pepper, to taste

Directions:
1. Toss all the meatball Ingredients: in a bowl and mix well.
2. Make small meatballs out this mixture and place them in the air fryer basket.
3. Press "Power Button" of Air Fry Oven and turn the dial to select the "Air Fry" mode.
4. Press the Time button and again turn the dial to set the cooking time to 25 minutes.
5. Now push the Temp button and rotate the dial to set the temperature at 375 degrees F.
6. Once preheated, place the air fryer basket inside and close its lid.
7. Serve warm.
- **Nutrition Info:** Calories 352 Total Fat 14 g Saturated Fat 2 g Cholesterol 65 mg Sodium 220 mg Total Carbs 15.8 g Fiber 0.2 g Sugar 1 g Protein 26 g

177.Roasted Stuffed Peppers

Servings: 4
Cooking Time: 20 Minutes
Ingredients:
- 4 ounces shredded cheddar cheese
- ½ tsp. Pepper
- ½ tsp. Salt
- 1 tsp. Worcestershire sauce
- ½ c. Tomato sauce
- 8 ounces lean ground beef
- 1 tsp. Olive oil
- 1 minced garlic clove
- ½ chopped onion
- 2 green peppers

Directions:
1. Preparing the ingredients. Ensure your instant crisp air fryer is preheated to 390 degrees. Spray with olive oil.
2. Cut stems off bell peppers and remove seeds. Cook in boiling salted water for 3 minutes.
3. Sauté garlic and onion together in a skillet until golden in color.

4. Take skillet off the heat. Mix pepper, salt, Worcestershire sauce, ¼ cup of tomato sauce, half of cheese and beef together.
5. Divide meat mixture into pepper halves. Top filled peppers with remaining cheese and tomato sauce.
6. Place filled peppers in the instant crisp air fryer.
7. Air frying. Close air fryer lid. Set temperature to 390°f, and set time to 20 minutes, bake 15-20 minutes.
- **Nutrition Info:** Calories: 295; Fat: 8g; Protein:23g; Sugar:2g

178.Bok Choy And Butter Sauce(1)

Servings: 4
Cooking Time: 12 Minutes
Ingredients:
- 2 bok choy heads; trimmed and cut into strips
- 1 tbsp. butter; melted
- 2 tbsp. chicken stock
- 1 tsp. lemon juice
- 1 tbsp. olive oil
- A pinch of salt and black pepper

Directions:
1. In a pan that fits your air fryer, mix all the ingredients, toss, introduce the pan in the air fryer and cook at 380°F for 15 minutes.
2. Divide between plates and serve as a side dish
- **Nutrition Info:** Calories: 141; Fat: 3g; Fiber: 2g; Carbs: 4g; Protein: 3g

179.Moroccan Pork Kebabs

Servings: 4
Cooking Time: 45 Minutes
Ingredients:
- 1/4 cup orange juice
- 1 tablespoon tomato paste
- 1 clove chopped garlic
- 1 tablespoon ground cumin
- 1/8 teaspoon ground cinnamon
- 4 tablespoons olive oil
- 1-1/2 teaspoons salt
- 3/4 teaspoon black pepper
- 1-1/2 pounds boneless pork loin
- 1 small eggplant
- 1 small red onion
- Pita bread (optional)
- 1/2 small cucumber
- 2 tablespoons chopped fresh mint
- Wooden skewers

Directions:
1. Start by placing wooden skewers in water to soak.
2. Cut pork loin and eggplant into 1- to 1-1/2-inch chunks.
3. Preheat toaster oven to 425°F.
4. Cut cucumber and onions into pieces and chop the mint.

5. In a large bowl, combine the orange juice, tomato paste, garlic, cumin, cinnamon, 2 tablespoons of oil, 1 teaspoon of salt, and 1/2 teaspoon of pepper.
6. Add the pork to this mixture and refrigerate for at least 30 minutes, but up to 8 hours.
7. Mix together vegetables, remaining oil, and salt and pepper.
8. Skewer the vegetables and bake for 20 minutes.
9. Add the pork to the skewers and bake for an additional 25 minutes.
10. Remove ingredients from skewers and sprinkle with mint; serve with flatbread if using.
- **Nutrition Info:** Calories: 465, Sodium: 1061 mg, Dietary Fiber: 5.6 g, Total Fat: 20.8 g, Total Carbs: 21.9 g, Protein: 48.2 g.

180.Herb-roasted Chicken Tenders

Servings: 2
Cooking Time: 10 Minutes
Ingredients:
- 7 ounces chicken tenders
- 1 tablespoon olive oil
- 1/2 teaspoon Herbes de Provence
- 2 tablespoons Dijon mustard
- 1 tablespoon honey
- Salt and pepper

Directions:
1. Start by preheating toaster oven to 450°F.
2. Brush bottom of pan with 1/2 tablespoon olive oil.
3. Season the chicken with herbs, salt, and pepper.
4. Place the chicken in a single flat layer in the pan and drizzle the remaining olive oil over it.
5. Bake for about 10 minutes.
6. While the chicken is baking, mix together the mustard and honey for a tasty condiment.
- **Nutrition Info:** Calories: 297, Sodium: 268 mg, Dietary Fiber: 0.8 g, Total Fat: 15.5 g, Total Carbs: 9.6 g, Protein: 29.8 g.

181.Ranch Chicken Wings

Servings: 3
Cooking Time: 10 Minutes
Ingredients:
- 1/4 cup almond meal
- 1/4 cup flaxseed meal
- 2 tablespoons butter, melted
- 6 tablespoons parmesan cheese, preferably freshly grated
- 1 tablespoon Ranch seasoning mix
- 2 tablespoons oyster sauce
- 6 chicken wings, bone-in

Directions:
1. Start by preheating your Air Fryer to 370 degrees F.
2. In a resealable bag, place the almond meal, flaxseed meal, butter, parmesan, Ranch seasoning mix, andoyster sauce. Add the chicken wings and shake to coat on all sides.
3. Arrange the chicken wings in the Air Fryer basket. Spritz the chicken wings with a nonstick cooking spray.
4. Cook for 11 minutes. Turn them over and cook an additional 11 minutes. Serve warm with your favorite dipping sauce, if desired. Enjoy!
- **Nutrition Info:** 285 Calories; 22g Fat; 3g Carbs; 12g Protein; 5g Sugars; 6g Fiber

182.Buttermilk Brined Turkey Breast

Servings: 8
Cooking Time: 20 Minutes
Ingredients:
- ¾ cup brine from a can of olives
- 3½ pounds boneless, skinless turkey breast
- 2 fresh thyme sprigs
- 1 fresh rosemary sprig
- ½ cup buttermilk

Directions:
1. Preheat the Air fryer to 350 degree F and grease an Air fryer basket.
2. Mix olive brine and buttermilk in a bowl until well combined.
3. Place the turkey breast, buttermilk mixture and herb sprigs in a resealable plastic bag.
4. Seal the bag and refrigerate for about 12 hours.
5. Remove the turkey breast from bag and arrange the turkey breast into the Air fryer basket.
6. Cook for about 20 minutes, flipping once in between.
7. Dish out the turkey breast onto a cutting board and cut into desired size slices to serve.
- **Nutrition Info:** Calories: 215, Fat: 3.5g, Carbohydrates: 9.4g, Sugar: 7.7g, Protein: 34.4g, Sodium: 2000mg

183.Turmeric Mushroom(3)

Servings: 4
Cooking Time: 12 Minutes
Ingredients:
- 1 lb. brown mushrooms
- 4 garlic cloves; minced
- ¼ tsp. cinnamon powder
- 1 tsp. olive oil
- ½ tsp. turmeric powder
- Salt and black pepper to taste

Directions:
1. In a bowl, combine all the ingredients and toss.
2. Put the mushrooms in your air fryer's basket and cook at 370°F for 15 minutes
3. Divide the mix between plates and serve as a side dish.
- **Nutrition Info:** Calories: 208; Fat: 7g; Fiber: 3g; Carbs: 5g; Protein: 7g

184.Country Comfort Corn Bread

Servings: 12
Cooking Time: 20 Minutes
Ingredients:
- 1 cup yellow cornmeal
- 1-1/2 cups oatmeal
- 1/4 teaspoon salt
- 1/4 cup granulated sugar
- 2 teaspoons baking powder
- 1 cup milk
- 1 large egg
- 1/2 cup applesauce

Directions:
1. Start by blending oatmeal into a fine powder.
2. Preheat toaster oven to 400°F.
3. Mix oatmeal, cornmeal, salt, sugar, and baking powder, and stir to blend.
4. Add milk, egg, and applesauce, and mix well.
5. Pour into a pan and bake for 20 minutes.
- **Nutrition Info:** Calories: 113, Sodium: 71 mg, Dietary Fiber: 1.9 g, Total Fat: 1.9 g, Total Carbs: 21.5 g, Protein: 3.4 g.

185.Lemon Pepper Turkey

Servings: 6
Cooking Time: 45 Minutes
Ingredients:
- 3 lbs. turkey breast
- 2 tablespoons oil
- 1 tablespoon Worcestershire sauce
- 1 teaspoon lemon pepper
- 1/2 teaspoon salt

Directions:
1. Whisk everything in a bowl and coat the turkey liberally.
2. Place the turkey in the Air fryer basket.
3. Press "Power Button" of Air Fry Oven and turn the dial to select the "Air Fry" mode.
4. Press the Time button and again turn the dial to set the cooking time to 45 minutes.
5. Now push the Temp button and rotate the dial to set the temperature at 375 degrees F.
6. Once preheated, place the air fryer basket inside and close its lid.
7. Serve warm.
- **Nutrition Info:** Calories 391 Total Fat 2.8 g Saturated Fat 0.6 g Cholesterol 330 mg Sodium 62 mg Total Carbs 36.5 g Fiber 9.2 g Sugar 4.5 g Protein 6.6

186.Marinated Chicken Parmesan

Servings: 4
Cooking Time: 20 Minutes
Ingredients:
- 2 cups breadcrumbs
- 1 teaspoon dried oregano
- 1/2 teaspoon garlic powder
- 4 teaspoons paprika
- 1/2 teaspoon salt
- 1/2 teaspoon black pepper
- 2 egg whites
- 1/2 cup skim milk
- 1/2 cup flour
- 4 (6 oz.) chicken breast halves, lb.ed
- Cooking spray
- 1 jar marinara sauce
- 3/4 cup mozzarella cheese, shredded
- 2 tablespoons Parmesan, shredded

Directions:
1. Whisk the flour with all the spices in a bowl and beat the eggs in another.
2. Coat the pounded chicken with flour then dip in the egg whites.
3. Dredge the chicken breast through the crumbs well.
4. Spread marinara sauce in a baking dish and place the crusted chicken on it.
5. Drizzle cheese on top of the chicken.
6. Press "Power Button" of Air Fry Oven and turn the dial to select the "Bake" mode.
7. Press the Time button and again turn the dial to set the cooking time to 20 minutes.
8. Now push the Temp button and rotate the dial to set the temperature at 400 degrees F.
9. Once preheated, place the baking pan inside and close its lid.
10. Serve warm.
- **Nutrition Info:** Calories 361 Total Fat 16.3 g Saturated Fat 4.9 g Cholesterol 114 mg Sodium 515 mg Total Carbs 19.3 g Fiber 0.1 g Sugar 18.2 g Protein 33.3 g

187.Spice-roasted Almonds

Servings: 32
Cooking Time: 10 Minutes
Ingredients:
- 1 tablespoon chili powder
- 1 tablespoon olive oil
- 1/2 teaspoon salt
- 1/2 teaspoon ground cumin
- 1/2 teaspoon ground coriander
- 1/4 teaspoon ground cinnamon
- 1/4 teaspoon black pepper
- 2 cups whole almonds

Directions:
1. Start by preheating toaster oven to 350°F.
2. Mix olive oil, chili powder, coriander, cinnamon, cumin, salt, and pepper.
3. Add almonds and toss together.
4. Transfer to a baking pan and bake for 10 minutes.
- **Nutrition Info:** Calories: 39, Sodium: 37 mg, Dietary Fiber: 0.8 g, Total Fat: 3.5 g, Total Carbs: 1.4 g, Protein: 1.3 g.

188.Spicy Green Crusted Chicken

Servings: 6
Cooking Time: 40 Minutes
Ingredients:
- 6 eggs, beaten
- 6 teaspoons parsley
- 4 teaspoons thyme

- 1 pound chicken pieces
- 6 teaspoons oregano
- Salt and freshly ground black pepper, to taste
- 4 teaspoons paprika

Directions:
1. Preheat the Air fryer to 360 degree F and grease an Air fryer basket.
2. Whisk eggs in a bowl and mix all the ingredients in another bowl except chicken pieces.
3. Dip the chicken in eggs and then coat generously with the dry mixture.
4. Arrange half of the chicken pieces in the Air fryer basket and cook for about 20 minutes.
5. Repeat with the remaining mixture and dish out to serve hot.
- **Nutrition Info:** Calories: 218, Fat: 10.4g, Carbohydrates: 2.6g, Sugar: 0.6g, Protein: 27.9g, Sodium: 128mg

189.Basic Roasted Tofu

Servings: 4
Cooking Time: 45 Minutes
Ingredients:
- 1 or more (16-ounce) containers extra-firm tofu
- 1 tablespoon sesame oil
- 1 tablespoon soy sauce
- 1 tablespoon rice vinegar
- 1 tablespoon water

Directions:
1. Start by drying the tofu: first pat dry with paper towels, then lay on another set of paper towels or a dish towel.
2. Put a plate on top of the tofu then put something heavy on the plate (like a large can of vegetables). Leave it there for at least 20 minutes.
3. While tofu is being pressed, whip up marinade by combining oil, soy sauce, vinegar, and water in a bowl and set aside.
4. Cut the tofu into squares or sticks. Place the tofu in the marinade for at least 30 minutes.
5. Preheat toaster oven to 350°F. Line a pan with parchment paper and add as many pieces of tofu as you can, giving each piece adequate space.
6. Bake 20–45 minutes; tofu is done when the outside edges look golden brown. Time will vary depending on tofu size and shape.
- **Nutrition Info:** Calories: 114, Sodium: 239 mg, Dietary Fiber: 1.1 g, Total Fat: 8.1 g, Total Carbs: 2.2 g, Protein: 9.5 g.

190.Butter Fish With Sake And Miso

Servings: 4
Cooking Time: 11 Minutes
Ingredients:
- 4 (7-ounce) pieces of butter fish
- 1/3 cup sake

- 1/3 cup mirin
- 2/3 cup sugar
- 1 cup white miso

Directions:
1. Start by combining sake, mirin, and sugar in a sauce pan and bring to a boil.
2. Allow to boil for 5 minutes, then reduce heat and simmer for another 10 minutes.
3. Remove from heat completely and mix in miso.
4. Marinate the fish in the mixture for as long as possible, up to 3 days if possible.
5. Preheat toaster oven to 450°F and bake fish for 8 minutes.
6. Switch your setting to Broil and broil another 2-3 minutes, until the sauce is caramelized.
- **Nutrition Info:** Calories: 529, Sodium: 2892 mg, Dietary Fiber: 3.7 g, Total Fat: 5.8 g, Total Carbs: 61.9 g, Protein: 53.4 g.

191.Okra And Green Beans Stew

Servings: 4
Cooking Time: 12 Minutes
Ingredients:
- 1 lb. green beans; halved
- 4 garlic cloves; minced
- 1 cup okra
- 3 tbsp. tomato sauce
- 1 tbsp. thyme; chopped.
- Salt and black pepper to taste.

Directions:
1. In a pan that fits your air fryer, mix all the ingredients, toss, introduce the pan in the air fryer and cook at 370°F for 15 minutes
2. Divide the stew into bowls and serve.
- **Nutrition Info:** Calories: 183; Fat: 5g; Fiber: 2g; Carbs: 4g; Protein: 8g

192.Orange Chicken Rice

Servings: 4
Cooking Time: 55 Minutes
Ingredients:
- 3 tablespoons olive oil
- 1 medium onion, chopped
- 1 3/4 cups chicken broth
- 1 cup brown basmati rice
- Zest and juice of 2 oranges
- Salt to taste
- 4 (6-oz.) boneless, skinless chicken thighs
- Black pepper, to taste
- 2 tablespoons fresh mint, chopped
- 2 tablespoons pine nuts, toasted

Directions:
1. Spread the rice in a casserole dish and place the chicken on top.
2. Toss the rest of the Ingredients: in a bowl and liberally pour over the chicken.
3. Press "Power Button" of Air Fry Oven and turn the dial to select the "Bake" mode.

4. Press the Time button and again turn the dial to set the cooking time to 55 minutes.
5. Now push the Temp button and rotate the dial to set the temperature at 350 degrees F.
6. Once preheated, place the casserole dish inside and close its lid.
7. Serve warm.
- **Nutrition Info:** Calories 231 Total Fat 20.1 g Saturated Fat 2.4 g Cholesterol 110 mg Sodium 941 mg Total Carbs 30.1 g Fiber 0.9 g Sugar 1.4 g Protein 14.6 g

193.Roasted Beet Salad With Oranges & Beet Greens

Servings: 6
Cooking Time: 1-1/2 Hours
Ingredients:
- 6 medium beets with beet greens attached
- 2 large oranges
- 1 small sweet onion, cut into wedges
- 1/3 cup red wine vinegar
- 1/4 cup extra-virgin olive oil
- 2 garlic cloves, minced
- 1/2 teaspoon grated orange peel

Directions:
1. Start by preheating toaster oven to 400°F.
2. Trim leaves from beets and chop, then set aside.
3. Pierce beets with a fork and place in a roasting pan.
4. Roast beets for 1-1/2 hours.
5. Allow beets to cool, peel, then cut into 8 wedges and put into a bowl.
6. Place beet greens in a sauce pan and cover with just enough water to cover. Heat until water boils, then immediately remove from heat.
7. Drain greens and press to remove liquid from greens, then add to beet bowl.
8. Remove peel and pith from orange and segment, adding each segment to the bowl.
9. Add onion to beet mixture. In a separate bowl mix together vinegar, oil, garlic and orange peel.
10. Combine both bowls and toss, sprinkle with salt and pepper.
11. Let stand for an hour before serving.
- **Nutrition Info:** Calories: 214, Sodium: 183 mg, Dietary Fiber: 6.5 g, Total Fat: 8.9 g, Total Carbs: 32.4 g, Protein: 4.7 g.

194.Simple Turkey Breast

Servings: 10
Cooking Time: 40 Minutes
Ingredients:
- 1: 8-poundsbone-in turkey breast
- Salt and black pepper, as required
- 2 tablespoons olive oil

Directions:
1. Preheat the Air fryer to 360 degree F and grease an Air fryer basket.

2. Season the turkey breast with salt and black pepper and drizzle with oil.
3. Arrange the turkey breast into the Air Fryer basket, skin side down and cook for about 20 minutes.
4. Flip the side and cook for another 20 minutes.
5. Dish out in a platter and cut into desired size slices to serve.
- **Nutrition Info:** Calories: 719, Fat: 35.9g, Carbohydrates: 0g, Sugar: 0g, Protein: 97.2g, Sodium: 386mg

195.Juicy Turkey Burgers

Servings: 8
Cooking Time: 25 Minutes
Ingredients:
- 1 lb ground turkey 85% lean / 15% fat
- ¼ cup unsweetened apple sauce
- ½ onion grated
- 1 Tbsp ranch seasoning
- 2 tsp Worcestershire Sauce
- 1 tsp minced garlic
- ¼ cup plain breadcrumbs
- Salt and pepper to taste

Directions:
1. Combine the onion, ground turkey, unsweetened apple sauce, minced garlic, breadcrumbs, ranch seasoning, Worchestire sauce, and salt and pepper. Mix them with your hands until well combined. Form 4 equally sized hamburger patties with them.
2. Place these burgers in the refrigerator for about 30 minutes to have them firm up a bit.
3. While preparing for cooking, select the Air Fry option. Set the temperature of 360°F and the cook time as required. Press start to begin preheating.
4. Once the preheating temperature is reached, place the burgers on the tray in the Air fryer basket, making sure they don't overlap or touch. Cook on for 15 minutes
5. flipping halfway through.
- **Nutrition Info:** Calories 183, Total Fat 3g, Total Carbs 11g, Protein 28g

196.Coriander Potatoes

Servings: 4
Cooking Time: 25 Minutes
Ingredients:
- 1 pound gold potatoes, peeled and cut into wedges
- Salt and black pepper to the taste
- 1 tablespoon tomato sauce
- 2 tablespoons coriander, chopped
- ½ teaspoon garlic powder
- 1 teaspoon chili powder
- 1 tablespoon olive oil

Directions:

1. In a bowl, combine the potatoes with the tomato sauce and the other Ingredients:, toss, and transfer to the air fryer's basket.
2. Cook at 370 degrees F for 25 minutes, divide between plates and serve as a side dish.
- **Nutrition Info:** Calories 210, fat 5, fiber 7, carbs 12, protein 5

197.Roasted Delicata Squash With Kale

Servings: 2
Cooking Time: 10 Minutes
Ingredients:
- 1 medium delicata squash
- 1 bunch kale
- 1 clove garlic
- 2 tablespoons olive oil
- Salt and pepper

Directions:
1. Start by preheating toaster oven to 425°F.
2. Clean squash and cut off each end. Cut in half and remove the seeds. Quarter the halves.
3. Toss the squash in 1 tablespoon of olive oil.
4. Place the squash on a greased baking sheet and roast for 25 minutes, turning halfway through.
5. Rinse kale and remove stems. Chop garlic.
6. Heat the leftover oil in a medium skillet and add kale and salt to taste.
7. Sauté the kale until it darkens, then mix in the garlic.
8. Cook for another minute then remove from heat and add 2 tablespoons of water.
9. Remove squash from oven and lay it on top of the garlic kale.
10. Top with salt and pepper to taste and serve.
- **Nutrition Info:** Calories: 159, Sodium: 28 mg, Dietary Fiber: 1.8 g, Total Fat: 14.2 g, Total Carbs: 8.2 g, Protein: 2.6 g.

198.Perfect Size French Fries

Servings: 1
Cooking Time: 30 Minutes
Ingredients:
- 1 medium potato
- 1 tablespoon olive oil
- Salt and pepper to taste

Directions:
1. Start by preheating your oven to 425°F.
2. Clean the potato and cut it into fries or wedges.
3. Place fries in a bowl of cold water to rinse.
4. Lay the fries on a thick sheet of paper towels and pat dry.
5. Toss in a bowl with oil, salt, and pepper.
6. Bake for 30 minutes.
- **Nutrition Info:** Calories: 284, Sodium: 13 mg, Dietary Fiber: 4.7 g, Total Fat: 14.2 g, Total Carbs: 37.3 g, Protein: 4.3 g.

199.Kale And Pine Nuts

Servings: 4
Cooking Time: 12 Minutes
Ingredients:
- 10 cups kale; torn
- 1/3 cup pine nuts
- 2 tbsp. lemon zest; grated
- 1 tbsp. lemon juice
- 2 tbsp. olive oil
- Salt and black pepper to taste.

Directions:
1. In a pan that fits the air fryer, combine all the ingredients, toss, introduce the pan in the machine and cook at 380°F for 15 minutes
2. Divide between plates and serve as a side dish.
- **Nutrition Info:** Calories: 121; Fat: 9g; Fiber: 2g; Carbs: 4g; Protein: 5g

200.Sweet Potato Rosti

Servings: 2
Cooking Time: 15 Minutes
Ingredients:
- ½ lb. sweet potatoes, peeled, grated and squeezed
- 1 tablespoon fresh parsley, chopped finely
- Salt and ground black pepper, as required
- 2 tablespoons sour cream

Directions:
1. In a large bowl, mix together the grated sweet potato, parsley, salt, and black pepper.
2. Press "Power Button" of Air Fry Oven and turn the dial to select the "Air Fry" mode.
3. Press the Time button and again turn the dial to set the cooking time to 15 minutes.
4. Now push the Temp button and rotate the dial to set the temperature at 355 degrees F.
5. Press "Start/Pause" button to start.
6. When the unit beeps to show that it is preheated, open the lid and lightly, grease the sheet pan.
7. Arrange the sweet potato mixture into the "Sheet Pan" and shape it into an even circle.
8. Insert the "Sheet Pan" in the oven.
9. Cut the potato rosti into wedges.
10. Top with the sour cream and serve immediately.
- **Nutrition Info:** Calories: 160 Cal Total Fat: 2.7 g Saturated Fat: 1.6 g Cholesterol: 5 mg Sodium: 95 mg Total Carbs: 32.3 g Fiber: 4.7 g Sugar: 0.6 g Protein: 2.2 g

201.Lime And Mustard Marinated Chicken

Servings: 4
Cooking Time: 10 Minutes
Ingredients:
- 1/2 teaspoon stone-ground mustard
- 1/2 teaspoon minced fresh oregano
- 1/3 cup freshly squeezed lime juice

- 2 small-sized chicken breasts, skin-on
- 1 teaspoon kosher salt
- 1teaspoon freshly cracked mixed peppercorns

Directions:
1. Preheat your Air Fryer to 345 degrees F.
2. Toss all of the above ingredients in a medium-sized mixing dish; allow it to marinate overnight.
3. Cook in the preheated Air Fryer for 26 minutes.
- **Nutrition Info:** 255 Calories; 15g Fat; 7g Carbs; 33g Protein; 8g Sugars; 3g Fiber

202.Air Fried Steak Sandwich

Servings: 4
Cooking Time: 16 Minutes
Ingredients:
- Large hoagie bun, sliced in half
- 6 ounces of sirloin or flank steak, sliced into bite-sized pieces
- ½ tablespoon of mustard powder
- ½ tablespoon of soy sauce
- 1 tablespoon of fresh bleu cheese, crumbled
- 8 medium-sized cherry tomatoes, sliced in half
- 1 cup of fresh arugula, rinsed and patted dry

Directions:
1. Preparing the ingredients. In a small mixing bowl, combine the soy sauce and onion powder; stir with a fork until thoroughly combined.
2. Lay the raw steak strips in the soy-mustard mixture, and fully immerse each piece to marinate.
3. Set the instant crisp air fryer to 320 degrees for 10 minutes.
4. Arrange the soy-mustard marinated steak pieces on a piece of tin foil, flat and not overlapping, and set the tin foil on one side of the instant crisp air fryer basket. The foil should not take up more than half of the surface.
5. Lay the hoagie-bun halves, crusty-side up and soft-side down, on the other half of the air-fryer.
6. Air frying. Close air fryer lid.
7. After 10 minutes, the instant crisp air fryer will shut off; the hoagie buns should be starting to crisp and the steak will have begun to cook.
8. Carefully, flip the hoagie buns so they are now crusty-side down and soft-side up; crumble a layer of the bleu cheese on each hoagie half.
9. With a long spoon, gently stir the marinated steak in the foil to ensure even coverage.
10. Set the instant crisp air fryer to 360 degrees for 6 minutes.

11. After 6 minutes, when the fryer shuts off, the bleu cheese will be perfectly melted over the toasted bread, and the steak will be juicy on the inside and crispy on the outside.
12. Remove the cheesy hoagie halves first, using tongs, and set on a serving plate; then cover one side with the steak, and top with the cherry-tomato halves and the arugula. Close with the other cheesy hoagie-half, slice into two pieces, and enjoy.
- **Nutrition Info:** Calories 284 Total fat 7.9 g Saturated fat 1.4 g Cholesterol 36 mg Sodium 704 mg Total carbs 46 g Fiber 3.6 g Sugar 5.5 g Protein 17.9 g

203.Philly Cheesesteak Egg Rolls

Servings: 4-5
Cooking Time: 20 Minutes
Ingredients:
- 1 egg
- 1 tablespoon milk
- 2 tablespoons olive oil
- 1 small red onion
- 1 small red bell pepper
- 1 small green bell pepper
- 1 pound thinly slice roast beef
- 8 ounces shredded pepper jack cheese
- 8 ounces shredded provolone cheese
- 8-10 egg roll skins
- Salt and pepper

Directions:
1. Start by preheating toaster oven to 425°F.
2. Mix together egg and milk in a shallow bowl and set aside for later use.
3. Chop onions and bell peppers into small pieces.
4. Heat the oil in a medium sauce pan and add the onions and peppers.
5. Cook onions and peppers for 2–3 minutes until softened.
6. Add roast beef to the pan and sauté for another 5 minutes.
7. Add salt and pepper to taste.
8. Add cheese and mix together until melted.
9. Remove from heat and drain liquid from pan.
10. Roll the egg roll skins flat.
11. Add equal parts of the mix to each egg roll and roll them up per the instructions on the package.
12. Brush each egg roll with the egg mixture.
13. Line a pan with parchment paper and lay egg rolls seam-side down with a gap between each roll.
14. Bake for 20–25 minutes, depending on your preference of egg roll crispness.
- **Nutrition Info:** Calories: 769, Sodium: 1114 mg, Dietary Fiber: 2.1 g, Total Fat: 39.9 g, Total Carbs: 41.4 g, Protein: 58.4 g.

204.Rolled Salmon Sandwich

Servings: 1
Cooking Time: 5 Minutes
Ingredients:
- 1 piece of flatbread
- 1 salmon filet
- Pinch of salt
- 1 tablespoon green onion, chopped
- 1/4 teaspoon dried sumac
- 1/2 teaspoon thyme
- 1/2 teaspoon sesame seeds
- 1/4 English cucumber
- 1 tablespoon yogurt

Directions:
1. Start by peeling and chopping the cucumber. Cut the salmon at a 45-degree angle into 4 slices and lay them flat on the flatbread.
2. Sprinkle salmon with salt to taste. Sprinkle onions, thyme, sumac, and sesame seeds evenly over the salmon.
3. Broil the salmon for at least 3 minutes, but longer if you want a more well-done fish.
4. While you broil your salmon, mix together the yogurt and cucumber. Remove your flatbread from the toaster oven and put it on a plate, then spoon the yogurt mix over the salmon.
5. Fold the sides of the flatbread in and roll it up for a gourmet lunch that you can take on the go.
- **Nutrition Info:** Calories: 347, Sodium: 397 mg, Dietary Fiber: 1.6 g, Total Fat: 12.4 g, Total Carbs: 20.6 g, Protein: 38.9 g.

DINNER RECIPES

205.Cajun Fish Fritters

Servings: 4
Cooking Time: 20 Minutes
Ingredients:
- 2 catfish fillets
- 1 cup parmesan cheese
- 3 ounces butter
- 1 teaspoon baking powder
- 1 teaspoon baking soda
- 1/2 cup buttermilk
- 1 teaspoon Cajun seasoning
- 1 cup Swiss cheese, shredded

Directions:
1. Bring a pot of salted water to a boil. Boil the fish fillets for 5 minutes or until it is opaque. Flake the fish into small pieces.
2. Mix the remaining ingredients in a bowl; add the fish and mix until well combined. Shape the fish mixture into 12 patties.
3. Cook in the preheated Air Fryer at 380 degrees F for 15 minutes. Work in batches. Enjoy!
- **Nutrition Info:** 478 Calories; 31g Fat; 22g Carbs; 28g Protein; 2g Sugars; 1g Fiber

206.Tasty Sausage Bacon Rolls

Servings: 4
Cooking Time: 1 Hour 44 Minutes
Ingredients:
- Sausage:
- 8 bacon strips
- 8 pork sausages
- Relish:
- 8 large tomatoes
- 1 clove garlic, peeled
- 1 small onion, peeled
- 3 tbsp chopped parsley
- A pinch of salt
- A pinch of pepper
- 2 tbsp sugar
- 1 tsp smoked paprika
- 1 tbsp white wine vinegar

Directions:
1. Start with the relish; add the tomatoes, garlic, and onion in a food processor. Blitz them for 10 seconds until the mixture is pulpy. Pour the pulp into a saucepan, add the vinegar, salt, pepper, and place it over medium heat.
2. Bring to simmer for 10 minutes; add the paprika and sugar. Stir with a spoon and simmer for 10 minutes until pulpy and thick. Turn off the heat, transfer the relish to a bowl and chill it for an hour. In 30 minutes after putting the relish in the refrigerator, move on to the sausages. Wrap each sausage with a bacon strip neatly and stick in a bamboo skewer at the end of the sausage to secure the bacon ends.

3. Open the Air Fryer, place 3 to 4 wrapped sausages in the fryer basket and cook for 12 minutes at 350 F. Ensure that the bacon is golden and crispy before removing them. Repeat the cooking process for the remaining wrapped sausages. Remove the relish from the refrigerator. Serve the sausages and relish with turnip mash.
- **Nutrition Info:** 346 Calories; 11g Fat; 4g Carbs; 32g Protein; 1g Sugars; 1g Fiber

207.Fish Cakes With Horseradish Sauce

Servings: 4
Cooking Time: 20 Minutes
Ingredients:
- Halibut Cakes:
- 1 pound halibut
- 2 tablespoons olive oil
- 1/2 teaspoon cayenne pepper
- 1/4 teaspoon black pepper
- Salt, to taste
- 2 tablespoons cilantro, chopped
- 1 shallot, chopped
- 2 garlic cloves, minced
- 1 cup Romano cheese, grated
- 1 egg, whisked
- 1 tablespoon Worcestershire sauce
- Mayo Sauce:
- 1 teaspoon horseradish, grated
- 1/2 cup mayonnaise

Directions:
1. Start by preheating your Air Fryer to 380 degrees F. Spritz the Air Fryer basket with cooking oil.
2. Mix all ingredients for the halibut cakes in a bowl; knead with your hands until everything is well incorporated.
3. Shape the mixture into equally sized patties. Transfer your patties to the Air Fryer basket. Cook the fish patties for 10 minutes, turning them over halfway through.
4. Mix the horseradish and mayonnaise. Serve the halibut cakes with the horseradish mayo.
- **Nutrition Info:** 532 Calories; 32g Fat; 3g Carbs; 28g Protein; 3g Sugars; 6g Fiber

208.Fragrant Pork Tenderloin

Servings: 3
Cooking Time: 15 Minutes
Ingredients:
- ½ teaspoon saffron
- 1 teaspoon sage
- ½ teaspoon ground cinnamon
- 1 teaspoon garlic powder
- 1 teaspoon onion powder
- 1-pound pork tenderloin
- 3 tablespoon butter
- 1 garlic clove, crushed
- 1 tablespoon apple cider vinegar

Directions:

1. Combine the saffron, sage, ground cinnamon, garlic powder, and onion powder together in the shallow bowl.
2. Then shake the spices gently to make them homogenous.
3. After this, coat the pork tenderloin in the spice mixture.
4. Rub the pork tenderloin with the crushed garlic and sprinkle the meat with the apple cider vinegar.
5. Leave the pork tenderloin for 10 minutes to marinate.
6. Meanwhile, preheat the air fryer to 320 F.
7. Put the pork tenderloin in the air fryer tray and place the butter over the meat.
8. Cook the meat for 15 minutes.
9. When the meat is cooked – let it chill briefly.
10. Slice the pork tenderloin and serve it.
11. Enjoy!
- **Nutrition Info:** calories 328, fat 16.9, fiber 0.5, carbs 2.2, protein 40

209.Hot Pork Skewers

Servings: 3 To 4
Cooking Time: 1 Hour 20 Minutes
Ingredients:
- 1 lb pork steak, cut in cubes
- ¼ cup soy sauce
- 2 tsp smoked paprika
- 1 tsp powdered chili
- 1 tsp garlic salt
- 1 tsp red chili flakes
- 1 tbsp white wine vinegar
- 3 tbsp steak sauce
- Skewing:
- 1 green pepper, cut in cubes
- 1 red pepper, cut in cubes
- 1 yellow squash, seeded and cut in cubes
- 1 green squash, seeded and cut in cubes
- Salt and black pepper to taste to season

Directions:
1. In a mixing bowl, add the pork cubes, soy sauce, smoked paprika, powdered chili, garlic salt, red chili flakes, white wine vinegar, and steak sauce. Mix them using a ladle. Refrigerate to marinate them for 1 hour.
2. After one hour, remove the marinated pork from the fridge and preheat the Air Fryer to 370 F.
3. On each skewer, stick the pork cubes and vegetables in the order that you prefer. Have fun doing this. Once the pork cubes and vegetables are finished, arrange the skewers in the fryer basket and grill them for 8 minutes. You can do them in batches. Once ready, remove them onto the serving platter and serve with salad.
- **Nutrition Info:** 456 Calories; 37g Fat; 1g Carbs; 21g Protein; 5g Sugars; 6g Fiber

210.Smoked Ham With Pears

Servings: 2

Cooking Time: 30 Minutes
Ingredients:
- 15 oz pears, halved
- 8 pound smoked ham
- 1 ½ cups brown sugar
- ¾ tbsp allspice
- 1 tbsp apple cider vinegar
- 1 tsp black pepper
- 1 tsp vanilla extract

Directions:
1. Preheat your air fryer to 330 f. In a bowl, mix pears, brown sugar, cider vinegar, vanilla extract, pepper, and allspice. Place the mixture in a frying pan and fry for 2-3 minutes. Pour the mixture over ham. Add the ham to the air fryer cooking basket and cook for 15 minutes. Serve ham with hot sauce, to enjoy!
- **Nutrition Info:** Calories: 550 Cal Total Fat: 29 g Saturated Fat: 0 g Cholesterol: 0 mg Sodium: 0 mg Total Carbs: 46 g Fiber: 0 g Sugar: 0 g Protein: 28 g

211.Spiced Salmon Kebabs

Servings: 3
Cooking Time: 15 Minutes
Ingredients:
- 2 tablespoons chopped fresh oregano
- 2 teaspoons sesame seeds
- 1 teaspoon ground cumin
- Salt and pepper to taste
- 1 ½ pounds salmon fillets
- 2 tablespoons olive oil
- 2 lemons, sliced into rounds

Directions:
1. Place the instant pot air fryer lid on and preheat the instant pot at 390 degrees F.
2. Place the grill pan accessory in the instant pot.
3. Create dry rub by combining the oregano, sesame seeds, cumin, salt, and pepper.
4. Rub the salmon fillets with the dry rub and brush with oil.
5. Place on the grill pan, close the air fryer lid and grill the salmon for 15 minutes.
6. Serve with lemon slices once cooked.
- **Nutrition Info:** Calories per serving 447 ; Carbs: 4.1g; Protein:47.6 g; Fat:26.6 g

212.Miso-glazed Salmon

Servings: 4
Cooking Time: 5 Minutes
Ingredients:
- 1/4 cup red or white miso
- 1/3 cup sake
- 1 tablespoon soy sauce
- 2 tablespoons vegetable oil
- 1/4 cup sugar
- 4 skinless salmon filets

Directions:
1. In a shallow bowl, mix together the miso, sake, oil, soy sauce, and sugar.

2. Toss the salmon in the mixture until thoroughly coated on all sides.
3. Preheat your toaster oven to "high" on broil mode.
4. Place salmon in a broiling pan and broil until the top is well charred—about 5 minutes.
- **Nutrition Info:** Calories: 401, Sodium: 315 mg, Dietary Fiber: 0 g, Total Fat: 19.2 g, Total Carbs: 14.1 g, Protein: 39.2 g.

213.Salmon Casserole

Servings: 8
Cooking Time: 12 Minutes
Ingredients:
- 7 oz Cheddar cheese, shredded
- ½ cup cream
- 1-pound salmon fillet
- 1 tablespoon dried dill
- 1 teaspoon dried parsley
- 1 teaspoon salt
- 1 teaspoon ground coriander
- ½ teaspoon ground black pepper
- 2 green pepper, chopped
- 4 oz chive stems, diced
- 7 oz bok choy, chopped
- 1 tablespoon olive oil

Directions:
1. Sprinkle the salmon fillet with the dried dill, dried parsley, ground coriander, and ground black pepper.
2. Massage the salmon fillet gently and leave it for 5 minutes to make the fish soaks the spices.
3. Meanwhile, sprinkle the air fryer casserole tray with the olive oil inside.
4. After this, cut the salmon fillet into the cubes.
5. Separate the salmon cubes into 2 parts.
6. Then place the first part of the salmon cubes in the casserole tray.
7. Sprinkle the fish with the chopped bok choy, diced chives, and chopped green pepper.
8. After this, place the second part of the salmon cubes over the vegetables.
9. Then sprinkle the casserole with the shredded cheese and heavy cream.
10. Preheat the air fryer to 380 F.
11. Cook the salmon casserole for 12 minutes.
12. When the dish is cooked – it will have acrunchy light brown crust.
13. Serve it and enjoy!
- **Nutrition Info:** calories 216, fat 14.4, fiber 1.1, carbs 4.3, protein 18.2

214.Air Fryer Roasted Broccoli

Servings: 4
Cooking Time: 10 Minutes
Ingredients:
- 1 tsp. herbes de provence seasoning (optional)
- 4 cups fresh broccoli
- 1 tablespoon olive oil

- Salt and pepper to taste

Directions:
1. Drizzle or spray broccoli with olive and sprinkle seasoning throughout
2. Spray air fryer basket with cooking oil, place broccoli and cook for 5-8 minutes on 360F
3. Open air fryer and examine broccoli after 5 minutes because different fryer brands cook at different rates.
- **Nutrition Info:** Calories 61 Fat 4g protein 3g net carbs 4g

215.Roasted Butternut Squash With Brussels Sprouts & Sweet Potato Noodles

Servings: 2
Cooking Time: 15 Minutes
Ingredients:
- Squash:
- 3 cups chopped butternut squash
- 2 teaspoons extra light olive oil
- 1/8 teaspoon sea salt
- Veggies:
- 5-6 Brussels sprouts
- 5 fresh shiitake mushrooms
- 2 cloves garlic
- 1/2 teaspoon black sesame seeds
- 1/2 teaspoon white sesame seeds
- A few sprinkles ground pepper
- A small pinch red pepper flakes
- 1 tablespoon extra light olive oil
- 1 teaspoon sesame oil
- 1 teaspoon onion powder
- 1 teaspoon garlic powder
- 1/4 teaspoon sea salt
- Noodles:
- 1 bundle sweet potato vermicelli
- 2-3 teaspoons low-sodium soy sauce

Directions:
1. Start by soaking potato vermicelli in water for at least 2 hours.
2. Preheat toaster oven to 375°F.
3. Place squash on a baking sheet with edges, then drizzle with olive oil and sprinkle with salt and pepper. Mix together well on pan.
4. Bake the squash for 30 minutes, mixing and flipping half way through.
5. Remove the stems from the mushrooms and chop the Brussels sprouts.
6. Chop garlic and mix the veggies.
7. Drizzle sesame and olive oil over the mixture, then add garlic powder, onion powder, sesame seeds, red pepper flakes, salt, and pepper.
8. Bake veggie mix for 15 minutes.
9. While the veggies bake, put noodles in a small sauce pan and add just enough water to cover.
10. Bring water to a rolling boil and boil noodles for about 8 minutes.

11. Drain noodles and combine with squash and veggies in a large bowl.
12. Drizzle with soy sauce, sprinkle with sesame seeds, and serve.
- **Nutrition Info:** Calories: 409, Sodium: 1124 mg, Dietary Fiber: 12.2 g, Total Fat: 15.6 g, Total Carbs: 69.3 g, Protein: 8.8 g.

216.Crispy Scallops

Servings: 4
Cooking Time: 6 Minutes
Ingredients:
- 18 sea scallops, cleaned and patted very dry
- 1/8 cup all-purpose flour
- 1 tablespoon 2% milk
- ½ egg
- ¼ cup cornflakes, crushed
- ½ teaspoon paprika
- Salt and black pepper, as required

Directions:
1. Preheat the Air fryer to 400 degree F and grease an Air fryer basket.
2. Mix flour, paprika, salt, and black pepper in a bowl.
3. Whisk egg with milk in another bowl and place the cornflakes in a third bowl.
4. Coat each scallop with the flour mixture, dip into the egg mixture and finally, dredge in the cornflakes.
5. Arrange scallops in the Air fryer basket and cook for about 6 minutes.
6. Dish out the scallops in a platter and serve hot.
- **Nutrition Info:** Calories: 150, Fat: 1.7g, Carbohydrates: 8g, Sugar: 0.4g, Protein: 24g, Sodium: 278mg

217.Garlic Butter Pork Chops

Servings: 4
Cooking Time: 8 Minutes
Ingredients:
- 4 pork chops
- 1 tablespoon coconut butter
- 2 teaspoons parsley
- 1 tablespoon coconut oil
- 2 teaspoons garlic, grated
- Salt and black pepper, to taste

Directions:
1. Preheat the Air fryer to 350 degree F and grease an Air fryer basket.
2. Mix all the seasonings, coconut oil, garlic, butter, and parsley in a bowl and coat the pork chops with it.
3. Cover the chops with foil and refrigerate to marinate for about 1 hour.
4. Remove the foil and arrange the chops in the Air fryer basket.
5. Cook for about 8 minutes and dish out in a bowl to serve warm.
- **Nutrition Info:** Calories: 311, Fat: 25.5g, Carbohydrates: 1.4g, Sugar: 0.3g, Protein: 18.4g, Sodium: 58mg

218.Creamy Breaded Shrimp

Servings: 3
Cooking Time: 20 Minutes
Ingredients:
- ¼ cup all-purpose flour
- 1 cup panko breadcrumbs
- 1 pound shrimp, peeled and deveined
- ½ cup mayonnaise
- ¼ cup sweet chili sauce
- 1 tablespoon Sriracha sauce

Directions:
1. Preheat the Air fryer to 400-degree F and grease an Air fryer basket.
2. Place flour in a shallow bowl and mix the mayonnaise, chili sauce, and Sriracha sauce in another bowl.
3. Place the breadcrumbs in a third bowl.
4. Coat each shrimp with the flour, dip into mayonnaise mixture and finally, dredge in the breadcrumbs.
5. Arrange half of the coated shrimps into the Air fryer basket and cook for about 10 minutes.
6. Dish out the coated shrimps onto serving plates and repeat with the remaining mixture.
- **Nutrition Info:** Calories: 540, Fat: 18.2g, Carbohydrates: 33.1g, Sugar: 10.6g, Protein: 36.8g, Sodium: 813mg

219.Scallops With Capers Sauce

Servings: 2
Cooking Time: 6 Minutes
Ingredients:
- 10: 1-ouncesea scallops, cleaned and patted very dry
- 2 tablespoons fresh parsley, finely chopped
- 2 teaspoons capers, finely chopped
- Salt and ground black pepper, as required
- ¼ cup extra-virgin olive oil
- 1 teaspoon fresh lemon zest, finely grated
- ½ teaspoon garlic, finely chopped

Directions:
1. Preheat the Air fryer to 390 degree F and grease an Air fryer basket.
2. Season the scallops evenly with salt and black pepper.
3. Arrange the scallops in the Air fryer basket and cook for about 6 minutes.
4. Mix parsley, capers, olive oil, lemon zest and garlic in a bowl.
5. Dish out the scallops in a platter and top with capers sauce.
- **Nutrition Info:** Calories: 344, Fat: 26.3g, Carbohydrates: 4.2g, Sugar: 0.1g, Protein: 24g, Sodium: 393mg

220.Baby Portabellas With Romano Cheese

Servings: 4
Cooking Time: 20 Minutes
Ingredients:

- 1 pound baby portabellas
- 1/2 cup almond meal
- 2 eggs
- 2 tablespoons milk
- 1 cup Romano cheese, grated
- Sea salt and ground black pepper
- 1/2 teaspoon shallot powder
- 1 teaspoon garlic powder
- 1/2 teaspoon cumin powder
- 1/2 teaspoon cayenne pepper

Directions:
1. Pat the mushrooms dry with a paper towel.
2. To begin, set up your breading station. Place the almond meal in a shallow dish. In a separate dish, whisk the eggs with milk.
3. Finally, place grated Romano cheese and seasonings in the third dish.
4. Start by dredging the baby portabellas in the almond meal mixture; then, dip them into the egg wash. Press the baby portabellas into Romano cheese, coating evenly.
5. Spritz the Air Fryer basket with cooking oil. Add the baby portabellas and cook at 400 degrees F for 6 minutes, flipping them halfway through the cooking time.
- **Nutrition Info:** 230 Calories; 13g Fat; 2g Carbs; 11g Protein; 8g Sugars; 6g Fiber

221.Beef, Olives And Tomatoes

Servings: 4
Cooking Time: 35 Minutes
Ingredients:
- 2pounds beef stew meat, cubed
- 1cup black olives, pitted and halved
- 1cup cherry tomatoes, halved
- 1tablespoon smoked paprika
- 3tablespoons olive oil
- 1teaspoon coriander, ground
- Salt and black pepper to the taste

Directions:
1. In the air fryer's pan, mix the beef with the olives and the other ingredients, toss and cook at 390 degrees F for 35 minutes.
2. Divide between plates and serve.
- **Nutrition Info:** Calories 291, Fat 12, Fiber 9, Carbs 20, Protein 26

222.Broccoli With Olives

Servings: 4
Cooking Time: 19 Minutes
Ingredients:
- 2 pounds broccoli, stemmed and cut into 1-inch florets
- 1/3 cup Kalamata olives, halved and pitted
- ¼ cup Parmesan cheese, grated
- 2 tablespoons olive oil
- Salt and ground black pepper, as required
- 2 teaspoons fresh lemon zest, grated

Directions:
1. Preheat the Air fryer to 400 ºF and grease an Air fryer basket.

2. Boil the broccoli for about 4 minutes and drain well.
3. Mix broccoli, oil, salt, and black pepper in a bowl and toss to coat well.
4. Arrange broccoli into the Air fryer basket and cook for about 15 minutes.
5. Stir in the olives, lemon zest and cheese and dish out to serve.
- **Nutrition Info:** Calories: 169, Fat: 10.2g, Carbohydrates: 16g, Sugar: 3.9g, Protein: 8.5g, Sodium: 254mg

223.Salsa Stuffed Eggplants

Servings: 2
Cooking Time: 25 Minutes
Ingredients:
- 1 large eggplant
- 8 cherry tomatoes, quartered
- ½ tablespoon fresh parsley
- 2 teaspoons olive oil, divided
- 2 teaspoons fresh lemon juice, divided
- 2 tablespoons tomato salsa
- Salt and black pepper, as required

Directions:
1. Preheat the Air fryer to 390 degree F and grease an Air fryer basket.
2. Arrange the eggplant into the Air fryer basket and cook for about 15 minutes.
3. Cut the eggplant in half lengthwise and drizzle evenly with one teaspoon of oil.
4. Set the Air fryer to 355 degree F and arrange the eggplant into the Air fryer basket, cut-side up.
5. Cook for another 10 minutes and dish out in a bowl.
6. Scoop out the flesh from the eggplant and transfer into a bowl.
7. Stir in the tomatoes, salsa, parsley, salt, black pepper, remaining oil, and lemon juice.
8. Squeeze lemon juice on the eggplant halves and stuff with the salsa mixture to serve.
- **Nutrition Info:** Calories: 192, Fat: 6.1g, Carbohydrates: 33.8g, Sugar: 20.4g, Protein: 6.9g, Sodium: 204mg

224.Indian Meatballs With Lamb

Servings: 8
Cooking Time: 14 Minutes
Ingredients:
- 1 garlic clove
- 1 tablespoon butter
- 4 oz chive stems
- ¼ tablespoon turmeric
- 1/3 teaspoon cayenne pepper
- 1 teaspoon ground coriander
- ¼ teaspoon bay leaf
- 1 teaspoon salt
- 1-pound ground lamb
- 1 egg
- 1 teaspoon ground black pepper

Directions:
1. Peel the garlic clove and mince it

2. Combine the minced garlic with the ground lamb.
3. Then sprinkle the meat mixture with the turmeric, cayenne pepper, ground coriander, bay leaf, salt, and ground black pepper.
4. Beat the egg in the forcemeat.
5. Then grate the chives and add them in the lamb forcemeat too.
6. Mix it up to make the smooth mass.
7. Then preheat the air fryer to 400 F.
8. Put the butter in the air fryer basket tray and melt it.
9. Then make the meatballs from the lamb mixture and place them in the air fryer basket tray.
10. Cook the dish for 14 minutes.
11. Stir the meatballs twice during the cooking.
12. Serve the cooked meatballs immediately.
13. Enjoy!
- **Nutrition Info:** calories 134, fat 6.2, fiber 0.4, carbs 1.8, protein 16.9

225.Creamy Lemon Turkey

Servings: 4
Cooking Time: 20 Minutes
Ingredients:
- 1/3 cup sour cream
- 2 cloves garlic, finely minced 1/3 tsp. lemon zest
- 2 small-sized turkey breasts, skinless and cubed 1/3 cup thickened cream
- 2 tablespoons lemon juice
- 1 tsp. fresh marjoram, chopped
- Salt and freshly cracked mixed peppercorns, to taste 1/2 cup scallion, chopped
- 1/2 can tomatoes, diced
- 1½ tablespoons canola oil

Directions:
1. Firstly, pat dry the turkey breast. Mix the remaining items; marinate the turkey for 2 hours.
2. Set the air fryer to cook at 355 °F. Brush the turkey with a nonstick spray; cook for 23 minutes, turning once. Serve with naan and enjoy!
- **Nutrition Info:** 260 Calories; 15.3g Fat; 8.9g Carbs; 28.6g Protein; 1.9g Sugars

226.Breaded Shrimp With Lemon

Servings: 3
Cooking Time: 14 Minutes
Ingredients:
- ½ cup plain flour
- 2 egg whites
- 1 cup breadcrumbs
- 1 pound large shrimp, peeled and deveined
- Salt and ground black pepper, as required
- ¼ teaspoon lemon zest
- ¼ teaspoon cayenne pepper
- ¼ teaspoon red pepper flakes, crushed

- 2 tablespoons vegetable oil

Directions:
1. Preheat the Air fryer to 400 degree F and grease an Air fryer basket.
2. Mix flour, salt, and black pepper in a shallow bowl.
3. Whisk the egg whites in a second bowl and mix the breadcrumbs, lime zest and spices in a third bowl.
4. Coat each shrimp with the flour, dip into egg whites and finally, dredge in the breadcrumbs.
5. Drizzle the shrimp evenly with olive oil and arrange half of the coated shrimps into the Air fryer basket.
6. Cook for about 7 minutes and dish out the coated shrimps onto serving plates.
7. Repeat with the remaining mixture and serve hot.
- **Nutrition Info:** Calories: 432, Fat: 11.3g, Carbohydrates: 44.8g, Sugar: 2.5g, Protein: 37.7g, Sodium: 526mg

227.Shrimp Scampi

Servings: 6
Cooking Time: 7 Minutes
Ingredients:
- 4 tablespoons salted butter
- 1 pound shrimp, peeled and deveined
- 2 tablespoons fresh basil, chopped
- 1 tablespoon fresh chives, chopped
- 1 tablespoon fresh lemon juice
- 1 tablespoon garlic, minced
- 2 teaspoons red pepper flakes, crushed
- 2 tablespoons dry white wine

Directions:
1. Preheat the Air fryer to 325 ºF and grease an Air fryer pan.
2. Heat butter, lemon juice, garlic, and red pepper flakes in a pan and return the pan to Air fryer basket.
3. Cook for about 2 minutes and stir in shrimp, basil, chives and wine.
4. Cook for about 5 minutes and dish out the mixture onto serving plates.
5. Serve hot.
- **Nutrition Info:** Calories: 250, Fat: 13.7g, Carbohydrates: 3.3g, Sugar: 0.3g, Protein: 26.3g, Sodium: 360mg

228.Kale And Brussels Sprouts

Servings: 8
Cooking Time: 7 Minutes
Ingredients:
- 1 lb. Brussels sprouts, trimmed
- 3 oz. mozzarella, shredded
- 2 cups kale, torn
- 1 tbsp. olive oil
- Salt and black pepper to taste.

Directions:
1. In a pan that fits the air fryer, combine all the Ingredients: except the mozzarella and toss.

2. Put the pan in the air fryer and cook at 380°F for 15 minutes
3. Divide between plates, sprinkle the cheese on top and serve.
- **Nutrition Info:** Calories: 170; Fat: 5g; Fiber: 3g; Carbs: 4g; Protein: 7g

229.Roasted Garlic Zucchini Rolls

Servings: 4
Cooking Time: 20 Minutes
Ingredients:
- 2 medium zucchinis
- ½ cup full-fat ricotta cheese
- ¼ white onion; peeled. And diced
- 2 cups spinach; chopped
- ¼ cup heavy cream
- ½ cup sliced baby portobello mushrooms
- ¾ cup shredded mozzarella cheese, divided.
- 2 tbsp. unsalted butter.
- 2 tbsp. vegetable broth.
- ½ tsp. finely minced roasted garlic
- ¼ tsp. dried oregano.
- ⅛ tsp. xanthan gum
- ¼ tsp. salt
- ½ tsp. garlic powder.

Directions:
1. Using a mandoline or sharp knife, slice zucchini into long strips lengthwise. Place strips between paper towels to absorb moisture. Set aside
2. In a medium saucepan over medium heat, melt butter. Add onion and sauté until fragrant. Add garlic and sauté 30 seconds.
3. Pour in heavy cream, broth and xanthan gum. Turn off heat and whisk mixture until it begins to thicken, about 3 minutes.
4. Take a medium bowl, add ricotta, salt, garlic powder and oregano and mix well. Fold in spinach, mushrooms and ½ cup mozzarella
5. Pour half of the sauce into a 6-inch round baking pan. To assemble the rolls, place two strips of zucchini on a work surface. Spoon 2 tbsp. of ricotta mixture onto the slices and roll up. Place seam side down on top of sauce. Repeat with remaining ingredients
6. Pour remaining sauce over the rolls and sprinkle with remaining mozzarella. Cover with foil and place into the air fryer basket. Adjust the temperature to 350 Degrees F and set the timer for 20 minutes. In the last 5 minutes, remove the foil to brown the cheese. Serve immediately.
- **Nutrition Info:** Calories: 245; Protein: 15g; Fiber: 8g; Fat: 19g; Carbs: 1g

230.Dinner Avocado Chicken Sliders

Servings: 4
Cooking Time: 20 Minutes
Ingredients:
- ½ pounds ground chicken meat 4 burger buns
- 1/2 cup Romaine lettuce, loosely packed
- ½ tsp. dried parsley flakes 1/3 tsp. mustard seeds
- 1 tsp. onion powder
- 1 ripe fresh avocado, mashed 1 tsp. garlic powder
- 1 ½ tablespoon extra-virgin olive oil
- 1 cloves garlic, minced Nonstick cooking spray
- Salt and cracked black pepper (peppercorns, to taste)

Directions:
1. Firstly, spritz an air fryer cooking basket with a nonstick cooking spray.
2. Mix ground chicken meat, mustard seeds, garlic powder, onion powder, parsley, salt, and black pepper until everything is thoroughly combined. Make sure not to overwork the meat to avoid tough chicken burgers.
3. Shape the meat mixture into patties and roll them in breadcrumbs; transfer your burgers to the prepared cooking basket. Brush the patties with the cooking spray.
4. Air-fry at 355 F for 9 minutes, working in batches. Slice burger buns into halves. In the meantime, combine olive oil with mashed avocado and pressed garlic.
5. To finish, lay Romaine lettuce and avocado spread on bun bottoms; now, add burgers and bun tops.
- **Nutrition Info:** 321 Calories; 18.7g Fat; 15.8g Carbs; 1.2g Sugars

231.Chili Pepper Lamb Chops

Servings: 6
Cooking Time: 10 Minutes
Ingredients:
- 21 oz. lamb chops
- 1 teaspoon chili pepper
- ½ teaspoon chili flakes
- 1 teaspoon onion powder
- 1 teaspoon garlic powder
- 1 teaspoon cayenne pepper
- 1 tablespoon olive oil
- 1 tablespoon butter
- ½ teaspoon lime zest

Directions:
1. Melt the butter and combine it with the olive oil.
2. Whisk the liquid and add chili pepper, chili flakes, onion powder, garlic powder, cayenne pepper, and lime zest.
3. Whisk it well
4. Then sprinkle the lamb chops with the prepared oily marinade.
5. Leave the meat for at least 5 minutes in the fridge.
6. Preheat the air fryer to 400 F.
7. Place the marinated lamb chops in the air fryer and cook them for 5 minutes.
8. After this, open the air fryer and turn the lamb chops into another side.
9. Cook the lamb chops for 5 minutes more.

10. When the meat is cooked – transfer it to the serving plates.
11. Enjoy!
- **Nutrition Info:** calories 227, fat 11.6, fiber 0.2, carbs 1, protein 28.1

232.Lemongrass Pork Chops

Servings: 3
Cooking Time: 2 Hrs 20 Minutes
Ingredients:
- 3 slices pork chops
- 2 garlic cloves, minced
- 1 ½ tbsp sugar
- 4 stalks lemongrass, trimmed and chopped
- 2 shallots, chopped
- 2 tbsp olive oil
- 1 ¼ tsp soy sauce
- 1 ¼ tsp fish sauce
- 1 ½ tsp black pepper

Directions:
1. In a bowl, add the garlic, sugar, lemongrass, shallots, olive oil, soy sauce, fish sauce, and black pepper; mix well. Add the pork chops, coat them with the mixture and allow to marinate for around 2 hours to get nice and savory.
2. Preheat the Air Fryer to 400 F. Cooking in 2 to 3 batches, remove and shake each pork chop from the marinade and place it in the fryer basket. Cook it for 7 minutes. Turn the pork chops with kitchen tongs and cook further for 5 minutes. Remove the chops and serve with a side of sautéed asparagus.
- **Nutrition Info:** 346 Calories; 11g Fat; 4g Carbs; 32g Protein; 1g Sugars; 1g Fiber

233.Fried Spicy Tofu

Servings: 4
Cooking Time: 20 Minutes
Ingredients:
- 16 ounces firm tofu, pressed and cubed
- 1 tablespoon vegan oyster sauce
- 1 tablespoon tamari sauce
- 1 teaspoon cider vinegar
- 1 teaspoon pure maple syrup
- 1 teaspoon sriracha
- 1/2 teaspoon shallot powder
- 1/2 teaspoon porcini powder
- 1 teaspoon garlic powder
- 1 tablespoon sesame oil
- 2 tablespoons golden flaxseed meal

Directions:
1. Toss the tofu with the oyster sauce, tamari sauce, vinegar, maple syrup, sriracha, shallot powder, porcini powder, garlic powder, and sesame oil. Let it marinate for 30 minutes.
2. Toss the marinated tofu with the flaxseed meal.
3. Cook at 360 degrees F for 10 minutes; turn them over and cook for 12 minutes more.
- **Nutrition Info:** 173 Calories; 13g Fat; 5g Carbs; 12g Protein; 8g Sugars; 1g Fiber

234.Flank Steak Beef

Servings: 4
Cooking Time: 20 Minutes
Ingredients:
- 1 pound flank steaks, sliced
- ¼ cup xanthum gum
- 2 teaspoon vegetable oil
- ½ teaspoon ginger
- ½ cup soy sauce
- 1 tablespoon garlic, minced
- ½ cup water
- ¾ cup swerve, packed

Directions:
1. Preheat the Air fryer to 390 degree F and grease an Air fryer basket.
2. Coat the steaks with xanthum gum on both the sides and transfer into the Air fryer basket.
3. Cook for about 10 minutes and dish out in a platter.
4. Meanwhile, cook rest of the ingredients for the sauce in a saucepan.
5. Bring to a boil and pour over the steak slices to serve.
- **Nutrition Info:** Calories: 372, Fat: 11.8g, Carbohydrates: 1.8g, Sugar: 27.3g, Protein: 34g, Sodium: 871mg

235.Tomato Stuffed Pork Roll

Servings: 4
Cooking Time: 15 Minutes
Ingredients:
- 1 scallion, chopped
- ¼ cup sun-dried tomatoes, chopped finely
- 2 tablespoons fresh parsley, chopped
- 4: 6-ouncepork cutlets, pounded slightly
- Salt and freshly ground black pepper, to taste
- 2 teaspoons paprika
- ½ tablespoon olive oil

Directions:
1. Preheat the Air fryer to 390 degree F and grease an Air fryer basket.
2. Mix scallion, tomatoes, parsley, salt and black pepper in a bowl.
3. Coat each cutlet with tomato mixture and roll up the cutlet, securing with cocktail sticks.
4. Coat the rolls with oil and rub with paprika, salt and black pepper.
5. Arrange the rolls in the Air fryer basket and cook for about 15 minutes, flipping once in between.
6. Dish out in a platter and serve warm.
- **Nutrition Info:** Calories: 244, Fat: 14.5g, Carbohydrates: 20.1g, Sugar: 1.7g, Protein: 8.2g, Sodium: 670mg

236.Effortless Beef Schnitzel

Servings: 2
Cooking Time: 25 Minutes
Ingredients:

- 2 tbsp vegetable oil
- 2 oz breadcrumbs
- 1 whole egg, whisked
- 1 thin beef schnitzel, cut into strips
- 1 whole lemon

Directions:
1. Preheat your fryer to 356 F. In a bowl, add breadcrumbs and oil and stir well to get a loose mixture. Dip schnitzel in egg, then dip in breadcrumbs coat well. Place the prepared schnitzel your Air Fryer's cooking basket and cook for 12 minutes. Serve with a drizzle of lemon juice.
- **Nutrition Info:** 346 Calories; 11g Fat; 4g Carbs; 32g Protein; 1g Sugars; 1g Fiber

237.Sage Sausages Balls

Servings: 4
Cooking Time: 20 Minutes
Ingredients:
- 3 ½ oz sausages, sliced
- Salt and black pepper to taste
- 1 cup onion, chopped
- 3 tbsp breadcrumbs
- ½ tsp garlic puree
- 1 tsp sage

Directions:
1. Preheat your air fryer to 340 f. In a bowl, mix onions, sausage meat, sage, garlic puree, salt and pepper. Add breadcrumbs to a plate. Form balls using the mixture and roll them in breadcrumbs. Add onion balls in your air fryer's cooking basket and cook for 15 minutes. Serve and enjoy!
- **Nutrition Info:** Calories: 162 Cal Total Fat: 12.1 g Saturated Fat: 0 g Cholesterol: 25 mg Sodium: 324 mg Total Carbs: 7.3 g Fiber: 0 g Sugar: 0 g Protein: 6 g

238.Bbq Pork Ribs

Servings: 2 To 3
Cooking Time: 5 Hrs 30 Minutes
Ingredients:
- 1 lb pork ribs
- 1 tsp soy sauce
- Salt and black pepper to taste
- 1 tsp oregano
- 1 tbsp + 1 tbsp maple syrup
- 3 tbsp barbecue sauce
- 2 cloves garlic, minced
- 1 tbsp cayenne pepper
- 1 tsp sesame oil

Directions:
1. Put the chops on a chopping board and use a knife to cut them into smaller pieces of desired sizes. Put them in a mixing bowl, add the soy sauce, salt, pepper, oregano, one tablespoon of maple syrup, barbecue sauce, garlic, cayenne pepper, and sesame oil. Mix well and place the pork in the fridge to marinate in the spices for 5 hours.

2. Preheat the Air Fryer to 350 F. Open the Air Fryer and place the ribs in the fryer basket. Slide the fryer basket in and cook for 15 minutes. Open the Air fryer, turn the ribs using tongs, apply the remaining maple syrup with a brush, close the Air Fryer, and continue cooking for 10 minutes.
- **Nutrition Info:** 346 Calories; 11g Fat; 4g Carbs; 32g Protein; 1g Sugars; 1g Fiber

239.Turkey Wontons With Garlic-parmesan Sauce

Servings: 8
Cooking Time: 20 Minutes
Ingredients:
- 8 ounces cooked turkey breasts, shredded 16 wonton wrappers
- 1½ tablespoons margarine, melted
- 1/3 cup cream cheese, room temperature 8 ounces Asiago cheese, shredded
- 3 tablespoons Parmesan cheese, grated
- 1 tsp. garlic powder
- Fine sea salt and freshly ground black pepper, to taste

Directions:
1. In a small-sized bowl, mix the margarine, Parmesan, garlic powder, salt, and black pepper; give it a good stir.
2. Lightly grease a mini muffin pan; lay 1 wonton wrapper in each mini muffin cup. Fill each cup with the cream cheese and turkey mixture.
3. Air-fry for 8 minutes at 335 °F. Immediately top with Asiago cheese and serve warm.
- **Nutrition Info:** 362 Calories;   13.5g Fat;   40.4g Carbs;   18.5g Protein;   1.2g Sugars

240.Okra With Green Beans

Servings: 2
Cooking Time: 20 Minutes
Ingredients:
- ½, 10-ouncesbag frozen cut okra
- ½, 10-ouncesbag frozen cut green beans
- ¼ cup nutritional yeast
- 3 tablespoons balsamic vinegar
- Salt and black pepper, to taste

Directions:
1. Preheat the Air fryer to 400 ºF and grease an Air fryer basket.
2. Mix the okra, green beans, nutritional yeast, vinegar, salt, and black pepper in a bowl and toss to coat well.
3. Arrange the okra mixture into the Air fryer basket and cook for about 20 minutes.
4. Dish out in a serving dish and serve hot.
- **Nutrition Info:** Calories: 126, Fat: 1.3g, Carbohydrates: 19.7g, Sugar: 2.1g, Protein: 11.9g, Sodium: 100mg

241.Beef With Apples And Plums

Servings: 4

Cooking Time: 30 Minutes

Ingredients:
- 2pounds beef stew meat, cubed
- 1cup apples, cored and cubed
- 1cup plums, pitted and halved
- 2tablespoons butter, melted
- Salt and black pepper to the taste
- ½ cup red wine
- 1tablespoon chives, chopped

Directions:
1. In the air fryer's pan, mix the beef with the apples and the other ingredients, toss, put the pan in the machine and cook at 390 degrees F for 30 minutes.
2. Divide the mix between plates and serve right away.
- **Nutrition Info:** Calories 290, Fat 12, Fiber 5, Carbs 19, Protein 28

242.Beef Roast

Servings: 4
Cooking Time:x

Ingredients:
- 2 lbs. beef roast
- 1 tbsp. smoked paprika
- 3 tbsp. garlic; minced
- 3 tbsp. olive oil
- Salt and black pepper to taste

Directions:
1. In a bowl, combine all the ingredients and coat the roast well.
2. Place the roast in your air fryer and cook at 390°F for 55 minutes. Slice the roast, divide it between plates and serve with a side salad

243.Sesame Seeds Bok Choy

Servings: 4
Cooking Time: 6 Minutes

Ingredients:
- 4 bunches baby bok choy, bottoms removed and leaves separated
- 1 teaspoon sesame seeds
- Olive oil cooking spray
- 1 teaspoon garlic powder

Directions:
1. Preheat the Air fryer to 325 ºF and grease an Air fryer basket.
2. Arrange the bok choy leaves into the Air fryer basket and spray with the cooking spray.
3. Sprinkle with garlic powder and cook for about 6 minutes, shaking twice in between.
4. Dish out in the bok choy onto serving plates and serve garnished with sesame seeds.
- **Nutrition Info:** Calories: 26, Fat: 0.7g, Carbohydrates: 4g, Sugar: 1.9g, Protein: 2.5g, Sodium: 98mg

244.Smoked Sausage And Bacon Shashlik

Servings: 4
Cooking Time: 20 Minutes

Ingredients:
- 1 pound smoked Polish beef sausage, sliced
- 1 tablespoon mustard
- 1 tablespoon olive oil
- 2 tablespoons Worcestershire sauce
- 2 bell peppers, sliced
- Salt and ground black pepper, to taste

Directions:
1. Toss the sausage with the mustard, olive, and Worcestershire sauce. Thread sausage and peppers onto skewers.
2. Sprinkle with salt and black pepper.
3. Cook in the preheated Air Fryer at 360 degrees Ffor 11 minutes. Brush the skewers with the reserved marinade.
- **Nutrition Info:** 422 Calories; 36g Fat; 9g Carbs; 18g Protein; 6g Sugars; 7g Fiber

245.Spicy Cauliflower Rice

Servings: 2
Cooking Time: 22 Minutes

Ingredients:
- 1 cauliflower head, cut into florets 1/2 tsp cumin
- 1/2 tsp chili powder
- 6 onion spring, chopped 2 jalapenos, chopped
- 4 tbsp olive oil
- 1 zucchini, trimmed and cut into cubes 1/2 tsp paprika
- 1/2 tsp garlic powder 1/2 tsp cayenne pepper 1/2 tsp pepper
- 1/2 tsp salt

Directions:
1. Preheat the air fryer to 370 F.
2. Add cauliflower florets into the food processor and process until it looks like rice.
3. Transfer cauliflower rice into the air fryer baking pan and drizzle with half oil.
4. Place pan in the air fryer and cook for 12 minutes, stir halfway through.
5. Heat remaining oil in a small pan over medium heat.
6. Add zucchini and cook for 5-8 minutes.
7. Add onion and jalapenos and cook for 5 minutes.
8. Add spices and stir well. Set aside.
9. Add cauliflower rice in the zucchini mixture and stir well.
10. Serve and enjoy.
- **Nutrition Info:** Calories 254 Fat 28 g Carbohydrates 12.3 g Sugar 5 g

246.Red Hot Chili Fish Curry

Servings: 4
Cooking Time: 20 Minutes

Ingredients:
- 2 tablespoons sunflower oil
- 1 pound fish, chopped
- 2 red chilies, chopped
- 1 tablespoon coriander powder
- 1 teaspoon red curry paste

- 1 cup coconut milk
- Salt and white pepper, to taste
- 1/2 teaspoon fenugreek seeds
- 1 shallot, minced
- 1 garlic clove, minced
- 1 ripe tomato, pureed

Directions:
1. Preheat your Air Fryer to 380 degrees F; brush the cooking basket with 1 tablespoon of sunflower oil.
2. Cook your fish for 10 minutes on both sides. Transfer to the baking pan that is previously greased with the remaining tablespoon of sunflower oil.
3. Add the remaining ingredients and reduce the heat to 350 degrees F. Continue to cook an additional 10 to 12 minutes or until everything is heated through. Enjoy!
- **Nutrition Info:** 298 Calories; 18g Fat; 4g Carbs; 23g Protein; 7g Sugars; 7g Fiber

247.Zingy Dilled Salmon

Servings: 2
Cooking Time: 20 Minutes
Ingredients:
- 2 salmon steaks
- Coarse sea salt, to taste
- 1/4 teaspoon freshly ground black pepper, or more to taste
- 1 tablespoon sesame oil
- Zest of 1 lemon
- 1 tablespoon fresh lemon juice
- 1 teaspoon garlic, minced
- 1/2 teaspoon smoked cayenne pepper
- 1/2 teaspoon dried dill

Directions:
1. Preheat your Air Fryer to 380 degrees F. Pat dry the salmon steaks with a kitchen towel.
2. In a ceramic dish, combine the remaining ingredients until everything is well whisked.
3. Add the salmon steaks to the ceramic dish and let them sit in the refrigerator for 1 hour. Now, place the salmon steaks in the cooking basket. Reserve the marinade.
4. Cook for 12 minutes, flipping halfway through the cooking time.
5. Meanwhile, cook the marinade in a small sauté pan over a moderate flame. Cook until the sauce has thickened.
6. Pour the sauce over the steaks and serve.
- **Nutrition Info:** 476 Calories; 18g Fat; 2g Carbs; 47g Protein; 8g Sugars; 4g Fiber

248.Beef Sausage With Grilled Broccoli

Servings: 4
Cooking Time: 20 Minutes
Ingredients:
- 1 pound beef Vienna sausage
- 1/2 cup mayonnaise
- 1 teaspoon yellow mustard
- 1 tablespoon fresh lemon juice
- 1 teaspoon garlic powder

- 1/4 teaspoon black pepper
- 1 pound broccoli

Directions:
1. Start by preheating your Air Fryer to 380 degrees F. Spritz the grill pan with cooking oil.
2. Cut the sausages into serving sized pieces. Cook the sausages for 15 minutes, shaking the basket occasionally to get all sides browned. Set aside.
3. In the meantime, whisk the mayonnaise with mustard, lemon juice, garlic powder, and black pepper. Toss the broccoli with the mayo mixture.
4. Turn up temperature to 400 degrees F. Cook broccoli for 6 minutes, turning halfway through the cooking time.
5. Serve the sausage with the grilled broccoli on the side.
- **Nutrition Info:** 477 Calories; 42g Fat; 3g Carbs; 19g Protein; 7g Sugars; 6g Fiber

249.Asparagus Frittata

Servings: 4
Cooking Time: 10 Minutes
Ingredients:
- 6 eggs
- 3 mushrooms, sliced
- 10 asparagus, chopped 1/4 cup half and half
- 2 tsp butter, melted
- 1 cup mozzarella cheese, shredded 1 tsp pepper
- 1 tsp salt

Directions:
1. Toss mushrooms and asparagus with melted butter and add into the air fryer basket.
2. Cook mushrooms and asparagus at 350 F for 5 minutes. Shake basket twice.
3. Meanwhile, in a bowl, whisk together eggs, half and half, pepper, and salt.
4. Transfer cook mushrooms and asparagus into the air fryer baking dish.
5. Pour egg mixture over mushrooms and asparagus.
6. Place dish in the air fryer and cook at 350 F for 5 minutes or until eggs are set.
7. Slice and serve.
- **Nutrition Info:** Calories 211 Fat 13 g Carbohydrates 4 g Sugar 1 g Protein 16 g Cholesterol 272 mg

250.Cod With Avocado Mayo Sauce

Servings: 2
Cooking Time: 20 Minutes
Ingredients:
- 2 cod fish fillets
- 1 egg
- Sea salt, to taste
- 2 teaspoons olive oil
- 1/2 avocado, peeled, pitted, and mashed
- 1 tablespoon mayonnaise
- 3 tablespoons sour cream

- 1/2 teaspoon yellow mustard
- 1 teaspoon lemon juice
- 1 garlic clove, minced
- 1/4 teaspoon black pepper
- 1/4 teaspoon salt
- 1/4 teaspoon hot pepper sauce

Directions:
1. Start by preheating your Air Fryer to 360 degrees F. Spritz the Air Fryer basket with cooking oil.
2. Pat dry the fish fillets with a kitchen towel. Beat the egg in a shallow bowl. Add in the salt and olive oil.
3. Dip the fish into the egg mixture, making sure to coat thoroughly. Cook in the preheated Air Fryer approximately 12 minutes.
4. Meanwhile, make the avocado sauce by mixing the remaining ingredients in a bowl. Place in your refrigerator until ready to serve.
5. Serve the fish fillets with chilled avocado sauce on the side.
- **Nutrition Info:** 344 Calories; 27g Fat; 8g Carbs; 21g Protein; 8g Sugars; 7g Fiber

251.Tasty Grilled Red Mullet

Servings: 8
Cooking Time: 15 Minutes
Ingredients:
- 8 whole red mullets, gutted and scales removed
- Salt and pepper to taste
- Juice from 1 lemon
- 1 tablespoon olive oil

Directions:
1. Place the instant pot air fryer lid on and preheat the instant pot at 390 degrees F.
2. Place the grill pan accessory in the instant pot.
3. Season the red mullet with salt, pepper, and lemon juice.
4. Place red mullets on the grill pan and brush with olive oil.
5. Close the air fryer lid and grill for 15 minutes.
- **Nutrition Info:** Calories: 152; Carbs: 0.9g; Protein: 23.1g; Fat: 6.2g

252.Cheese Breaded Pork

Servings: 6
Cooking Time: 15 Minutes
Ingredients:
- 6 pork chops
- 6 tbsp seasoned breadcrumbs
- 2 tbsp parmesan cheese, grated
- 1 tbsp melted butter
- ½ cup mozzarella cheese, shredded
- 1 tbsp marinara sauce

Directions:
1. Preheat your air fryer to 390 f. Grease the cooking basket with cooking spray. In a

small bowl, mix breadcrumbs and parmesan cheese. In another microwave proof bowl, add butter and melt in the microwave.
2. Brush the pork with butter and dredge into the breadcrumbs. Add pork to the cooking basket and cook for 6 minutes. Turnover and top with marinara sauce and shredded mozzarella; cook for 3 more minutes
- **Nutrition Info:** Calories: 431 Cal Total Fat: 0 g Saturated Fat: 0 g Cholesterol: 0 mg Sodium: 0 mg Total Carbs: 0 g Fiber: 0 g Sugar: 0 g Protein: 0 g

253.Sweet Chicken Breast

Servings: 4
Cooking Time: 12 Minutes
Ingredients:
- 1-pound chicken breast, boneless, skinless
- 3 tablespoon Stevia extract
- 1 teaspoon ground white pepper
- ½ teaspoon paprika
- 1 teaspoon cayenne pepper
- 1 teaspoon lemongrass
- 1 teaspoon lemon zest
- 1 tablespoon apple cider vinegar
- 1 tablespoon butter

Directions:
1. Sprinkle the chicken breast with the apple cider vinegar.
2. After this, rub the chicken breast with the ground white pepper, paprika, cayenne pepper, lemongrass, and lemon zest.
3. Leave the chicken breast for 5 minutes to marinate.
4. After this, rub the chicken breast with the stevia extract and leave it for 5 minutes more.
5. Preheat the air fryer to 380 F.
6. Rub the prepared chicken breast with the butter and place it in the air fryer basket tray.
7. Cook the chicken breast for 12 minutes.
8. Turn the chicken breast into another side after 6 minutes of cooking.
9. Serve the dish hot!
10. Enjoy!
- **Nutrition Info:** calories 160, fat 5.9, fiber 0.4, carbs 1, protein 24.2

254.Corned Beef With Carrots

Servings: 3
Cooking Time: 35 Minutes
Ingredients:
- 1 tbsp beef spice
- 1 whole onion, chopped
- 4 carrots, chopped
- 12 oz bottle beer
- 1½ cups chicken broth
- 4 pounds corned beef

Directions:
1. Preheat your air fryer to 380 f. Cover beef with beer and set aside for 20 minutes.

Place carrots, onion and beef in a pot and heat over high heat. Add in broth and bring to a boil. Drain boiled meat and veggies; set aside.

2. Top with beef spice. Place the meat and veggies in your air fryer's cooking basket and cook for 30 minutes.

- **Nutrition Info:** Calories: 464 Cal Total Fat: 17 g Saturated Fat: 6.8 g Cholesterol: 91.7 mg Sodium: 1904.2 mg Total Carbs: 48.9 g Fiber: 7.2 g Sugar: 5.8 g Protein: 30.6 g

255.Pesto & White Wine Salmon

Servings: 4
Cooking Time: 10 Minutes
Ingredients:

- 1-1/4 pounds salmon filet
- 2 tablespoons white wine
- 2 tablespoons pesto
- 1 lemon

Directions:

1. Cut the salmon into 4 pieces and place on a greased baking sheet.
2. Slice the lemon into quarters and squeeze 1 quarter over each piece of salmon.
3. Drizzle wine over salmon and set aside to marinate while preheating the toaster oven on broil.
4. Spread pesto over each piece of salmon.
5. Broil for at least 10 minutes, or until the fish is cooked to desired doneness and the pesto is browned.

- **Nutrition Info:** Calories: 236, Sodium: 111 mg, Dietary Fiber: 0.9 g, Total Fat: 12.1 g, Total Carbs: 3.3 g, Protein: 28.6 g.

256.Broccoli Stuffed Peppers

Servings: 2
Cooking Time: 40 Minutes
Ingredients:

- 4 eggs
- 1/2 cup cheddar cheese, grated
- 2 bell peppers, cut in half and remove seeds
- 1/2 tsp garlic powder
- 1 tsp dried thyme
- 1/4 cup feta cheese, crumbled 1/2 cup broccoli, cooked
- 1/4 tsp pepper 1/2 tsp salt

Directions:

1. Preheat the air fryer to 325 F.
2. Stuff feta and broccoli into the bell peppers halved.
3. Beat egg in a bowl with seasoning and pour egg mixture into the pepper halved over feta and broccoli.
4. Place bell pepper halved into the air fryer basket and cook for 35-40 minutes.
5. Top with grated cheddar cheese and cook until cheese melted.
6. Serve and enjoy.

- **Nutrition Info:** Calories 340 Fat 22 g Carbohydrates 12 g Sugar 8.2 g Protein 22 g Cholesterol 374 mg

257.Grandma's Meatballs With Spicy Sauce

Servings: 4
Cooking Time: 20 Minutes
Ingredients:

- 4 tablespoons pork rinds
- 1/3 cup green onion
- 1 pound beef sausage meat
- 3 garlic cloves, minced
- 1/3 teaspoon ground black pepper
- Sea salt, to taste
- For the sauce:
- 2 tablespoons Worcestershire sauce
- 1/3 yellow onion, minced
- Dash of Tabasco sauce
- 1/3 cup tomato paste
- 1 teaspoon cumin powder
- 1/2 tablespoon balsamic vinegar

Directions:

1. Knead all of the above ingredients until everything is well incorporated.
2. Roll into balls and cook in the preheated Air Fryer at 365 degrees for 13 minutes.
3. In the meantime, in a saucepan, cook the ingredients for the sauce until thoroughly warmed. Serve your meatballs with the tomato sauce and enjoy!

- **Nutrition Info:** 360 Calories; 23g Fat; 6g Carbs; 23g Protein; 4g Sugars; 2g Fiber

258.Oven-fried Herbed Chicken

Servings: 2
Cooking Time: 15 Minutes
Ingredients:

- 1/2 cup buttermilk
- 2 cloves garlic, minced
- 1-1/2 teaspoons salt
- 1 tablespoon oil
- 1/2 pound boneless, skinless chicken breasts
- 1 cup rolled oats
- 1/2 teaspoon red pepper flakes
- 1/2 cup grated parmesan cheese
- 1/4 cup fresh basil leaves or rosemary needles
- Olive oil spray

Directions:

1. Mix together buttermilk, oil, 1/2 teaspoon salt, and garlic in a shallow bowl.
2. Roll chicken in buttermilk and refrigerate in bowl overnight.
3. Preheat your toaster oven to 425°F.
4. Mix together the oats, red pepper, salt, parmesan, and basil, and mix roughly to break up oats.
5. Place the mixture on a plate.
6. Remove the chicken from the buttermilk mixture and let any excess drip off.
7. Roll the chicken in the oat mixture and transfer to a baking sheet lightly coated with olive oil spray.

8. Spray the chicken with oil spray and bake for 15 minutes.
- **Nutrition Info:** Calories: 651, Sodium: 713 mg, Dietary Fiber: 4.4 g, Total Fat: 31.2 g, Total Carbs: 34.1 g, Protein: 59.5 g.

259.Award Winning Breaded Chicken

Servings: 4
Cooking Time: 20 Minutes
Ingredients:
- 1 1/2 tsp.s olive oil
- 1 tsp. red pepper flakes, crushed 1/3 tsp. chicken bouillon granules 1/3 tsp. shallot powder
- 1 1/2 tablespoons tamari soy sauce 1/3 tsp. cumin powder
- 1½ tablespoons mayo 1 tsp. kosher salt
- For the chicken:
- 2 beaten eggs Breadcrumbs
- 1½ chicken breasts, boneless and skinless 1 ½ tablespoons plain flour

Directions:
1. Margarine fly the chicken breasts, and then, marinate them for at least 55 minutes. Coat the chicken with plain flour; then, coat with the beaten eggs; finally, roll them in the breadcrumbs.
2. Lightly grease the cooking basket. Air-fry the breaded chicken at 345 °F for 12 minutes, flipping them halfway.
- **Nutrition Info:** 262 Calories; 14.9g Fat; 2.7g Carbs; 27.5g Protein; 0.3g Sugars

260.Traditional English Fish And Chips

Servings: 4
Cooking Time: 17 Minutes
Ingredients:
- 1 3/4 pounds potatoes
- 4 tablespoons olive oil
- 1-1/4 teaspoons kosher salt
- 1-1/4 teaspoons black pepper
- 8 sprigs fresh thyme
- 4 (6-ounce) pieces cod
- 1 lemon
- 1 clove garlic
- 2 tablespoons capers

Directions:
1. Start by preheating toaster oven to 450°F.
2. Cut potatoes into 1-inch chunks.
3. Place potatoes, 2 tablespoons oil, salt, and thyme in a baking tray and toss to combine.
4. Spread in a flat layer and bake for 30 minutes.
5. Wrap mixture in foil to keep warm.
6. Wipe tray with a paper towel and then lay cod in the tray.
7. Slice the lemon and top cod with lemon, salt, pepper, and thyme.
8. Drizzle rest of the oil over the cod and bake for 12 minutes.

9. Place cod and potatoes on separate pans and bake together for an additional 5 minutes.
10. Combine and serve.
- **Nutrition Info:** Calories: 442, Sodium: 1002 mg, Dietary Fiber: 5.4 g, Total Fat: 15.8 g, Total Carbs: 32.7 g, Protein: 42.5 g.

261.Cheesy Shrimp

Servings: 4
Cooking Time: 20 Minutes
Ingredients:
- 2/3 cup Parmesan cheese, grated
- 2 pounds shrimp, peeled and deveined
- 4 garlic cloves, minced
- 2 tablespoons olive oil
- 1 teaspoon dried basil
- ½ teaspoon dried oregano
- 1 teaspoon onion powder
- ½ teaspoon red pepper flakes, crushed
- Ground black pepper, as required
- 2 tablespoons fresh lemon juice

Directions:
1. Preheat the Air fryer to 350 degree F and grease an Air fryer basket.
2. Mix Parmesan cheese, garlic, olive oil, herbs, and spices in a large bowl.
3. Arrange half of the shrimp into the Air fryer basket in a single layer and cook for about 10 minutes.
4. Dish out the shrimps onto serving plates and drizzle with lemon juice to serve hot.
- **Nutrition Info:** Calories: 386, Fat: 14.2g, Carbohydrates: 5.3g, Sugar: 0.4g, Protein: 57.3g, Sodium: 670mg

262.Garlic Lamb Shank

Servings: 5
Cooking Time: 24 Minutes
Ingredients:
- 17 oz. lamb shanks
- 2 tablespoon garlic, peeled
- 1 teaspoon kosher salt
- 1 tablespoon dried parsley
- 4 oz chive stems, chopped
- ½ cup chicken stock
- 1 teaspoon butter
- 1 teaspoon dried rosemary
- 1 teaspoon nutmeg
- ½ teaspoon ground black pepper

Directions:
1. Chop the garlic roughly.
2. Make the cuts in the lamb shank and fill the cuts with the chopped garlic.
3. Then sprinkle the lamb shank with the kosher salt, dried parsley, dried rosemary, nutmeg, and ground black pepper.
4. Stir the spices on the lamb shank gently.
5. Then put the butter and chicken stock in the air fryer basket tray.
6. Preheat the air fryer to 380 F.
7. Put the chives in the air fryer basket tray.

8. Add the lamb shank and cook the meat for 24 minutes.
9. When the lamb shank is cooked – transfer it to the serving plate and sprinkle with the remaining liquid from the cooked meat.
10. Enjoy!
- **Nutrition Info:** calories 205, fat 8.2, fiber 0.8, carbs 3.8, protein 27.2

263.Roasted Tuna On Linguine

Servings: 2
Cooking Time: 20 Minutes
Ingredients:
- 1pound fresh tuna fillets
- Salt and pepper to taste
- 1 tablespoon olive oil
- 12 ounces linguine, cooked according to package Directions:
- 2 cups parsley leaves, chopped
- 1 tablespoon capers, chopped
- Juice from 1 lemon

Directions:
1. Place the instant pot air fryer lid on and preheat the instant pot at 390 degrees F.
2. Place the grill pan accessory in the instant pot.
3. Season the tuna with salt and pepper. Brush with oil.
4. Place on the grill pan, close the air fryer lid and grill for 20 minutes.
5. Once the tuna is cooked, shred using forks and place on top of cooked linguine. Add parsley and capers. Season with salt and pepper and add lemon juice.
- **Nutrition Info:** Calories: 520; Carbs: 60.6g; Protein: 47.7g; Fat: 9.6g

264.Coconut Crusted Shrimp

Servings: 3
Cooking Time: 40 Minutes
Ingredients:
- 8 ounces coconut milk
- ½ cup sweetened coconut, shredded
- ½ cup panko breadcrumbs
- 1 pound large shrimp, peeled and deveined
- Salt and black pepper, to taste

Directions:
1. Preheat the Air fryer to 350-degree F and grease an Air fryer basket.
2. Place the coconut milk in a shallow bowl.
3. Mix coconut, breadcrumbs, salt, and black pepper in another bowl.
4. Dip each shrimp into coconut milk and finally, dredge in the coconut mixture.
5. Arrange half of the shrimps into the Air fryer basket and cook for about 20 minutes.
6. Dish out the shrimps onto serving plates and repeat with the remaining mixture to serve.
- **Nutrition Info:** Calories: 408, Fats: 23.7g, Carbohydrates: 11.7g, Sugar: 3.4g, Proteins: 31g, Sodium: 253mg

265.Venetian Liver

Servings: 6
Cooking Time: 15-30;
Ingredients:
- 500g veal liver
- 2 white onions
- 100g of water
- 2 tbsp vinegar
- Salt and pepper to taste

Directions:
1. Chop the onion and put it inside the pan with the water. Set the air fryer to 1800C and cook for 20 minutes.
2. Add the liver cut into small pieces and vinegar, close the lid, and cook for an additional 10 minutes.
3. Add salt and pepper.
- **Nutrition Info:** Calories 131, Fat 14.19 g, Carbohydrates 16.40 g, Sugars 5.15 g, Protein 25.39 g, Cholesterol 350.41 mg

266.Grilled Chicken Tikka Masala

Servings: 4
Cooking Time: 20 Minutes
Ingredients:
- 1 tsp. Tikka Masala 1 tsp. fine sea salt
- 2 heaping tsps. whole grain mustard
- 2 tsps. coriander, ground 2 tablespoon olive oil
- 2 large-sized chicken breasts, skinless and halved lengthwise
- 2 tsp.s onion powder
- 1½ tablespoons cider vinegar Basmati rice, steamed
- 1/3 tsp. red pepper flakes, crushed

Directions:
1. Preheat the air fryer to 335 °For 4 minutes.
2. Toss your chicken together with the other ingredients, minus basmati rice. Let it stand at least 3 hours.
3. Cook for 25 minutes in your air fryer; check for doneness because the time depending on the size of the piece of chicken.
4. Serve immediately over warm basmati rice. Enjoy!
- **Nutrition Info:** 319 Calories; 20.1g Fat; 1.9g Carbs; 30.5g Protein; 0.1g Sugars

267.Sage Beef

Servings: 4
Cooking Time: 30 Minutes
Ingredients:
- 2pounds beef stew meat, cubed
- 1tablespoon sage, chopped
- 2tablespoons butter, melted
- ½ teaspoon coriander, ground
- ½ tablespoon garlic powder
- 1teaspoon Italian seasoning
- Salt and black pepper to the taste

Directions:

1. In the air fryer's pan, mix the beef with the sage, melted butter and the other ingredients, introduce the pan in the fryer and cook at 360 degrees F for 30 minutes.
2. Divide everything between plates and serve.
- **Nutrition Info:** Calories 290, Fat 11, Fiber 6, Carbs 20, Protein 29

268.Scallops With Spinach

Servings: 2
Cooking Time: 10 Minutes
Ingredients:
- 1: 12-ouncespackage frozen spinach, thawed and drained
- 8 jumbo sea scallops
- Olive oil cooking spray
- 1 tablespoon fresh basil, chopped
- Salt and ground black pepper, as required
- ¾ cup heavy whipping cream
- 1 tablespoon tomato paste
- 1 teaspoon garlic, minced

Directions:
1. Preheat the Air fryer to 350 degree F and grease an Air fryer pan.
2. Season the scallops evenly with salt and black pepper.
3. Mix cream, tomato paste, garlic, basil, salt, and black pepper in a bowl.
4. Place spinach at the bottom of the Air fryer pan, followed by seasoned scallops and top with the cream mixture.
5. Transfer into the Air fryer and cook for about 10 minutes.
6. Dish out in a platter and serve hot.
- **Nutrition Info:** Calories: 203, Fat: 18.3g, Carbohydrates: 12.3g, Sugar: 1.7g, Protein: 26.4g, Sodium: 101mg

269.Clam With Lemons On The Grill

Servings: 6
Cooking Time: 6 Minutes
Ingredients:
- 4 pounds littleneck clams
- Salt and pepper to taste
- 1 clove of garlic, minced
- ½ cup parsley, chopped
- 1 teaspoon crushed red pepper flakes
- 5 tablespoons olive oil
- 1 loaf crusty bread, halved
- ½ cup Parmesan cheese, grated

Directions:
1. Place the instant pot air fryer lid on and preheat the instant pot at 390 degrees F.
2. Place the grill pan accessory in the instant pot.
3. Place the clams on the grill pan, close the air fryer lid and cook for 6 minutes.
4. Once the clams have opened, take them out and extract the meat.
5. Transfer the meat into a bowl and season with salt and pepper.

6. Stir in the garlic, parsley, red pepper flakes, and olive oil.
7. Serve on top of bread and sprinkle with Parmesan cheese.
- **Nutrition Info:** Calories: 341; Carbs: 26g; Protein:48.3g; Fat: 17.2g

270.Herbed Carrots

Servings: 8
Cooking Time: 14 Minutes
Ingredients:
- 6 large carrots, peeled and sliced lengthwise
- 2 tablespoons olive oil
- ½ tablespoon fresh oregano, chopped
- ½ tablespoon fresh parsley, chopped
- Salt and black pepper, to taste
- 2 tablespoons olive oil, divided
- ½ cup fat-free Italian dressing
- Salt, to taste

Directions:
1. Preheat the Air fryer to 360-degree F and grease an Air fryer basket.
2. Mix the carrot slices and olive oil in a bowl and toss to coat well.
3. Arrange the carrot slices in the Air fryer basket and cook for about 12 minutes.
4. Dish out the carrot slices onto serving plates and sprinkle with herbs, salt and black pepper.
5. Transfer into the Air fryer basket and cook for 2 more minutes.
6. Dish out and serve hot.
- **Nutrition Info:** Calories: 93, Fat: 7.2g, Carbohydrates: 7.3g, Sugar: 3.8g, Protein: 0.7g, Sodium: 252mg

271.Green Beans And Mushroom Casserole

Servings: 6
Cooking Time: 12 Minutes
Ingredients:
- 24 ounces fresh green beans, trimmed
- 2 cups fresh button mushrooms, sliced
- 1/3 cup French fried onions
- 3 tablespoons olive oil
- 2 tablespoons fresh lemon juice
- 1 teaspoon ground sage
- 1 teaspoon garlic powder
- 1 teaspoon onion powder
- Salt and black pepper, to taste

Directions:
1. Preheat the Air fryer to 400 ºF and grease an Air fryer basket.
2. Mix the green beans, mushrooms, oil, lemon juice, sage, and spices in a bowl and toss to coat well.
3. Arrange the green beans mixture into the Air fryer basket and cook for about 12 minutes.
4. Dish out in a serving dish and top with fried onions to serve.

- **Nutrition Info:** Calories: 65, Fat: 1.6g, Carbohydrates: 11g, Sugar: 2.4g, Protein: 3g, Sodium: 52mg

272.Sirloin Steak With Cremini Mushroom Sauce

Servings: 5
Cooking Time: 20 Minutes
Ingredients:
- 2 tablespoons butter
- 2 pounds sirloin, cut into four pieces
- Salt and cracked black pepper, to taste
- 1 teaspoon cayenne pepper
- 1/2 teaspoon dried rosemary
- 1/2 teaspoon dried dill
- 1/4 teaspoon dried thyme
- 1 pound Cremini mushrooms, sliced
- 1 cup sour cream
- 1 teaspoon mustard
- 1/2 teaspoon curry powder

Directions:
1. Start by preheating your Air Fryer to 396 degrees F. Grease a baking pan with butter.
2. Add the sirloin, salt, black pepper, cayenne pepper, rosemary, dill, and thyme to the baking pan. Cook for 9 minutes.
3. Next, stir in the mushrooms, sour cream, mustard, and curry powder. Continue to cook another 5 minutes or until everything is heated through.
4. Spoon onto individual serving plates.
- **Nutrition Info:** 349 Calories; 12g Fat; 4g Carbs; 49g Protein; 6g Sugars; 4g Fiber

MEAT RECIPES

273.Salsa Beef Meatballs

Servings:4
Cooking Time: 10 Minutes
Ingredients:
- 1 pound (454 g) ground beef (85% lean)
- ½ cup salsa
- ¼ cup diced green or red bell peppers
- 1 large egg, beaten
- ¼ cup chopped onions
- ½ teaspoon chili powder
- 1 clove garlic, minced
- ½ teaspoon ground cumin
- 1 teaspoon fine sea salt
- Lime wedges, for serving
- Cooking spray

Directions:
1. Spritz the air fryer basket with cooking spray.
2. Combine all the ingredients in a large bowl. Stir to mix well.
3. Divide and shape the mixture into 1-inch balls. Arrange the balls in the pan and spritz with cooking spray.
4. Put the air fryer basket on the baking pan and slide into Rack Position 2, select Air Fry, set temperature to 350ºF (180ºC) and set time to 10 minutes.
5. Flip the balls with tongs halfway through.
6. When cooking is complete, the balls should be well browned.
7. Transfer the balls on a plate and squeeze the lime wedges over before serving.

274.Beef And Tomato Sauce Meatloaf

Servings:4
Cooking Time: 25 Minutes
Ingredients:
- 1½ pounds (680 g) ground beef
- 1 cup tomato sauce
- ½ cup bread crumbs
- 2 egg whites
- ½ cup grated Parmesan cheese
- 1 diced onion
- 2 tablespoons chopped parsley
- 2 tablespoons minced ginger
- 2 garlic cloves, minced
- ½ teaspoon dried basil
- 1 teaspoon cayenne pepper
- Salt and ground black pepper, to taste
- Cooking spray

Directions:
1. Spritz the baking pan with cooking spray.
2. Combine all the ingredients in a large bowl. Stir to mix well.
3. Pour the meat mixture in the prepared pan and press with a spatula to make it firm.
4. Slide the baking pan into Rack Position 1, select Convection Bake, set temperature to 360ºF (182ºC) and set time to 25 minutes.

5. When cooking is complete, the beef should be well browned.
6. Serve immediately.

275.Crispy Southern Fried Chicken

Servings: 4
Cooking Time: 25 Minutes
Ingredients:
- 1 tsp. cayenne pepper
- 2 tbsp. mustard powder
- 2 tbsp. oregano
- 2 tbsp. thyme
- 3 tbsp. coconut milk
- 1 beaten egg
- ¼ C. cauliflower
- ¼ C. gluten-free oats
- 8 chicken drumsticks

Directions:
1. Preparing the Ingredients. Ensure the Cuisinart air fryer oven is preheated to 350 degrees.
2. Lay out chicken and season with pepper and salt on all sides.
3. Add all other ingredients to a blender, blending till a smooth-like breadcrumb mixture is created. Place in a bowl and add a beaten egg to another bowl.
4. Dip chicken into breadcrumbs, then into the egg, and breadcrumbs once more.
5. Air Frying. Place coated drumsticks into the Cuisinart air fryer oven. Set temperature to 350°F, and set time to 20 minutes and cook 20 minutes. Bump up the temperature to 390 degrees and cook another 5 minutes till crispy.
- **Nutrition Info:** CALORIES: 504; FAT: 18G; PROTEIN:35G; SUGAR:5G

276.Crispy Lamb Chops

Servings: 5
Cooking Time: 15 Minutes
Ingredients:
- 10 lamb chop cutlets, bone in & fat removed
- 1 cup bread crumbs
- 1 tbsp. parmesan cheese, grated
- 2 eggs
- ¼ tsp salt
- ¼ tsp pepper
- Nonstick cooking spray

Directions:
1. In a shallow dish, combine breadcrumbs and parmesan.
2. In a separate shallow dish, whisk eggs with salt and pepper.
3. Place baking pan in position 2 of the oven. Lightly spray fryer basket with cooking spray.
4. Dip chops first in egg mixture then in breadcrumbs to coat both sides. Place in single layer in the basket, these will need to be cooked in batches.

5. Place basket on the baking pan and set oven to air fry on 350°F for 6 minutes. Cook chops turning them over halfway through cooking time. Repeat with remaining chops and serve.
- **Nutrition Info:** Calories 233, Total Fat 9g, Saturated Fat 3g, Total Carbs 16g, Net Carbs 15g, Protein 22g, Sugar 1g, Fiber 1g, Sodium 386mg, Potassium 348mg, Phosphorus 240mg

277.Beef Chimichangas

Servings: 4
Cooking Time: 10 Minutes
Ingredients:
- 1 lb. ground beef
- 1 tbsp. taco seasoning
- 1/3 cup salsa
- 4 flour tortillas
- 16 oz. refried beans
- 1 cup Mexican cheese blend, grated
- 1 cup lettuce, shredded
- 1 tbsp. olive oil

Directions:
1. Heat a medium skillet over medium heat. Add beef and taco seasoning and cook, breaking up with spatula, until meat is no longer pink. Stir in salsa and remove from heat.
2. Place tortillas, one at a time, on work surface and spread with 1/3 cup beans, leaving a 1-inch border.
3. Top with beef mixture, cheese and lettuce. Fold one edge of the tortilla to the middle, then the opposite edge so they overlap slightly. Fold other two ends towards middle until you have a rectangular pocket.
4. Place the baking pan in position 2 of the oven. Lightly brush Chimichangas with oil and place in fryer basket. Place on baking pan.
5. Set oven to air fry on 400°F for 10 minutes. Cook until Chimichangas are golden brown and crispy. Serve immediately with your favorite toppings.
- **Nutrition Info:** Calories 638, Total Fat 22g, Saturated Fat 9g, Total Carbs 58g, Net Carbs 42g, Protein 52g, Sugar 3g, Fiber 12g, Sodium 928mg, Potassium 1045mg, Phosphorus 650mg

278.Meatballs(6)

Servings: 8
Cooking Time: 25 Minutes
Ingredients:
- 3 eggs
- 2 lbs ground beef
- 2 tsp cumin
- 5 garlic cloves, minced
- 1 onion, grated
- 1 cup breadcrumbs
- 1/2 cup fresh parsley, minced
- 1 tsp cinnamon
- 2 tsp dried oregano
- 1 tsp pepper
- 2 tsp salt

Directions:
1. Fit the Cuisinart oven with the rack in position
2. Add all ingredients into the large mixing bowl and mix until well combined.
3. Make small meatballs from mixture and place in baking pan.
4. Set to bake at 400 F for 30 minutes. After 5 minutes place the baking pan in the preheated oven.
5. Serve and enjoy.
- **Nutrition Info:** Calories 302 Fat 9.7 g Carbohydrates 12.9 g Sugar 1.6 g Protein 38.8 g Cholesterol 163 mg

279.Kielbasa Sausage With Pineapple And Bell Peppers

Servings:2 To 4
Cooking Time: 10 Minutes
Ingredients:
- ¾ pound (340 g) kielbasa sausage, cut into ½-inch slices
- 1 (8-ounce / 227-g) can pineapple chunks in juice, drained
- 1 cup bell pepper chunks
- 1 tablespoon barbecue seasoning
- 1 tablespoon soy sauce
- Cooking spray

Directions:
1. Spritz the air fryer basket with cooking spray.
2. Combine all the ingredients in a large bowl. Toss to mix well.
3. Pour the sausage mixture in the basket.
4. Put the air fryer basket on the baking pan and slide into Rack Position 2, select Air Fry, set temperature to 390ºF (199ºC) and set time to 10 minutes.
5. After 5 minutes, remove from the oven. Stir the sausage mixture. Return to the oven and continue cooking.
6. When cooking is complete, the sausage should be lightly browned and the bell pepper and pineapple should be soft.
7. Serve immediately.

280.Lettuce Chicken Tacos With Peanut Sauce

Servings:4
Cooking Time: 6 Minutes
Ingredients:
- 1 pound (454 g) ground chicken
- 2 cloves garlic, minced
- ¼ cup diced onions
- ¼ teaspoon sea salt
- Cooking spray
- Peanut Sauce:

- ¼ cup creamy peanut butter, at room temperature
- 2 tablespoons tamari
- 1½ teaspoons hot sauce
- 2 tablespoons lime juice
- 2 tablespoons grated fresh ginger
- 2 tablespoons chicken broth
- 2 teaspoons sugar
- For Serving:
- 2 small heads butter lettuce, leaves separated
- Lime slices (optional)

Directions:
1. Spritz the baking pan with cooking spray.
2. Combine the ground chicken, garlic, and onions in the baking pan, then sprinkle with salt. Use a fork to break the ground chicken and combine them well.
3. Slide the baking pan into Rack Position 1, select Convection Bake, set temperature to 350ºF (180ºC) and set time to 5 minutes.
4. Stir them halfway through the cooking time.
5. When cooking is complete, the chicken should be lightly browned.
6. Meanwhile, combine the ingredients for the sauce in a small bowl. Stir to mix well.
7. Pour the sauce in the pan of chicken, then bake for 1 more minute or until heated through.
8. Unfold the lettuce leaves on a large serving plate, then divide the chicken mixture on the lettuce leaves. Drizzle with lime juice and serve immediately.

281.Veal Marinade Cutlet

Servings:x
Cooking Time:x
Ingredients:
- 2 cups sliced veal
- 1 big capsicum (Cut this capsicum into big cubes)
- 1 onion (Cut it into quarters. Now separate the layers carefully.)
- 5 tbsp. gram flour
- A pinch of salt to taste
- For the filling:
- 2 cup fresh green coriander
- ½ cup mint leaves
- 4 tsp. fennel
- 2 tbsp. ginger-garlic paste
- 1 small onion
- Salt to taste
- 3 tbsp. lemon juice

Directions:
1. You will first need to make the sauce. Add the ingredients to a blender and make a thick paste. Slit the pieces of veal and stuff half the paste into the cavity obtained. Take the remaining paste and add it to the gram flour and salt. Toss the pieces of veal in this mixture and set aside. Apply a little bit of the mixture on the capsicum and onion.

2. Place these on a stick along with the veal pieces. Pre heat the Breville smart oven at 290 Fahrenheit for around 5 minutes. Open the basket.
3. Arrange the satay sticks properly. Close the basket. Keep the sticks with the veal at 180 degrees for around half an hour while the sticks with the vegetables are to be kept at the same temperature for only 7 minutes. Turn the sticks in between so that one side does not get burnt and also to provide a uniform cook.

282.Lemon-pepper Chicken Wings

Servings: 4
Cooking Time: 20 Minutes
Ingredients:
- 8 whole chicken wings
- Juice of ½ lemon
- ½ teaspoon garlic powder
- 1 teaspoon onion powder
- Salt
- Pepper
- ¼ cup low-fat buttermilk
- ½ cup all-purpose flour
- Cooking oil

Directions:
1. Preparing the Ingredients. Place the wings in a sealable plastic bag. Drizzle the wings with the lemon juice. Season the wings with the garlic powder, onion powder, and salt and pepper to taste.
2. Seal the bag. Shake thoroughly to combine the seasonings and coat the wings.
3. Pour the buttermilk and the flour into separate bowls large enough to dip the wings.
4. Spray the Oven rack/basket with cooking oil.
5. One at a time, dip the wings in the buttermilk and then the flour.
6. Air Frying. Place the wings in the Oven rack/basket. It is okay to stack them on top of each other. Spray the wings with cooking oil, being sure to spray the bottom layer. Place the Rack on the middle-shelf of the Cuisinart air fryer oven. Cook for 5 minutes.
7. Remove the basket and shake it to ensure all of the pieces will cook fully.
8. Return the basket to the Cuisinart air fryer oven and continue to cook the chicken. Repeat shaking every 5 minutes until a total of 20 minutes has passed.
9. Cool before serving.
- **Nutrition Info:** CALORIES: 347; FAT: 12G; PROTEIN:46G; FIBER:1G

283.Veal Patti With Boiled Peas

Servings:x
Cooking Time:x
Ingredients:
- ½ lb. minced veal
- ½ cup breadcrumbs

- A pinch of salt to taste
- ½ cup of boiled peas
- ¼ tsp. ginger finely chopped
- 1 green chili finely chopped
- 1 tsp. lemon juice
- 1 tbsp. fresh coriander leaves. Chop them finely
- ¼ tsp. red chili powder
- ¼ tsp. cumin powder
- ¼ tsp. dried mango powder

Directions:
1. Take a container and into it pour all the masalas, onions, green chilies, peas, coriander leaves, lemon juice, and ginger and 1-2 tbsp. breadcrumbs. Add the minced veal as well. Mix all the ingredients well. Mold the mixture into round patties. Press them gently. Now roll them out carefully.
2. Pre heat the Breville smart oven at 250 Fahrenheit for 5 minutes. Open the basket of the Fryer and arrange the patties in the basket. Close it carefully. Keep the fryer at 150 degrees for around 10 or 12 minutes. In between the cooking process, turn the patties over to get a uniform cook. Serve hot with mint sauce.

284. Turkey Meatballs

Servings: 4
Cooking Time: 25 Minutes
Ingredients:
- 1 lb ground chicken
- 2 garlic cloves, minced
- 1/2 cup parmesan cheese, grated
- 1/2 cup breadcrumbs
- 1 egg, lightly beaten
- 2 tbsp cilantro, chopped
- 1 tbsp olive oil
- 1/2 tsp red pepper flakes
- 1/4 cup shallots, chopped
- Pepper
- Salt

Directions:
1. Fit the Cuisinart oven with the rack in position
2. Add all ingredients into the large bowl and mix until well combined.
3. Make small balls from the meat mixture and place them into the baking pan.
4. Set to bake at 400 F for 30 minutes. After 5 minutes place the baking pan in the preheated oven.
5. Serve and enjoy.
- **Nutrition Info:** Calories 361 Fat 16.2 g Carbohydrates 12.6 g Sugar 1 g Protein 40 g Cholesterol 150 mg

285. Teriyaki Rump Steak With Broccoli And Capsicum

Servings:4
Cooking Time: 13 Minutes
Ingredients:

- ½ pound (227 g) rump steak
- $^1/_3$ cup teriyaki marinade
- 1½ teaspoons sesame oil
- ½ head broccoli, cut into florets
- 2 red capsicums, sliced
- Fine sea salt and ground black pepper, to taste
- Cooking spray

Directions:
1. Toss the rump steak in a large bowl with teriyaki marinade. Wrap the bowl in plastic and refrigerate to marinate for at least an hour.
2. Spritz the air fryer basket with cooking spray.
3. Discard the marinade and transfer the steak in the pan. Spritz with cooking spray.
4. Put the air fryer basket on the baking pan and slide into Rack Position 2, select Air Fry, set temperature to 400ºF (205ºC) and set time to 13 minutes.
5. Flip the steak halfway through.
6. When cooking is complete, the steak should be well browned.
7. Meanwhile, heat the sesame oil in a nonstick skillet over medium heat. Add the broccoli and capsicum. Sprinkle with salt and ground black pepper. Sauté for 5 minutes or until the broccoli is tender.
8. Transfer the air fried rump steak on a plate and top with the sautéed broccoli and capsicum. Serve hot.

286. Ranch Chicken Thighs

Servings: 4
Cooking Time: 30 Minutes
Ingredients:
- 2 lbs chicken thighs
- 1 oz ranch seasoning
- 1 cup cheddar cheese, shredded
- 1/2 cup mayonnaise
- 2 tsp garlic, minced

Directions:
1. Fit the Cuisinart oven with the rack in position
2. Place chicken thighs into the baking dish.
3. Mix together mayonnaise, garlic, cheddar cheese, and ranch seasoning and pour over chicken thighs.
4. Set to bake at 400 F for 35 minutes. After 5 minutes place the baking dish in the preheated oven.
5. Serve and enjoy.
- **Nutrition Info:** Calories 684 Fat 36 g Carbohydrates 7.8 g Sugar 2 g Protein 73 g Cholesterol 239 mg

287. Stuffed Pork Loin

Servings: 8
Cooking Time: 35 Minutes
Ingredients:
- 3 tbsp. butter
- 2 onions, sliced thin

- ½ cup beef broth
- 3 lb. pork loin, center cut
- 2 tbsp. extra virgin olive oil
- 1 tsp salt
- 1/4 tsp pepper
- 1 tsp Italian seasoning
- 2 cups gruyere cheese, grated
- Nonstick cooking spray

Directions:
1. Melt butter in a large skillet over med-high heat. Add onions and broth and cook until onions are brown and tender, about 15 minutes. Transfer to bowl and keep warm.
2. Butterfly the pork making sure you do not cut all the way through. Open up the tenderloin, cover with plastic wrap and pound to 1/3-inch thick.
3. In a small bowl, combine salt, pepper, and Italian seasoning. Rub both sides of pork with mixture.
4. Spread half the cooked onions on one side of pork and top with half the cheese. Tightly roll up pork and tie with butcher string.
5. Heat oil in skillet. Add the tenderloin and brown on all sides.
6. Set the oven to convection bake on 425°F for 35 minutes.
7. Lightly spray the baking pan with cooking spray and place pork on it. After the oven has preheated for 5 minutes, place the baking pan in position 1 and cook 30 minutes. Basting occasionally with juice from the pan.
8. Top pork with remaining onions and cheese. Increase heat to broil and cook another 5 minutes, or until cheese is melted and golden brown. Let rest 5 minutes before slicing and serving.
- **Nutrition Info:** Calories 448, Total Fat 24g, Saturated Fat 11g, Total Carbs 3g, Net Carbs 0g, Protein 55g, Sugar 1g, Fiber 0g, Sodium 715mg, Potassium 795mg, Phosphorus 665mg

288.Pork Neck With Salad

Servings: 2
Cooking Time: 12 Minutes
Ingredients:
- For Pork:
- 1 tablespoon soy sauce
- 1 tablespoon fish sauce
- ½ tablespoon oyster sauce
- ½ pound pork neck
- For Salad:
- 1 ripe tomato, sliced tickly
- 8-10 Thai shallots, sliced
- 1 scallion, chopped
- 1 bunch fresh basil leaves
- 1 bunch fresh cilantro leaves
- For Dressing:
- 3 tablespoons fish sauce
- 2 tablespoons olive oil

- 1 teaspoon apple cider vinegar
- 1 tablespoon palm sugar
- 2 bird eye chili
- 1 tablespoon garlic, minced

Directions:
1. Preparing the Ingredients. For pork in a bowl, mix together all ingredients except pork.
2. Add pork neck and coat with marinade evenly.   Refrigerate for about 2-3 hours.
3. Preheat the Cuisinart air fryer oven to 340 degrees F.
4. Air Frying.   Place the pork neck onto a grill pan. Cook for about 12 minutes.
5. Meanwhile, in a large salad bowl, mix together all salad ingredients.
6. In a bowl, add all dressing ingredients and beat till well combined.
7. Remove pork neck from Air fryer oven and cut into desired slices.
8. Place pork slices over salad.

289.Roast Duck

Servings: 6
Cooking Time: 1 Hour
Ingredients:
- 3 lb. duck
- 1 tsp salt
- 3 tbsp. crushed red pepper flakes
- 3 tbsp. soy sauce, divided
- 3 tbsp. honey
- 2 tbsp. rice vinegar

Directions:
1. Wash the duck and pat dry with paper towels. Place in an 8x11-inch baking dish.
2. In a small bowl, stir together salt and pepper flakes. Rub over the skin of the duck. Sprinkle 2 tablespoons soy sauce over duck. Cover and refrigerate 2 hours.
3. Place rack in position 1 and set oven to convection bake on 375°F for 5 minutes.
4. In a small bowl, whisk together honey, vinegar, and remaining soy sauce. Brush over duck.
5. Once the oven has preheated, place duck inside and cook 1 hour. Serve.
- **Nutrition Info:** Calories 519, Total Fat 35g, Saturated Fat 11g, Total Carbs 11g, Net Carbs 10g, Protein 40g, Sugar 9g, Fiber 1g, Sodium 772mg, Potassium 652mg, Phosphorus 401mg

290.Roasted Pepper Chicken Thighs

Servings: 4
Cooking Time: 55 Minutes
Ingredients:
- 8 chicken thighs
- 1 1/2 lbs potatoes, cut into small chunks
- 6 garlic cloves, crushed
- 1/4 cup capers, drained
- 10 oz jar roasted red peppers, drained and sliced
- 2 cups grape tomatoes

- 4 tbsp olive oil
- 1 tsp dried oregano
- Pepper
- Salt

Directions:
1. Fit the Cuisinart oven with the rack in position
2. Season chicken with pepper and salt.
3. Heat 2 tablespoons of olive oil in a pan over medium heat.
4. Add chicken to the pan and sear until brown from all the sides.
5. Transfer chicken in baking pan.
6. Add tomato, potatoes, capers, oregano, garlic, and red peppers around the chicken. Drizzle with remaining olive oil.
7. Set to bake at 400 F for 60 minutes. After 5 minutes place the baking pan in the preheated oven.
8. Serve and enjoy.
- **Nutrition Info:** Calories 542 Fat 21.9 g Carbohydrates 45.1 g Sugar 4.4 g Protein 35.6 g Cholesterol 89 mg

291.Homemade Tarragon Chicken

Servings:4
Cooking Time: 25 Minutes
Ingredients:
- 1 lb chicken breasts
- ½ tbsp butter, melted
- Salt and black pepper to taste
- ¼ tsp dried tarragon

Directions:
1. Preheat Breville on Bake function to 380 F. Place each chicken breast on a 12x12 inches foil. Drizzle with butter and sprinkle with tarragon, salt, and pepper. Wrap the foil around the chicken in a loose way to create a flow of air. Bake for 15 minutes. Carefully unwrap and serve.

292.Dijon Garlic Pork Tenderloin

Servings: 6
Cooking Time: 10 Minutes
Ingredients:
- 1 C. breadcrumbs
- Pinch of cayenne pepper
- 3 crushed garlic cloves
- 2 tbsp. ground ginger
- 2 tbsp. Dijon mustard
- 2 tbsp. raw honey
- 4 tbsp. water
- 2 tsp. salt
- 1 pound pork tenderloin, sliced into 1-inch rounds

Directions:
1. Preparing the Ingredients. With pepper and salt, season all sides of tenderloin.
2. Combine cayenne pepper, garlic, ginger, mustard, honey, and water until smooth.

3. Dip pork rounds into the honey mixture and then into breadcrumbs, ensuring they all get coated well.
4. Place coated pork rounds into your Cuisinart air fryer oven.
5. Air Frying. Set temperature to 400°F, and set time to 10 minutes. Cook 10 minutes at 400 degrees. Flip and then cook an additional 5 minutes until golden in color.
- **Nutrition Info:** CALORIES: 423; FAT: 18G; PROTEIN:31G; SUGAR:3G

293.Meatballs(5)

Servings: 6
Cooking Time: 20 Minutes
Ingredients:
- 2 lbs ground beef
- 1 egg, lightly beaten
- 1 tsp cinnamon
- 2 tsp cumin
- 2 tsp coriander
- 1 tsp garlic, minced
- 1 tbsp fresh basil, chopped
- 1/4 cup fresh parsley, minced
- 1 tsp smoked paprika
- 1 tsp oregano
- 1 onion, grated
- 1/4 tsp pepper
- 1/2 tsp salt

Directions:
1. Fit the Cuisinart oven with the rack in position
2. Add all ingredients into the large mixing bowl and mix until well combined.
3. Make small balls from the meat mixture and place it into the parchment-lined baking pan.
4. Set to bake at 400 F for 25 minutes. After 5 minutes place the baking pan in the preheated oven.
5. Serve and enjoy.
- **Nutrition Info:** Calories 306 Fat 10.4 g Carbohydrates 3.1 g Sugar 0.9 g Protein 47.3 g Cholesterol 162 mg

294.Barbecue Flavored Pork Ribs

Servings: 6
Cooking Time: 15 Minutes
Ingredients:
- ¼ cup honcy, divided
- ¾ cup BBQ sauce
- 2 tablespoons tomato ketchup
- 1 tablespoon Worcestershire sauce
- 1 tablespoon soy sauce
- ½ teaspoon garlic powder
- Freshly ground white pepper, to taste
- 1¾ pound pork ribs

Directions:
1. Preparing the Ingredients. In a large bowl, mix together 3 tablespoons of honey and remaining ingredients except pork ribs.

2. Refrigerate to marinate for about 20 minutes.
3. Preheat the Cuisinart air fryer oven to 355 degrees F.
4. Place the ribs in an Air fryer rack/basket.
5. Air Frying. Cook for about 13 minutes.
6. Remove the ribs from the Cuisinart air fryer oven and coat with remaining honey.
7. Serve hot.

295.Morning Ham & Cheese Sandwich

Servings: 4
Cooking Time: 15 Minutes
Ingredients:
- 8 slices whole wheat bread
- 4 slices lean pork ham
- 4 slices cheese
- 8 slices tomato

Directions:
1. Lay four slices of bread on a flat surface. Spread the slices with cheese, tomato, turkey, and ham. Cover with the remaining slices to form sandwiches. Add the sandwiches to the cooking basket and cook for 10 minutes at 360 F on Air Fry function. Serve.

296.Meatballs(18)

Servings: 4
Cooking Time: 15 Minutes
Ingredients:
- 1 lb ground pork
- 1 tsp paprika
- 1 tsp garlic powder
- 1 tsp onion powder
- 1/2 tsp ground cumin
- 1/2 tsp coriander
- 1/2 tsp dried thyme
- Pepper
- Salt

Directions:
1. Fit the Cuisinart oven with the rack in position
2. Add all ingredients into the mixing bowl and mix until well combined.
3. Make small balls from the meat mixture and place them into the baking pan.
4. Set to bake at 400 F for 20 minutes. After 5 minutes place the baking pan in the preheated oven.
5. Serve and enjoy.
- **Nutrition Info:** Calories 170 Fat 4.1 g Carbohydrates 1.5 g Sugar 0.4 g Protein 30 g Cholesterol 83 mg

297.Honey & Garlic Chicken Thighs

Servings: 4
Cooking Time: 30 Minutes
Ingredients:
- 4 thighs, skin-on
- 3 tbsp honey
- 2 tbsp Dijon mustard

- ½ tbsp garlic powder
- Salt and black pepper to taste

Directions:
1. In a bowl, mix honey, mustard, garlic, salt, and black pepper. Coat the thighs in the mixture and arrange them on the greased basket. Fit in the baking tray and cook for 16 minutes at 400 F on Air Fry function, turning once halfway through. Serve warm.

298.Stuffed Bell Peppers

Servings: 6
Cooking Time: 15 Minutes
Ingredients:
- 6 green bell peppers, cut off tops & remove seeds
- 1 lb. lean ground beef
- 1 tbsp. olive oil
- ¼ cup green onion, chopped
- ¼ cup fresh parsley, chopped
- ½ tsp sage
- ½ tsp garlic salt
- 1 cup rice, cooked
- 1 cup marinara sauce
- Nonstick cooking spray
- ¼ cup mozzarella cheese, grated

Directions:
1. Heat a medium skillet over med-high heat. Add ground beef and cook, breaking up with spatula, until no longer pink. Drain off fat.
2. Add oil, onion, and seasonings and stir to mix.
3. Stir in rice and marinara and mix well.
4. Spoon beef mixture into the bell peppers.
5. Place the baking pan in position 2 of the oven. Lightly spray fryer basket with cooking spray.
6. Place peppers in basket and place on baking pan. Set oven to air fry on 355°F for 10 minutes.
7. Remove basket and sprinkle cheese over tops of peppers. Return to oven and cook another 5 minutes, or until peppers are tended and cheese is melted. Serve immediately.
- **Nutrition Info:** Calories 398, Total Fat 16g, Saturated Fat 5g, Total Carbs 35g, Net Carbs 31g, Protein 26g, Sugar 4g, Fiber 4g, Sodium 114mg, Potassium 674mg, Phosphorus 272mg

299.Chili Pork Chops With Tomatoes & Rice

Servings: 4
Cooking Time: 40 Minutes + Marinating Time
Ingredients:
- 4 pork chops
- 1 lime juice
- Salt and black pepper to taste
- 1 tsp garlic powder
- 1 ½ cups white rice, cooked

- 2 tbsp olive oil
- 1 can (14.5 oz) tomato sauce
- 1 onion, chopped
- 3 garlic cloves, minced
- ½ tsp oregano
- 1 tsp chipotle chili

Directions:
1. Season pork with salt, pepper, and garlic powder. In a bowl, mix onion, garlic, chipotle, oregano, and tomato sauce. Add in the pork. Let sit for 1 hour. Then remove from the mixture and place in the basket. Fit in the baking tray and cook for 25 minutes on Air Fry at 350 F. Serve with rice.

300.Lechon Kawali

Servings:4
Cooking Time: 30 Minutes
Ingredients:
- 1 pound (454 g) pork belly, cut into three thick chunks
- 6 garlic cloves
- 2 bay leaves
- 2 tablespoons soy sauce
- 1 teaspoon kosher salt
- 1 teaspoon ground black pepper
- 3 cups water
- Cooking spray

Directions:
1. Put all the ingredients in a pressure cooker, then put the lid on and cook on high for 15 minutes.
2. Natural release the pressure and release any remaining pressure, transfer the tender pork belly on a clean work surface. Allow to cool under room temperature until you can handle.
3. Generously Spritz the air fryer basket with cooking spray.
4. Cut each chunk into two slices, then put the pork slices in the pan.
5. Put the air fryer basket on the baking pan and slide into Rack Position 2, select Air Fry, set temperature to 400ºF (205ºC) and set time to 15 minutes.
6. After 7 minutes, remove from the oven. Flip the pork. Return to the oven and continue cooking.
7. When cooking is complete, the pork fat should be crispy.
8. Serve immediately.

301.Comforting Red Wine Steak

Servings:x
Cooking Time:x
Ingredients:
- 2 (8-oz) sirloin steaks, trimmed of fat
- Salt and freshly ground black pepper, to taste
- 4 Tbsp extra-virgin olive oil, divided
- 1 lb. fingerling potatoes, rinsed, halved
- 3 Tbsp shallots, minced

- 2 tsp chopped fresh thyme
- ¾ cup red wine

Directions:
1. Pat the steaks dry with a paper towel. Season generously with salt and pepper. Let them rest at room temperature for 15 to 20 minutes before cooking.
2. In Breville smart oven over medium heat, heat 1 Tbsp of olive oil.
3. Add the potatoes, season with salt and pepper, and toss. Cook covered over low heat for 20 to 30 minutes. Set aside.
4. Heat Breville smart oven over high heat. Add the remaining 3 Tbsp of oil, then lower the heat to medium-high.
5. Add the steaks and cook for 4 minutes on each side for medium-rare, or longer as desired. Remove from the pot and set aside.
6. Add the shallots and thyme to the pot.
7. Add the wine and cook until the liquid is almost evaporated, 1 to 2 minutes. Season with salt and pepper, and stir with a whisk.
8. Spoon the sauce over the steaks, and serve with the potatoes.

302.Pineapple Chicken Kabobs With Sesame Seeds

Servings:4
Cooking Time: 20 Minutes
Ingredients:
- 1 lb chicken tenders
- ½ cup soy sauce
- ½ cup pineapple juice
- ¼ cup sesame oil
- 2 cloves garlic, chopped
- 1 tbsp fresh ginger, grated
- 4 scallions, chopped
- 2 tbsp toasted sesame seeds

Directions:
1. Preheat your Breville oven on AirFry function to 390 F. Thread the chicken pieces onto the skewers and trim any fat. In a bowl, mix all the remaining ingredients. Dip in the skewered chicken and place in the cooking basket. Press Start and cook for12-14 minutes. Serve.

303.Balsamic Chicken With Mozzarella Cheese

Servings:4
Cooking Time: 25 Minutes
Ingredients:
- 4 chicken breasts, cubed
- 4 fresh basil leaves
- ¼ cup balsamic vinegar
- 2 tomatoes, chopped
- 1 tbsp butter, melted
- 4 mozzarella cheese, grated

Directions:
1. In a bowl, mix butter and balsamic vinegar. Add in the chicken and toss to coat. Transfer to a baking tray and press Start.

Cook for 20 minutes at 400 F on AirFry function. Top with mozzarella cheese and Bake until the cheese melts. Top with basil and tomatoes and serve.

304.Mango Chicken With Avocado

Servings:2
Cooking Time: 20 Minutes + Marinating Time
Ingredients:
- 2 chicken breasts, cubed
- 1 mango, cubed
- 1 avocado, pitted and sliced
- 1 chili pepper, chopped
- 5 tbsp balsamic vinegar
- 2 tbsp olive oil
- 2 garlic cloves, minced
- ¼ tsp dried oregano
- 1 tbsp fresh parsley, chopped
- ¼ tsp mustard powder

Directions:
1. In a blender, add mango, chili pepper, mustard powder, garlic, oregano, olive oil, and balsamic vinegar and pulse until smooth. Pour the liquid over chicken and let marinate for 3 hours.
2. Preheat Breville on AirFry function to 350 F. Transfer the chicken to the basket and press Start.Cook for 14-16 minutes. Top with avocado and parsley and serve.

305.Garlic Pork Roast

Servings: 4
Cooking Time: 55 Minutes
Ingredients:
- 2 lbs pork sirloin roast
- 6 garlic cloves, sliced
- 2 tbsp olive oil
- 1/2 tsp pepper
- 1 tsp salt

Directions:
1. Fit the Cuisinart oven with the rack in position
2. Using a sharp knife make slits on top of the roast and stuff sliced garlic in each slit.
3. Season pork roast with pepper and salt.
4. Heat oil in a pan over medium-high heat.
5. Place roast in a pan and brown from all the sides.
6. Transfer roast in a baking pan.
7. Set to bake at 300 F for 60 minutes. After 5 minutes place the baking pan in the preheated oven.
8. Slice and serve.
- **Nutrition Info:** Calories 537 Fat 28.4 g Carbohydrates 1.7 g Sugar 0.1 g Protein 65 g Cholesterol 195 mg

306.Cheesy Chicken Fritters

Servings: 17 Fritters
Cooking Time: 20 Minutes
Ingredients:
- Chicken Fritters:

- ½ tsp. salt
- 1/8 tsp. pepper
- 1 ½ tbsp. fresh dill
- 1 1/3 C. shredded mozzarella cheese
- 1/3 C. coconut flour
- 1/3 C. vegan mayo
- 2 eggs
- 1 ½ pounds chicken breasts
- Garlic Dip:
- 1/8 tsp. pepper
- ¼ tsp. salt
- ½ tbsp. lemon juice
- 1 pressed garlic cloves
- 1/3 C. vegan mayo

Directions:
1. Preparing the Ingredients. Slice chicken breasts into 1/3" pieces and place in a bowl. Add all remaining fritter ingredients to the bowl and stir well. Cover and chill 2 hours or overnight.
2. Ensure your air fryer oven is preheated to 350 degrees. Spray basket with a bit of olive oil.
3. Air Frying. Add marinated chicken to the Cuisinart air fryer oven. Set temperature to 350°F, and set time to 20 minutes and cook 20 minutes, making sure to turn halfway through cooking process.
4. To make the dipping sauce, combine all the dip ingredients until smooth.
- **Nutrition Info:** CALORIES: 467; FAT: 27G; PROTEIN:21G; SUGAR:3G

307.Roasted Lamb Chops With Potatoes

Servings:4
Cooking Time: 20 Minutes
Ingredients:
- 8 (½-inch thick) lamb loin chops (about 2 pounds / 907 g)
- 2 teaspoons kosher salt or 1 teaspoon fine salt, divided
- ¾ cup plain whole milk yogurt
- 2 garlic cloves, minced or smashed
- 1 tablespoon freshly grated ginger (1- or 2-inch piece) or 1 teaspoon ground ginger
- 1 teaspoon curry powder
- 1 teaspoon smoked paprika
- ½ teaspoon cayenne pepper
- 12 ounces (340 g) small red potatoes, quartered
- Cooking spray

Directions:
1. Sprinkle the lamb chops on both sides with 1 teaspoon of kosher salt and set aside.
2. Meanwhile, make the marinade by stirring together the yogurt, garlic, ginger, curry powder, paprika, cayenne pepper, and remaining 1 teaspoon of kosher salt in a large bowl.
3. Transfer 2 tablespoons of the marinade to a resealable plastic bag, leaving those 2 tablespoons in the bowl. Place the lamb

chops in the bag. Squeeze out as much air as possible and squish the bag around so that the chops are well coated with the marinade. Set aside.

4. Add the potatoes to the bowl and toss until well coated. Spritz the air fryer basket with cooking spray. Arrange the potatoes in the basket.
5. Put the air fryer basket on the baking pan and slide into Rack Position 2, select Roast, set temperature to 375ºF (190ºC), and set time to 10 minutes.
6. Once cooking is complete, remove from the oven.
7. Remove the chops from the marinade, draining off all but a thin coat. Return them to the baking pan.
8. Select Convection Broil, set the temperature to High, and set the time for 10 minutes.
9. After 5 minutes, remove from the oven and turn over the chops and potatoes. Return to the oven and continue cooking until the lamb read 145ºF (63ºC) on a meat thermometer. If you want it more well done, continue cooking for another few minutes.
10. Serve warm.

308.Lamb Rack With Pistachio

Servings:2
Cooking Time: 20 Minutes
Ingredients:
- ½ cup finely chopped pistachios
- 1 teaspoon chopped fresh rosemary
- 3 tablespoons panko bread crumbs
- 2 teaspoons chopped fresh oregano
- 1 tablespoon olive oil
- Salt and freshly ground black pepper, to taste
- 1 lamb rack, bones fat trimmed and frenched
- 1 tablespoon Dijon mustard

Directions:
1. Put the pistachios, rosemary, bread crumbs, oregano, olive oil, salt, and black pepper in a food processor. Pulse to combine until smooth.
2. Rub the lamb rack with salt and black pepper on a clean work surface, then place it in the basket.
3. Put the air fryer basket on the baking pan and slide into Rack Position 2, select Air Fry, set temperature to 380ºF (193ºC) and set time to 12 minutes.
4. Flip the lamb halfway through.
5. When cooking is complete, the lamb should be lightly browned.
6. Transfer the lamb on a plate and brush with Dijon mustard on the fat side, then sprinkle with the pistachios mixture over the lamb rack to coat well.
7. Put the lamb rack back to the oven and air fry for 8 more minutes or until the internal

temperature of the rack reaches at least 145ºF (63ºC).

8. Remove the lamb rack from the oven with tongs and allow to cool for 5 minutes before slicing to serve.

309.Cheesy Pork Chops With Marinara Sauce

Servings:4
Cooking Time: 15 Minutes
Ingredients:
- 4 pork chops
- 1 cup breadcrumbs
- 2 tbsp Parmesan cheese, grated
- 1 tbsp butter, melted
- ½ cup mozzarella cheese, shredded
- ½ cup marinara sauce

Directions:
1. Preheat Breville oven to 400 F on AirFry function. In a bowl, mix breadcrumbs and Parmesan. Brush the pork with butter and dredge into the breadcrumbs. Add to the greased basket and cook for 8 minutes. Top with marinara sauce and mozzarella. Cook for 5 more minutes. Serve.

310.Meatballs(13)

Servings: 4
Cooking Time: 20 Minutes
Ingredients:
- 1 lb ground turkey
- 1/4 cup basil, chopped
- 3 tbsp scallions, chopped
- 1 egg, lightly beaten
- 1/2 cup almond flour
- 1/2 tsp red pepper, crushed
- 1 tbsp lemongrass, chopped
- 1 1/2 tbsp fish sauce
- 2 garlic cloves, minced

Directions:
1. Fit the Cuisinart oven with the rack in position 2.
2. Line the air fryer basket with parchment paper.
3. Add all ingredients into a large bowl and mix until well combined.
4. Make small balls from meat mixture and place in the air fryer basket then place the air fryer basket in the baking pan.
5. Place a baking pan on the oven rack. Set to air fry at 380 F for 20 minutes.
6. Serve and enjoy.
- **Nutrition Info:** Calories 269 Fat 15.4 g Carbohydrates 3.4 g Sugar 1.3 g Protein 33.9 g Cholesterol 157 mg

311.Air Fried Golden Wasabi Spam

Servings:3
Cooking Time: 12 Minutes
Ingredients:
- $^2/_3$ cup all-purpose flour
- 2 large eggs

- 1½ tablespoons wasabi paste
- 2 cups panko bread crumbs
- 6 ½-inch-thick spam slices
- Cooking spray

Directions:
1. Spritz the air fryer basket with cooking spray.
2. Pour the flour in a shallow plate. Whisk the eggs with wasabi in a large bowl. Pour the panko in a separate shallow plate.
3. Dredge the spam slices in the flour first, then dunk in the egg mixture, and then roll the spam over the panko to coat well. Shake the excess off.
4. Arrange the spam slices in the pan and spritz with cooking spray.
5. Put the air fryer basket on the baking pan and slide into Rack Position 2, select Air Fry, set temperature to 400ºF (205ºC) and set time to 12 minutes.
6. Flip the spam slices halfway through.
7. When cooking is complete, the spam slices should be golden and crispy.
8. Serve immediately.

312.Chicken Momo's Recipe

Servings:x
Cooking Time:x
Ingredients:
- 1 ½ cup all-purpose flour
- ½ tsp. salt
- 5 tbsp. water
- 2 cups minced chicken
- 2 tbsp. oil
- 2 tsp. ginger-garlic paste
- 2 tsp. soya sauce
- 2 tsp. vinegar

Directions:
1. Squeeze the dough and cover it with plastic wrap and set aside. Next, cook the ingredients for the filling and try to ensure that the beef is covered well with the sauce.
2. Roll the dough and cut it into a square. Place the filling in the center. Now, wrap the dough to cover the filling and pinch the edges together. Pre heat the Breville smart oven at 200° F for 5 minutes. Place the wontons in the fry basket and close it. Let them cook at the same temperature for another 20 minutes. Recommended sides are chili sauce or ketchup.

313.Coconut Chicken Tenders

Servings: 4
Cooking Time: 20 Minutes
Ingredients:
- 1 lb chicken breast, skinless, boneless & cut into strips
- 1 egg, lightly beaten
- 1/4 cup shredded coconut
- 1/2 cup almond meal
- 1/2 tsp garlic powder

- 1/2 tsp cayenne pepper
- 1 tsp paprika
- 1/4 tsp black pepper
- 1/2 tsp sea salt

Directions:
1. Fit the Cuisinart oven with the rack in position
2. In a shallow dish, mix almond meal, shredded coconut, paprika, cayenne pepper, garlic powder, pepper, and salt.
3. In a separate bowl, whisk the egg.
4. Dip each chicken strip in egg then coat with almond meal mixture,
5. Place coat chicken strips in a parchment-lined baking pan.
6. Set to bake at 400 F for 25 minutes. After 5 minutes place the baking pan in the preheated oven.
7. Serve and enjoy.
- **Nutrition Info:** Calories 235 Fat 11.7 g Carbohydrates 4.2 g Sugar 1.1 g Protein 28.3 g Cholesterol 114 mg

314.Bacon-wrapped Chicken Breasts

Servings:2
Cooking Time: 20 Minutes
Ingredients:
- 2 chicken breasts
- 8 oz onion and chive cream cheese
- 1 tbsp butter
- 6 turkey bacon
- Salt to taste
- 1 tbsp fresh parsley, chopped
- Juice from ½ lemon

Directions:
1. Preheat on AirFry function to 390 F. Stretch out the bacon slightly and lay them in 2 sets; 3 bacon strips together on each side. Place the chicken breast on each bacon set and use a knife to smear cream cheese on both.
2. Share the butter on top and sprinkle with salt. Wrap the bacon around the chicken and secure the ends into the wrap. Place the wrapped chicken in the basket and press Start.
3. Cook for 14 minutes. Remove the chicken onto a serving platter and top with parsley and lemon juice. Serve with steamed greens.

315.White Wine Chicken Wings

Servings:2
Cooking Time: 30 Minutes
Ingredients:
- 8 chicken wings
- ½ tbsp sugar
- 2 tbsp cornflour
- ½ tbsp white wine
- 1 tbsp fresh ginger, grated
- ½ tbsp olive oil

Directions:
1. In a bowl, mix olive oil, ginger, white wine, and sugar. Add in the chicken wings and

toss to coat. Roll up in the flour. Place the chicken in the frying basket and press Start. Cook for 20 minutes until crispy on the outside at 320 F on AirFry function. Serve warm.

316.Chicken Oregano Fingers

Servings:x
Cooking Time:x
Ingredients:
- 1 lb. boneless chicken breast cut into Oregano Fingers
- 2 cup dry breadcrumbs
- 2 tsp. oregano
- 1 ½ tbsp. ginger-garlic paste
- 4 tbsp. lemon juice
- 2 tsp. salt
- 1 tsp. pepper powder
- 1 tsp. red chili powder
- 6 tbsp. corn flour
- 4 eggs

Directions:
1. Mix all the ingredients for the marinade and put the chicken Oregano Fingers inside and let it rest overnight.
2. Mix the breadcrumbs, oregano and red chili flakes well and place the marinated Oregano Fingers on this mixture. Cover it with plastic wrap and leave it till right before you serve to cook.
3. Pre heat the Breville smart oven at 160 degrees Fahrenheit for 5 minutes. Place the Oregano Fingers in the fry basket and close it. Let them cook at the same temperature for another 15 minutes or so. Toss the Oregano Fingers well so that they are cooked uniformly.

317.Pork Belly Strips

Servings: 4
Cooking Time: 15 Minutes
Ingredients:
- 1 lb pork belly strips
- 1/4 tsp paprika
- 1/2 tsp garlic powder
- Pepper
- Salt

Directions:
1. Fit the Cuisinart oven with the rack in position 2.
2. Toss pork belly strips with paprika, garlic powder, pepper, and salt.
3. Place pork strips in the air fryer basket then place an air fryer basket in the baking pan.
4. Place a baking pan on the oven rack. Set to air fry at 390 F for 15 minutes.
5. Serve and enjoy.
- **Nutrition Info:** Calories 162 Fat 6 g Carbohydrates 0.3 g Sugar 0.1 g Protein 24.2 g Cholesterol 65 mg

318.Herb Beef Tips

Servings: 6
Cooking Time: 20 Minutes
Ingredients:
- 2 lbs sirloin steak, cut into 1-inch cubes
- 1/4 tsp red chili flakes
- 1/2 tsp pepper
- 1/2 tsp dried thyme
- 1 tsp onion powder
- 1 tsp dried oregano
- 2 tbsp lemon juice
- 2 tbsp water
- 1/4 cup olive oil
- 1 cup parsley, chopped
- 1 tsp garlic, minced
- 1/2 tsp salt

Directions:
1. Fit the Cuisinart oven with the rack in position
2. Add all ingredients into the zip-lock bag, seal bag shake well and place in the refrigerator for 1 hour.
3. Place marinated steak cubes into the parchment-lined baking pan.
4. Set to bake at 400 F for 25 minutes. After 5 minutes place the baking pan in the preheated oven.
5. Serve and enjoy.
- **Nutrition Info:** Calories 361 Fat 18 g Carbohydrates 1.6 g Sugar 0.4 g Protein 46.3 g Cholesterol 135 mg

319.Chili Cheese Pork With Sauce

Servings:x
Cooking Time:x
Ingredients:
- 1 lb. pork (Cut in to long strips)
- 2 ½ tsp. ginger-garlic paste
- 1 tsp. red chili sauce
- ¼ tsp. salt
- ¼ tsp. red chili powder/black pepper
- ¼ tsp. Ajinomoto
- 1-2 tsp. red chili flakes
- A few drops of edible orange food coloring
- 2 tbsp. olive oil
- 1 ½ tsp. ginger garlic paste
- ½ tbsp. red chili sauce
- 2 tbsp. tomato ketchup
- 2 tsp. soya sauce
- 1-2 tbsp. honey

Directions:
1. Mix all the ingredients for the marinade and put the pork Oregano Fingers inside and let it rest overnight. Mix the breadcrumbs, oregano and red chili flakes well and place the marinated Oregano Fingers on this mixture. Cover it with plastic wrap and leave it till right before you serve to cook.
2. Pre heat the Breville smart oven at 160 degrees Fahrenheit for 5 minutes.
3. Place the Oregano Fingers in the fry basket and close it. Let them cook at the same

temperature for another 15 minutes or so. Toss the Oregano Fingers well so that they are cooked uniformly.

320.Garlic Chicken Wings

Servings: 2
Cooking Time: 25 Minutes
Ingredients:
- 1 lb chicken wings
- 2 tbsp butter, melted
- 1 tbsp garlic, minced

Directions:
1. Fit the Cuisinart oven with the rack in position 2.
2. In a large bowl, mix butter and garlic. Add chicken wings and toss to coat.
3. Add marinated chicken wings to the air fryer basket then place an air fryer basket in the baking pan.
4. Place a baking pan on the oven rack. Set to air fry at 360 F for 25 minutes.
5. Serve and enjoy.
- **Nutrition Info:** Calories 539 Fat 28.4 g Carbohydrates 1.4 g Sugar 0.1 g Protein 66 g Cholesterol 232 mg

321.Sriracha Beef And Broccoli

Servings:4
Cooking Time: 15 Minutes
Ingredients:
- 12 ounces (340 g) broccoli, cut into florets (about 4 cups)
- 1 pound (454 g) flat iron steak, cut into thin strips
- ½ teaspoon kosher salt
- ¾ cup soy sauce
- 1 teaspoon Sriracha sauce
- 3 tablespoons freshly squeezed orange juice
- 1 teaspoon cornstarch
- 1 medium onion, thinly sliced

Directions:
1. Line the baking pan with aluminum foil. Place the broccoli on top and sprinkle with 3 tablespoons of water. Seal the broccoli in the foil in a single layer.
2. Slide the baking pan into Rack Position 2, select Roast, set temperature to 375ºF (190ºC), and set time to 6 minutes.
3. While the broccoli steams, sprinkle the steak with the salt. In a small bowl, whisk together the soy sauce, Sriracha, orange juice, and cornstarch. Place the onion and beef in a large bowl.
4. When cooking is complete, remove from the oven. Open the packet of broccoli and use tongs to transfer the broccoli to the bowl with the beef and onion, discarding the foil and remaining water. Pour the sauce over the beef and vegetables and toss to coat. Place the mixture in the baking pan.
5. Select Roast, set temperature to 375ºF (190ºC), and set time to 9 minutes.

6. After about 4 minutes, remove from the oven and gently toss the ingredients. Return to the oven and continue cooking.
7. When cooking is complete, the sauce should be thickened, the vegetables tender, and the beef barely pink in the center. Serve warm.

322.Rosemary Turkey Scotch Eggs

Servings:4
Cooking Time: 12 Minutes
Ingredients:
- 1 egg
- 1 cup panko bread crumbs
- ½ teaspoon rosemary
- 1 pound (454 g) ground turkey
- 4 hard-boiled eggs, peeled
- Salt and ground black pepper, to taste
- Cooking spray

Directions:
1. Spritz the air fryer basket with cooking spray.
2. Whisk the egg with salt in a bowl. Combine the bread crumbs with rosemary in a shallow dish.
3. Stir the ground turkey with salt and ground black pepper in a separate large bowl, then divide the ground turkey into four portions.
4. Wrap each hard-boiled egg with a portion of ground turkey. Dredge in the whisked egg, then roll over the breadcrumb mixture.
5. Place the wrapped eggs in the basket and spritz with cooking spray.
6. Put the air fryer basket on the baking pan and slide into Rack Position 2, select Air Fry, set temperature to 400ºF (205ºC) and set time to 12 minutes.
7. Flip the eggs halfway through.
8. When cooking is complete, the scotch eggs should be golden brown and crunchy.
9. Serve immediately.

323.Air Fryer Chicken Tenders

Servings: 4
Cooking Time: 16 Minutes
Ingredients:
- 1 lb chicken tenders
- For rub:
- 1/2 tbsp dried thyme
- 1 tbsp garlic powder
- 1 tbsp paprika
- 1/2 tbsp onion powder
- 1/2 tsp cayenne pepper
- Pepper
- Salt

Directions:
1. Fit the Cuisinart oven with the rack in position 2.
2. In a bowl, add all rub ingredients and mix well.
3. Add chicken tenders into the bowl and coat well.

4. Place chicken tenders in the air fryer basket then place an air fryer basket in the baking pan.
5. Place a baking pan on the oven rack. Set to air fry at 370 F for 16 minutes.
6. Serve and enjoy.
- **Nutrition Info:** Calories 232 Fat 8.7 g Carbohydrates 3.6 g Sugar 1 g Protein 33.6 g Cholesterol 101 mg

324.Sweet Chicken Drumsticks

Servings: 2
Cooking Time: 20 Minutes + Marinating Time
Ingredients:
- 2 chicken drumsticks, skin removed
- 2 tbsp olive oil
- 2 tbsp honey
- ½ tbsp garlic, minced

Directions:
1. Add all the ingredients to a resealable bag; massage until well-coated. Allow the chicken to marinate for 30 minutes in the fridge.
2. Preheat Cuisinart on Air Fry function to 390 F. Remove the chicken drumsticks from the fridge and add them to the greased basket. Fit in the baking tray and cook for 15 minutes, shaking once. Serve hot.

325.Garlic Lemony Chicken Breast

Servings:2
Cooking Time: 20 Minutes
Ingredients:
- 1 chicken breast
- 2 lemon, juiced and rind reserved
- 1 tbsp chicken seasoning
- 1 tbsp garlic puree
- A handful of peppercorns
- Salt and black pepper to taste

Directions:
1. Place a silver foil sheet on a flat surface. Add all seasonings alongside the lemon rind. Lay the chicken breast onto a chopping board and trim any fat and little bones; season.
2. Rub the chicken seasoning on both sides. Place on the foil sheet and seal tightly; flatten with a rolling pin. Place the breast in the basket and cook for 15 minutes at 350 F on AirFry function.

326.Chinese-style Broccoli & Beef Steak

Servings:4
Cooking Time: 25 Minutes
Ingredients:
- ¾ lb circular beef steak, cut into strips
- 1 lb broccoli, cut into florets
- ⅓ cup oyster sauce
- 2 tbsp sesame oil
- ⅓ cup sherry
- 1 tsp soy sauce
- 1 tsp white sugar
- 1 tsp cornstarch

- 1 tbsp olive oil
- 1 garlic clove, minced

Directions:
1. In a bowl, mix cornstarch, sherry, oyster sauce, sesame oil, soy sauce, sugar, garlic, ginger and add in the beef steaks; toss to coat. Marinate for 45 minutes.
2. Preheat Breville oven to 390 F on AirFry function. Place the steaks in the frying basket and cook for 20 minutes. Serve warm with green salad.

327.Mini Pot Pies

Servings: 16
Cooking Time: 20 Minutes
Ingredients:
- 2 cans large flaky biscuits, refrigerated
- 6 oz. turkey, cooked & chopped fine
- 3 ½ cups turkey gravy
- 2 cups mixed vegetables
- 1 cup cheddar cheese, grated

Directions:
1. Place baking pan in position 1 of the oven. Spray 3 6-cup muffin tins with cooking spray.
2. Gently pull each biscuit until it is double in size. Press into prepared tins, pressing up the sides until edge is at, or above, the top of the cup.
3. In a large bowl, stir together turkey, gravy, and vegetables. Spoon mixture into biscuits. Top with cheese.
4. Set oven to bake on 350°F for 25 minutes. After 5 minutes, place muffin tin, one at a time, in the oven and bake until golden brown, about 20-22 minutes. Repeat with remaining tins. Serve warm.
- **Nutrition Info:** Calories 324, Total Fat 8g, Saturated Fat 2g, Total Carbs 24g, Net Carbs 23g, Protein 9g, Sugar 1g, Fiber 1g, Sodium 790mg, Potassium 210mg, Phosphorus 232mg

328.Italian Veggie Chicken

Servings: 4
Cooking Time: 30 Minutes
Ingredients:
- 4 chicken breasts
- 1 cup mozzarella cheese, shredded
- 6 bacon slices, cooked & chopped
- 8 oz can artichoke hearts, sliced
- 1 cup cherry tomatoes, cut in half
- 1 zucchini, sliced
- 1 tbsp dried basil
- 1/4 tsp salt

Directions:
1. Fit the Cuisinart oven with the rack in position
2. Place chicken breasts into the casserole dish and sprinkle with basil and salt.
3. Spread artichoke hearts, cherry tomatoes, and zucchini on top of chicken.

4. Sprinkle shredded cheese and bacon on top of vegetables.
5. Set to bake at 375 F for 35 minutes. After 5 minutes place the casserole dish in the preheated oven.
6. Serve and enjoy.
- **Nutrition Info:** Calories 484 Fat 24.2 g Carbohydrates 6.9 g Sugar 2.5 g Protein 56.8 g Cholesterol 165 mg

329.Tonkatsu

Servings:4
Cooking Time: 10 Minutes
Ingredients:
- $^2/_3$ cup all-purpose flour
- 2 large egg whites
- 1 cup panko bread crumbs
- 4 (4-ounce / 113-g) center-cut boneless pork loin chops (about ½ inch thick)
- Cooking spray

Directions:
1. Pour the flour in a bowl. Whisk the egg whites in a separate bowl. Spread the bread crumbs on a large plate.
2. Dredge the pork loin chops in the flour first, press to coat well, then shake the excess off and dunk the chops in the eggs whites, and then roll the chops over the bread crumbs. Shake the excess off.
3. Arrange the pork chops in the basket and spritz with cooking spray.
4. Put the air fryer basket on the baking pan and slide into Rack Position 2, select Air Fry, set temperature to 375ºF (190ºC) and set time to 10 minutes.
5. After 5 minutes, remove from the oven. Flip the pork chops. Return to the oven and continue cooking.
6. When cooking is complete, the pork chops should be crunchy and lightly browned.
7. Serve immediately.

330.Spice-coated Steaks With Cucumber And Snap Pea Salad

Servings:4
Cooking Time: 15 Minutes
Ingredients:
- 1 (1½-pound / 680-g) boneless top sirloin steak, trimmed and halved crosswise
- 1½ teaspoons chili powder
- 1½ teaspoons ground cumin
- ¾ teaspoon ground coriander
- ⅛ teaspoon cayenne pepper
- ⅛ teaspoon ground cinnamon
- 1¼ teaspoons plus ⅛ teaspoon salt, divided
- ½ teaspoon plus ⅛ teaspoon ground black pepper, divided
- 1 teaspoon plus 1½ tablespoons extra-virgin olive oil, divided
- 3 tablespoons mayonnaise
- 1½ tablespoons white wine vinegar
- 1 tablespoon minced fresh dill

- 1 small garlic clove, minced
- 8 ounces (227 g) sugar snap peas, strings removed and cut in half on bias
- ½ English cucumber, halved lengthwise and sliced thin
- 2 radishes, trimmed, halved and sliced thin
- 2 cups baby arugula

Directions:
1. In a bowl, mix chili powder, cumin, coriander, cayenne pepper, cinnamon, 1¼ teaspoons salt and ½ teaspoon pepper until well combined.
2. Add the steaks to another bowl and pat dry with paper towels. Brush with 1 teaspoon oil and transfer to the bowl of spice mixture. Roll over to coat thoroughly.
3. Arrange the coated steaks in the basket, spaced evenly apart.
4. Put the air fryer basket on the baking pan and slide into Rack Position 2, select Air Fry, set temperature to 400ºF (205ºC) and set time to 15 minutes.
5. Flip the steak halfway through to ensure even cooking.
6. When cooking is complete, an instant-read thermometer inserted in the thickest part of the meat should register at least 145ºF (63ºC).
7. Transfer the steaks to a clean work surface and wrap with aluminum foil. Let stand while preparing salad.
8. Make the salad: In a large bowl, stir together 1½ tablespoons olive oil, mayonnaise, vinegar, dill, garlic, ⅛ teaspoon salt, and ⅛ teaspoon pepper. Add snap peas, cucumber, radishes and arugula. Toss to blend well.
9. Slice the steaks and serve with the salad.

331.Olive Caper Chicken

Servings: 4
Cooking Time: 18 Minutes
Ingredients:
- 4 chicken breast, boneless and halves
- 12 olives, pitted and halved
- 2 cups cherry tomatoes
- 3 tbsp olive oil
- 3 tbsp capers, rinsed and drained
- Pepper
- Salt

Directions:
1. Fit the Cuisinart oven with the rack in position
2. In a bowl, toss tomatoes, capers, olives with 2 tablespoons of oil. Set aside.
3. Season chicken with pepper and salt.
4. Heat remaining oil in a pan over high heat.
5. Place chicken in the pan and cook for 4 minutes.
6. Transfer chicken in baking dish. Top with tomato mixture.

7. Set to bake at 450 F for 23 minutes. After 5 minutes place the baking dish in the preheated oven.
8. Serve and enjoy.
- **Nutrition Info:** Calories 251 Fat 15 g Carbohydrates 4.7 g Sugar 2.4 g Protein 24.8 g Cholesterol 72 mg

332.Meatballs(1)

Servings: 6
Cooking Time: 20 Minutes
Ingredients:
- 8 oz ground beef
- 1/2 onion, diced
- 1 egg, lightly beaten
- 1/4 cup parmesan cheese, grated
- 1/2 cup breadcrumbs
- 1/4 cup parsley, chopped
- 1 tsp garlic, minced
- 8 oz ground pork
- Pepper
- Salt

Directions:
1. Fit the Cuisinart oven with the rack in position
2. Add all ingredients into the mixing bowl and mix until well combined.
3. Make small balls from the meat mixture and place them into the baking pan.
4. Set to bake at 400 F for 25 minutes. After 5 minutes place the baking pan in the preheated oven.
5. Serve and enjoy.
- **Nutrition Info:** Calories 188 Fat 5.7 g Carbohydrates 7.9 g Sugar 1 g Protein 24.9 g Cholesterol 91 mg

333.Perfect Beef Hash Brown Bake

Servings: 4
Cooking Time: 40 Minutes
Ingredients:
- 1 lb ground beef
- 2 cups cheddar cheese, shredded
- 1 cup milk
- 10 oz can cream of mushroom soup
- 30 oz frozen shredded hash browns
- 1 tsp garlic powder
- 1 tbsp onion, minced
- Pepper
- Salt

Directions:
1. Fit the Cuisinart oven with the rack in position
2. In a pan, brown ground beef with garlic powder, onion, pepper, and salt. Drain.
3. In a bowl, mix meat, shredded cheese, milk, soup, and hash browns.
4. Pour meat mixture into the greased 9*13-inch baking dish.
5. Set to bake at 350 F for 45 minutes. After 5 minutes place the baking dish in the preheated oven.

6. Serve and enjoy.
- **Nutrition Info:** Calories 514 Fat 28.3 g Carbohydrates 11.4 g Sugar 4.8 g Protein 51.6 g Cholesterol 168 mg

334.Jalapeno Basil Lamb Patties

Servings: 4
Cooking Time: 8 Minutes
Ingredients:
- 1 lb ground lamb
- 5 basil leaves, minced
- 8 mint leaves, minced
- 1/4 cup fresh parsley, chopped
- 1 tsp dried oregano
- 1 cup goat cheese, crumbled
- 1 tbsp garlic, minced
- 1 jalapeno pepper, minced
- 1/4 tsp pepper
- 1/2 tsp kosher salt

Directions:
1. Fit the Cuisinart oven with the rack in position
2. Add all ingredients into the mixing bowl and mix until well combined.
3. Make the equal shape of patties from the meat mixture and place it into the baking pan.
4. Set to bake at 450 F for 13 minutes. After 5 minutes place the baking pan in the preheated oven.
5. Serve and enjoy.
- **Nutrition Info:** Calories 296 Fat 13.9 g Carbohydrates 3.7 g Sugar 0.5 g Protein 37.5 g Cholesterol 118 mg

335.Simple Air Fried Chicken Wings

Servings:4
Cooking Time: 15 Minutes
Ingredients:
- 1 tablespoon olive oil
- 8 whole chicken wings
- Chicken seasoning or rub, to taste
- 1 teaspoon garlic powder
- Freshly ground black pepper, to taste

Directions:
1. Grease the basket with olive oil.
2. On a clean work surface, rub the chicken wings with chicken seasoning and rub, garlic powder, and ground black pepper.
3. Arrange the well-coated chicken wings in the basket.
4. Put the air fryer basket on the baking pan and slide into Rack Position 2, select Air Fry, set temperature to 400ºF (205ºC) and set time to 15 minutes.
5. Flip the chicken wings halfway through.
6. When cooking is complete, the internal temperature of the chicken wings should reach at least 165ºF (74ºC).
7. Remove the chicken wings from the oven. Serve immediately.

336.Parmesan Herb Meatballs

Servings: 6
Cooking Time: 20 Minutes
Ingredients:

- 1 lb ground beef
- 1/2 small onion, minced
- 2 garlic cloves, minced
- 1 egg, lightly beaten
- 1 1/2 tbsp fresh basil, chopped
- 1 tbsp fresh parsley, chopped
- 1/2 tbsp fresh rosemary, chopped
- 1/4 cup parmesan cheese, grated
- 1/2 cup breadcrumbs
- Pepper
- Salt

Directions:

1. Fit the Cuisinart oven with the rack in position
2. Add all ingredients into the mixing bowl and mix until well combined.
3. Make small balls from the meat mixture and place them into the baking pan.
4. Set to bake at 375 F for 25 minutes. After 5 minutes place the baking pan in the preheated oven.
5. Serve and enjoy.
- **Nutrition Info:** Calories 204 Fat 6.8 g Carbohydrates 7.8 g Sugar 0.9 g Protein 26.5 g Cholesterol 98 mg

337.Ricotta And Parsley Stuffed Turkey Breasts

Servings: 4
Cooking Time: 25 Minutes
Ingredients:

- 1 turkey breast, quartered
- 1 cup Ricotta cheese
- 1/4 cup fresh Italian parsley, chopped
- 1 teaspoon garlic powder
- 1/2 teaspoon cumin powder
- 1 egg, beaten
- 1 teaspoon paprika
- Salt and ground black pepper, to taste
- Crushed tortilla chips
- 1 ½ tablespoons extra-virgin olive oil

Directions:

1. Preparing the Ingredients. Firstly, flatten out each piece of turkey breast with a rolling pin. Prepare three mixing bowls.
2. In a shallow bowl, combine Ricotta cheese with the parsley, garlic powder, and cumin powder.
3. Place the Ricotta/parsley mixture in the middle of each piece. Repeat with the remaining pieces of the turkey breast and roll them up.
4. In another shallow bowl, whisk the egg together with paprika. In the third shallow bowl, combine the salt, pepper, and crushed tortilla chips.
5. Dip each roll in the whisked egg, then, roll them over the tortilla chips mixture.

6. Transfer prepared rolls to the Oven rack/basket. Drizzle olive oil over all. Place the Rack on the middle-shelf of the Cuisinart air fryer oven.
7. Air Frying. Cook at 350 degrees F for 25 minutes, working in batches. Serve warm, garnished with some extra parsley, if desired.

338.Smoked Ham With Sweet Glaze

Servings:4
Cooking Time: 30 Minutes
Ingredients:

- 2 pears, chopped
- 1 lb smoked ham
- 1 ½ cups brown sugar
- ¾ tbsp allspice
- 1 tbsp balsamic vinegar
- 1 tsp black pepper

Directions:

1. Preheat Breville oven to 330 F on AirFry function. Place pears, brown sugar, balsamic vinegar, allspices, and pepper in a small pot over medium heat. Stir and bring to a boil then reduce the heat to low. Simmer for 8-10 minutes until the glaze is thickened.
2. Place the ham in a greased baking dish. With a knife, score only the fatty surface of the ham in a diamond pattern. Pour the pear mixture over the ham and cook for 20-25 minutes until golden and glazed. Let sit for a few minutes before slicing and serving.

339.Chicken And Ham Meatballs With Dijon Sauce

Servings:4
Cooking Time: 15 Minutes
Ingredients:

- Meatballs:
- ½ pound (227 g) ham, diced
- ½ pound (227 g) ground chicken
- ½ cup grated Swiss cheese
- 1 large egg, beaten
- 3 cloves garlic, minced
- ¼ cup chopped onions
- 1½ teaspoons sea salt
- 1 teaspoon ground black pepper
- Cooking spray
- Dijon Sauce:
- 3 tablespoons Dijon mustard
- 2 tablespoons lemon juice
- ¼ cup chicken broth, warmed
- ¾ teaspoon sea salt
- ¼ teaspoon ground black pepper
- Chopped fresh thyme leaves, for garnish

Directions:

1. Spritz the air fryer basket with cooking spray.
2. Combine the ingredients for the meatballs in a large bowl. Stir to mix well, then shape the mixture in twelve 1½-inch meatballs.

3. Arrange the meatballs in the basket.
4. Put the air fryer basket on the baking pan and slide into Rack Position 2, select Air Fry, set temperature to 390ºF (199ºC) and set time to 15 minutes.
5. Flip the balls halfway through.
6. When cooking is complete, the balls should be lightly browned.
7. Meanwhile, combine the ingredients, except for the thyme leaves, for the sauce in a small bowl. Stir to mix well.
8. Transfer the cooked meatballs on a large plate, then baste the sauce over. Garnish with thyme leaves and serve.

340.Asian Pork Shoulder

Servings: 4
Cooking Time: 15 Minutes
Ingredients:
- 1 lb pork shoulder, boneless
- 1 tbsp wine
- 1 tbsp sugar
- 2 tbsp soy sauce
- 4 tbsp honey
- 1 tsp Chinese five-spice
- 2 tsp ginger, minced
- 2 tsp garlic, minced

Directions:
1. Fit the Cuisinart oven with the rack in position 2.
2. Add all ingredients except pork into the large zip-lock bag and mix well.
3. Add pork and seal the bag and place it in the fridge overnight.
4. Remove pork from marinade and place in an air fryer basket then place an air fryer basket in baking pan.
5. Place a baking pan on the oven rack. Set to air fry at 390 F for 15 minutes.
6. Serve and enjoy.
- **Nutrition Info:** Calories 419 Fat 24.3 g Carbohydrates 22.1 g Sugar 20.5 g Protein 27.1 g Cholesterol 102 mg

FISH & SEAFOOD RECIPES

341.Seafood Spring Rolls

Servings:4
Cooking Time: 20 Minutes
Ingredients:
- 1 tablespoon olive oil
- 2 teaspoons minced garlic
- 1 cup matchstick cut carrots
- 2 cups finely sliced cabbage
- 2 (4-ounce / 113-g) cans tiny shrimp, drained
- 4 teaspoons soy sauce
- Salt and freshly ground black pepper, to taste
- 16 square spring roll wrappers
- Cooking spray

Directions:
1. Spray the air fryer basket with cooking spray. Set aside.
2. Heat the olive oil in a medium skillet over medium heat until it shimmers.
3. Add the garlic to the skillet and cook for 30 seconds. Stir in the cabbage and carrots and sauté for about 5 minutes, stirring occasionally, or until the vegetables are lightly tender.
4. Fold in the shrimp and soy sauce and sprinkle with salt and pepper, then stir to combine. Sauté for another 2 minutes, or until the moisture is evaporated. Remove from the heat and set aside to cool.
5. Put a spring roll wrapper on a work surface and spoon 1 tablespoon of the shrimp mixture onto the lower end of the wrapper.
6. Roll the wrapper away from you halfway, and then fold in the right and left sides, like an envelope. Continue to roll to the very end, using a little water to seal the edge. Repeat with the remaining wrappers and filling.
7. Place the spring rolls in the air fryer basket in a single layer, leaving space between each spring roll. Mist them lightly with cooking spray.
8. Put the air fryer basket on the baking pan and slide into Rack Position 2, select Air Fry, set temperature to 375ºF (190ºC), and set time to 10 minutes.
9. Flip the rolls halfway through the cooking time.
10. When cooking is complete, the spring rolls will be heated through and start to brown. If necessary, continue cooking for 5 minutes more. Remove from the oven and cool for a few minutes before serving.

342.Lemon Salmon

Servings:2
Cooking Time: 20 Minutes
Ingredients:
- 2 salmon fillets
- Salt to taste
- Zest of 1 lemon

Directions:
1. Rub the fillets with salt and lemon zest. Place them in the frying basket and spray with cooking spray. Press Start and cook the salmon in the preheated Breville oven for 14 minutes at 360 F on AirFry function. Serve with steamed asparagus and a drizzle of lemon juice.

343.Lemony Tuna

Servings: 4
Cooking Time: 10 Minutes
Ingredients:
- 2 (6-ounce) cans water packed plain tuna
- 2 teaspoons Dijon mustard
- ½ cup breadcrumbs
- 1 tablespoon fresh lime juice
- 2 tablespoons fresh parsley, chopped
- 1 egg
- Chefman of hot sauce
- 3 tablespoons canola oil
- Salt and freshly ground black pepper, to taste

Directions:
1. Preparing the Ingredients. Drain most of the liquid from the canned tuna.
2. In a bowl, add the fish, mustard, crumbs, citrus juice, parsley, and hot sauce and mix till well combined. Add a little canola oil if it seems too dry. Add egg, salt and stir to combine. Make the patties from tuna mixture. Refrigerate the tuna patties for about 2 hours.
3. Air Frying. Preheat the air fryer oven to 355 degrees F. Cook for about 10-12 minutes.

344.Lemon-garlic Butter Lobster

Servings: 2
Cooking Time: 15 Minutes
Ingredients:
- 4 oz lobster tails
- 1 tsp garlic, minced
- 1 tbsp butter
- Salt and black pepper to taste
- ½ tbsp lemon Juice

Directions:
1. Add all the ingredients to a food processor except for lobster and blend well. Wash lobster and halve using a meat knife; clean the skin of the lobster and cover with the marinade.
2. Preheat your Cuisinart to 380 F on Air Fry function. Place the lobster in the cooking basket and fit in the baking tray; cook for 10 minutes. Serve with fresh herbs.

345.Garlic-butter Shrimp With Vegetables

Servings:4
Cooking Time: 15 Minutes
Ingredients:

- 1 pound (454 g) small red potatoes, halved
- 2 ears corn, shucked and cut into rounds, 1 to 1½ inches thick
- 2 tablespoons Old Bay or similar seasoning
- ½ cup unsalted butter, melted
- 1 (12- to 13-ounce / 340- to 369-g) package kielbasa or other smoked sausages
- 3 garlic cloves, minced
- 1 pound (454 g) medium shrimp, peeled and deveined

Directions:
1. Place the potatoes and corn in a large bowl.
2. Stir together the butter and Old Bay seasoning in a small bowl. Drizzle half the butter mixture over the potatoes and corn, tossing to coat. Spread out the vegetables in the baking pan.
3. Slide the baking pan into Rack Position 2, select Roast, set temperature to 350ºF (180ºC), and set time to 15 minutes.
4. Meanwhile, cut the sausages into 2-inch lengths, then cut each piece in half lengthwise. Put the sausages and shrimp in a medium bowl and set aside.
5. Add the garlic to the bowl of remaining butter mixture and stir well.
6. After 10 minutes, remove the pan and pour the vegetables into the large bowl. Drizzle with the garlic butter and toss until well coated. Arrange the vegetables, sausages, and shrimp in the pan.
7. Return to the oven and continue cooking. After 5 minutes, check the shrimp for doneness. The shrimp should be pink and opaque. If they are not quite cooked through, roast for an additional 1 minute.
8. When done, remove from the oven and serve on a plate.

346.Oyster Club Sandwich

Servings:x
Cooking Time:x
Ingredients:
- 2 slices of white bread
- 1 tbsp. softened butter
- ½ lb. shelled oyster
- 1 small capsicum
- For Barbeque Sauce:
- ¼ tbsp. Worcestershire sauce
- ½ tsp. olive oil
- ½ flake garlic crushed
- ¼ cup chopped onion
- ¼ tsp. mustard powder
- 1 tbsp. tomato ketchup
- ½ tbsp. sugar
- ¼ tbsp. red chili sauce
- ½ cup water.
- A pinch of salt and black pepper to taste

Directions:
1. Take the slices of bread and remove the edges. Now cut the slices horizontally. Cook the ingredients for the sauce and wait till it

thickens. Now, add the oyster to the sauce and stir till it obtains the flavors.
2. Roast the capsicum and peel the skin off. Cut the capsicum into slices. Mix the ingredients together and apply it to the bread slices. Pre-heat the Breville smart oven for 5 minutes at 300 Fahrenheit. Open the basket of the Fryer and place the prepared Classic Sandwiches in it such that no two Classic Sandwiches are touching each other. Now keep the fryer at 250 degrees for around 15 minutes.
3. Turn the Classic Sandwiches in between the cooking process to cook both slices. Serve the Classic Sandwiches with tomato ketchup or mint sauce.

347.Cajun Red Snapper

Servings: 2
Cooking Time: 12 Minutes
Ingredients:
- 8 oz red snapper fillets
- 2 tbsp parmesan cheese, grated
- 1/4 cup breadcrumbs
- 1/2 tsp Cajun seasoning
- 1/4 tsp Worcestershire sauce
- 1 garlic clove, minced
- 1/4 cup butter

Directions:
1. Fit the Cuisinart oven with the rack in position
2. Melt butter in a pan over low heat. Add Cajun seasoning, garlic, and Worcestershire sauce into the melted butter and stir well.
3. Brush fish fillets with melted butter and place into the baking dish.
4. Mix together parmesan cheese and breadcrumbs and sprinkle over fish fillets.
5. Set to bake at 400 F for 17 minutes. After 5 minutes place the baking dish in the preheated oven.
6. Serve and enjoy.
- **Nutrition Info:** Calories 424 Fat 27 g Carbohydrates 10.6 g Sugar 1 g Protein 33.9 g Cholesterol 119 mg

348.Herbed Salmon With Roasted Asparagus

Servings:2
Cooking Time: 12 Minutes
Ingredients:
- 2 teaspoons olive oil, plus additional for drizzling
- 2 (5-ounce / 142-g) salmon fillets, with skin
- Salt and freshly ground black pepper, to taste
- 1 bunch asparagus, trimmed
- 1 teaspoon dried tarragon
- 1 teaspoon dried chives
- Fresh lemon wedges, for serving

Directions:

1. Rub the olive oil all over the salmon fillets. Sprinkle with salt and pepper to taste.
2. Put the asparagus on the foil-lined baking pan and place the salmon fillets on top, skin-side down.
3. Slide the baking pan into Rack Position 2, select Roast, set temperature to 425ºF (220ºC), and set time to 12 minutes.
4. When cooked, the fillets should register 145ºF (63ºC) on an instant-read thermometer. Remove from the oven and cut the salmon fillets in half crosswise, then use a metal spatula to lift flesh from skin and transfer to a serving plate. Discard the skin and drizzle the salmon fillets with additional olive oil. Scatter with the herbs.
5. Serve the salmon fillets with roasted asparagus spears and lemon wedges on the side.

349.Garlic Shrimp With Parsley

Servings:4
Cooking Time: 5 Minutes
Ingredients:
- 18 shrimp, shelled and deveined
- 2 garlic cloves, peeled and minced
- 2 tablespoons extra-virgin olive oil
- 2 tablespoons freshly squeezed lemon juice
- ½ cup fresh parsley, coarsely chopped
- 1 teaspoon onion powder
- 1 teaspoon lemon-pepper seasoning
- ½ teaspoon hot paprika
- ½ teaspoon salt
- ¼ teaspoon cumin powder

Directions:
1. Toss all the ingredients in a mixing bowl until the shrimp are well coated.
2. Cover and allow to marinate in the refrigerator for 30 minutes.
3. When ready, transfer the shrimp to the air fryer basket.
4. Put the air fryer basket on the baking pan and slide into Rack Position 2, select Air Fry, set temperature to 400ºF (205ºC), and set time to 5 minutes.
5. When cooking is complete, the shrimp should be pink on the outside and opaque in the center. Remove from the oven and serve warm.

350.Moist & Juicy Baked Cod

Servings: 2
Cooking Time: 10 Minutes
Ingredients:
- 1 lb cod fillets
- 1 1/2 tbsp olive oil
- 3 dashes cayenne pepper
- 1 tbsp fresh lemon juice
- 1/4 tsp salt

Directions:
1. Fit the Cuisinart oven with the rack in position
2. Place fish fillets in a baking pan.

3. Drizzle with oil and lemon juice and sprinkle with cayenne pepper and salt.
4. Set to bake at 400 F for 15 minutes. After 5 minutes place the baking pan in the preheated oven.
5. Serve and enjoy.
- **Nutrition Info:** Calories 275 Fat 12.7 g Carbohydrates 0.4 g Sugar 0.2 g Protein 40.6 g Cholesterol 111 mg

351.Roasted Halibut Steaks With Parsley

Servings:4
Cooking Time: 10 Minutes
Ingredients:
- 1 pound (454 g) halibut steaks
- ¼ cup vegetable oil
- 2½ tablespoons Worcester sauce
- 2 tablespoons honey
- 2 tablespoons vermouth
- 1 tablespoon freshly squeezed lemon juice
- 1 tablespoon fresh parsley leaves, coarsely chopped
- Salt and pepper, to taste
- 1 teaspoon dried basil

Directions:
1. Put all the ingredients in a large mixing dish and gently stir until the fish is coated evenly. Transfer the fish to the air fryer basket.
2. Put the air fryer basket on the baking pan and slide into Rack Position 2, select Roast, set temperature to 390ºF (199ºC), and set time to 10 minutes.
3. Flip the fish halfway through cooking time.
4. When cooking is complete, the fish should reach an internal temperature of at least 145ºF (63ºC) on a meat thermometer. Remove from the oven and let the fish cool for 5 minutes before serving.

352.Quick Shrimp Bowl

Servings: 4
Cooking Time: 15 Minutes
Ingredients:
- 1 ¼ pounds tiger shrimp
- ¼ tsp cayenne pepper
- ½ tsp old bay seasoning
- ¼ tsp smoked paprika
- A pinch of salt
- 1 tbsp olive oil

Directions:
1. Preheat your Cuisinart oven to 390 F on Air Fry function. In a bowl, mix all the ingredients. Place the mixture in your the cooking basket and fit in the baking tray; cook for 5 minutes, flipping once. Serve drizzled with lemon juice.

353.Seafood Mac N Cheese

Servings: 8
Cooking Time: 30 Minutes
Ingredients:
- Nonstick cooking spray

- 16 oz. macaroni
- 7 tbsp. butter, divided
- ¾ lb. medium shrimp, peel, devein, & cut in ½-inch pieces
- ½ cup Italian panko bread crumbs
- 1 cup onion, chopped fine
- 1 ½ tsp garlic, diced fine
- 1/3 cup flour
- 3 cups milk
- 1/8 tsp nutmeg
- ½ tsp Old Bay seasoning
- 1 tsp salt
- ¾ tsp pepper
- 1 1/3 cup Parmesan cheese, grated
- 1 1/3 cup Swiss cheese, grated
- 1 1/3 cup sharp cheddar cheese, grated
- ½ lb. lump crab meat, cooked

Directions:
1. Place wire rack in position 1 of the oven. Spray a 7x11-inch baking dish with cooking spray.
2. Cook macaroni according to package directions, shortening cooking time by 2 minutes. Drain and rinse with cold water.
3. Melt 1 tablespoon butter in a large skillet over med-high heat. Add shrimp and cook, stirring, until they turn pink. Remove from heat.
4. Melt remaining butter in a large saucepan over medium heat. Once melted, transfer 2 tablespoons to a small bowl and mix in bread crumbs.
5. Add onions and garlic to saucepan and cook, stirring, until they soften.
6. Whisk in flour and cook 1 minute, until smooth.
7. Whisk in milk until there are no lumps. Bring to a boil, reduce heat and simmer until thickened, whisking constantly.
8. Whisk in seasonings. Stir in cheese until melted and smooth. Fold in macaroni and seafood. Transfer to prepared dish. Sprinkle bread crumb mixture evenly over top.
9. Set oven to bake on 400°F for 25 minutes. After 5 minutes, place dish on the rack and bake 20 minutes, until topping is golden brown and sauce is bubbly. Let cool 5 minutes before serving.
- **Nutrition Info:** Calories 672, Total Fat 26g, Saturated Fat 15g, Total Carbs 68g, Net Carbs 61g, Protein 39g, Sugar 7g, Fiber 7g, Sodium 996mg, Potassium 921mg, Phosphorus 714mg

354.Crab Cakes With Bell Peppers

Servings:4
Cooking Time: 10 Minutes
Ingredients:
- 8 ounces (227 g) jumbo lump crab meat
- 1 egg, beaten
- Juice of ½ lemon
- ¹/₃ cup bread crumbs

- ¼ cup diced green bell pepper
- ¼ cup diced red bell pepper
- ¼ cup mayonnaise
- 1 tablespoon Old Bay seasoning
- 1 teaspoon flour
- Cooking spray

Directions:
1. Make the crab cakes: Place all the ingredients except the flour and oil in a large bowl and stir until well incorporated.
2. Divide the crab mixture into four equal portions and shape each portion into a patty with your hands. Top each patty with a sprinkle of ¼ teaspoon of flour.
3. Arrange the crab cakes in the air fryer basket and spritz them with cooking spray.
4. Put the air fryer basket on the baking pan and slide into Rack Position 2, select Air Fry, set temperature to 375ºF (190ºC), and set time to 10 minutes.
5. Flip the crab cakes halfway through.
6. When cooking is complete, the cakes should be cooked through. Remove from the oven and divide the crab cakes among four plates and serve.

355.Perfect Crab Cakes

Servings: 6
Cooking Time: 30 Minutes
Ingredients:
- 16 oz lump crab meat
- 1/4 cup celery, diced
- 1/4 cup onion, diced
- 1 cup crushed crackers
- 1 tsp old bay seasoning
- 1 tsp brown mustard
- 2/3 cup mashed avocado

Directions:
1. Fit the Cuisinart oven with the rack in position
2. Add all ingredients into the bowl and mix until just combined.
3. Make small patties from mixture and place in parchment-lined baking pan.
4. Set to bake at 350 F for 35 minutes. After 5 minutes place the baking dish in the preheated oven.
5. Serve and enjoy.
- **Nutrition Info:** Calories 84 Fat 7.7 g Carbohydrates 4.6 g Sugar 0.8 g Protein 11.5 g Cholesterol 43 mg

356.Crispy Paprika Fish Fillets(1)

Servings: 4
Cooking Time: 15 Minutes
Ingredients:
- 1/2 cup seasoned breadcrumbs
- 1 tablespoon balsamic vinegar
- 1/2 teaspoon seasoned salt
- 1 teaspoon paprika
- 1/2 teaspoon ground black pepper
- 1 teaspoon celery seed

- 2 fish fillets, halved
- 1 egg, beaten

Directions:
1. Preparing the Ingredients. Add the breadcrumbs, vinegar, salt, paprika, ground black pepper, and celery seeds to your food processor. Process for about 30 seconds.
2. Coat the fish fillets with the beaten egg; then, coat them with the breadcrumbs mixture.
3. Air Frying. Cook at 350 degrees F for about 15 minutes.

357.Cajun Salmon With Lemon

Servings:1
Cooking Time: 10 Minutes
Ingredients:
- 1 salmon fillet
- ¼ tsp brown sugar
- Juice of ½ lemon
- 1 tbsp cajun seasoning
- 2 lemon wedges
- 1 tbsp fresh parsley, chopped

Directions:
1. Preheat Breville on Bake function to 350 F. Combine sugar and lemon and coat in the salmon. Sprinkle with the Cajun seasoning as well. Place a parchment paper on a baking tray and press Start. Cook for 14-16 minutes. Serve with lemon wedges and chopped parsley.

358.Carp Fritters

Servings:x
Cooking Time:x
Ingredients:
- 10 carp filets
- 3 onions chopped
- 5 green chilies-roughly chopped
- 1 ½ tbsp. ginger paste
- 1 ½ tsp. garlic paste
- 1 ½ tsp. salt
- 3 tsp. lemon juice
- 2 tsp. garam masala
- 3 eggs
- 2 ½ tbsp. white sesame seeds

Directions:
1. Grind the ingredients except for the egg and form a smooth paste. Coat the filets in the paste. Now, beat the eggs and add a little salt to it.
2. Dip the coated filets in the egg mixture and then transfer to the sesame seeds and coat the florets well. Place the vegetables on a stick.
3. Pre heat the Breville smart oven at 160 degrees Fahrenheit for around 5 minutes. Place the sticks in the basket and let them cook for another 25 minutes at the same temperature. Turn the sticks over in between the cooking process to get a uniform cook.

359.Mediterranean Sole

Servings: 6
Cooking Time: 20 Minutes
Ingredients:
- Nonstick cooking spray
- 2 tbsp. olive oil
- 8 scallions, sliced thin
- 2 cloves garlic, diced fine
- 4 tomatoes, chopped
- ½ cup dry white wine
- 2 tbsp. fresh parsley, chopped fine
- 1 tsp oregano
- 1 tsp pepper
- 2 lbs. sole, cut in 6 pieces
- 4 oz. feta cheese, crumbled

Directions:
1. Place the rack in position 1 of the oven. Spray an 8x11-inch baking dish with cooking spray.
2. Heat the oil in a medium skillet over medium heat. Add scallions and garlic and cook until tender, stirring frequently.
3. Add the tomatoes, wine, parsley, oregano, and pepper. Stir to mix. Simmer for 5 minutes, or until sauce thickens. Remove from heat.
4. Pour half the sauce on the bottom of the prepared dish. Lay fish on top then pour remaining sauce over the top. Sprinkle with feta.
5. Set the oven to bake on 400°F for 25 minutes. After 5 minutes, place the baking dish on the rack and cook 15-18 minutes or until fish flakes easily with a fork. Serve immediately.
- **Nutrition Info:** Calories 220, Total Fat 12g, Saturated Fat 4g, Total Carbs 6g, Net Carbs 4g, Protein 22g, Sugar 4g, Fiber 2g, Sodium 631mg, Potassium 540mg, Phosphorus 478mg

360.Healthy Haddock

Servings: 2
Cooking Time: 25 Minutes
Ingredients:
- 1 lb haddock fillets
- 1/4 cup parsley, chopped
- 1 lemon juice
- 1/4 cup brown sugar
- 1/4 cup onion, diced
- 1 tsp ginger, grated
- 3/4 cup soy sauce
- Pepper
- Salt

Directions:
1. Fit the Cuisinart oven with the rack in position
2. Add fish fillets and remaining ingredients into the large bowl and coat well and place in the refrigerator for 1 hour.
3. Place marinated fish fillets into the baking dish.

4. Set to bake at 325 F for 30 minutes. After 5 minutes place the baking dish in the preheated oven.
5. Serve and enjoy.
- **Nutrition Info:** Calories 391 Fat 2.5 g Carbohydrates 28 g Sugar 20.4 g Protein 61.7 g Cholesterol 168 mg

361.Parsley Catfish Fillets

Servings:4
Cooking Time: 25 Minutes
Ingredients:
- 4 catfish fillets, rinsed and dried
- ¼ cup seasoned fish fry
- 1 tbsp olive oil
- 1 tbsp fresh parsley, chopped

Directions:
1. Add seasoned fish fry and fillets in a large Ziploc bag; massage well to coat. Place the fillets in the Breville basket and cook for 14-16 minutes at 360 F on AirFry function. Top with parsley.

362.Easy Scallops

Servings:2
Cooking Time: 4 Minutes
Ingredients:
- 12 medium sea scallops, rinsed and patted dry
- 1 teaspoon fine sea salt
- ¾ teaspoon ground black pepper, plus more for garnish
- Fresh thyme leaves, for garnish (optional)
- Avocado oil spray

Directions:
1. Coat the air fryer basket with avocado oil spray.
2. Place the scallops in a medium bowl and spritz with avocado oil spray. Sprinkle the salt and pepper to season.
3. Transfer the seasoned scallops to the basket, spacing them apart.
4. Put the air fryer basket on the baking pan and slide into Rack Position 2, select Air Fry, set temperature to 390ºF (199ºC), and set time to 4 minutes.
5. Flip the scallops halfway through the cooking time.
6. When cooking is complete, the scallops should reach an internal temperature of just 145ºF (63ºC) on a meat thermometer. Sprinkle the pepper and thyme leaves on top for garnish, if desired. Serve immediately.

363.Sweet And Savory Breaded Shrimp

Servings: 2
Cooking Time: 20 Minutes
Ingredients:
- ½ pound of fresh shrimp, peeled from their shells and rinsed
- 2 raw eggs

- ½ cup of breadcrumbs (we like Panko, but any brand or home recipe will do)
- ½ white onion, peeled and rinsed and finely chopped
- 1 teaspoon of ginger-garlic paste
- ½ teaspoon of turmeric powder
- ½ teaspoon of red chili powder
- ½ teaspoon of cumin powder
- ½ teaspoon of black pepper powder
- ½ teaspoon of dry mango powder
- Pinch of salt

Directions:
1. Preparing the Ingredients. Cover the basket of the Cuisinart air fryer oven with a lining of tin foil, leaving the edges uncovered to allow air to circulate through the basket.
2. Preheat the Cuisinart air fryer oven to 350 degrees.
3. In a large mixing bowl, beat the eggs until fluffy and until the yolks and whites are fully combined.
4. Dunk all the shrimp in the egg mixture, fully submerging.
5. In a separate mixing bowl, combine the bread crumbs with all the dry ingredients until evenly blended.
6. One by one, coat the egg-covered shrimp in the mixed dry ingredients so that fully covered, and place on the foil-lined air-fryer basket.
7. Air Frying. Set the air-fryer timer to 20 minutes.
8. Halfway through the cooking time, shake the handle of the air-fryer so that the breaded shrimp jostles inside and fry-coverage is even.
9. After 20 minutes, when the fryer shuts off, the shrimp will be perfectly cooked and their breaded crust golden-brown and delicious! Using tongs, remove from the air fryer oven and set on a serving dish to cool.

364.Browned Shrimp Patties

Servings:4
Cooking Time: 12 Minutes
Ingredients:
- ½ pound (227 g) raw shrimp, shelled, deveined, and chopped finely
- 2 cups cooked sushi rice
- ¼ cup chopped red bell pepper
- ¼ cup chopped celery
- ¼ cup chopped green onion
- 2 teaspoons Worcestershire sauce
- ½ teaspoon salt
- ½ teaspoon garlic powder
- ½ teaspoon Old Bay seasoning
- ½ cup plain bread crumbs
- Cooking spray

Directions:
1. Put all the ingredients except the bread crumbs and oil in a large bowl and stir to incorporate.

2. Scoop out the shrimp mixture and shape into 8 equal-sized patties with your hands, no more than ½-inch thick. Roll the patties in the bread crumbs on a plate and spray both sides with cooking spray. Place the patties in the air fryer basket.
3. Put the air fryer basket on the baking pan and slide into Rack Position 2, select Air Fry, set temperature to 390°F (199°C), and set time to 12 minutes.
4. Flip the patties halfway through the cooking time.
5. When cooking is complete, the outside should be crispy brown. Divide the patties among four plates and serve warm.

365.Salmon Fritters

Servings:x
Cooking Time:x
Ingredients:
- 2 tbsp. garam masala
- 1 lb. fileted Salmon
- 3 tsp ginger finely chopped
- 1-2 tbsp. fresh coriander leaves
- 2 or 3 green chilies finely chopped
- 1 ½ tbsp. lemon juice
- Salt and pepper to taste

Directions:
1. Mix the ingredients in a clean bowl.
2. Mold this mixture into round and flat French Cuisine Galettes.
3. Wet the French Cuisine Galettes slightly with water.
4. Pre heat the Breville smart oven at 160 degrees Fahrenheit for 5 minutes. Place the French Cuisine Galettes in the fry basket and let them cook for another 25 minutes at the same temperature. Keep rolling them over to get a uniform cook. Serve either with mint sauce or ketchup.

366.Delicious Crab Cakes

Servings: 5
Cooking Time: 10 Minutes
Ingredients:
- 18 oz can crab meat, drained
- 2 1/2 tbsp mayonnaise
- 2 eggs, lightly beaten
- 1/4 cup breadcrumbs
- 1 1/2 tsp dried parsley
- 1 tbsp dried celery
- 1 tsp Old bay seasoning
- 1 1/2 tbsp Dijon mustard
- Pepper
- Salt

Directions:
1. Fit the Cuisinart oven with the rack in position 2.
2. Add all ingredients into the mixing bowl and mix until well combined.
3. Make patties from mixture and place in the air fryer basket then place an air fryer basket in the baking pan.

4. Place a baking pan on the oven rack. Set to air fry at 320 F for 10 minutes.
5. Serve and enjoy.
- **Nutrition Info:** Calories 138 Fat 4.7 g Carbohydrates 7.8 g Sugar 2.7 g Protein 16.8 g Cholesterol 127 mg

367.Parmesan Fish With Pine Nuts

Servings: 4
Cooking Time: 15 Minutes
Ingredients:
- 2 tbsp fresh basil, chopped
- 2 garlic cloves, minced
- 2 tbsp olive oil
- 1 tbsp Parmesan cheese, grated
- salt and black pepper to taste
- 2 tbsp pine nuts
- 4 white fish fillets
- 2 tbsp olive oil

Directions:
1. Preheat Cuisinart on Air Fry function to 350 F. Season the fish with salt and pepper. Place in the greased basket and fit in the baking tray. Cook the fillets for 8 minutes, flipping once. In a bowl, add basil, olive oil, pine nuts, garlic, and Parmesan cheese; mix well. Serve with the fish.

368.Buttery Crab Legs

Servings:4
Cooking Time: 15 Minutes
Ingredients:
- 3 pounds crab legs
- 1 cup butter, melted

Directions:
1. Preheat Breville on AirFry function to 380 F. Dip the crab legs in salted water and let stay for a few minutes. Drain, pat dry, and place the legs in the basket and press Start. Cook for 10 minutes. Pour the butter over crab legs and serve.

369.Herbed Scallops With Vegetables

Servings:4
Cooking Time: 9 Minutes
Ingredients:
- 1 cup frozen peas
- 1 cup green beans
- 1 cup frozen chopped broccoli
- 2 teaspoons olive oil
- ½ teaspoon dried oregano
- ½ teaspoon dried basil
- 12 ounces (340 g) sea scallops, rinsed and patted dry

Directions:
1. Put the peas, green beans, and broccoli in a large bowl. Drizzle with the olive oil and toss to coat well. Transfer the vegetables to the air fryer basket.
2. Put the air fryer basket on the baking pan and slide into Rack Position 2, select Air Fry,

set temperature to 400ºF (205ºC), and set time to 5 minutes.

3. When cooking is complete, the vegetables should be fork-tender. Transfer the vegetables to a serving bowl. Scatter with the oregano and basil and set aside.
4. Place the scallops in the basket.
5. Put the air fryer basket on the baking pan and slide into Rack Position 2, select Air Fry, set temperature to 400ºF (205ºC), and set time to 4 minutes.
6. When cooking is complete, the scallops should be firm and just opaque in the center. Remove from the oven to the bowl of vegetables and toss well. Serve warm.

370.Shrimp And Cherry Tomato Kebabs

Servings:4
Cooking Time: 5 Minutes
Ingredients:
- 1½ pounds (680 g) jumbo shrimp, cleaned, shelled and deveined
- 1 pound (454 g) cherry tomatoes
- 2 tablespoons butter, melted
- 1 tablespoons Sriracha sauce
- Sea salt and ground black pepper, to taste
- 1 teaspoon dried parsley flakes
- ½ teaspoon dried basil
- ½ teaspoon dried oregano
- ½ teaspoon mustard seeds
- ½ teaspoon marjoram
- Special Equipment:
- 4 to 6 wooden skewers, soaked in water for 30 minutes

Directions:
1. Put all the ingredients in a large bowl and toss to coat well.
2. Make the kebabs: Thread, alternating jumbo shrimp and cherry tomatoes, onto the wooden skewers. Place the kebabs in the air fryer basket.
3. Put the air fryer basket on the baking pan and slide into Rack Position 2, select Air Fry, set temperature to 400ºF (205ºC), and set time to 5 minutes.
4. When cooking is complete, the shrimp should be pink and the cherry tomatoes should be softened. Remove from the oven. Let the shrimp and cherry tomato kebabs cool for 5 minutes and serve hot.

371.Blackened Mahi Mahi

Servings: 4
Cooking Time: 12 Minutes
Ingredients:
- 4 mahi-mahi fillets
- 1 tsp cumin
- 1 tsp paprika
- 1/2 tsp cayenne pepper
- 1 tsp oregano
- 1 tsp garlic powder
- 1 tsp onion powder
- 1/2 tsp pepper
- 3 tbsp olive oil
- 1/2 tsp salt

Directions:
1. Fit the Cuisinart oven with the rack in position
2. Brush fish fillets with oil and place them into the baking dish.
3. Mix together the remaining ingredients and sprinkle over fish fillets.
4. Set to bake at 450 F for 17 minutes. After 5 minutes place the baking dish in the preheated oven.
5. Serve and enjoy.
- **Nutrition Info:** Calories 189 Fat 11.7 g Carbohydrates 2.1 g Sugar 0.5 g Protein 19.4 g Cholesterol 86 mg

372.Sesame Seeds Coated Fish

Servings:5
Cooking Time: 8 Minutes
Ingredients:
- 3 tablespoons plain flour
- 2 eggs
- ½ cup sesame seeds, toasted
- ½ cup breadcrumbs
- 1/8 teaspoon dried rosemary, crushed
- Pinch of salt
- Pinch of black pepper
- 3 tablespoons olive oil
- 5 frozen fish fillets (white fish of your choice)

Directions:
1. Preparing the Ingredients. In a shallow dish, place flour. In a second shallow dish, beat the eggs. In a third shallow dish, add remaining ingredients except fish fillets and mix till a crumbly mixture forms.
2. Coat the fillets with flour and shake off the excess flour.
3. Next, dip the fillets in the egg.
4. Then coat the fillets with sesame seeds mixture generously.
5. Preheat the Cuisinart air fryer oven to 390 degrees F.
6. Air Frying. Line an Air fryer rack/basket with a piece of foil. Arrange the fillets into prepared basket.
7. Cook for about 14 minutes, flipping once after 10 minutes.

373.Homemade Fish Sticks

Servings: 8 Fish Sticks
Cooking Time: 8 Minutes
Ingredients:
- 8 ounces (227 g) fish fillets (pollock or cod), cut into ½×3-inch strips
- Salt, to taste (optional)
- ½ cup plain bread crumbs
- Cooking spray

Directions:
1. Season the fish strips with salt to taste, if desired.

2. Place the bread crumbs on a plate. Roll the fish strips in the bread crumbs to coat. Spritz the fish strips with cooking spray.
3. Arrange the fish strips in the air fryer basket in a single layer.
4. Put the air fryer basket on the baking pan and slide into Rack Position 2, select Air Fry, set temperature to 390ºF (199ºC), and set time to 8 minutes.
5. When cooking is complete, they should be golden brown. Remove from the oven and cool for 5 minutes before serving.

374.Miso White Fish Fillets

Servings: 2
Cooking Time: 10 Minutes
Ingredients:
- 2 cod fish fillets
- 2 tbsp brown sugar
- 2 tbsp miso
- 1 tbsp garlic, chopped

Directions:
1. Fit the Cuisinart oven with the rack in position 2.
2. Add all ingredients to the zip-lock bag and marinate fish in the refrigerator overnight.
3. Place marinated fish fillets in the air fryer basket then place an air fryer basket in the baking pan.
4. Place a baking pan on the oven rack. Set to air fry at 350 F for 10 minutes.
5. Serve and enjoy.
- **Nutrition Info:** Calories 9 Fat 0.1 g Carbohydrates 0.5 g Sugar 0.3 g Protein 1.5 g Cholesterol 3 mg

375.Carp Best Homemade Croquette

Servings:x
Cooking Time:x
Ingredients:
- 1 lb. Carp filets
- 3 onions chopped
- 5 green chilies-roughly chopped
- 1 ½ tbsp. ginger paste
- 1 ½ tsp garlic paste
- 1 ½ tsp salt
- 3 tsp lemon juice
- 2 tsp garam masala
- 4 tbsp. chopped coriander
- 3 tbsp. cream
- 2 tbsp. coriander powder
- 4 tbsp. fresh mint chopped
- 3 tbsp. chopped capsicum
- 3 eggs
- 2 ½ tbsp. white sesame seeds

Directions:
1. Take all the ingredients mentioned under the first heading and mix them in a bowl. Grind them thoroughly to make a smooth paste. Take the eggs in a different bowl and beat them. Add a pinch of salt and leave them aside. Mold the fish mixture into small balls and flatten them into round and flat Best Homemade Croquettes. Dip these Best Homemade Croquettes in the egg and salt mixture and then in the mixture of breadcrumbs and sesame seeds.
2. Leave these Best Homemade Croquettes in the fridge for an hour or so to set. Pre heat the Breville smart oven at 160 degrees Fahrenheit for around 5 minutes. Place the Best Homemade Croquettes in the basket and let them cook for another 25 minutes at the same temperature. Turn the Best Homemade Croquettes over in between the cooking process to get a uniform cook. Serve the Best Homemade Croquettes with mint sauce.

376.Crispy Crab Legs

Servings: 4
Cooking Time: 15 Minutes
Ingredients:
- 3 pounds crab legs
- ½ cup butter, melted

Directions:
1. Preheat Cuisinart on Air Fry function to 380 F. Cover the crab legs with salted water and let them stay for a few minutes. Drain, pat them dry, and place the legs in the basket. Fit in the baking tray and brush with some butter; cook for 10 minutes, flipping once. Drizzle with the remaining butter and serve.

377.Baked Lemon Swordfish

Servings: 2
Cooking Time: 10 Minutes
Ingredients:
- 12 oz swordfish fillets
- 1/8 tsp crushed red pepper
- 1 garlic clove, minced
- 2 tsp fresh parsley, chopped
- 3 tbsp olive oil
- 1/2 tsp lemon zest, grated
- 1/2 tsp ginger, grated

Directions:
1. Fit the Cuisinart oven with the rack in position
2. In a small bowl, mix 2 tbsp oil, lemon zest, red pepper, ginger, garlic, and parsley.
3. Season fish fillets with salt.
4. Heat remaining oil in a pan over medium-high heat.
5. Place fish fillets in the pan and cook until browned, about 2-3 minutes.
6. Transfer fish fillets in a baking dish.
7. Set to bake at 400 F for 15 minutes. After 5 minutes place the baking dish in the preheated oven.
8. Pour oil mixture over fish fillets and serve.
- **Nutrition Info:** Calories 449 Fat 29.8 g Carbohydrates 1.1 g Sugar 0.1 g Protein 43.4 g Cholesterol 85 mg

378.Roasted Scallops With Snow Peas

Servings:4
Cooking Time: 8 Minutes
Ingredients:
- 1 pound (454 g) sea scallops
- 3 tablespoons hoisin sauce
- ½ cup toasted sesame seeds
- 6 ounces (170 g) snow peas, trimmed
- 3 teaspoons vegetable oil, divided
- 1 teaspoon soy sauce
- 1 teaspoon sesame oil
- 1 cup roasted mushrooms

Directions:
1. Brush the scallops with the hoisin sauce. Put the sesame seeds in a shallow dish. Roll the scallops in the sesame seeds until evenly coated.
2. Combine the snow peas with 1 teaspoon of vegetable oil, the sesame oil, and soy sauce in a medium bowl and toss to coat.
3. Grease the baking pan with the remaining 2 teaspoons of vegetable oil. Put the scallops in the middle of the pan and arrange the snow peas around the scallops in a single layer.
4. Slide the baking pan into Rack Position 2, select Roast, set temperature to 375ºF (190ºC), and set time to 8 minutes.
5. After 5 minutes, remove the pan and flip the scallops. Fold in the mushrooms and stir well. Return the pan to the oven and continue cooking.
6. When done, remove from the oven and cool for 5 minutes. Serve warm.

379.Quick Tuna Patties

Servings: 10
Cooking Time: 10 Minutes
Ingredients:
- 15 oz can tuna, drained and flaked
- 3 tbsp parmesan cheese, grated
- 1/2 cup breadcrumbs
- 1 tbsp lemon juice
- 2 eggs, lightly beaten
- 1/2 tsp dried mixed herbs
- 1/2 tsp garlic powder
- 2 tbsp onion, minced
- 1 celery stalk, chopped
- Pepper
- Salt

Directions:
1. Fit the Cuisinart oven with the rack in position 2.
2. Add all ingredients into the mixing bowl and mix until well combined.
3. Make patties from mixture and place in the air fryer basket then place the air fryer basket in the baking pan.
4. Place a baking pan on the oven rack. Set to air fry at 360 F for 10 minutes.
5. Serve and enjoy.

- **Nutrition Info:** Calories 90 Fat 1.8 g Carbohydrates 4.4 g Sugar 0.6 g Protein 13.2 g Cholesterol 47 mg

380.Prawn Fried Baked Pastry

Servings:x
Cooking Time:x
Ingredients:
- 2 tbsp. unsalted butter
- 1 ½ cup all-purpose flour
- A pinch of salt to taste
- Add as much water as required to make the dough stiff and firm
- 1 lb. prawn
- ¼ cup boiled peas
- 1 tsp. powdered ginger
- 1 or 2 green chilies that are finely chopped or mashed
- ½ tsp. cumin
- 1 tsp. coarsely crushed coriander
- 1 dry red chili broken into pieces
- A small amount of salt (to taste)
- ½ tsp. dried mango powder
- ½ tsp. red chili power.
- 1-2 tbsp. coriander.

Directions:
1. You will first need to make the outer covering. In a large bowl, add the flour, butter and enough water to knead it into dough that is stiff. Transfer this to a container and leave it to rest for five minutes. Place a pan on medium flame and add the oil. Roast the mustard seeds and once roasted, add the coriander seeds and the chopped dry red chilies. Add all the dry ingredients for the filling and mix the ingredients well.
2. Add a little water and continue to stir the ingredients. Make small balls out of the dough and roll them out. Cut the rolled-out dough into halves and apply a little water on the edges to help you fold the halves into a cone. Add the filling to the cone and close up the samosa. Pre-heat the Breville smart oven for around 5 to 6 minutes at 300 Fahrenheit. Place all the samosas in the fry basket and close the basket properly.
3. Keep the Breville smart oven at 200 degrees for another 20 to 25 minutes. Around the halfway point, open the basket and turn the samosas over for uniform cooking. After this, fry at 250 degrees for around 10 minutes in order to give them the desired golden-brown color. Serve hot. Recommended sides are tamarind or mint sauce.

381.Simple Salmon Patties

Servings: 2
Cooking Time: 7 Minutes
Ingredients:
- 8 oz salmon fillet, minced

- 1 egg, lightly beaten
- 1/4 tsp garlic powder
- 1/4 tsp onion powder
- 1/8 tsp paprika
- 2 tbsp breadcrumbs
- Pepper
- Salt

Directions:
1. Fit the Cuisinart oven with the rack in position 2.
2. Add all ingredients into the bowl and mix until well combined.
3. Make patties from mixture and place in the air fryer basket then place an air fryer basket in the baking pan.
4. Place a baking pan on the oven rack. Set to air fry at 390 F for 7 minutes.
5. Serve and enjoy.
- **Nutrition Info:** Calories 211 Fat 9.6 g Carbohydrates 5.6 g Sugar 0.8 g Protein 25.8 g Cholesterol 132 mg

382.Tuna Sandwich

Servings:x
Cooking Time:x
Ingredients:
- 2 slices of white bread
- 1 tbsp. softened butter
- 1 tin tuna
- 1 small capsicum
- For Barbeque Sauce:
- ¼ tbsp. Worcestershire sauce
- ½ tsp. olive oil
- ¼ tsp. mustard powder
- ½ flake garlic crushed
- ¼ cup chopped onion
- ½ tbsp. sugar
- 1 tbsp. tomato ketchup
- ½ cup water.
- ¼ tbsp. red chili sauce
- A pinch of salt and black pepper to taste

Directions:
1. Take the slices of bread and remove the edges. Now cut the slices horizontally. Cook the ingredients for the sauce and wait till it thickens. Now, add the lamb to the sauce and stir till it obtains the flavors. Roast the capsicum and peel the skin off. Cut the capsicum into slices. Mix the ingredients together and apply it to the bread slices.
2. Pre-heat the Breville smart oven for 5 minutes at 300 Fahrenheit. Open the basket of the Fryer and place the prepared Classic Sandwiches in it such that no two Classic Sandwiches are touching each other. Now keep the fryer at 250 degrees for around 15 minutes. Turn the Classic Sandwiches in between the cooking process to cook both slices. Serve the Classic Sandwiches with tomato ketchup or mint sauce.

383.Flavorful Baked Halibut

Servings: 4
Cooking Time: 12 Minutes
Ingredients:
- 1 lb halibut fillets
- 1/4 tsp garlic powder
- 1/4 tsp paprika
- 1/4 tsp smoked paprika
- 1/4 tsp pepper
- 1/4 cup olive oil
- 1 lemon juice
- 1/2 tsp salt

Directions:
1. Fit the Cuisinart oven with the rack in position
2. Place fish fillets into the baking dish.
3. In a small bowl, mix lemon juice, oil, paprika, smoked paprika, garlic powder, and salt.
4. Brush lemon juice mixture over fish fillets.
5. Set to bake at 425 F for 17 minutes. After 5 minutes place the baking dish in the preheated oven.
6. Serve and enjoy.
- **Nutrition Info:** Calories 236 Fat 15.3 g Carbohydrates 0.4 g Sugar 0.1 g Protein 24 g Cholesterol 36 mg

384.Easy Blackened Shrimp

Servings: 6
Cooking Time: 10 Minutes
Ingredients:
- 1 lb shrimp, deveined
- 1 tbsp olive oil
- 1/4 tsp pepper
- 2 tsp blackened seasoning
- 1/4 tsp salt

Directions:
1. Fit the Cuisinart oven with the rack in position
2. Toss shrimp with oil, pepper, blackened seasoning, and salt.
3. Transfer shrimp into the baking pan.
4. Set to bake at 400 F for 15 minutes. After 5 minutes place the baking pan in the preheated oven.
5. Serve and enjoy.
- **Nutrition Info:** Calories 167 Fat 4.3 g Carbohydrates 10.5 g Sugar 0 g Protein 20.6 g Cholesterol 159 mg

385.Spicy Orange Shrimp

Servings:4
Cooking Time: 12 Minutes
Ingredients:
- $^1/_3$ cup orange juice
- 3 teaspoons minced garlic
- 1 teaspoon Old Bay seasoning
- ¼ to ½ teaspoon cayenne pepper
- 1 pound (454 g) medium shrimp, thawed, deveined, peeled, with tails off, and patted dry
- Cooking spray

Directions:
1. Stir together the orange juice, garlic, Old Bay seasoning, and cayenne pepper in a medium bowl. Add the shrimp to the bowl and toss to coat well.
2. Cover the bowl with plastic wrap and marinate in the refrigerator for 30 minutes.
3. Spritz the air fryer basket with cooking spray. Place the shrimp in the pan and spray with cooking spray.
4. Put the air fryer basket on the baking pan and slide into Rack Position 2, select Air Fry, set temperature to 400ºF (205ºC), and set time to 12 minutes.
5. Flip the shrimp halfway through the cooking time.
6. When cooked, the shrimp should be opaque and crisp. Remove from the oven and serve hot.

386.Crispy Crab And Fish Cakes

Servings:4
Cooking Time: 12 Minutes
Ingredients:
- 8 ounces (227 g) imitation crab meat
- 4 ounces (113 g) leftover cooked fish (such as cod, pollock, or haddock)
- 2 tablespoons minced celery
- 2 tablespoons minced green onion
- 2 tablespoons light mayonnaise
- 1 tablespoon plus 2 teaspoons Worcestershire sauce
- ¾ cup crushed saltine cracker crumbs
- 2 teaspoons dried parsley flakes
- 1 teaspoon prepared yellow mustard
- ½ teaspoon garlic powder
- ½ teaspoon dried dill weed, crushed
- ½ teaspoon Old Bay seasoning
- ½ cup panko bread crumbs
- Cooking spray

Directions:
1. Pulse the crab meat and fish in a food processor until finely chopped.
2. Transfer the meat mixture to a large bowl, along with the celery, green onion, mayo, Worcestershire sauce, cracker crumbs, parsley flakes, mustard, garlic powder, dill weed, and Old Bay seasoning. Stir to mix well.
3. Scoop out the meat mixture and form into 8 equal-sized patties with your hands.
4. Place the panko bread crumbs on a plate. Roll the patties in the bread crumbs until they are evenly coated on both sides. Put the patties in the baking pan and spritz them with cooking spray.
5. Slide the baking pan into Rack Position 1, select Convection Bake, set temperature to 390ºF (199ºC), and set time to 12 minutes.
6. Flip the patties halfway through the cooking time.
7. When cooking is complete, they should be golden brown and cooked through. Remove

the pan from the oven. Divide the patties among four plates and serve.

387.Parmesan-crusted Salmon Patties

Servings:4
Cooking Time: 13 Minutes
Ingredients:
- 1 pound (454 g) salmon, chopped into ½-inch pieces
- 2 tablespoons coconut flour
- 2 tablespoons grated Parmesan cheese
- 1½ tablespoons milk
- ½ white onion, peeled and finely chopped
- ½ teaspoon butter, at room temperature
- ½ teaspoon chipotle powder
- ½ teaspoon dried parsley flakes
- $1/3$ teaspoon ground black pepper
- $1/3$ teaspoon smoked cayenne pepper
- 1 teaspoon fine sea salt

Directions:
1. Put all the ingredients for the salmon patties in a bowl and stir to combine well.
2. Scoop out 2 tablespoons of the salmon mixture and shape into a patty with your palm, about ½ inch thick. Repeat until all the mixture is used. Transfer to the refrigerator for about 2 hours until firm.
3. When ready, arrange the salmon patties in the baking pan.
4. Slide the baking pan into Rack Position 1, select Convection Bake, set temperature to 395ºF (202ºC), and set time to 13 minutes.
5. Flip the patties halfway through the cooking time.
6. When cooking is complete, the patties should be golden brown. Remove from the oven and cool for 5 minutes before serving.

388.Italian Cod

Servings: 4
Cooking Time: 20 Minutes
Ingredients:
- 1 1/2 lbs cod fillet
- 1/4 cup olives, sliced
- 1 lb cherry tomatoes, halved
- 2 garlic cloves, crushed
- 1 small onion, chopped
- 1 tbsp olive oil
- 1/4 cup of water
- 1 tsp Italian seasoning
- Pepper
- Salt

Directions:
1. Fit the Cuisinart oven with the rack in position
2. Place fish fillets, olives, tomatoes, garlic, and onion in a baking dish. Drizzle with oil.
3. Sprinkle with Italian seasoning, pepper, and salt. Pour water into the dish.
4. Set to bake at 400 F for 25 minutes. After 5 minutes place the baking dish in the preheated oven.

5. Serve and enjoy.
- **Nutrition Info:** Calories 210 Fat 6.5 g Carbohydrates 7.2 g Sugar 3.8 g Protein 31.7 g Cholesterol 84 mg

389.Panko-crusted Tilapia

Servings: 3
Cooking Time: 10 Minutes
Ingredients:
- 2 tsp. Italian seasoning
- 2 tsp. lemon pepper
- 1/3 C. panko breadcrumbs
- 1/3 C. egg whites
- 1/3 C. almond flour
- 3 tilapia fillets
- Olive oil

Directions:
1. Preparing the Ingredients. Place panko, egg whites, and flour into separate bowls. Mix lemon pepper and Italian seasoning in with breadcrumbs.
2. Pat tilapia fillets dry. Dredge in flour, then egg, then breadcrumb mixture.
3. Air Frying. Add to the Oven rack/basket and spray lightly with olive oil. Place the Rack on the middle-shelf of the Cuisinart air fryer oven.
4. Cook 10-11 minutes at 400 degrees, making sure to flip halfway through cooking.
- **Nutrition Info:** CALORIES: 256; FAT: 9G; PROTEIN:39G; SUGAR:5G

390.Crispy Coated Scallops

Servings: 4
Cooking Time: 10 Minutes
Ingredients:
- Nonstick cooking spray
- 1 lb. sea scallops, patted dry
- 1 teaspoon onion powder
- ½ tsp pepper
- 1 egg
- 1 tbsp. water
- ¼ cup Italian bread crumbs
- Paprika
- 1 tbsp. fresh lemon juice

Directions:
1. Lightly spray fryer basket with cooking spray. Place baking pan in position 2 of the oven.
2. Sprinkle scallops with onion powder and pepper.
3. In a shallow dish, whisk together egg and water.
4. Place bread crumbs in a separate shallow dish.
5. Dip scallops in egg then bread crumbs coating them lightly. Place in fryer basket and lightly spray with cooking spray. Sprinkle with paprika.
6. Place the basket on the baking pan and set oven to air fryer on 400°F. Bake 10-12 minutes until scallops are firm on the inside

and golden brown on the outside. Drizzle with lemon juice and serve.
- **Nutrition Info:** Calories 122, Total Fat 2g, Saturated Fat 1g, Total Carbs 10g, Net Carbs 9g, Protein 16g, Sugar 1g, Fiber 1g, Sodium 563mg, Potassium 282mg, Phosphorus 420mg

391.Mustard-crusted Sole Fillets

Servings:4
Cooking Time: 10 Minutes
Ingredients:
- 5 teaspoons low-sodium yellow mustard
- 1 tablespoon freshly squeezed lemon juice
- 4 (3.5-ounce / 99-g) sole fillets
- 2 teaspoons olive oil
- ½ teaspoon dried marjoram
- ½ teaspoon dried thyme
- ⅛ teaspoon freshly ground black pepper
- 1 slice low-sodium whole-wheat bread, crumbled

Directions:
1. Whisk together the mustard and lemon juice in a small bowl until thoroughly mixed and smooth. Spread the mixture evenly over the sole fillets, then transfer the fillets to the baking pan.
2. In a separate bowl, combine the olive oil, marjoram, thyme, black pepper, and bread crumbs and stir to mix well. Gently but firmly press the mixture onto the top of fillets, coating them completely.
3. Slide the baking pan into Rack Position 1, select Convection Bake, set temperature to 320ºF (160ºC), and set time to 10 minutes.
4. When cooking is complete, the fish should reach an internal temperature of 145ºF (63ºC) on a meat thermometer. Remove from the oven and serve on a plate.

392.Panko Crab Sticks With Mayo Sauce

Servings:4
Cooking Time: 12 Minutes
Ingredients:
- Crab Sticks:
- 2 eggs
- 1 cup flour
- $^1/_3$ cup panko bread crumbs
- 1 tablespoon old bay seasoning
- 1 pound (454 g) crab sticks
- Cooking spray
- Mayo Sauce:
- ½ cup mayonnaise
- 1 lime, juiced
- 2 garlic cloves, minced

Directions:
1. In a bowl, beat the eggs. In a shallow bowl, place the flour. In another shallow bowl, thoroughly combine the panko bread crumbs and old bay seasoning.
2. Dredge the crab sticks in the flour, shaking off any excess, then in the beaten eggs,

finally press them in the bread crumb mixture to coat well.

3. Arrange the crab sticks in the air fryer basket and spray with cooking spray.
4. Put the air fryer basket on the baking pan and slide into Rack Position 2, select Air Fry, set temperature to 390ºF (199ºC), and set time to 12 minutes.
5. Flip the crab sticks halfway through the cooking time.
6. Meanwhile, make the sauce by whisking together the mayo, lime juice, and garlic in a small bowl.
7. When cooking is complete, remove from the oven. Serve the crab sticks with the mayo sauce on the side.

393.Golden Beer-battered Cod

Servings:4
Cooking Time: 15 Minutes
Ingredients:
- 2 eggs
- 1 cup malty beer
- 1 cup all-purpose flour
- ½ cup cornstarch
- 1 teaspoon garlic powder
- Salt and pepper, to taste
- 4 (4-ounce / 113-g) cod fillets
- Cooking spray

Directions:
1. In a shallow bowl, beat together the eggs with the beer. In another shallow bowl, thoroughly combine the flour and cornstarch. Sprinkle with the garlic powder, salt, and pepper.
2. Dredge each cod fillet in the flour mixture, then in the egg mixture. Dip each piece of fish in the flour mixture a second time.
3. Spritz the air fryer basket with cooking spray. Arrange the cod fillets in the pan in a single layer.
4. Put the air fryer basket on the baking pan and slide into Rack Position 2, select Air Fry, set temperature to 400ºF (205ºC), and set time to 15 minutes.
5. Flip the fillets halfway through the cooking time.
6. When cooking is complete, the cod should reach an internal temperature of 145ºF (63ºC) on a meat thermometer and the outside should be crispy. Let the fish cool for 5 minutes and serve.

394.Rosemary Garlic Shrimp

Servings: 4
Cooking Time: 10 Minutes
Ingredients:
- 1 lb shrimp, peeled and deveined
- 2 garlic cloves, minced
- 1/2 tbsp fresh rosemary, chopped
- 1 tbsp olive oil
- Pepper
- Salt

Directions:
1. Fit the Cuisinart oven with the rack in position
2. Add shrimp and remaining ingredients in a large bowl and toss well.
3. Pour shrimp mixture into the baking dish.
4. Set to bake at 400 F for 15 minutes. After 5 minutes place the baking dish in the preheated oven.
5. Serve and enjoy.
- **Nutrition Info:** Calories 168 Fat 5.5 g Carbohydrates 2.5 g Sugar 0 g Protein 26 g Cholesterol 239 mg

395.Baked Flounder Fillets

Servings:2
Cooking Time: 12 Minutes
Ingredients:
- 2 flounder fillets, patted dry
- 1 egg
- ½ teaspoon Worcestershire sauce
- ¼ cup almond flour
- ¼ cup coconut flour
- ½ teaspoon coarse sea salt
- ½ teaspoon lemon pepper
- ¼ teaspoon chili powder
- Cooking spray

Directions:
1. In a shallow bowl, beat together the egg with Worcestershire sauce until well incorporated.
2. In another bowl, thoroughly combine the almond flour, coconut flour, sea salt, lemon pepper, and chili powder.
3. Dredge the fillets in the egg mixture, shaking off any excess, then roll in the flour mixture to coat well.
4. Spritz the baking pan with cooking spray. Place the fillets in the pan.
5. Slide the baking pan into Rack Position 1, select Convection Bake, set temperature to 390ºF (199ºC), and set time to 12 minutes.
6. After 7 minutes, remove from the oven and flip the fillets and spray with cooking spray. Return the pan to the oven and continue cooking for 5 minutes, or until the fish is flaky.
7. When cooking is complete, remove from the oven and serve warm.

396.Parmesan-crusted Hake With Garlic Sauce

Servings:3
Cooking Time: 10 Minutes
Ingredients:
- Fish:
- 6 tablespoons mayonnaise
- 1 tablespoon fresh lime juice
- 1 teaspoon Dijon mustard
- 1 cup grated Parmesan cheese
- Salt, to taste

- ¼ teaspoon ground black pepper, or more to taste
- 3 hake fillets, patted dry
- Nonstick cooking spray
- Garlic Sauce:
- ¼ cup plain Greek yogurt
- 2 tablespoons olive oil
- 2 cloves garlic, minced
- ½ teaspoon minced tarragon leaves

Directions:
1. Mix the mayo, lime juice, and mustard in a shallow bowl and whisk to combine. In another shallow bowl, stir together the grated Parmesan cheese, salt, and pepper.
2. Dredge each fillet in the mayo mixture, then roll them in the cheese mixture until they are evenly coated on both sides.
3. Spray the air fryer basket with nonstick cooking spray. Place the fillets in the pan.
4. Put the air fryer basket on the baking pan and slide into Rack Position 2, select Air Fry, set temperature to 395ºF (202ºC), and set time to 10 minutes.
5. Flip the fillets halfway through the cooking time.
6. Meanwhile, in a small bowl, whisk all the ingredients for the sauce until well incorporated.
7. When cooking is complete, the fish should flake apart with a fork. Remove the fillets from the oven and serve warm alongside the sauce.

397.Fired Shrimp With Mayonnaise Sauce

Servings:4
Cooking Time: 7 Minutes
Ingredients:
- Shrimp
- 12 jumbo shrimp
- ½ teaspoon garlic salt
- ¼ teaspoon freshly cracked mixed peppercorns
- Sauce:
- 4 tablespoons mayonnaise
- 1 teaspoon grated lemon rind
- 1 teaspoon Dijon mustard
- 1 teaspoon chipotle powder
- ½ teaspoon cumin powder

Directions:
1. In a medium bowl, season the shrimp with garlic salt and cracked mixed peppercorns.
2. Place the shrimp in the air fryer basket.
3. Put the air fryer basket on the baking pan and slide into Rack Position 2, select Air Fry, set temperature to 395ºF (202ºC), and set time to 7 minutes.
4. After 5 minutes, remove from the oven and flip the shrimp. Return to the oven and continue cooking for 2 minutes more, or until they are pink and no longer opaque.
5. Meanwhile, stir together all the ingredients for the sauce in a small bowl until well mixed.

6. When cooking is complete, remove the shrimp from the oven and serve alongside the sauce.

398.Cheesy Tilapia Fillets

Servings: 4
Cooking Time: 15 Minutes
Ingredients:
- ¾ cup grated Parmesan cheese
- 1 tbsp olive oil
- 2 tsp paprika
- 1 tbsp chopped parsley
- ¼ tsp garlic powder
- 4 tilapia fillets

Directions:
1. Preheat Cuisinart on Air Fry function to 350 F. Mix parsley, Parmesan cheese, garlic, and paprika in a bowl. Brush the olive oil over the fillets and then coat with the Parmesan mixture. Place the tilapia onto a lined baking sheet and cook for 8-10 minutes, turning once. Serve.

399.Easy Salmon Patties

Servings: 6 Patties
Cooking Time: 11 Minutes
Ingredients:
- 1 (14.75-ounce / 418-g) can Alaskan pink salmon, drained and bones removed
- ½ cup bread crumbs
- 1 egg, whisked
- 2 scallions, diced
- 1 teaspoon garlic powder
- Salt and pepper, to taste
- Cooking spray

Directions:
1. Stir together the salmon, bread crumbs, whisked egg, scallions, garlic powder, salt, and pepper in a large bowl until well incorporated.
2. Divide the salmon mixture into six equal portions and form each into a patty with your hands.
3. Arrange the salmon patties in the air fryer basket and spritz them with cooking spray.
4. Put the air fryer basket on the baking pan and slide into Rack Position 2, select Air Fry, set temperature to 400ºF (205ºC), and set time to 10 minutes.
5. Flip the patties once halfway through.
6. When cooking is complete, the patties should be golden brown and cooked through. Remove the patties from the oven and serve on a plate.

400.Blackened Tuna Steaks

Servings:x
Cooking Time:x
Ingredients:
- 2 Tbsp canola oil
- 4 (8-oz) tuna steaks, preferably sushi-grade
- Blackening Spice:

- ½ cup freshly ground black pepper
- 2 Tbsp kosher salt
- 1 Tbsp cardamom
- 1 Tbsp ground cinnamon
- 1 Tbsp nutmeg
- 1 Tbsp ground cloves
- 1 tsp coriander
- 1 tsp cumin
- 1 tsp cayenne pepper
- ½ tsp celery salt

Directions:
1. First prepare the blackening spice by combining all the spices.
2. Preheat Breville smart oven.
3. Place oil inside the pot and wait until smoking.
4. Sprinkle blackening mixture on top of both sides of tuna steaks (about
5. -2 Tbsp of blackening spice, depending on how spicy you want your steaks).
6. Add tuna into Breville smart oven and cook about 3 minutes each side. The tuna should be browned on the outside and rare on the inside.

401.Lobster Grandma's Easy To Cook Wontons

Servings:x
Cooking Time:x
Ingredients:
- 1 ½ cup all-purpose flour
- ½ tsp. salt
- 5 tbsp. water
- For filling:
- 2 cups minced lobster
- 2 tbsp. oil
- 2 tsp. ginger-garlic paste
- 2 tsp. soya sauce
- 2 tsp. vinegar

Directions:
1. Squeeze the dough and cover it with plastic wrap and set aside. Next, cook the ingredients for the filling and try to ensure that the lobster is covered well with the sauce.
2. Roll the dough and place the filling in the center. Now, wrap the dough to cover the filling and pinch the edges together.
3. Pre heat the Breville smart oven at 200° F for 5 minutes. Place the wontons in the fry basket and close it. Let them cook at the same temperature for another 20 minutes. Recommended sides are chili sauce or ketchup.

402.Garlic Butter Shrimp Scampi

Servings:4
Cooking Time: 8 Minutes
Ingredients:
- Sauce:
- ¼ cup unsalted butter
- 2 tablespoons fish stock or chicken broth
- 2 cloves garlic, minced
- 2 tablespoons chopped fresh basil leaves
- 1 tablespoon lemon juice
- 1 tablespoon chopped fresh parsley, plus more for garnish
- 1 teaspoon red pepper flakes
- Shrimp:
- 1 pound (454 g) large shrimp, peeled and deveined, tails removed
- Fresh basil sprigs, for garnish

Directions:
1. Put all the ingredients for the sauce in the baking pan and stir to incorporate.
2. Put the air fryer basket on the baking pan and slide into Rack Position 2, select Air Fry, set temperature to 350ºF (180ºC), and set time to 8 minutes.
3. After 3 minutes, remove from the oven and add the shrimp to the baking pan, flipping to coat in the sauce. Return to the oven and continue cooking for 5 minutes until the shrimp are pink and opaque. Stir the shrimp twice during cooking.
4. When cooking is complete, remove from the oven. Serve garnished with the parsley and basil sprigs.

403.Roasted Nicoise Salad

Servings:4
Cooking Time: 15 Minutes
Ingredients:
- 10 ounces (283 g) small red potatoes, quartered
- 8 tablespoons extra-virgin olive oil, divided
- 1 teaspoon kosher salt, divided
- ½ pound (227 g) green beans, trimmed
- 1 pint cherry tomatoes
- 1 teaspoon Dijon mustard
- 3 tablespoons red wine vinegar
- Freshly ground black pepper, to taste
- 1 (9-ounce / 255-g) bag spring greens, washed and dried if needed
- 2 (5-ounce / 142-g) cans oil-packed tuna, drained
- 2 hard-cooked eggs, peeled and quartered
- $^1/_3$ cup kalamata olives, pitted

Directions:
1. In a large bowl, drizzle the potatoes with 1 tablespoon of olive oil and season with ¼ teaspoon of kosher salt. Transfer to the baking pan.
2. Slide the baking pan into Rack Position 2, select Roast, set temperature to 375ºF (190ºC), and set time to 15 minutes.
3. Meanwhile, in a mixing bowl, toss the green beans and cherry tomatoes with 1 tablespoon of olive oil and ¼ teaspoon of kosher salt until evenly coated.
4. After 10 minutes, remove the pan and fold in the green beans and cherry tomatoes. Return the pan to the oven and continue cooking.

5. Meanwhile, make the vinaigrette by whisking together the remaining 6 tablespoons of olive oil, mustard, vinegar, the remaining ½ teaspoon of kosher salt, and black pepper in a small bowl. Set aside.
6. When done, remove from the oven. Allow the vegetables to cool for 5 minutes.
7. Spread out the spring greens on a plate and spoon the tuna into the center of the greens. Arrange the potatoes, green beans, cheery tomatoes, and eggs around the tuna. Serve drizzled with the vinaigrette and scattered with the olives.

404.Herbed Salmon With Asparagus

Servings: 2
Cooking Time: 12 Minutes
Ingredients:
- 2 teaspoons olive oil, plus additional for drizzling
- 2 (5-ounce / 142-g) salmon fillets, with skin
- Salt and freshly ground black pepper, to taste
- 1 bunch asparagus, trimmed
- 1 teaspoon dried tarragon
- 1 teaspoon dried chives
- Fresh lemon wedges, for serving

Directions:
1. Rub the olive oil all over the salmon fillets. Sprinkle with salt and pepper to taste.
2. Put the asparagus on the foil-lined baking pan and place the salmon fillets on top, skin-side down.
3. Slide the baking pan into Rack Position 1, select Convection Bake, set temperature to 350ºF (180ºC), and set time to 12 minutes.
4. When cooked, the fillets should register 145ºF (63ºC) on an instant-read thermometer. Remove from the oven and cut the salmon fillets in half crosswise, then use a metal spatula to lift flesh from skin and transfer to a serving plate. Discard the skin and drizzle the salmon fillets with additional olive oil. Scatter with the herbs.
5. Serve the salmon fillets with asparagus spears and lemon wedges on the side.

405.Garlicky Cod Fillets

Servings:4
Cooking Time: 12 Minutes
Ingredients:
- 1 teaspoon olive oil
- 4 cod fillets
- ¼ teaspoon fine sea salt
- ¼ teaspoon ground black pepper, or more to taste
- 1 teaspoon cayenne pepper
- ½ cup fresh Italian parsley, coarsely chopped
- ½ cup nondairy milk
- 1 Italian pepper, chopped
- 4 garlic cloves, minced
- 1 teaspoon dried basil

- ½ teaspoon dried oregano

Directions:
1. Lightly coat the sides and bottom of the baking pan with the olive oil. Set aside.
2. In a large bowl, sprinkle the fillets with salt, black pepper, and cayenne pepper.
3. In a food processor, pulse the remaining ingredients until smoothly puréed.
4. Add the purée to the bowl of fillets and toss to coat, then transfer to the prepared baking pan.
5. Slide the baking pan into Rack Position 1, select Convection Bake, set temperature to 380ºF (193ºC), and set time to 12 minutes.
6. When cooking is complete, the fish should flake when pressed lightly with a fork. Remove from the oven and serve warm.

406.Seafood Pizza

Servings:x
Cooking Time:x
Ingredients:
- One pizza base
- Grated pizza cheese (mozzarella cheese preferably) for topping
- Some pizza topping sauce
- Use cooking oil for brushing and topping purposes
- ingredients for topping:
- 2 onions chopped
- 2 cups mixed seafood
- 2 capsicums chopped
- 2 tomatoes that have been deseeded and chopped
- 1 tbsp. (optional) mushrooms/corns
- 2 tsp. pizza seasoning
- Some cottage cheese that has been cut into small cubes (optional)

Directions:
1. Put the pizza base in a pre-heated Breville smart oven for around 5 minutes. (Pre heated to 340 Fahrenheit). Take out the base. Pour some pizza sauce on top of the base at the center. Using a spoon spread the sauce over the base making sure that you leave some gap around the circumference. Grate some mozzarella cheese and sprinkle it over the sauce layer. Take all the vegetables and the seafood and mix them in a bowl. Add some oil and seasoning.
2. Also add some salt and pepper according to taste. Mix them properly. Put this topping over the layer of cheese on the pizza. Now sprinkle some more grated cheese and pizza seasoning on top of this layer. Pre heat the Breville smart oven at 250 Fahrenheit for around 5 minutes.
3. Open the fry basket and place the pizza inside. Close the basket and keep the fryer at 170 degrees for another 10 minutes. If you feel that it is undercooked you may put it at the same temperature for another 2 minutes or so.

407.Maryland Crab Cakes

Servings: 6
Cooking Time: 10 Minutes
Ingredients:
- Nonstick cooking spray
- 2 eggs
- 1 cup Panko bread crumbs
- 1 stalk celery, chopped
- 3 tbsp. mayonnaise
- 1 tsp Worcestershire sauce
- ¼ cup mozzarella cheese, grated
- 1 tsp Italian seasoning
- 1 tbsp. fresh parsley, chopped
- 1 tsp pepper
- ¾ lb. lump crabmeat, drained

Directions:
1. Place baking pan in position 2 of the oven. Lightly spray the fryer basket with cooking spray.
2. In a large bowl, combine all ingredients except crab meat, mix well.
3. Fold in crab carefully so it retains some chunks. Form mixture into 12 patties.
4. Place patties in a single layer in the fryer basket. Place the basket on the baking pan.
5. Set oven to air fryer on 350°F for 10 minutes. Cook until golden brown, turning over halfway through cooking time. Serve immediately.
- **Nutrition Info:** Calories 172, Total Fat 8g, Saturated Fat 2g, Total Carbs 14g, Net Carbs 13g, Protein 16g, Sugar 1g, Fiber 1g, Sodium 527mg, Potassium 290mg, Phosphorus 201mg

408.Sweet & Spicy Lime Salmon

Servings: 6
Cooking Time: 15 Minutes
Ingredients:
- 1 1/2 lbs salmon fillets
- 3 tbsp brown sugar
- 2 tbsp fresh lime juice
- 1/3 cup olive oil
- 1/2 tsp red pepper flakes
- 2 garlic cloves, minced
- Pepper
- Salt

Directions:
1. Fit the Cuisinart oven with the rack in position
2. Place salmon on a prepared baking sheet and season with pepper and salt.
3. In a small bowl, whisk oil, red pepper flakes, garlic, brown sugar, and lime juice.
4. Pour oil mixture over salmon.
5. Set to bake at 350 F for 20 minutes. After 5 minutes place the baking dish in the preheated oven.
6. Serve and enjoy.
- **Nutrition Info:** Calories 269 Fat 18.3 g Carbohydrates 6.1 g Sugar 4.7 g Protein 22.2 g Cholesterol 50 mg

409.Mediterranean Baked Eggs With Spinach

Servings:2
Cooking Time: 10 Minutes
Ingredients:
- 2 tablespoons olive oil
- 4 eggs, whisked
- 5 ounces (142 g) fresh spinach, chopped
- 1 medium-sized tomato, chopped
- 1 teaspoon fresh lemon juice
- ½ teaspoon ground black pepper
- ½ teaspoon coarse salt
- ½ cup roughly chopped fresh basil leaves, for garnish

Directions:
1. Generously grease the baking pan with olive oil.
2. Stir together the remaining ingredients except the basil leaves in the greased baking pan until well incorporated.
3. Slide the baking pan into Rack Position 1, select Convection Bake, set temperature to 280ºF (137ºC), and set time to 10 minutes.
4. When cooking is complete, the eggs should be completely set and the vegetables should be tender. Remove from the oven and serve garnished with the fresh basil leaves.

410.Sweet And Spicy Broccoli

Servings:4
Cooking Time: 15 To 20 Minutes
Ingredients:
- ½ teaspoon olive oil, plus more for greasing
- 1 pound (454 g) fresh broccoli, cut into florets
- ½ tablespoon minced garlic
- Salt, to taste
- Sauce:
- 1½ tablespoons soy sauce
- 2 teaspoons hot sauce or sriracha
- 1½ teaspoons honey
- 1 teaspoon white vinegar
- Freshly ground black pepper, to taste

Directions:
1. Grease the air fryer basket with olive oil.
2. Add the broccoli florets, ½ teaspoon of olive oil, and garlic to a large bowl and toss well. Season with salt to taste.
3. Put the broccoli in the basket in a single layer.
4. Put the air fryer basket on the baking pan and slide into Rack Position 2, select Air Fry, set temperature to 400ºF (205ºC), and set time to 15 minutes.
5. Stir the broccoli florets three times during cooking.
6. Meanwhile, whisk together all the ingredients for the sauce in a small bowl until well incorporated. If the honey doesn't

incorporate well, microwave the sauce for 10 to 20 seconds until the honey is melted.
7. When cooking is complete, the broccoli should be lightly browned and crispy. Continue cooking for 5 minutes, if desired. Remove from the oven to a serving bowl. Pour over the sauce and toss to combine. Add more salt and pepper, if needed. Serve warm.

411.Hearty Roasted Veggie Salad

Servings:2
Cooking Time: 20 Minutes
Ingredients:
- 1 potato, chopped
- 1 carrot, sliced diagonally
- 1 cup cherry tomatoes
- ½ small beetroot, sliced
- ¼ onion, sliced
- ½ teaspoon turmeric
- ½ teaspoon cumin
- ¼ teaspoon sea salt
- 2 tablespoons olive oil, divided
- A handful of arugula
- A handful of baby spinach
- Juice of 1 lemon
- 3 tablespoons canned chickpeas, for serving
- Parmesan shavings, for serving

Directions:
1. Combine the potato, carrot, cherry tomatoes, beetroot, onion, turmeric, cumin, salt, and 1 tablespoon of olive oil in a large bowl and toss until well coated.
2. Arrange the veggies in the air fryer basket.
3. Put the air fryer basket on the baking pan and slide into Rack Position 2, select Roast, set temperature to 370ºF (188ºC) and set time to 20 minutes.
4. Stir the vegetables halfway through.
5. When cooking is complete, the potatoes should be golden brown.
6. Let the veggies cool for 5 to 10 minutes in the oven.
7. Put the arugula, baby spinach, lemon juice, and remaining 1 tablespoon of olive oil in a salad bowl and stir to combine. Mix in the roasted veggies and toss well.
8. Scatter the chickpeas and Parmesan shavings on top and serve immediately.

412.Chili Veggie Skewers

Servings: 4
Cooking Time: 20 Minutes
Ingredients:
- 2 tbsp cornflour
- 1 cup canned white beans, drained
- ⅓ cup grated carrots
- 2 boiled and mashed potatoes
- ¼ cup chopped fresh mint leaves
- ½ tsp garam masala powder
- ½ cup paneer

- 1 green chili
- 1-inch piece of fresh ginger
- 3 garlic cloves
- Salt to taste

Directions:
1. Preheat Cuisinart on Air Fry function to 390 F. Place the beans, carrots, garlic, ginger, chili, paneer, and mint in a food processor; process until smooth. Transfer to a bowl. Add in the mashed potatoes, cornflour, salt, and garam masala powder and mix until fully incorporated.
2. Divide the mixture into 12 equal pieces. Shape each of the pieces around a skewer. Cook in your Cuisinart for 10 minutes, turning once. Serve.

413.Chinese Spring Rolls

Servings:4
Cooking Time: 15 Minutes
Ingredients:
- ½ head cabbage, grated
- 2 carrots, grated
- 1 tsp fresh ginger, minced
- 1 garlic clove, minced
- 1 tsp sesame oil
- 1 tsp soy sauce
- 1 tsp sesame seeds
- ½ tsp salt
- 1 tsp olive oil
- 1 package spring roll wrappers

Directions:
1. Combine all ingredients in a bowl. Divide the mixture between the roll sheets and roll them up; arrange on a baking tray. Press Start and cook in the Breville for 5 minutes on Bake function at 370 F.

414.Cheesy Spinach Toasties

Servings:x
Cooking Time:x
Ingredients:
- 1 tsp. coarsely crushed green chilies
- 2 tbsp. grated pizza cheese
- 1 cup milk
- 2 toasted bread slices cut into triangles
- 1 tbsp. butter
- 1 tbsp. all-purpose flour
- 1 small onion finely chopped
- 1 2 flakes garlic finely chopped
- Half a bunch of spinach that has been boiled and crushed (does not have to
- be crushed finely)
- 1 tbsp. fresh cream
- Some salt and pepper to taste

Directions:
1. Take a pan and melt some butter in it. Also add some onions and garlic.
2. Now keep roasting them in the butter until the onions are caramelized or attain a golden-brown color.

3. Into this pan add the required amount of all-purpose flour. Continue to roast for 3 minutes or so. Add milk and keep stirring until you bring it to a boil.
4. Add green chilies, cream, spinach and seasoning. Mix the ingredients properly and let it cook until the mixture thickens. Toast some bread. Apply the paste made in the previous step on the bread.
5. Sprinkle some grated cheese on top of the paste.
6. Pre heat the Breville smart oven at 290 Fahrenheit for around 4 minutes. Put the toasts in the Fry basket and let it continue to cook for another 10 minutes at the same temperature.

415.Parmesan Breaded Zucchini Chips

Servings: 5
Cooking Time: 20 Minutes
Ingredients:
- For the zucchini chips:
- 2 medium zucchini
- 2 eggs
- ⅓ cup bread crumbs
- ⅓ cup grated Parmesan cheese
- Salt
- Pepper
- Cooking oil
- For the lemon aioli:
- ½ cup mayonnaise
- ½ tablespoon olive oil
- Juice of ½ lemon
- 1 teaspoon minced garlic
- Salt
- Pepper

Directions:
1. Preparing the Ingredients. To make the zucchini chips:
2. Slice the zucchini into thin chips (about ⅛ inch thick) using a knife or mandoline.
3. In a small bowl, beat the eggs. In another small bowl, combine the bread crumbs, Parmesan cheese, and salt and pepper to taste.
4. Spray the Oven rack/basket with cooking oil.
5. Dip the zucchini slices one at a time in the eggs and then the bread crumb mixture. You can also sprinkle the bread crumbs onto the zucchini slices with a spoon.
6. Place the zucchini chips in the Oven rack/basket, but do not stack. Place the Rack on the middle-shelf of the Cuisinart air fryer oven.
7. Air Frying. Cook in batches. Spray the chips with cooking oil from a distance (otherwise, the breading may fly off). Cook for 10 minutes.
8. Remove the cooked zucchini chips from the air fryer oven, then repeat step 5 with the remaining zucchini.
9. To make the lemon aioli:

10. While the zucchini is cooking, combine the mayonnaise, olive oil, lemon juice, and garlic in a small bowl, adding salt and pepper to taste. Mix well until fully combined.
11. Cool the zucchini and serve alongside the aioli.
- **Nutrition Info:** CALORIES: 192; FAT: 13G; PROTEIN: 6

416.Dill Baby Carrots With Honey

Servings:4
Cooking Time: 20 Minutes
Ingredients:
- 1 lb baby carrots
- 1 tsp dried dill
- 1 tbsp olive oil
- 1 tbsp honey
- Salt and black pepper to taste

Directions:
1. Preheat Breville Oven to 360 F on AirFry function. In a bowl, mix oil, carrots, and honey; stir to coat. Season with dill, pepper, and salt. Place the carrots in the basket and cook for 15 minutes.

417.Cabbage Fritters(2)

Servings:x
Cooking Time:x
Ingredients:
- 1 ½ tsp. salt
- 3 tsp. lemon juice
- 2 tsp. garam masala
- 3 eggs
- 2 ½ tbsp. white sesame seeds
- 10 leaves cabbage
- 3 onions chopped
- 5 green chilies-roughly chopped
- 1 ½ tbsp. ginger paste
- 1 ½ tsp. garlic paste

Directions:
1. Grind the ingredients except for the egg and form a smooth paste. Coat the leaves in the paste. Now, beat the eggs and add a little salt to it.
2. Dip the coated leaves in the egg mixture and then transfer to the sesame seeds and coat the florets well. Place the vegetables on a stick.
3. Pre heat the Breville smart oven at 160 degrees Fahrenheit for around 5 minutes. Place the sticks in the basket and let them cook for another 25 minutes at the same temperature. Turn the sticks over in between the cooking process to get a uniform cook.

418.Cabbage Steaks With Fennel Seeds

Servings:3
Cooking Time: 25 Minutes
Ingredients:
- 1 cabbage head

- 1 tbsp garlic paste
- Salt and black pepper to taste
- 2 tbsp olive oil
- 2 tsp fennel seeds

Directions:
1. Preheat Breville on AirFry function to 350 F. Slice the cabbage into 1 ½-inch slice. In a small bowl, combine all the other ingredients; brush cabbage with the mixture. Arrange the steaks on a greased baking dish and press Start. Cook for 15 minutes.

419.Roasted Asparagus With Eggs And Tomatoes

Servings:4
Cooking Time: 12 Minutes
Ingredients:
- 2 pounds (907 g) asparagus, trimmed
- 3 tablespoons extra-virgin olive oil, divided
- 1 teaspoon kosher salt, divided
- 1 pint cherry tomatoes
- 4 large eggs
- ¼ teaspoon freshly ground black pepper

Directions:
1. Put the asparagus in the baking pan and drizzle with 2 tablespoons of olive oil, tossing to coat. Season with ½ teaspoon of kosher salt.
2. Slide the baking pan into Rack Position 2, select Roast, set temperature to 375ºF (190ºC), and set time to 12 minutes.
3. Meanwhile, toss the cherry tomatoes with the remaining 1 tablespoon of olive oil in a medium bowl until well coated.
4. After 6 minutes, remove the pan and toss the asparagus. Evenly spread the asparagus in the middle of the pan. Add the tomatoes around the perimeter of the pan. Return the pan to the oven and continue cooking.
5. After 2 minutes, remove from the oven.
6. Carefully crack the eggs, one at a time, over the asparagus, spacing them out. Season with the remaining ½ teaspoon of kosher salt and the pepper. Return the pan to the oven and continue cooking. Cook for an additional 3 to 7 minutes, or until the eggs are cooked to your desired doneness.
7. When done, divide the asparagus and eggs among four plates. Top each plate evenly with the tomatoes and serve.

420.Air Fried Carrots, Yellow Squash & Zucchini

Servings: 4
Cooking Time: 35 Minutes
Ingredients:
- 1 tbsp. chopped tarragon leaves
- ½ tsp. white pepper
- 1 tsp. salt
- 1 pound yellow squash
- 1 pound zucchini

- 6 tsp. olive oil
- ½ pound carrots

Directions:
1. Preparing the Ingredients. Stem and root the end of squash and zucchini and cut in ¾-inch half-moons. Peel and cut carrots into 1-inch cubes
2. Combine carrot cubes with 2 teaspoons of olive oil, tossing to combine.
3. Air Frying. Pour into the Oven rack/basket. Place the Rack on the middle-shelf of the Cuisinart air fryer oven. Set temperature to 400°F, and set time to 5 minutes.
4. As carrots cook, drizzle remaining olive oil over squash and zucchini pieces, then season with pepper and salt. Toss well to coat.
5. Add squash and zucchini when the timer for carrots goes off. Cook 30 minutes, making sure to toss 2-3 times during the cooking process.
6. Once done, take out veggies and toss with tarragon. Serve up warm!
- **Nutrition Info:** CALORIES: 122; FAT: 9G; PROTEIN: 6G; SUGAR:0G

421.Teriyaki Cauliflower

Servings:4
Cooking Time: 14 Minutes
Ingredients:
- ½ cup soy sauce
- $^1/_3$ cup water
- 1 tablespoon brown sugar
- 1 teaspoon sesame oil
- 1 teaspoon cornstarch
- 2 cloves garlic, chopped
- ½ teaspoon chili powder
- 1 big cauliflower head, cut into florets

Directions:
1. Make the teriyaki sauce: In a small bowl, whisk together the soy sauce, water, brown sugar, sesame oil, cornstarch, garlic, and chili powder until well combined.
2. Place the cauliflower florets in a large bowl and drizzle the top with the prepared teriyaki sauce and toss to coat well.
3. Put the cauliflower florets in the air fryer basket.
4. Put the air fryer basket on the baking pan and slide into Rack Position 2, select Air Fry, set temperature to 340ºF (171ºC) and set time to 14 minutes.
5. Stir the cauliflower halfway through.
6. When cooking is complete, the cauliflower should be crisp-tender.
7. Let the cauliflower cool for 5 minutes before serving.

422.Roasted Vegetables With Basil

Servings:2
Cooking Time: 20 Minutes
Ingredients:
- 1 small eggplant, halved and sliced

- 1 yellow bell pepper, cut into thick strips
- 1 red bell pepper, cut into thick strips
- 2 garlic cloves, quartered
- 1 red onion, sliced
- 1 tablespoon extra-virgin olive oil
- Salt and freshly ground black pepper, to taste
- ½ cup chopped fresh basil, for garnish
- Cooking spray

Directions:
1. Grease the baking pan with cooking spray.
2. Place the eggplant, bell peppers, garlic, and red onion in the greased baking pan. Drizzle with the olive oil and toss to coat well. Spritz any uncoated surfaces with cooking spray.
3. Slide the baking pan into Rack Position 1, select Convection Bake, set temperature to 350ºF (180ºC), and set time to 20 minutes.
4. Flip the vegetables halfway through the cooking time.
5. When done, remove from the oven and sprinkle with salt and pepper.
6. Sprinkle the basil on top for garnish and serve.

423.Burger Cutlet

Servings:x
Cooking Time:x
Ingredients:
- 1 tbsp. fresh coriander leaves. Chop them finely
- ¼ tsp. red chili powder
- ½ cup of boiled peas
- ¼ tsp. cumin powder
- 1 large potato boiled and mashed
- ½ cup breadcrumbs
- A pinch of salt to taste
- ¼ tsp. ginger finely chopped
- 1 green chili finely chopped
- 1 tsp. lemon juice
- ¼ tsp. dried mango powder

Directions:
1. Mix the ingredients together and ensure that the flavors are right. You will now make round cutlets with the mixture and roll them out well.
2. Pre heat the Breville smart oven at 250 Fahrenheit for 5 minutes. Open the basket of the Fryer and arrange the cutlets in the basket. Close it carefully. Keep the fryer at 150 degrees for around 10 or 12 minutes. In between the cooking process, turn the cutlets over to get a uniform cook. Serve hot with mint sauce.

424.Masala Vegetable Skewers

Servings:4
Cooking Time: 20 Minutes
Ingredients:
- 2 tbsp cornflour
- 1 cup canned white beans, drained

- ⅓ cup carrots, grated
- 2 potatoes, boiled and mashed
- ¼ cup fresh mint leaves, chopped
- ½ tsp garam masala powder
- ½ cup paneer
- 1 green chili
- 1-inch piece of fresh ginger
- 3 garlic cloves
- Salt to taste

Directions:
1. Preheat Breville on AirFry function to 390 F. Place the beans, carrots, garlic, ginger, chili, paneer, and mint in a food processor and blend until smooth. Transfer to a bowl.
2. Add in the mashed potatoes, cornflour, salt, and garam masala powder and mix until fully incorporated. Divide the mixture into 12 equal pieces. Thread each of the pieces onto a skewer. Press Start and cook skewers for 10 minutes. Serve.

425.Cheese And Mushroom Spicy Lemon Kebab

Servings:x
Cooking Time:x
Ingredients:
- 1-2 tbsp. all-purpose flour for coating purposes
- 1-2 tbsp. mint
- 1 cup molten cheese
- 1 onion that has been finely chopped
- ½ cup milk
- 2 cups sliced mushrooms
- 1-2 green chilies chopped finely
- ¼ tsp. red chili powder
- A pinch of salt to taste
- ½ tsp. dried mango powder
- ¼ tsp. black salt

Directions:
1. Take the mushroom slices and add the grated ginger and the cut green chilies. Grind this mixture until it becomes a thick paste.
2. Keep adding water as and when required. Now add the onions, mint, the breadcrumbs and all the various masalas required. Mix this well until you get a soft dough. Now take small balls of this mixture (about the size of a lemon) and mold them into the shape of flat and round kebabs. Here is where the milk comes into play.
3. Pour a very small amount of milk onto each kebab to wet it. Now roll the kebab in the dry breadcrumbs. Pre heat the Breville smart oven for 5 minutes at 300 Fahrenheit. Take out the basket. Arrange the kebabs in the basket leaving gaps between them so that no two kebabs are touching each other. Keep the fryer at 340 Fahrenheit for around half an hour.
4. Half way through the cooking process, turn the kebabs over so that they can be cooked

properly. Recommended sides for this dish are mint sauce, tomato ketchup or yoghurt sauce.

426.Spicy Sweet Potato Friespotato Fries

Servings: 4
Cooking Time: 37 Minutes
Ingredients:
- 2 tbsp. sweet potato fry seasoning mix
- 2 tbsp. olive oil
- 2 sweet potatoes
- Seasoning Mix:
- 2 tbsp. salt
- 1 tbsp. cayenne pepper
- 1 tbsp. dried oregano
- 1 tbsp. fennel
- 2 tbsp. coriander

Directions:
1. Preparing the Ingredients. Slice both ends off sweet potatoes and peel. Slice lengthwise in half and again crosswise to make four pieces from each potato.
2. Slice each potato piece into 2-3 slices, then slice into fries.
3. Grind together all of seasoning mix ingredients and mix in the salt.
4. Ensure the Cuisinart air fryer oven is preheated to 350 degrees.
5. Toss potato pieces in olive oil, sprinkling with seasoning mix and tossing well to coat thoroughly.
6. Air Frying. Add fries to air fryer rack/basket. Set temperature to 350°F, and set time to 27 minutes. Select START/STOP to begin.
7. Take out the basket and turn fries. Turn off air fryer oven and let cook 10-12 minutes till fries are golden.
- **Nutrition Info:** CALORIES: 89; FAT: 14G; PROTEIN: 8Gs; SUGAR:3

427.Stuffed Mushrooms

Servings: 12
Cooking Time: 8 Minutes
Ingredients:
- 2 Rashers Bacon, Diced
- ½ Onion, Diced
- ½ Bell Pepper, Diced
- 1 Small Carrot, Diced
- 24 Medium Size Mushrooms (Separate the caps & stalks)
- 1 cup Shredded Cheddar Plus Extra for the Top
- ½ cup Sour Cream

Directions:
1. Preparing the Ingredients. Chop the mushrooms stalks finely and fry them up with the bacon, onion, pepper and carrot at 350 ° for 8 minutes.
2. When the veggies are fairly tender, stir in the sour cream & the cheese. Keep on the heat until the cheese has melted and everything is mixed nicely.

3. Now grab the mushroom caps and heap a plop of filling on each one.
4. Place in the fryer basket and top with a little extra cheese.

428.Garlicky Veggie Bake

Servings: 3
Cooking Time: 25 Minutes
Ingredients:
- 3 turnips, sliced
- 1 large red onion, cut into rings
- 1 large zucchini, sliced
- Salt and black pepper to taste
- 2 cloves garlic, crushed
- 1 bay leaf, cut in 6 pieces
- 1 tbsp olive oil

Directions:
1. Place the turnips, onion, and zucchini in a bowl. Toss with olive oil, salt, and pepper.
2. Preheat Cuisinart on Air Fry function to 380 F. Place the veggies into a baking pan. Slip the bay leaves in the different parts of the slices and tuck the garlic cloves in between the slices. Cook for 15 minutes. Serve warm with as a side to a meat dish or salad.

429.Chili Sweet Potato Fries

Servings:4
Cooking Time: 30 Minutes
Ingredients:
- ½ tsp salt
- ½ tsp garlic powder
- ½ tsp chili powder
- ¼ tsp ground cumin
- 3 tbsp olive oil
- 3 sweet potatoes, cut into thick strips

Directions:
1. In a bowl, mix salt, garlic powder, chili powder, and cumin, and whisk in oil. Coat in the potato strips and arrange them on the basket, without overcrowding. Press Start and cook for 20-25 minutes at 380 F on AirFry function or until crispy. Serve hot.

430.Mushroom French Cuisine Galette

Servings:x
Cooking Time:x
Ingredients:
- 2 or 3 green chilies finely chopped
- 1 ½ tbsp. lemon juice
- Salt and pepper to taste
- 2 tbsp. garam masala
- 2 cups sliced mushrooms
- 1 ½ cup coarsely crushed peanuts
- 3 tsp. ginger finely chopped
- 1-2 tbsp. fresh coriander leaves

Directions:
1. Mix the ingredients in a clean bowl.
2. Mold this mixture into round and flat French Cuisine Galettes.

3. Wet the French Cuisine Galettes slightly with water. Coat each French Cuisine Galette with the crushed peanuts.
4. Pre heat the Breville smart oven at 160 degrees Fahrenheit for 5 minutes. Place the French Cuisine Galettes in the fry basket and let them cook for another 25 minutes at the same temperature. Keep rolling them over to get a uniform cook. Serve either with mint sauce or ketchup.

431.Caramelized Eggplant With Yogurt Sauce

Servings:2
Cooking Time: 15 Minutes
Ingredients:
- 1 medium eggplant, quartered and cut crosswise into ½-inch-thick slices
- 2 tablespoons vegetable oil
- Kosher salt and freshly ground black pepper, to taste
- ½ cup plain yogurt (not Greek)
- 2 tablespoons harissa paste
- 1 garlic clove, grated
- 2 teaspoons honey

Directions:
1. Toss the eggplant slices with the vegetable oil, salt, and pepper in a large bowl until well coated.
2. Lay the eggplant slices in the air fryer basket.
3. Put the air fryer basket on the baking pan and slide into Rack Position 2, select Air Fry, set temperature to 400ºF (205ºC), and set time to 15 minutes.
4. Stir the slices two to three times during cooking.
5. Meanwhile, make the yogurt sauce by whisking together the yogurt, harissa paste, and garlic in a small bowl.
6. When cooking is complete, the eggplant slices should be golden brown. Spread the yogurt sauce on a platter, and pile the eggplant slices over the top. Serve drizzled with the honey.

432.Carrots & Shallots With Yogurt

Servings:4
Cooking Time: 25 Minutes
Ingredients:
- 2 tsp olive oil
- 2 shallots, chopped
- 3 carrots, sliced
- Salt to taste
- ¼ cup yogurt
- 2 garlic cloves, minced
- 3 tbsp parsley, chopped

Directions:
1. In a bowl, mix sliced carrots, salt, garlic, shallots, parsley, and yogurt. Sprinkle with oil. Place the veggies in the basket and press Start. Cook for 15 minutes on AirFry

function at 370 F. Serve with basil and garlic mayo.

433.Cumin And Cayenne Spicy Sweet Potatoes

Servings: 4
Cooking Time: 30 Minutes
Ingredients:
- ½ tsp garlic powder
- ½ tsp cayenne pepper
- ¼ tsp cumin
- 3 tbsp olive oil
- 3 sweet potatoes, cut into ½-inch thick wedges
- 2 tbsp chopped fresh parsley
- Sea salt to taste

Directions:
1. In a bowl, mix olive oil, salt, garlic powder, chili powder, and cumin. Add in potatoes and toss to coat. Arrange them on the basket and fit in the baking tray.
2. Cook in your Cuisinart for 20 minutes at 380 F on Air Fry function. Toss every 5 minutes. Sprinkle with parsley and serve.

434.Cheddar & Tempeh Stuffed Mushrooms

Servings: 3 To 4
Cooking Time: 20 Minutes
Ingredients:
- 14 mushroom caps
- 1 clove garlic, minced
- Salt and pepper to taste
- 4 slices tempeh, chopped
- ¼ cup grated Cheddar cheese
- 1 tbsp olive oil
- 1 tbsp chopped parsley

Directions:
1. Preheat on Air Fry function to 390 F. In a bowl, add olive oil, tempeh, cheddar cheese, parsley, salt, pepper, and garlic. Mix well with a spoon. Fill the mushroom caps with the tempeh mixture.
2. Place the stuffed mushrooms in the basket and fit in the baking tray; cook for 8 minutes. Once golden and crispy, plate them and serve with green salad.

435.Cottage Cheese French Cuisine Galette

Servings:x
Cooking Time:x
Ingredients:
- 1-2 tbsp. fresh coriander leaves
- 2 or 3 green chilies finely chopped
- 1 ½ tbsp. lemon juice
- Salt and pepper to taste
- 2 tbsp. garam masala
- 2 cups grated cottage cheese
- 1 ½ cup coarsely crushed peanuts
- 3 tsp. ginger finely chopped

Directions:
1. Mix the ingredients in a clean bowl.

2. Mold this mixture into round and flat French Cuisine Galettes.
3. Wet the French Cuisine Galettes slightly with water. Coat each French Cuisine Galette with the crushed peanuts.
4. Pre heat the Breville smart oven at 160 degrees Fahrenheit for 5 minutes. Place the French Cuisine Galettes in the fry basket and let them cook for another 25 minutes at the same temperature. Keep rolling them over to get a uniform cook. Serve either with mint sauce or ketchup.

436.Cheesy Asparagus And Potato Platter

Servings:5
Cooking Time: 26 Minutes
Ingredients:
- 4 medium potatoes, cut into wedges
- Cooking spray
- 1 bunch asparagus, trimmed
- 2 tablespoons olive oil
- Salt and pepper, to taste
- Cheese Sauce:
- ¼ cup crumbled cottage cheese
- ¼ cup buttermilk
- 1 tablespoon whole-grain mustard
- Salt and black pepper, to taste

Directions:
1. Spritz the air fryer basket with cooking spray.
2. Put the potatoes in the air fryer basket.
3. Put the air fryer basket on the baking pan and slide into Rack Position 2, select Roast, set temperature to 400ºF (205ºC) and set time to 20 minutes.
4. Stir the potatoes halfway through.
5. When cooking is complete, the potatoes should be golden brown.
6. Remove the potatoes from the oven to a platter. Cover the potatoes with foil to keep warm. Set aside.
7. Place the asparagus in the air fryer basket and drizzle with the olive oil. Sprinkle with salt and pepper.
8. Put the air fryer basket on the baking pan and slide into Rack Position 2, select Roast, set temperature to 400ºF (205ºC) and set time to 6 minutes. Stir the asparagus halfway through.
9. When cooking is complete, the asparagus should be crispy.
10. Meanwhile, make the cheese sauce by stirring together the cottage cheese, buttermilk, and mustard in a small bowl. Season as needed with salt and pepper.
11. Transfer the asparagus to the platter of potatoes and drizzle with the cheese sauce. Serve immediately.

437.Tofu & Pea Cauli Rice

Servings:4
Cooking Time: 30 Minutes
Ingredients:

- Tofu:
- ½ block tofu
- ½ cup onions, chopped
- 2 tbsp soy sauce
- 1 tsp turmeric
- 1 cup carrots, chopped
- Cauliflower:
- 3 cups cauliflower rice
- 2 tbsp soy sauce
- ½ cup broccoli, chopped
- 2 garlic cloves, minced
- 1 ½ tsp toasted sesame oil
- 1 tbsp fresh ginger, minced
- ½ cup frozen peas
- 1 tbsp rice vinegar

Directions:
1. Preheat Breville on AirFry function to 370 F. Crumble the tofu and combine it with all tofu ingredients. Place in a baking dish and cook for 10 minutes.
2. Meanwhile, place all cauliflower ingredients in a large bowl; mix to combine. Add the cauliflower mixture to the tofu and stir to combine. Press Start and cook for 12 minutes. Serve.

438.Veg Momo's Recipe

Servings:x
Cooking Time:x
Ingredients:
- 2 tsp. ginger-garlic paste
- 2 tsp. soya sauce
- 2 tsp. vinegar
- 1 ½ cup all-purpose flour
- ½ tsp. salt or to taste
- 5 tbsp. water
- 2 cup carrots grated
- 2 cup cabbage grated
- 2 tbsp. oil

Directions:
1. Squeeze the dough and cover it with plastic wrap and set aside. Next, cook the ingredients for the filling and try to ensure that the vegetables are covered well with the sauce.
2. Roll the dough and cut it into a square. Place the filling in the center. Now, wrap the dough to cover the filling and pinch the edges together.
3. Pre heat the Breville smart oven at 200° F for 5 minutes. Place the gnocchi's in the fry basket and close it. Let them cook at the same temperature for another 20 minutes. Recommended sides are chili sauce or ketchup.

439.Stuffed Portobello Mushrooms With Vegetables

Servings:4
Cooking Time: 8 Minutes
Ingredients:
- 4 portobello mushrooms, stem removed

- 1 tablespoon olive oil
- 1 tomato, diced
- ½ green bell pepper, diced
- ½ small red onion, diced
- ½ teaspoon garlic powder
- Salt and black pepper, to taste
- ½ cup grated Mozzarella cheese

Directions:
1. Using a spoon to scoop out the gills of the mushrooms and discard them. Brush the mushrooms with the olive oil.
2. In a mixing bowl, stir together the remaining ingredients except the Mozzarella cheese. Using a spoon to stuff each mushroom with the filling and scatter the Mozzarella cheese on top.
3. Arrange the mushrooms in the air fryer basket.
4. Put the air fryer basket on the baking pan and slide into Rack Position 2, select Roast, set temperature to 330ºF (166ºC) and set time to 8 minutes.
5. When cooking is complete, the cheese should be melted.
6. Serve warm.

440.Garlicky Sesame Carrots

Servings:4 To 6
Cooking Time: 16 Minutes
Ingredients:
- 1 pound (454 g) baby carrots
- 1 tablespoon sesame oil
- ½ teaspoon dried dill
- Pinch salt
- Freshly ground black pepper, to taste
- 6 cloves garlic, peeled
- 3 tablespoons sesame seeds

Directions:
1. In a medium bowl, drizzle the baby carrots with the sesame oil. Sprinkle with the dill, salt, and pepper and toss to coat well.
2. Place the baby carrots in the air fryer basket.
3. Put the air fryer basket on the baking pan and slide into Rack Position 2, select Roast, set temperature to 380ºF (193ºC), and set time to 16 minutes.
4. After 8 minutes, remove from the oven and stir in the garlic. Return the pan to the oven and continue roasting for 8 minutes more.
5. When cooking is complete, the carrots should be lightly browned. Remove from the oven and serve sprinkled with the sesame seeds.

441.Pineapple Spicy Lemon Kebab

Servings:x
Cooking Time:x
Ingredients:
- 4 tbsp. chopped coriander
- 3 tbsp. cream
- 3 tbsp. chopped capsicum
- 3 eggs

- 2 ½ tbsp. white sesame seeds
- 2 cups cubed pineapples
- 3 onions chopped
- 5 green chilies-roughly chopped
- 1 ½ tbsp. ginger paste
- 1 ½ tsp. garlic paste
- 1 ½ tsp. salt
- 3 tsp. lemon juice
- 2 tsp. garam masala

Directions:
1. Grind the ingredients except for the egg and form a smooth paste. Coat the pineapples in the paste. Now, beat the eggs and add a little salt to it.
2. Dip the coated vegetables in the egg mixture and then transfer to the sesame seeds and coat the pineapples well. Place the vegetables on a stick.
3. Pre heat the Breville smart oven at 160 degrees Fahrenheit for around 5 minutes. Place the sticks in the basket and let them cook for another 25 minutes at the same temperature. Turn the sticks over in between the cooking process to get a uniform cook.

442.Cauliflower Spicy Lemon Kebab

Servings:x
Cooking Time:x
Ingredients:
- 3 tsp. lemon juice
- 2 tsp. garam masala
- 3 eggs
- 2 ½ tbsp. white sesame seeds
- 2 cups cauliflower florets
- 3 onions chopped
- 5 green chilies-roughly chopped
- 1 ½ tbsp. ginger paste
- 1 ½ tsp. garlic paste
- 1 ½ tsp. salt

Directions:
1. Grind the ingredients except for the egg and form a smooth paste. Coat the florets in the paste. Now, beat the eggs and add a little salt to it.
2. Dip the coated florets in the egg mixture and then transfer to the sesame seeds and coat the florets well. Place the vegetables on a stick.
3. Pre heat the Breville smart oven at 160 degrees Fahrenheit for around 5 minutes. Place the sticks in the basket and let them cook for another 25 minutes at the same temperature. Turn the sticks over in between the cooking process to get a uniform cook.

443.Honey Chili Potatoes

Servings:x
Cooking Time:x
Ingredients:

- 1 capsicum, cut into thin and long pieces (lengthwise)
- 2 tbsp. olive oil
- 2 onions. Cut them into halves.
- 1 ½ tbsp. sweet chili sauce
- 1 ½ tsp. ginger garlic paste
- ½ tbsp. red chili sauce.
- 2 tbsp. tomato ketchup
- 3 big potatoes (Cut into strips or cubes)
- 2 ½ tsp. ginger-garlic paste
- ¼ tsp. salt
- 1 tsp. red chili sauce
- ¼ tsp. red chili powder/black pepper
- A few drops of edible orange food coloring
- 2 tsp. soya sauce
- 2 tsp. vinegar
- A pinch of black pepper powder
- 1-2 tsp. red chili flakes

Directions:
1. Create the mix for the potato Oregano Fingers and coat the chicken well with it.
2. Pre heat the Breville smart oven at 250 Fahrenheit for 5 minutes or so. Open the basket of the Fryer. Place the Oregano Fingers inside the basket. Now let the fryer stay at 290 Fahrenheit for another 20 minutes. Keep tossing the Oregano Fingers periodically through the cook to get a uniform cook.
3. Add the ingredients to the sauce and cook it with the vegetables till it thickens. Add the Oregano Fingers to the sauce and cook till the flavors have blended.

444.Parmesan Coated Green Beans

Servings:4
Cooking Time: 20 Minutes
Ingredients:
- 1 cup panko breadcrumbs
- 2 whole eggs, beaten
- ½ cup Parmesan cheese, grated
- ½ cup flour
- 1 tsp cayenne pepper powder
- 1 ½ pounds green beans
- Salt to taste

Directions:
1. Preheat Breville on AirFry function to 380 F. In a bowl, mix breadcrumbs, Parmesan cheese, cayenne pepper powder, salt, and pepper. Flour the green beans and dip them in eggs. Dredge beans in the Parmesan-panko mix. Place in the cooking basket and cook for 15 minutes Serve.

445.Palak French Cuisine Galette

Servings:x
Cooking Time:x
Ingredients:
- 1-2 tbsp. fresh coriander leaves
- 2 or 3 green chilies finely chopped
- 1 ½ tbsp. lemon juice
- Salt and pepper to taste

- 2 tbsp. garam masala
- 2 cups Palak leaves
- 1 ½ cup coarsely crushed peanuts
- 3 tsp. ginger finely chopped

Directions:
1. Mix the ingredients in a clean bowl.
2. Mold this mixture into round and flat French Cuisine Galettes.
3. Wet the French Cuisine Galettes slightly with water. Coat each French Cuisine Galette with the crushed peanuts.
4. Pre heat the Breville smart oven at 160 degrees Fahrenheit for 5 minutes. Place the French Cuisine Galettes in the fry basket and let them cook for another 25 minutes at the same temperature. Keep rolling them over to get a uniform cook. Serve either with mint sauce or ketchup.

446.Stuffed Portobellos With Peppers And Cheese

Servings:4
Cooking Time: 15 Minutes
Ingredients:
- 4 tablespoons sherry vinegar or white wine vinegar
- 6 garlic cloves, minced, divided
- 1 tablespoon fresh thyme leaves
- 1 teaspoon Dijon mustard
- 1 teaspoon kosher salt, divided
- ¼ cup plus 3¼ teaspoons extra-virgin olive oil, divided
- 8 portobello mushroom caps, each about 3 inches across, patted dry
- 1 small red or yellow bell pepper, thinly sliced
- 1 small green bell pepper, thinly sliced
- 1 small onion, thinly sliced
- ¼ teaspoon red pepper flakes
- Freshly ground black pepper, to taste
- 4 ounces (113 g) shredded Fontina cheese

Directions:
1. Stir together the vinegar, 4 minced garlic cloves, thyme, mustard, and ½ teaspoon of kosher salt in a small bowl. Slowly pour in ¼ cup of olive oil, whisking constantly, or until an emulsion is formed. Reserve 2 tablespoons of the marinade and set aside.
2. Put the mushrooms in a resealable plastic bag and pour in the marinade. Seal and shake the bag, coating the mushrooms in the marinade. Transfer the mushrooms to the baking pan, gill-side down.
3. Put the remaining 2 minced garlic cloves, bell peppers, onion, red pepper flakes, remaining ½ teaspoon of salt, and black pepper in a medium bowl. Drizzle with the remaining 3¼ teaspoons of olive oil and toss well. Transfer the bell pepper mixture to the pan.
4. Slide the baking pan into Rack Position 2, select Roast, set temperature to 375ºF (190ºC), and set time to 12 minutes.

5. After 7 minutes, remove the pan and stir the peppers and flip the mushrooms. Return the pan to the oven and continue cooking for 5 minutes.
6. Remove from the oven and place the pepper mixture onto a cutting board and coarsely chop.
7. Brush both sides of the mushrooms with the reserved 2 tablespoons marinade. Stuff the caps evenly with the pepper mixture. Scatter the cheese on top.
8. Select Convection Broil, set temperature to High, and set time to 3 minutes.
9. When done, the mushrooms should be tender and the cheese should be melted.
10. Serve warm.

447.Jalapeño & Tomato Gratin

Servings: 4
Cooking Time: 35 Minutes
Ingredients:
- 1 (16 oz) can jalapeño peppers
- 1 cup cheddar cheese, shredded
- 1 cup Monterey Jack cheese, shredded
- 2 tbsp all-purpose flour
- 2 large eggs, beaten
- ½ cup milk
- 1 can tomato sauce

Directions:
1. Preheat Cuisinart on Air Fry function to 380 F. Arrange the jalapeño peppers on the greased Air Fryer baking pan and top with half of the cheese.
2. In a medium bowl, combine the eggs, milk, and flour and pour the mixture over the chilies. Cook in your Cuisinart for 20 minutes. Take out the chilies and pour the tomato sauce over them. Return and cook for 15 more minutes. Sprinkle with the remaining cheese and serve.

448.Garlicky Fennel Cabbage Steaks

Servings: 3
Cooking Time: 25 Minutes
Ingredients:
- 1 cabbage head
- 1 tbsp garlic paste
- 1 tsp salt
- 2 tbsp olive oil
- ½ tsp black pepper
- 2 tsp fennel seeds

Directions:
1. Preheat Cuisinart on Air Fry function to 350 F. Slice the cabbage into 1 ½-inch slices. In a small bowl, combine all the other ingredients; brush cabbage with the mixture. Arrange the steaks on a greased baking dish and cook for 15 minutes, flipping once. Serve.

449.Feta & Scallion Triangles

Servings:4
Cooking Time: 20 Minutes

Ingredients:
- 4 oz feta cheese, crumbled
- 2 sheets filo pastry
- 1 egg yolk, beaten
- 2 tbsp fresh parsley, finely chopped
- 1 scallion, finely chopped
- 2 tbsp olive oil
- Salt and black pepper to taste

Directions:
1. In a bowl, mix the yolk with the cheese, parsley, and scallion. Season with salt and black pepper. Cut each filo sheet in 3 strips. Put a teaspoon of the feta mixture on the bottom. Roll the strip in a spinning spiral way until the filling of the inside mixture is completely wrapped in a triangle.
2. Preheat Breville on Bake function to 360 F. Brush the surface of filo with olive oil. Place up to 5 triangles in the oven and press Start. Cook for 5 minutes. Lower the temperature to 330 F, cook for 3 more minutes or until golden brown.

450.Radish Flat Cakes

Servings:x
Cooking Time:x
Ingredients:
- 1-2 tbsp. fresh coriander leaves
- 2 or 3 green chilies finely chopped
- 1 ½ tbsp. lemon juice
- Salt and pepper to taste
- 2 tbsp. garam masala
- 2 cups sliced radish
- 3 tsp. ginger finely chopped

Directions:
1. Mix the ingredients in a clean bowl and add water to it. Make sure that the paste is not too watery but is enough to apply on the radish.
2. Pre heat the Breville smart oven at 160 degrees Fahrenheit for 5 minutes. Place the French Cuisine Galettes in the fry basket and let them cook for another 25 minutes at the same temperature. Keep rolling them over to get a uniform cook. Serve either with mint sauce or ketchup.

451.Masala French Cuisine Galette

Servings:x
Cooking Time:x
Ingredients:
- 1 ½ tbsp. lemon juice
- Salt and pepper to taste
- 1-2 tbsp. fresh coriander leaves
- 2 or 3 green chilies finely chopped
- 2 tbsp. garam masala
- 2 medium potatoes boiled and mashed
- 1 ½ cup coarsely crushed peanuts
- 3 tsp. ginger finely chopped

Directions:
1. Mix the ingredients in a clean bowl.

2. Mold this mixture into round and flat French Cuisine Galettes.
3. Wet the French Cuisine Galettes slightly with water. Coat each French Cuisine Galette with the crushed peanuts.
4. Pre heat the Breville smart oven at 160 degrees Fahrenheit for 5 minutes. Place the French Cuisine Galettes in the fry basket and let them cook for another 25 minutes at the same temperature. Keep rolling them over to get a uniform cook. Serve either with mint sauce or ketchup.

452.Cheese-walnut Stuffed Mushrooms

Servings:4
Cooking Time: 10 Minutes
Ingredients:
- 4 large portobello mushrooms
- 1 tablespoon canola oil
- ½ cup shredded Mozzarella cheese
- $^1/_3$ cup minced walnuts
- 2 tablespoons chopped fresh parsley
- Cooking spray

Directions:
1. Spritz the air fryer basket with cooking spray.
2. On a clean work surface, remove the mushroom stems. Scoop out the gills with a spoon and discard. Coat the mushrooms with canola oil. Top each mushroom evenly with the shredded Mozzarella cheese, followed by the minced walnuts.
3. Arrange the mushrooms in the basket.
4. Put the air fryer basket on the baking pan and slide into Rack Position 2, select Roast, set temperature to 350ºF (180ºC) and set time to 10 minutes.
5. When cooking is complete, the mushroom should be golden brown.
6. Transfer the mushrooms to a plate and sprinkle the parsley on top for garnish before serving.

453.Vegetable Dumpling

Servings:x
Cooking Time:x
Ingredients:
- 2 tbsp. oil
- 2 tsp. ginger-garlic paste
- 2 tsp. soya sauce
- 2 tsp. vinegar
- 1 ½ cup all-purpose flour
- ½ tsp. salt or to taste
- 5 tbsp. water
- 2 cup carrots grated
- 2 cup cabbage grated

Directions:
1. Squeeze the dough and cover it with plastic wrap and set aside. Next, cook the ingredients for the filling and try to ensure that the vegetables are covered well with the sauce.

2. Roll the dough and place the filling in the center. Now, wrap the dough to cover the filling and pinch the edges together. Pre heat the Breville smart oven at 200° F for 5 minutes. Place the dumplings in the fry basket and close it. Let them cook at the same temperature for another 20 minutes. Recommended sides are chili sauce or ketchup.

454.White Lentil French Cuisine Galette

Servings:x
Cooking Time:x
Ingredients:
- 1 ½ tbsp. lemon juice
- Salt and pepper to taste
- 2 cup white lentil soaked
- 3 tsp. ginger finely chopped
- 1-2 tbsp. fresh coriander leaves
- 2 or 3 green chilies finely chopped

Directions:
1. Wash the soaked lentils and mix it with the rest of the ingredients in a clean bowl.
2. Mold this mixture into round and flat French Cuisine Galettes.
3. Wet the French Cuisine Galettes slightly with water.
4. Pre heat the Breville smart oven at 160 degrees Fahrenheit for 5 minutes. Place the French Cuisine Galettes in the fry basket and let them cook for another 25 minutes at the same temperature. Keep rolling them over to get a uniform cook. Serve either with mint sauce or ketchup.

455.Roasted Bell Peppers With Garlic

Servings:4
Cooking Time: 22 Minutes
Ingredients:
- 1 green bell pepper, sliced into 1-inch strips
- 1 red bell pepper, sliced into 1-inch strips
- 1 orange bell pepper, sliced into 1-inch strips
- 1 yellow bell pepper, sliced into 1-inch strips
- 2 tablespoons olive oil, divided
- ½ teaspoon dried marjoram
- Pinch salt
- Freshly ground black pepper, to taste
- 1 head garlic

Directions:
1. Toss the bell peppers with 1 tablespoon of olive oil in a large bowl until well coated. Season with the marjoram, salt, and pepper. Toss again and set aside.
2. Cut off the top of a head of garlic. Place the garlic cloves on a large square of aluminum foil. Drizzle the top with the remaining 1 tablespoon of olive oil and wrap the garlic cloves in foil.
3. Transfer the garlic to the air fryer basket.
4. Put the air fryer basket on the baking pan and slide into Rack Position 2, select Roast,

set temperature to 330ºF (166ºC) and set time to 15 minutes.
5. After 15 minutes, remove from the oven and add the bell peppers. Return to the oven and set time to 7 minutes.
6. When cooking is complete or until the garlic is soft and the bell peppers are tender.
7. Transfer the cooked bell peppers to a plate. Remove the garlic and unwrap the foil. Let the garlic rest for a few minutes. Once cooled, squeeze the roasted garlic cloves out of their skins and add them to the plate of bell peppers. Stir well and serve immediately.

456.French Bean Toast

Servings:x
Cooking Time:x
Ingredients:
- 1 tsp. sugar for every 2 slices
- Crushed cornflakes
- 2 cups baked beans
- Bread slices (brown or white)
- 1 egg white for every 2 slices

Directions:
1. Put two slices together and cut them along the diagonal.
2. In a bowl, whisk the egg whites and add some sugar.
3. Dip the bread triangles into this mixture and then coat them with the crushed cornflakes.
4. Pre heat the Breville smart oven at 180° C for 4 minutes. Place the coated bread triangles in the fry basket and close it. Let them cook at the same temperature for another 20 minutes at least. Halfway through the process, turn the triangles over so that you get a uniform cook. Top with baked beans and serve.

457.Yam French Cuisine Galette

Servings:x
Cooking Time:x
Ingredients:
- 1 ½ tbsp. lemon juice
- Salt and pepper to taste
- 2 cups minced yam
- 3 tsp. ginger finely chopped
- 1-2 tbsp. fresh coriander leaves
- 2 or 3 green chilies finely chopped

Directions:
1. Mix the ingredients in a clean bowl.
2. Mold this mixture into round and flat French Cuisine Galettes.
3. Wet the French Cuisine Galettes slightly with water.
4. Pre heat the Breville smart oven at 160 degrees Fahrenheit for 5 minutes. Place the French Cuisine Galettes in the fry basket and let them cook for another 25 minutes at the same temperature. Keep rolling them

over to get a uniform cook. Serve either with mint sauce or ketchup.

458.Cauliflower Gnocchi's

Servings:x
Cooking Time:x
Ingredients:
- 2 tbsp. oil
- 2 tsp. ginger-garlic paste
- 2 tsp. soya sauce
- 2 tsp. vinegar
- 1 ½ cup all-purpose flour
- ½ tsp. salt
- 5 tbsp. water
- 2 cups grated cauliflower

Directions:
1. Squeeze the dough and cover it with plastic wrap and set aside. Next, cook the ingredients for the filling and try to ensure that the cauliflower is covered well with the sauce.
2. Roll the dough and place the filling in the center. Now, wrap the dough to cover the filling and pinch the edges together.
3. Pre heat the Breville smart oven at 200° F for 5 minutes. Place the gnocchi's in the fry basket and close it. Let them cook at the same temperature for another 20
4. minutes. Recommended sides are chili sauce or ketchup.

459.Cheese With Spinach Enchiladas

Servings: 4
Cooking Time: 20 Minutes
Ingredients:
- 8 corn tortillas, warm
- 2 cups mozzarella cheese, shredded
- 1 cup ricotta cheese
- 1 cup spinach, torn
- 1 garlic clove, minced
- ½ cup sliced onions
- ½ cup sour cream
- 1 tbsp butter
- 1 can enchilada sauce

Directions:
1. Warm olive oil In a saucepan over medium heat and sauté garlic and onion for 3 minutes until soft. Stir in the spinach and cook for 5 more minutes until wilted. Remove from the heat and stir in the ricotta cheese, sour cream, and half of the mozzarella cheese.
2. Spoon ¼ cup of the spinach mixture in the middle of each tortilla. Roll up and place seam side down in a baking dish. Pour the enchilada sauce over the tortillas and sprinkle with the remaining cheese. Cook in your Cuisinart for 15 minutes at 380 F on Air Fry function.

460.Fried Root Vegetable Medley With Thyme

Servings:4
Cooking Time: 22 Minutes
Ingredients:
- 2 carrots, sliced
- 2 potatoes, cut into chunks
- 1 rutabaga, cut into chunks
- 1 turnip, cut into chunks
- 1 beet, cut into chunks
- 8 shallots, halved
- 2 tablespoons olive oil
- Salt and black pepper, to taste
- 2 tablespoons tomato pesto
- 2 tablespoons water
- 2 tablespoons chopped fresh thyme

Directions:
1. Toss the carrots, potatoes, rutabaga, turnip, beet, shallots, olive oil, salt, and pepper in a large mixing bowl until the root vegetables are evenly coated.
2. Place the root vegetables in the air fryer basket.
3. Put the air fryer basket on the baking pan and slide into Rack Position 2, select Air Fry, set temperature to 400ºF (205ºC) and set time to 22 minutes.
4. Stir the vegetables twice during cooking.
5. When cooking is complete, the vegetables should be tender.
6. Meanwhile, in a small bowl, whisk together the tomato pesto and water until smooth.
7. When ready, remove the root vegetables from the oven to a platter. Drizzle with the tomato pesto mixture and sprinkle with the thyme. Serve immediately.

461.Easy Cheesy Vegetable Quesadilla

Servings:1
Cooking Time: 10 Minutes
Ingredients:
- 1 teaspoon olive oil
- 2 flour tortillas
- ¼ zucchini, sliced
- ¼ yellow bell pepper, sliced
- ¼ cup shredded gouda cheese
- 1 tablespoon chopped cilantro
- ½ green onion, sliced

Directions:
1. Coat the air fryer basket with 1 teaspoon of olive oil.
2. Arrange a flour tortilla in the basket and scatter the top with zucchini, bell pepper, gouda cheese, cilantro, and green onion. Place the other flour tortilla on top.
3. Put the air fryer basket on the baking pan and slide into Rack Position 2, select Air Fry, set temperature to 390ºF (199ºC), and set time to 10 minutes.
4. When cooking is complete, the tortillas should be lightly browned and the vegetables should be tender. Remove from

the oven and cool for 5 minutes before slicing into wedges.

462.Gorgonzola Cheese & Pumpkin Salad

Servings:2
Cooking Time: 30 Minutes + Chilling Time
Ingredients:
- ½ lb pumpkin
- 2 oz gorgonzola cheese, crumbled
- 2 tbsp pine nuts, toasted
- 1 tbsp olive oil
- ½ cup baby spinach
- 1 spring onion, sliced
- 2 radishes, thinly sliced
- 1 tsp apple cider vinegar

Directions:
1. Preheat Breville on Bake function to 360 F. Peel the pumpkin and chop it into small pieces. Place in a greased baking dish and bake for 20 minutes. Let cool.
2. Add baby spinach, radishes, and spring onion in a serving bowl and toss with olive oil and vinegar. Top with the pumpkin and gorgonzola cheese and sprinkle with the pine nuts to serve.

463.Asian-inspired Broccoli

Servings:2
Cooking Time: 10 Minutes
Ingredients:
- 12 ounces (340 g) broccoli florets
- 2 tablespoons Asian hot chili oil
- 1 teaspoon ground Sichuan peppercorns (or black pepper)
- 2 garlic cloves, finely chopped
- 1 (2-inch) piece fresh ginger, peeled and finely chopped
- Kosher salt and freshly ground black pepper

Directions:
1. Toss the broccoli florets with the chili oil, Sichuan peppercorns, garlic, ginger, salt, and pepper in a mixing bowl until thoroughly coated.
2. Transfer the broccoli florets to the air fryer basket.
3. Put the air fryer basket on the baking pan and slide into Rack Position 2, select Air Fry, set temperature to 375ºF (190ºC), and set time to 10 minutes.
4. Stir the broccoli florets halfway through the cooking time.
5. When cooking is complete, the broccoli florets should be lightly browned and tender. Remove the broccoli from the oven and serve on a plate.

464.Crispy Tofu Sticks

Servings:4
Cooking Time: 14 Minutes
Ingredients:
- 2 tablespoons olive oil, divided
- ½ cup flour
- ½ cup crushed cornflakes
- Salt and black pepper, to taste
- 14 ounces (397 g) firm tofu, cut into ½-inch-thick strips

Directions:
1. Grease the air fryer basket with 1 tablespoon of olive oil.
2. Combine the flour, cornflakes, salt, and pepper on a plate.
3. Dredge the tofu strips in the flour mixture until they are completely coated. Transfer the tofu strips to the greased basket.
4. Drizzle the remaining 1 tablespoon of olive oil over the top of tofu strips.
5. Put the air fryer basket on the baking pan and slide into Rack Position 2, select Air Fry, set temperature to 360ºF (182ºC), and set time to 14 minutes.
6. Flip the tofu strips halfway through the cooking time.
7. When cooking is complete, the tofu strips should be crispy. Remove from the oven and serve warm.

465.Cheesy Ravioli Lunch

Servings:6
Cooking Time: 15 Minutes
Ingredients:
- 1 package cheese ravioli
- 2 cup Italian breadcrumbs
- ¼ cup Parmesan cheese, grated
- 1 cup buttermilk
- 1 tsp olive oil
- ¼ tsp garlic powder

Directions:
1. Preheat Breville on AirFry function to 390 F. In a bowl, combine breadcrumbs, Parmesan cheese, garlic, and olive oil. Dip the ravioli in the buttermilk and coat with the breadcrumb mixture.
2. Line a baking sheet with parchment paper and arrange the ravioli on it. Press Start and cook for 5 minutes. Serve with marinara jar sauce.

466.Gourd French Cuisine Galette

Servings:x
Cooking Time:x
Ingredients:
- 2 or 3 green chilies finely chopped
- 1 ½ tbsp. lemon juice
- Salt and pepper to taste
- 2 tbsp. garam masala
- 2 cups sliced gourd
- 1 ½ cup coarsely crushed peanuts
- 3 tsp. ginger finely chopped
- 1-2 tbsp. fresh coriander leaves

Directions:
1. Mix the ingredients in a clean bowl.
2. Mold this mixture into round and flat French Cuisine Galettes.

3. Wet the French Cuisine Galettes slightly with water. Coat each French Cuisine Galette with the crushed peanuts.
4. Pre heat the Breville smart oven at 160 degrees Fahrenheit for 5 minutes. Place the French Cuisine Galettes in the fry basket and let them cook for another 25 minutes at the same temperature. Keep rolling them over to get a uniform cook. Serve either with mint sauce or ketchup

467.Stuffed Capsicum Baskets

Servings:x
Cooking Time:x
Ingredients:
- 1 green chili finely chopped
- 2 or 3 large potatoes boiled and mashed
- 1 ½ tbsp. chopped coriander leaves
- 1 tsp. fenugreek
- 1 tsp. dried mango powder
- 3-4 long capsicum
- ½ tsp. salt
- ½ tsp. pepper powder
- For filling:
- 1 medium onion finely chopped
- 1 tsp. cumin powder
- Salt and pepper to taste
- 3 tbsp. grated cheese
- 1 tsp. red chili flakes
- ½ tsp. oregano
- ½ tsp. basil
- ½ tsp. parsley

Directions:
1. Take all the ingredients under the heading "Filling" and mix them together in a bowl.
2. Remove the stem of the capsicum. Cut off the caps. Remove the seeds as well. Sprinkle some salt and pepper on the inside of the capsicums. Leave them aside for some time.
3. Now fill the hollowed-out capsicums with the filling prepared but leave a small space at the top. Sprinkle grated cheese and also add the seasoning.
4. Pre heat the Breville smart oven at 140 degrees Fahrenheit for 5 minutes. Put the capsicums in the fry basket and close it. Let them cook at the same temperature for another 20 minutes. Turn them over in between to prevent over cooking.

468.Cottage Cheese And Mushroom Mexican Burritos

Servings:x
Cooking Time:x
Ingredients:
- ½ cup mushrooms thinly sliced
- 1 cup cottage cheese cut in too long and slightly thick Oregano Fingers
- A pinch of salt to taste
- ½ tsp. red chili flakes
- 1 tsp. freshly ground peppercorns
- ½ cup pickled jalapenos
- 1-2 lettuce leaves shredded.
- ½ cup red kidney beans (soaked overnight)
- ½ small onion chopped
- 1 tbsp. olive oil
- 2 tbsp. tomato puree
- ¼ tsp. red chili powder
- 1 tsp. of salt to taste
- 4-5 flour tortillas
- 1 or 2 spring onions chopped finely. Also cut the greens.
- Take one tomato. Remove the seeds and chop it into small pieces.
- 1 green chili chopped.
- 1 cup of cheddar cheese grated.
- 1 cup boiled rice (not necessary).
- A few flour tortillas to put the filing in.

Directions:
1. Cook the beans along with the onion and garlic and mash them finely.
2. Now, make the sauce you will need for the burrito. Ensure that you create a slightly thick sauce.
3. For the filling, you will need to cook the ingredients well in a pan and ensure that the vegetables have browned on the outside.
4. To make the salad, toss the ingredients together. Place the tortilla and add a layer of sauce, followed by the beans and the filling at the center. Before you roll it, you will need to place the salad on top of the filling.
5. Pre-heat the Breville smart oven for around 5 minutes at 200 Fahrenheit. Open the fry basket and keep the burritos inside. Close the basket properly. Let the Air
6. Fryer remain at 200 Fahrenheit for another 15 minutes or so. Halfway through, remove the basket and turn all the burritos over in order to get a uniform cook.

469.Classic Baked Potatoes

Servings:4
Cooking Time: 30 Minutes
Ingredients:
- 1 lb potatoes
- 2 garlic cloves, minced
- Salt and black pepper to taste
- 1 tsp rosemary
- 1 tsp butter, melted

Directions:
1. Preheat Breville oven to 360 F on AirFry function. Prick the potatoes with a fork. Place into frying basket and press Start. Cook for 25 minutes. Cut the potatoes in half and top with butter and rosemary. Season with salt and pepper and serve.

470.Apricot Spicy Lemon Kebab

Servings:x
Cooking Time:x
Ingredients:
- 3 tsp. lemon juice
- 2 tsp. garam masala

- 3 eggs
- 2 ½ tbsp. white sesame seeds
- 2 cups fresh apricots
- 3 onions chopped
- 5 green chilies-roughly chopped
- 1 ½ tbsp. ginger paste
- 1 ½ tsp. garlic paste
- 1 ½ tsp. salt

Directions:
1. Grind the ingredients except for the egg and form a smooth paste. Coat the apricots in the paste. Now, beat the eggs and add a little salt to it.
2. Dip the coated apricots in the egg mixture and then transfer to the sesame seeds and coat the apricots well. Place the vegetables on a stick.
3. Pre heat the Breville smart oven at 160 degrees Fahrenheit for around 5 minutes. Place the sticks in the basket and let them cook for another 25 minutes at the same temperature. Turn the sticks over in between the cooking process to get a uniform cook.

471.Spicy Kung Pao Tofu

Servings:4
Cooking Time: 10 Minutes
Ingredients:
- $^1/_3$ cup Asian-Style sauce
- 1 teaspoon cornstarch
- ½ teaspoon red pepper flakes, or more to taste
- 1 pound (454 g) firm or extra-firm tofu, cut into 1-inch cubes
- 1 small carrot, peeled and cut into ¼-inch-thick coins
- 1 small green bell pepper, cut into bite-size pieces
- 3 scallions, sliced, whites and green parts separated
- 3 tablespoons roasted unsalted peanuts

Directions:
1. In a large bowl, whisk together the sauce, cornstarch, and red pepper flakes. Fold in the tofu, carrot, pepper, and the white parts of the scallions and toss to coat. Spread the mixture evenly in the baking pan.
2. Slide the baking pan into Rack Position 2, select Roast, set temperature to 375ºF (190ºC), and set time to 10 minutes.
3. Stir the ingredients once halfway through the cooking time.
4. When done, remove from the oven. Serve sprinkled with the peanuts and scallion greens.

472.Asparagus Spicy Lemon Kebab

Servings:x
Cooking Time:x
Ingredients:
- 3 tsp. lemon juice

- 2 tsp. garam masala
- 3 eggs
- 2 ½ tbsp. white sesame seeds
- 2 cups sliced asparagus
- 3 onions chopped
- 5 green chilies-roughly chopped
- 1 ½ tbsp. ginger paste
- 1 ½ tsp. garlic paste
- 1 ½ tsp. salt

Directions:
1. Grind the ingredients except for the egg and form a smooth paste. Coat the asparagus in the paste. Now, beat the eggs and add a little salt to it.
2. Dip the coated apricots in the egg mixture and then transfer to the sesame seeds and coat the asparagus. Place the vegetables on a stick.
3. Pre heat the Breville smart oven at 160 degrees Fahrenheit for around 5 minutes. Place the sticks in the basket and let them cook for another 25 minutes at the same temperature. Turn the sticks over in between the cooking process to get a uniform cook.

473.Cheddar & Bean Burritos

Servings:4
Cooking Time: 30 Minutes
Ingredients:
- 4 flour tortillas
- 1 cup grated cheddar cheese
- 1 (8 oz) can black beans, drained
- 1 tsp taco seasoning

Directions:
1. Preheat Breville on Bake function to 350 F. Mix the black beans with the taco seasoning. Divide the bean mixture between the tortillas and top with cheddar cheese. Roll the burritos and arrange them on a lined baking dish. Place in the oven and press Start. Cook for 5 minutes.

474.Simple Ricotta & Spinach Balls

Servings: 4
Cooking Time: 20 Minutes
Ingredients:
- 14 oz store-bought crescent dough
- 1 cup steamed spinach
- 1 cup crumbled ricotta cheese
- ¼ tsp garlic powder
- 1 tsp chopped oregano
- ¼ tsp salt

Directions:
1. Preheat Cuisinart on Air Fry function to 350 F. Roll the dough onto a lightly floured flat surface. Combine the ricotta cheese, spinach, oregano, salt, and garlic powder together in a bowl. Cut the dough into 4 equal pieces.
2. Divide the spinach/feta mixture between the dough pieces. Make sure to place the filling in the center. Fold the dough and

secure with a fork. Place onto a lined baking dish and then in your Cuisinart oven. Cook for 12 minutes until lightly browned. Serve.

475.Mozzarella Eggplant Patties

Servings: 1
Cooking Time: 10 Minutes
Ingredients:
- 1 hamburger bun
- 1 eggplant, sliced
- 1 mozzarella slice, chopped
- 1 red onion cut into 3 rings
- 1 lettuce leaf
- ½ tbsp tomato sauce
- 1 pickle, sliced

Directions:
1. Preheat Cuisinart on Bake function to 330 F. Place the eggplant slices in a greased baking tray and cook for 6 minutes. Take out the tray and top the eggplant with mozzarella cheese and cook for 30 more seconds. Spread tomato sauce on one half of the bun. Place the lettuce leaf on top of the sauce. Place the cheesy eggplant on top of the lettuce. Top with onion rings and pickles and then with the other bun half to serve.

476.Sago French Cuisine Galette

Servings:x
Cooking Time:x
Ingredients:
- 2 or 3 green chilies finely chopped
- 1 ½ tbsp. lemon juice
- Salt and pepper to taste
- 2 cup sago soaked
- 1 ½ cup coarsely crushed peanuts
- 3 tsp. ginger finely chopped
- 1-2 tbsp. fresh coriander leaves

Directions:
1. Wash the soaked sago and mix it with the rest of the ingredients in a clean bowl.
2. Mold this mixture into round and flat French Cuisine Galettes.
3. Wet the French Cuisine Galettes slightly with water. Coat each French Cuisine Galette with the crushed peanuts.
4. Pre heat the Breville smart oven at 160 degrees Fahrenheit for 5 minutes. Place the French Cuisine Galettes in the fry basket and let them cook for another 25 minutes at the same temperature. Keep rolling them over to get a uniform cook. Serve either with mint sauce or ketchup.

SNACKS AND DESSERTS RECIPES

477.Roasted Veggie Bowl

Servings: 2
Cooking Time: 35 Minutes
Ingredients:
- ¼ medium white onion; peeled.and sliced ¼-inch thick
- ½ medium green bell pepper; seeded and sliced ¼-inch thick
- 1 cup broccoli florets
- 1 cup quartered Brussels sprouts
- ½ cup cauliflower florets
- 1 tbsp. coconut oil
- ½ tsp. garlic powder.
- ½ tsp. cumin
- 2 tsp. chili powder

Directions:
1. Toss all ingredients together in a large bowl until vegetables are fully coated with oil and seasoning. Pour vegetables into the air fryer basket.
2. Adjust the temperature to 360 Degrees F and set the timer for 15 minutes. Shake two- or three-times during cooking. Serve warm.
- **Nutrition Info:** Calories: 121; Protein: 4.3g; Fiber: 5.2g; Fat: 7.1g; Carbs: 13.1g

478.Strawberry Cobbler

Servings: 6
Cooking Time: 45 Minutes
Ingredients:
- 2 cups strawberries, diced
- 1 cup milk
- 1 cup self-rising flour
- 1 1/4 cup sugar
- 1 tsp vanilla
- 1/2 cup butter, melted

Directions:
1. Fit the Cuisinart oven with the rack in position
2. In a bowl, mix together flour and 1 cup sugar.
3. Add milk and whisk until smooth.
4. Add vanilla and butter and mix well.
5. Pour mixture into the greased baking dish and sprinkle with strawberries and top with remaining sugar.
6. Set to bake at 350 F for 50 minutes. After 5 minutes place the baking dish in the preheated oven.
7. Serve and enjoy.
- **Nutrition Info:** Calories 405 Fat 16.5 g Carbohydrates 63.4 g Sugar 46 g Protein 4 g Cholesterol 44 mg

479.Yogurt Cake(2)

Servings: 12
Cooking Time: 30 Minutes
Ingredients:
- 6 eggs, whisked
- 1 teaspoon vanilla extract
- 1 teaspoon baking powder
- 9 ounces coconut flour
- 4 tablespoons stevia
- 8 ounces Greek yogurt

Directions:
1. In a bowl, mix all the ingredients and whisk well.
2. Pour this into a cake pan that fits the air fryer lined with parchment paper, put the pan in the air fryer and cook at 330 degrees F for 30 minutes.
- **Nutrition Info:** calories 181, fat 13, fiber 2, carbs 4, protein 5

480.Chocolate Chip Pan Cookie

Servings: 4
Cooking Time: 15 Minutes
Ingredients:
- ½ cup blanched finely ground almond flour.
- 1 large egg.
- ¼ cup powdered erythritol
- 2 tbsp. unsalted butter; softened.
- 2 tbsp. low-carb, sugar-free chocolate chips
- ½ tsp. unflavored gelatin
- ½ tsp. baking powder.
- ½ tsp. vanilla extract.

Directions:
1. Take a large bowl, mix almond flour and erythritol. Stir in butter, egg and gelatin until combined.
2. Stir in baking powder and vanilla and then fold in chocolate chips.
3. Pour batter into 6-inch round baking pan. Place pan into the air fryer basket.
4. Adjust the temperature to 300 Degrees F and set the timer for 7 minutes
5. When fully cooked, the top will be golden brown and a toothpick inserted in center will come out clean. Let cool at least 10 minutes.
- **Nutrition Info:** Calories: 188; Protein: 5.6g; Fiber: 2.0g; Fat: 15.7g; Carbs: 16.8g

481.Mixed Berry Compote With Coconut Chips

Servings: 6
Cooking Time: 15 Minutes
Ingredients:
- 1 tablespoon butter
- 12 ounces mixed berries
- 1/3 cup granulated swerve
- 1/4 teaspoon grated nutmeg
- 1/4 teaspoon ground cloves
- 1/2 teaspoon ground cinnamon
- 1 teaspoon pure vanilla extract
- 1/2 cup coconut chips

Directions:
1. Start by preheating your Air Fryer to 330 degrees F. Grease a baking pan with butter.

2. Place all ingredients, except for the coconut chips, in a baking pan. Bake in the preheated Air Fryer for 20 minutes.
3. Serve in individual bowls, garnished with coconut chips.
- **Nutrition Info:** 76 Calories; 3g Fat; 5g Carbs; 6g Protein; 1g Sugars; 1g Fiber

482.Apple Treat With Raisins

Servings:4
Cooking Time: 15 Minutes
Ingredients:
- 4 apples, cored
- 1 ½ oz almonds
- ¾ oz raisins
- 2 tbsp sugar

Directions:
1. Preheat Breville on Bake function to 360 F. In a bowl, mix sugar, almonds, and raisins and blend the mixture using a hand mixer. Fill cored apples with the almond mixture. Place the prepared apples in the basket and press Start. Bake for 10 minutes. Serve with powdered sugar.

483.Tomato Bites

Servings: 6
Cooking Time: 15 Minutes
Ingredients:
- 6 tomatoes; halved
- 2 oz. watercress
- 3 oz. cheddar cheese; grated
- 1 tbsp. olive oil
- 3 tsp. sugar-free apricot jam
- 2 tsp. oregano; dried
- A pinch of salt and black pepper

Directions:
1. Spread the jam on each tomato half, sprinkle oregano, salt and pepper and drizzle the oil all over them
2. Introduce them in the fryer's basket, sprinkle the cheese on top and cook at 360°F for 20 minutes
3. Arrange the tomatoes on a platter, top each half with some watercress and serve as an appetizer.
- **Nutrition Info:** Calories: 131; Fat: 7g; Fiber: 2g; Carbs: 4g; Protein: 7g

484.Italian Pork Skewers

Servings:x
Cooking Time:x
Ingredients:
- ¼ cup finely minced onion
- 1 teaspoon dried Italian seasoning
- ½ teaspoon salt
- teaspoon pepper
- 2 pounds pork tenderloin
- ¼ cup balsamic vinegar
- ¼ cup olive oil

Directions:

1. Trim excess fat from tenderloin. Cut pork, on a slant, into ¼-inch-thick slices, each about 4 inches long. In large bowl, combine remaining ingredients and mix well with wire whisk. Add tenderloin slices and mix gently to coat. Cover and refrigerate for 2 to 3 hours. Meanwhile, soak 8-inch wooden skewers in cold water.
2. Remove pork from marinade and thread onto soaked skewers. Flash freeze on baking sheet in single layer. When frozen solid, pack skewers in rigid containers, with layers separated by waxed paper. Label skewers and freeze.
3. To thaw and reheat: Thaw overnight in refrigerator. Cook skewers 4 to 6 inches from medium coals on grill, or broil 4 to 6 inches from heat source, for about 4 to 6 minutes or until cooked (160ºF on an instant-read thermometer), turning once.

485.Shrimp Cheese Quiches

Servings:x
Cooking Time:x
Ingredients:
- 1 (6-ounce) can tiny shrimp, drained
- ½ teaspoon dried marjoram leaves
- ½ teaspoon salt
- ½ teaspoon pepper
- ¾ cup shredded Havarti cheese
- 2 9-inch Pie Crusts
- ½ cup chopped leek, rinsed
- 1 tablespoon olive oil
- 2 eggs
- ½ cup cream

Directions:
1. Using a 2-inch cookie cutter, cut 36 rounds from pie crusts. Place each in a 1¾-inch mini muffin cup, pressing to bottom and sides. Set aside.
2. Sauté leek in olive oil until tender. Beat eggs with cream in medium bowl. Add drained shrimp, cooked leek, marjoram, salt, and pepper, and mix well.
3. Sprinkle 1 teaspoon cheese into each muffin cup and fill cups with shrimp mixture. Bake at 375ºF for 15 to 18 minutes or until pastry is golden and filling is set. Cool in refrigerator until cold, then freeze.
4. Freeze in single layer on baking sheet. When frozen solid, pack in rigid containers, using waxed paper to separate layers. Label and freeze.
5. To reheat: Place frozen quiches on baking sheet and bake at 375ºF for 8 to 11 minutes or until hot.

486.Baked Apple

Servings: 4
Cooking Time: 20 Minutes
Ingredients:
- ¼ C. water
- ¼ tsp. nutmeg

- ¼ tsp. cinnamon
- 1 ½ tsp. melted ghee
- 2 tbsp. raisins
- 2 tbsp. chopped walnuts
- 1 medium apple

Directions:
1. Preparing the Ingredients. Preheat your air fryer oven to 350 degrees.
2. Slice an apple in half and discard some of the flesh from the center.
3. Place into frying pan.
4. Mix remaining ingredients together except water. Spoon mixture to the middle of apple halves.
5. Pour water overfilled apples.
6. Air Frying. Place pan with apple halves into the Cuisinart air fryer oven, bake 20 minutes.
- **Nutrition Info:** CALORIES: 199; FAT:9G; PROTEIN:1G; SUGAR:3G

487.Eggplant Stacks

Servings: 4
Cooking Time: 15 Minutes
Ingredients:
- 2 large tomatoes; cut into ¼-inch slices
- ¼ cup fresh basil, sliced
- 4 oz. fresh mozzarella; cut into ½-oz. slices
- 1 medium eggplant; cut into ¼-inch slices
- 2 tbsp. olive oil

Directions:
1. In a 6-inch round baking dish, place four slices of eggplant on the bottom. Place a slice of tomato on top of each eggplant round, then mozzarella, then eggplant. Repeat as necessary.
2. Drizzle with olive oil. Cover dish with foil and place dish into the air fryer basket. Adjust the temperature to 350 Degrees F and set the timer for 12 minutes.
3. When done, eggplant will be tender. Garnish with fresh basil to serve.
- **Nutrition Info:** Calories: 195; Protein: 8.5g; Fiber: 5.2g; Fat: 12.7g; Carbs: 12.7g

488.Sweet And Sour Meatballs

Servings:x
Cooking Time:x
Ingredients:
- ¼ cup apple cider vinegar
- 1 (10-ounce) can condensed tomato soup
- cup sugar
- 1 (8-ounce) can pineapple tidbits, undrained
- 1-pound ground beef
- 1 egg
- ½ cup grated Parmesan cheese
- ¼ cup dry bread crumbs

Directions:
1. Preheat oven to 350ºF. In medium bowl, combine ground beef, egg, cheese, and bread crumbs and mix well to blend. Form

into 1-inch meatballs and place on baking sheet. Bake at 350ºF for 20 to 25 minutes or until no longer pink in center. Chill meatballs in refrigerator until thoroughly cold.
2. In a medium bowl, combine vinegar, soup, sugar, and pineapple tidbits and juice. Mix well and pour into 1-gallon-size zipper-lock freezer bag. Add meatballs, seal bag, and turn gently to mix. Label bag and freeze.
3. To thaw and reheat: Thaw overnight in refrigerator. Pour meatballs and sauce into large skillet and cook over medium heat until sauce comes to a boil. Reduce heat, cover, and simmer meatballs for 8 to 10 minutes or until thoroughly heated, stirring occasionally.

489.Tasty Broccoli Fritters

Servings: 4
Cooking Time: 30 Minutes
Ingredients:
- 3 cups broccoli florets, steam & chopped
- 2 eggs, lightly beaten
- 2 garlic cloves, minced
- 2 cups cheddar cheese, shredded
- 1/4 cup breadcrumbs
- 1/2 tsp Italian seasoning
- Pepper
- Salt

Directions:
1. Fit the Cuisinart oven with the rack in position
2. Add all ingredients into the large bowl and mix until well combined.
3. Make patties from broccoli mixture and place in baking pan.
4. Set to bake at 375 F for 35 minutes. After 5 minutes place the baking pan in the preheated oven.
5. Serve and enjoy.
- **Nutrition Info:** Calories 313 Fat 21.7 g Carbohydrates 10.9 g Sugar 2.1 g Protein 19.8 g Cholesterol 142 mg

490.Walnut Zucchini Bread

Servings: 8
Cooking Time: 20 Minutes
Ingredients:
- 1½ cups all-purpose flour
- ½ teaspoon baking soda
- ½ teaspoon baking powder
- ½ tablespoon ground cinnamon
- ½ teaspoon salt
- 2¼ cups white sugar
- ½ cup vegetable oil
- 1½ eggs
- 1½ teaspoons vanilla extract
- 1 cup zucchini, grated
- ½ cup walnuts, chopped

Directions:

1. In a bowl and mix together the flour, baking powder, baking soda, cinnamon, and salt.
2. In another large bowl, add the sugar, oil, eggs, and vanilla extract and whisk until well combined.
3. Add the flour mixture and mix until just combined.
4. Gently, fold in the zucchini and walnuts.
5. Place the mixture into a lightly greased loaf pan.
6. Press "Power Button" of Air Fry Oven and turn the dial to select the "Air Crisp" mode.
7. Press the Time button and again turn the dial to set the cooking time to 20 minutes.
8. Now push the Temp button and rotate the dial to set the temperature at 320 degrees F.
9. Press "Start/Pause" button to start.
10. When the unit beeps to show that it is preheated, open the lid.
11. Arrange the pan in "Air Fry Basket" and insert in the oven.
12. Place the pan onto a wire rack to cool for about 10 minutes.
13. Carefully, invert the bread onto wire rack to cool completely before slicing.
14. Cut the bread into desired-sized slices and serve.
- **Nutrition Info:** Calories 483 Total Fat 19.3 g Saturated Fat 3.2 g Cholesterol 31mg Sodium 241 mg Total Carbs 76 g Fiber 1.6 g Sugar 56.8 g Protein 5.5 g

491. Caramelized Peaches

Servings:4
Cooking Time: 10 To 13 Minutes
Ingredients:
- 2 tablespoons sugar
- ¼ teaspoon ground cinnamon
- 4 peaches, cut into wedges
- Cooking spray

Directions:
1. Toss the peaches with the sugar and cinnamon in a medium bowl until evenly coated.
2. Lightly spray the air fryer basket with cooking spray. Place the peaches in the basket in a single layer. Lightly mist the peaches with cooking spray.
3. Put the air fryer basket on the baking pan and slide into Rack Position 2, select Air Fry, set temperature to 350ºF (180ºC), and set time to 10 minutes.
4. After 5 minutes, remove from the oven and flip the peaches. Return to the oven and continue cooking for 5 minutes.
5. When cooking is complete, the peaches should be caramelized. If necessary, continue cooking for 3 minutes. Remove from the oven. Let the peaches cool for 5 minutes and serve warm.

492. Apple-toffee Upside-down Cake

Servings: 9

Cooking Time: 30 Minutes
Ingredients:
- Almond butter, ¼ cup
- Sunflower oil, ¼ cup
- Chopped walnuts, ½ cup
- Coconut sugar, 1 cup
- Water, ¾ cup
- Mixed spice, 1 ½ tsps.
- Plain flour, 1 cup
- Zest from 1 lemon
- Baking soda, 1 tsp.
- Vinegar, 1 tsp.
- Cored and sliced, 3

Directions:
1. Preheat the air fryer to 3900 F.
2. In a skillet, melt the almond butter and 3 tablespoons sugar. Pour mixture over a baking dish that will fit in the air fryer. Arrange the slices of apples on top. Set aside.
3. In a mixing bowl, combine flour, ¾ cup sugar, and baking soda. Add the mixed spice.
4. In another bowl, mix the oil, water, vinegar, and lemon zest. Stir in the chopped walnuts.
5. Combine the wet ingredients to dry ingredients until well combined.
6. Pour over the tin with apple slices.
7. Leave to cook for 30 minutes.
- **Nutrition Info:** Calories: 335 Carbs: 39.6g Protein: 3.8g Fat: 17.9g

493. Mouthwatering Chocolate Soufflé

Servings:2
Cooking Time: 25 Minutes
Ingredients:
- 2 eggs, whites and yolks separated
- ¼ cup butter, melted
- 2 tbsp flour
- 3 tbsp sugar
- 3 oz chocolate, melted
- ½ tsp vanilla extract

Directions:
1. Preheat Breville on Bake function to 330 F. Beat the yolks along with the sugar and vanilla extract; stir in butter, chocolate, and flour. Whisk the whites until a stiff peak forms.
2. Working in batches, gently combine the egg whites with the chocolate mixture. Divide the batter between two greased ramekins. Press Start. Bake for 14-18 minutes.

494. Lemon Ricotta Cake

Servings:6
Cooking Time: 25 Minutes
Ingredients:
- 17.5 ounces (496 g) ricotta cheese
- 5.4 ounces (153 g) sugar
- 3 eggs, beaten
- 3 tablespoons flour
- 1 lemon, juiced and zested
- 2 teaspoons vanilla extract

Directions:

1. In a large mixing bowl, stir together all the ingredients until the mixture reaches a creamy consistency.
2. Pour the mixture into the baking pan.
3. Slide the baking pan into Rack Position 1, select Convection Bake, set temperature to 320ºF (160ºC), and set time to 25 minutes.
4. When cooking is complete, a toothpick inserted in the center should come out clean.
5. Allow to cool for 10 minutes on a wire rack before serving.

495.Choco Lava Cakes

Servings:4
Cooking Time: 20 Minutes
Ingredients:
- 3 ½ oz butter, melted
- 3 ½ tbsp sugar
- 1 ½ tbsp self-rising flour
- 3 ½ oz dark chocolate, melted
- 2 eggs

Directions:
1. Preheat Breville on Bake function to 375 F. Beat eggs and sugar until frothy. Stir in butter and chocolate; gently fold in the flour.
2. Divide the mixture between 4 buttered ramekins and press Start. Bake in the fryer for 10 minutes. Let cool for 2 minutes before turning the cakes upside down onto serving plates.

496.Spicy Cauliflower Florets

Servings: 4
Cooking Time: 15 Minutes
Ingredients:
- 1 medium cauliflower head, cut into florets
- 1/2 tsp old bay seasoning
- 1/4 tsp paprika
- 1/4 tsp cayenne
- 1/4 tsp chili powder
- 1 tbsp garlic, minced
- 3 tbsp olive oil
- Pepper
- Salt

Directions:
1. Fit the Cuisinart oven with the rack in position 2.
2. In a bowl, toss cauliflower with remaining ingredients.
3. Add cauliflower florets in air fryer basket then place air fryer basket in baking pan.
4. Place a baking pan on the oven rack. Set to air fry at 400 F for 15 minutes.
5. Serve and enjoy.
- **Nutrition Info:** Calories 130 Fat 10.7 g Carbohydrates 8.6 g Sugar 3.5 g Protein 3 g Cholesterol 0 mg

497.Cinnamon S'mores

Servings: 12 S'mores
Cooking Time: 3 Minutes
Ingredients:

- 12 whole cinnamon graham crackers, halved
- 2 (1.55-ounce / 44-g) chocolate bars, cut into 12 pieces
- 12 marshmallows

Directions:
1. Arrange 12 graham cracker squares in the baking pan in a single layer.
2. Top each square with a piece of chocolate.
3. Slide the baking pan into Rack Position 1, select Convection Bake, set temperature to 350ºF (180ºC), and set time to 3 minutes.
4. Bake for 2 minutes. Remove the pan and place a marshmallow on each piece of melted chocolate. Bake for another 1 minute.
5. Remove from the oven to a serving plate.
6. Serve topped with the remaining graham cracker squares

498.Crispy Eggplant Bites

Servings: 4
Cooking Time: 20 Minutes
Ingredients:
- 1 eggplant, cut into 1-inch pieces
- 1 tsp garlic powder
- 2 tbsp olive oil
- 1/2 tsp Italian seasoning
- 1 tsp paprika
- 1/2 tsp red pepper

Directions:
1. Fit the Cuisinart oven with the rack in position 2.
2. Add all ingredients into the large mixing bowl and toss well.
3. Transfer eggplant mixture in air fryer basket then places air fryer basket in baking pan.
4. Place a baking pan on the oven rack. Set to air fry at 375 F for 20 minutes.
5. Serve and enjoy.
- **Nutrition Info:** Calories 99 Fat 7.5 g Carbohydrates 8.7 g Sugar 4.5 g Protein 1.5 g Cholesterol 0 mg

499.Poppy Seed Pound Cake

Servings: 8
Cooking Time: 20 Minutes
Ingredients:
- Large eggs, 2.
- Coconut milk, ½ cup
- Unsalted butter, 1/3 cup
- Vanilla extract, ¼ tsp.
- Psyllium husk powder, 2 tbsps.
- Baking powder, 1 ½ tsps.
- Poppy seeds, 2 tbsps.
- Almond flour, 1 ½ cup

Directions:
1. Preheat the air fryer for 5 minutes.
2. In a mixing bowl, combine all ingredients.
3. Use a hand mixer to mix everything.

4. Pour into a small loaf pan that will fit in the air fryer.
5. Bake for 20 minutes at 3750 F or until a toothpick inserted in the middle comes out clean.
- **Nutrition Info:** Calories: 145 Carbs: 3.6 Protein: 2.1g Fat: 13.6g

500.Strawberry Tart

Servings:x
Cooking Time:x
Ingredients:
- 2 cups sliced strawberries
- 1 cup fresh cream
- 3 tbsp. butter
- 1 ½ cup plain flour
- 3 tbsp. unsalted butter
- 2 tbsp. powdered sugar
- 2 cups cold water

Directions:
1. In a large bowl, mix the flour, cocoa powder, butter and sugar with your Oregano Fingers. The mixture should resemble breadcrumbs. Squeeze the dough using the cold milk and wrap it and leave it to cool for ten minutes. Roll the dough out into the pie and prick the sides of the pie.
2. Mix the ingredients for the filling in a bowl. Make sure that it is a little
3. thick. Preheat the fryer to 300 Fahrenheit for five minutes. You will need to place the tin in the basket and cover it. When the pastry has turned golden brown, you will need to remove the tin and let it cool. Cut into slices and serve with a dollop of cream.

501.Rice Pudding

Servings:x
Cooking Time:x
Ingredients:
- 3 tbsp. powdered sugar
- 2 tbsp. rice
- 2 cups milk
- 2 tbsp. custard powder
- 3 tbsp. unsalted butter

Directions:
1. Boil the milk and the sugar in a pan and add the custard powder and stir till you get a thick mixture. Add the rice to the bowl and ensure that the mixture becomes slightly thicker.
2. Preheat the fryer to 300 Fahrenheit for five minutes. Place the dish in the basket and reduce the temperature to 250 Fahrenheit. Cook for ten minutes and set aside to cool.

502.Orange Citrus Blend

Servings:x
Cooking Time:x
Ingredients:
- 3 tbsp. powdered sugar
- 3 tbsp. unsalted butter
- 2 oranges (sliced)
- 2 persimmons (sliced)
- 2 cups milk
- 2 cups almond flour
- 2 tbsp. custard powder

Directions:
1. Boil the milk and the sugar in a pan and add the custard powder followed by the almond flour and stir till you get a thick mixture. Add the sliced fruits to the mixture.
2. Preheat the fryer to 300 Fahrenheit for five minutes. Place the dish in the basket and reduce the temperature to 250 Fahrenheit. Cook for ten minutes and set aside to cool.

503.Healthy Broccoli Tots

Servings: 4
Cooking Time: 12 Minutes
Ingredients:
- 1 lb broccoli, cooked & chopped
- 1/2 tsp garlic powder
- 1/2 cup almond flour
- 1/4 cup ground flaxseed
- 1 tsp salt

Directions:
1. Fit the Cuisinart oven with the rack in position 2.
2. Add broccoli into the food processor and process until it looks like rice.
3. Transfer broccoli to a large mixing bowl.
4. Add remaining ingredients into the bowl and mix until well combined.
5. Make tots from broccoli mixture and place in the air fryer basket then place an air fryer basket in the baking pan.
6. Place a baking pan on the oven rack. Set to air fry at 375 F for 12 minutes.
7. Serve and enjoy.
- **Nutrition Info:** Calories 97 Fat 4.3 g Carbohydrates 10.5 g Sugar 2.3 g Protein 5.3 g Cholesterol 0 mg

504.Bbq Pulled Mushrooms

Servings: 2
Cooking Time: 15 Minutes
Ingredients:
- 4 large portobello mushrooms
- ½ cup low-carb, sugar-free barbecue sauce
- 1 tbsp. salted butter; melted.
- 1 tsp. paprika
- ¼ tsp. onion powder.
- ¼ tsp. ground black pepper
- 1 tsp. chili powder

Directions:
1. Remove stem and scoop out the underside of each mushroom. Brush the caps with butter and sprinkle with pepper, chili powder, paprika and onion powder.
2. Place mushrooms into the air fryer basket. Adjust the temperature to 400 Degrees F and set the timer for 8 minutes.

3. When the timer beeps, remove mushrooms from the basket and place on a cutting board or work surface. Using two forks, gently pull the mushrooms apart, creating strands.
4. Place mushroom strands into a 4-cup round baking dish with barbecue sauce. Place dish into the air fryer basket.
5. Adjust the temperature to 350 Degrees F and set the timer for 4 minutes. Stir halfway through the cooking time. Serve warm.
- **Nutrition Info:** Calories: 108; Protein: 3.3g; Fiber: 2.7g; Fat: 5.9g; Carbs: 10.9g

505.Tofu Steaks

Servings: 4
Cooking Time: 35 Minutes
Ingredients:
- 1 package tofu, press and remove excess liquid
- 2 tbsp lemon zest
- 3 garlic cloves, minced
- 1/4 cup olive oil
- 1/4 tsp dried thyme
- 1/4 cup lemon juice
- Pepper
- Salt

Directions:
1. Fit the Cuisinart oven with the rack in position 2.
2. Cut tofu into eight pieces.
3. In a bowl, mix together olive oil, thyme, lemon juice, lemon zest, garlic, pepper, and salt.
4. Add tofu into the bowl and coat well and place it in the refrigerator overnight.
5. Place marinated tofu in an air fryer basket then places an air fryer basket in the baking pan.
6. Place a baking pan on the oven rack. Set to air fry at 350 F for 35 minutes.
7. Serve and enjoy.
- **Nutrition Info:** Calories 139 Fat 14.1 g Carbohydrates 2.3 g Sugar 0.7 g Protein 2.9 g Cholesterol 0 mg

506.Cheddar Dill Mushrooms

Servings: 6
Cooking Time: 5 Minutes
Ingredients:
- 9 oz mushrooms, cut stems
- 6 oz mozzarella cheese, shredded
- 1 tbsp butter
- 1 tsp dried parsley
- 1/2 tsp salt

Directions:
1. Fit the Cuisinart oven with the rack in position 2.
2. Add parsley, cheese, butter, and salt into the bowl and mix until well combined.
3. Stuff cheese mixture into the mushroom caps and place in the air fryer basket then place an air fryer basket in the baking pan.

4. Place a baking pan on the oven rack. Set to air fry at 400 F for 5 minutes.
5. Serve and enjoy.
- **Nutrition Info:** Calories 141 Fat 11.5 g Carbohydrates 1.9 g Sugar 0.9 g Protein 8.5 g Cholesterol 35 mg

507.Cherry Apple Risotto

Servings: 4
Cooking Time: 12 Minutes
Ingredients:
- 1 tablespoon of butter
- ¼ cup of brown sugar
- ½ cup of apple juice
- 1½ cups of milk
- ¾ cup of Arborio rice, boiled
- 1 apple, diced
- 2 pinches salt
- ¾ teaspoon of cinnamon powder
- ¼ cup of dried cherries
- 1½ tablespoons of almonds, roasted and sliced
- ¼ cup of whipped cream

Directions:
1. Set the Instant Vortex on Air fryer to 375 degrees F for 12 minutes. Combine rice with butter, sugar, apple juice, milk, apple, salt, and cinnamon in a bowl. Pour the rice mixture into the cooking tray. Insert the cooking tray in the Vortex when it displays "Add Food". Toss the food when it displays "Turn Food". Remove from the oven when cooking time is complete. Top with the dried cherries, almonds, and whipped cream to serve.
- **Nutrition Info:** Calories: 317 Cal Total Fat: 8.5 g Saturated Fat: 0 g Cholesterol: 0 mg Sodium: 0 mg Total Carbs: 54.8 g Fiber: 0 g Sugar: 0 g Protein: 6.2 g

508.Three Berry Crumble

Servings:x
Cooking Time:x
Ingredients:
- ¾ cup brown sugar
- ¾ cup old fashioned oats
- ½ cup chopped almonds
- 1 tsp cinnamon
- 6 cups of fresh mixed berries (blueberries, raspberries), washed and dried
- ¼ cup sugar
- ¼ cup flour
- 1 Tbsp lemon juice
- ¾ cup flour
- 1 stick cold butter, cut into cubes

Directions:
1. Preheat oven to 375°F.
2. Lightly toss the berries, sugar, flour and lemon juice inside your Breville smart oven.
3. In a bowl, mix the flour, brown sugar, oats, almonds and cinnamon.

4. Incorporate cold butter with your fingertips into the oat mixture until small clumps form.
5. Pour topping onto fruit and bake for 45 minutes to 1 hour, until bubbles form and top appears browned and crispy.
6. Serve with vanilla ice cream right out of Breville smart oven.

509.Strawberry And Rhubarb Crumble

Servings:6
Cooking Time: 12 To 17 Minutes
Ingredients:
- 1½ cups sliced fresh strawberries
- $^1/_3$ cup sugar
- ¾ cup sliced rhubarb
- $^2/_3$ cup quick-cooking oatmeal
- ¼ cup packed brown sugar
- ½ cup whole-wheat pastry flour
- ½ teaspoon ground cinnamon
- 3 tablespoons unsalted butter, melted

Directions:
1. Place the strawberries, sugar, and rhubarb in the baking pan and toss to coat.
2. Combine the oatmeal, brown sugar, pastry flour, and cinnamon in a medium bowl.
3. Add the melted butter to the oatmeal mixture and stir until crumbly. Sprinkle this generously on top of the strawberries and rhubarb.
4. Slide the baking pan into Rack Position 1, select Convection Bake, set temperature to 370ºF (188ºC), and set the time to 12 minutes.
5. Bake until the fruit is bubbly and the topping is golden brown. Continue cooking for an additional 2 to 5 minutes if needed.
6. When cooking is complete, remove from the oven and serve warm.

510.Fried Peaches

Servings: 4
Cooking Time: 15 Minutes
Ingredients:
- 4 ripe peaches (1/2 a peach = 1 serving)
- 1 1/2 cups flour
- Salt
- 2 egg yolks
- 3/4 cups cold water
- 1 1/2 tablespoons olive oil
- 2 tablespoons brandy
- 4 egg whites
- Cinnamon/sugar mix

Directions:
1. Preparing the Ingredients. Mix flour, egg yolks, and salt in a mixing bowl. Slowly mix in water, then add brandy. Set the mixture aside for 2 hours and go do something for 1 hour 45 minutes.
2. Boil a large pot of water and cut an X at the bottom of each peach. While the water boils, fill another large bowl with water and ice. Boil each peach for about a minute, then plunge it in the ice bath. Now the peels

should basically fall off the peach. Beat the egg whites and mix into the batter mix. Dip each peach in the mix to coat.
3. Air Frying. Cook at 360 degrees for 10 Minutes.
4. Prepare a plate with cinnamon/sugar mix, roll peaches in the mix and serve.
- **Nutrition Info:** CALORIES: 306; FAT:.3G; PROTEIN:10G; FIBER:2.7G

511.Crack Dip

Servings: 15
Cooking Time: 15 Minutes
Ingredients:
- 8 oz cream cheese
- 1/8 tsp cayenne
- 1/3 cup green onion, chopped
- 1/3 cup bacon bits, cooked
- 1/3 cup sour cream
- ¾ cup ranch dressing

Directions:
1. Fit the Cuisinart oven with the rack in position 2.
2. Add all ingredients into the bowl and mix well and pour into the greased baking dish.
3. Set to bake at 350 F for 20 minutes. After 5 minutes place the baking dish in the preheated oven.
4. Serve and enjoy.
- **Nutrition Info:** Calories 168 Fat 16 g Carbohydrates 1 g Sugar 0 g Protein 3 g Cholesterol 8 mg

512.Almond Blueberry Bars

Servings: 4
Cooking Time: 50 Minutes
Ingredients:
- 1/4 cup blueberries
- 3 tbsp coconut oil
- 2 tbsp coconut flour
- 1/2 cup almond flour
- 3 tbsp water
- 1 tbsp chia seeds
- 1 tsp vanilla
- 1 tsp fresh lemon juice
- 2 tbsp erythritol
- 1/4 cup almonds, sliced
- 1/4 cup coconut flakes

Directions:
1. Fit the Cuisinart oven with the rack in position
2. Line baking dish with parchment paper and set aside.
3. In a small bowl, mix together water and chia seeds. Set aside.
4. In a bowl, combine together all ingredients. Add chia mixture and stir well.
5. Pour mixture into the prepared baking dish and spread evenly.
6. Set to bake at 300 F for 55 minutes. After 5 minutes place the baking dish in the preheated oven.

7. Slice and serve.
- **Nutrition Info:** Calories 208 Fat 18.2 g Carbohydrates 9.1 g Sugar 2.3 g Protein 3.6 g Cholesterol 0 mg

513.Tasty Jalapeno Poppers

Servings: 4
Cooking Time: 13 Minutes
Ingredients:
- 4 jalapeno peppers, slice in half and deseeded
- 4 oz goat cheese, crumbled
- 1/4 tsp chili powder
- 2 tbsp chunky salsa
- Pepper
- Salt

Directions:
1. Fit the Cuisinart oven with the rack in position 2.
2. In a small bowl, mix together cheese, chunky salsa, chili powder, pepper, and salt.
3. Stuff cheese mixture into each jalapeno half and place in the air fryer basket then place the air fryer basket in the baking pan.
4. Place a baking pan on the oven rack. Set to air fry at 350 F for 13 minutes.
5. Serve and enjoy.
- **Nutrition Info:** Calories 68 Fat 5.1 g Carbohydrates 2.5 g Sugar 1.6 g Protein 3.6 g Cholesterol 20 mg

514.Sweet And Salty Snack Mix

Servings: About 10 Cups
Cooking Time: 10 Minutes
Ingredients:
- 3 tablespoons butter, melted
- ½ cup honey
- 1 teaspoon salt
- 2 cups granola
- 2 cups sesame sticks
- 2 cups crispy corn puff cereal
- 2 cups mini pretzel crisps
- 1 cup cashews
- 1 cup pepitas
- 1 cup dried cherries

Directions:
1. In a small mixing bowl, mix together the butter, honey, and salt until well incorporated.
2. In a large bowl, combine the granola, sesame sticks, corn puff cereal and pretzel crisps, cashews, and pepitas. Drizzle with the butter mixture and toss until evenly coated. Transfer the snack mix to the air fryer basket.
3. Put the air fryer basket on the baking pan and slide into Rack Position 2, select Air Fry, set temperature to 370ºF (188ºC), and set time to 10 minutes.
4. Stir the snack mix halfway through the cooking time.

5. When cooking is complete, they should be lightly toasted. Remove from the oven and allow to cool completely. Scatter with the dried cherries and mix well. Serve immediately.

515.Lemon-raspberry Muffins

Servings:6
Cooking Time: 15 Minutes
Ingredients:
- 2 cups almond flour
- ¾ cup Swerve
- 1¼ teaspoons baking powder
- $^1/_3$ teaspoon ground allspice
- $^1/_3$ teaspoon ground anise star
- ½ teaspoon grated lemon zest
- ¼ teaspoon salt
- 2 eggs
- 1 cup sour cream
- ½ cup coconut oil
- ½ cup raspberries

Directions:
1. Line a muffin pan with 6 paper liners.
2. In a mixing bowl, mix the almond flour, Swerve, baking powder, allspice, anise, lemon zest, and salt.
3. In another mixing bowl, beat the eggs, sour cream, and coconut oil until well mixed. Add the egg mixture to the flour mixture and stir to combine. Mix in the raspberries.
4. Scrape the batter into the prepared muffin cups, filling each about three-quarters full.
5. Put the muffin pan into Rack Position 1, select Convection Bake, set temperature to 345ºF (174ºC), and set time to 15 minutes.
6. When cooking is complete, the tops should be golden and a toothpick inserted in the middle should come out clean.
7. Allow the muffins to cool for 10 minutes in the muffin pan before removing and serving.

516.Fudgy Chocolate Brownies

Servings:8
Cooking Time: 21 Minutes
Ingredients:
- 1 stick butter, melted
- 1 cup Swerve
- 2 eggs
- 1 cup coconut flour
- ½ cup unsweetened cocoa powder
- 2 tablespoons flaxseed meal
- 1 teaspoon baking powder
- 1 teaspoon vanilla essence
- A pinch of salt
- A pinch of ground cardamom
- Cooking spray

Directions:
1. Spray the baking pan with cooking spray.
2. Beat together the melted butter and Swerve in a large mixing dish until fluffy. Whisk in the eggs.

3. Add the coconut flour, cocoa powder, flaxseed meal, baking powder, vanilla essence, salt, and cardamom and stir with a spatula until well incorporated. Spread the mixture evenly into the prepared baking pan.
4. Slide the baking pan into Rack Position 1, select Convection Bake, set temperature to 350ºF (180ºC), and set time to 21 minutes.
5. When cooking is complete, a toothpick inserted in the center should come out clean.
6. Remove from the oven and place on a wire rack to cool completely. Cut into squares and serve immediately.

517.Famous New York Cheesecake

Servings: 8
Cooking Time: 15 Minutes
Ingredients:
- 1 ½ cups almond flour
- 3 ounces swerve
- 1/2 stick butter, melted
- 20 ounces full-fat cream cheese
- 1/2 cup heavy cream
- 1 ¼ cups granulated swerve
- 3 eggs, at room temperature
- 1 tablespoon vanilla essence
- 1 teaspoon grated lemon zest

Directions:
1. Coat the sides and bottom of a baking pan with a little flour.
2. In a mixing bowl, combine the almond flour and swerve. Add the melted butter and mix until your mixture looks like breadcrumbs.
3. Press the mixture into the bottom of the prepared pan to form an even layer. Bake at 330 degrees F for 7 minutes until golden brown. Allow it to cool completely on a wire rack.
4. Meanwhile, in a mixer fitted with the paddle attachment, prepare the filling by mixing the soft cheese, heavy cream, and granulated swerve; beat until creamy and fluffy.
5. Crack the eggs into the mixing bowl, one at a time; add the vanilla and lemon zest and continue to mix until fully combined.
6. Pour the prepared topping over the cooled crust and spread evenly.
7. Bake in the preheated Air Fryer at 330 degrees F for 25 to 30 minutes; leave it in the Air Fryer to keep warm for another 30 minutes.
8. Cover your cheesecake with plastic wrap. Place in your refrigerator and allow it to cool at least 6 hours or overnight. Serve well chilled.
- **Nutrition Info:** 245 Calories; 22g Fat; 5g Carbs; 8g Protein; 1g Sugars; 5g Fiber

518.Coconut Chip Mixed Berry Crisp

Servings:6

Cooking Time: 20 Minutes
Ingredients:
- 1 tablespoon butter, melted
- 12 ounces (340 g) mixed berries
- $^1/_3$ cup granulated Swerve
- 1 teaspoon pure vanilla extract
- ½ teaspoon ground cinnamon
- ¼ teaspoon ground cloves
- ¼ teaspoon grated nutmeg
- ½ cup coconut chips, for garnish

Directions:
1. Coat the baking pan with melted butter.
2. Put the remaining ingredients except the coconut chips in the prepared baking pan.
3. Slide the baking pan into Rack Position 1, select Convection Bake, set temperature to 330ºF (166ºC), and set time to 20 minutes.
4. When cooking is complete, remove from the oven. Serve garnished with the coconut chips.

519.Peanut Butter Cookies

Servings: 8
Cooking Time: 30 Minutes
Ingredients:
- 1 large egg.
- ⅓ cup granular erythritol.
- 1 cup no-sugar-added smooth peanut butter.
- 1 tsp. vanilla extract.

Directions:
1. Take a large bowl, mix all ingredients until smooth. Continue stirring for 2 additional minutes and the mixture will begin to thicken.
2. Roll the mixture into eight balls and press gently down to flatten into 2-inch round disks.
3. Cut a piece of parchment to fit your air fryer and place it into the basket. Place the cookies onto the parchment, working in batches as necessary.
4. Adjust the temperature to 320 Degrees F and set the timer for 8 minutes.
5. Flip the cookies at the 6-minute mark. Serve completely cooled.
- **Nutrition Info:** Calories: 210; Protein: 8.8g; Fiber: 2.0g; Fat: 17.5g; Carbs: 14.1g

520.Homemade Bbq Chicken Pizza

Servings:1
Cooking Time: 8 Minutes
Ingredients:
- 1 piece naan bread
- ¼ cup Barbecue sauce
- ¼ cup shredded Monterrey Jack cheese
- ¼ cup shredded Mozzarella cheese
- ½ chicken herby sausage, sliced
- 2 tablespoons red onion, thinly sliced
- Chopped cilantro or parsley, for garnish
- Cooking spray

Directions:

1. Spritz the bottom of naan bread with cooking spray, then transfer to the air fryer basket.
2. Brush with the Barbecue sauce. Top with the cheeses, sausage, and finish with the red onion.
3. Put the air fryer basket on the baking pan and slide into Rack Position 2, select Air Fry, set temperature to 400ºF (205ºC), and set time to 8 minutes.
4. When cooking is complete, the cheese should be melted. Remove from the oven. Garnish with the chopped cilantro or parsley before slicing to serve.

521.Currant Cookies

Servings: 6
Cooking Time: 15 Minutes
Ingredients:
- ½ cup currants
- ½ cup swerve
- 2 cups almond flour
- ½ cup ghee; melted
- 1 tsp. vanilla extract
- 2 tsp. baking soda

Directions:
1. Take a bowl and mix all the ingredients and whisk well.
2. Spread this on a baking sheet lined with parchment paper, put the pan in the air fryer and cook at 350°F for 30 minutes
3. Cool down; cut into rectangles and serve.
- **Nutrition Info:** Calories: 172; Fat: 5g; Fiber: 2g; Carbs: 3g; Protein: 5g

522.Air Fryer Cinnamon Rolls

Servings: 8
Cooking Time: 5 Minutes
Ingredients:
- 1 ½ tbsp. cinnamon
- ¾ C. brown sugar
- ¼ C. melted coconut oil
- 1 pound frozen bread dough, thawed
- Glaze:
- ½ tsp. vanilla
- 1 ¼ C. powdered erythritol
- 2 tbsp. softened ghee
- 3   ounces softened cream cheese

Directions:
1. Preparing the Ingredients. Lay out bread dough and roll out into a rectangle. Brush melted ghee over dough and leave a 1-inch border along edges.
2. Mix cinnamon and sweetener together and then sprinkle over the dough.
3. Roll dough tightly and slice into 8 pieces. Let sit 1-2 hours to rise.
4. To make the glaze, simply mix ingredients together till smooth.
5. Air Frying. Once rolls rise, place into the Cuisinart air fryer oven and cook 5 minutes at 350 degrees.

6. Serve rolls drizzled in cream cheese glaze. Enjoy!
- **Nutrition Info:** CALORIES: 390; FAT:8G; PROTEIN:1G; SUGAR:7G

523.Mini Pecan Pies

Servings: 8
Cooking Time: 10 Minutes
Ingredients:
- Nonstick cooking spray
- 1 sheet puff pastry, thawed
- 4 tbsp. brown sugar
- ½ stick butter, melted
- 2 tbsp. maple syrup
- ½ cup pecans, chopped fine

Directions:
1. Place baking pan in position 2. Lightly spray fryer basket with cooking spray.
2. In a plastic bowl, stir together butter, syrup and pecans. Freeze 10 minutes.
3. Unfold pastry on a lightly floured surface. Gently roll it out. Cut in 8 equal triangles.
4. Spoon 2 teaspoons of pecan mixture onto the right side of rectangles, leaving a border. Fold left side over filling and seal edges with a fork. Pierce the tops of each pie.
5. Place half the pies in the fryer basket and put it on the baking pan. Set oven to air fryer on 375°F for 10 minutes. Cook pies 7 minutes or until puffed and golden brown. Repeat with remaining pies. Serve warm.
- **Nutrition Info:** Calories 161, Total Fat 13g, Saturated Fat 4g, Total Carbs 10g, Net Carbs 9g, Protein 1g, Sugar 7g, Fiber 1g, Sodium 62mg, Potassium 48mg, Phosphorus 24mg

524.Vanilla And Oats Pudding

Servings:x
Cooking Time:x
Ingredients:
- 2 tbsp. custard powder
- 3 tbsp. powdered sugar
- 3 tbsp. unsalted butter
- 2 cups vanilla powder
- 2 cups milk
- 1 cup oats

Directions:
1. Boil the milk and the sugar in a pan and add the custard powder followed by the vanilla powder followed by the oats and stir till you get a thick mixture.
2. Preheat the fryer to 300 Fahrenheit for five minutes. Place the dish in the basket and reduce the temperature to 250 Fahrenheit. Cook for ten minutes and set aside to cool.

525.Shrimp Toasts With Sesame Seeds

Servings:4 To 6
Cooking Time: 8 Minutes
Ingredients:
- ½ pound (227 g) raw shrimp, peeled and deveined

- 1 egg, beaten
- 2 scallions, chopped, plus more for garnish
- 2 tablespoons chopped fresh cilantro
- 2 teaspoons grated fresh ginger
- 1 to 2 teaspoons sriracha sauce
- 1 teaspoon soy sauce
- ½ teaspoon toasted sesame oil
- 6 slices thinly sliced white sandwich bread
- ½ cup sesame seeds
- Cooking spray
- Thai chili sauce, for serving

Directions:
1. In a food processor, add the shrimp, egg, scallions, cilantro, ginger, sriracha sauce, soy sauce and sesame oil, and pulse until chopped finely. You'll need to stop the food processor occasionally to scrape down the sides. Transfer the shrimp mixture to a bowl.
2. On a clean work surface, cut the crusts off the sandwich bread. Using a brush, generously brush one side of each slice of bread with shrimp mixture.
3. Place the sesame seeds on a plate. Press bread slices, shrimp-side down, into sesame seeds to coat evenly. Cut each slice diagonally into quarters.
4. Spritz the air fryer basket with cooking spray. Spread the coated slices in a single layer in the basket.
5. Put the air fryer basket on the baking pan and slide into Rack Position 2, select Air Fry, set temperature to 400ºF (205ºC), and set time to 8 minutes.
6. Flip the bread slices halfway through.
7. When cooking is complete, they should be golden and crispy. Remove from the oven to a plate and let cool for 5 minutes. Top with the chopped scallions and serve warm with Thai chili sauce.

526.Breaded Bananas With Chocolate Sauce

Servings:6
Cooking Time: 7 Minutes
Ingredients:
- ¼ cup cornstarch
- ¼ cup plain bread crumbs
- 1 large egg, beaten
- 3 bananas, halved crosswise
- Cooking spray
- Chocolate sauce, for serving

Directions:
1. Place the cornstarch, bread crumbs, and egg in three separate bowls.
2. Roll the bananas in the cornstarch, then in the beaten egg, and finally in the bread crumbs to coat well.
3. Spritz the air fryer basket with cooking spray.
4. Arrange the banana halves in the basket and mist them with cooking spray.

5. Put the air fryer basket on the baking pan and slide into Rack Position 2, select Air Fry, set temperature to 350ºF (180ºC), and set time to 7 minutes.
6. After about 5 minutes, flip the bananas and continue to air fry for another 2 minutes.
7. When cooking is complete, remove the bananas from the oven to a serving plate. Serve with the chocolate sauce drizzled over the top.

527.Muffins And Jam

Servings:x
Cooking Time:x
Ingredients:
- 1 tbsp. unsalted butter
- 2 cups buttermilk
- Parchment paper
- 1 cup + 2 tbsp. powdered sugar
- 1 ½ cups + 2 tbsp. all-purpose flour
- 1 tsp. baking powder
- ½ tsp. baking soda
- 2 tbsp. jam

Directions:
1. In a bowl, add the flour and the buttermilk. Fold the mixture using a spatula. Add the jam and whisk the ingredients to ensure that the jam has thinned. Add the remaining ingredients to the bowl and continue to mix the ingredients. Do not mix too much.
2. Grease the muffin cups and line them with the parchment paper. Transfer the mixture into the cups and set them aside. Preheat the fryer to 300 Fahrenheit for five minutes. Place the muffin cups in the basket and reduce the temperature to 250 Fahrenheit. Cool in the basket and serve warm.

528.Rosemary Russet Potato Chips

Servings: 4
Cooking Time: 1 Hour
Ingredients:
- 4 russet potatoes
- ½ tsp. salt
- 1 tbsp. olive oil
- 2 tsps. chopped rosemary

Directions:
1. Rinse the potatoes and scrub to clean. Peel and cut them in a lengthwise manner similar to thin chips.
2. Put them in a bowl and soak in water for 30 minutes.
3. Pat the potato chips with paper towels to dry.
4. Toss the chips in a bowl with olive oil. Transfer them to the cooking basket.
5. Cook for 30 minutes at 330 ºF. Shake several times during the cooking process.
6. Toss the cooked chips in a bowl with salt and rosemary while warm.
- **Nutrition Info:** Calories: 322 Fat: 3.69g Carbs: 66g Protein: 7.5g

529.Creamy Chicken Dip

Servings: 6
Cooking Time: 20 Minutes
Ingredients:
- 2 cups chicken, cooked and shredded
- 8 oz cream cheese, softened
- 3 tbsp hot sauce
- 1/4 tsp garlic powder
- 3/4 cup sour cream
- 1/4 tsp onion powder

Directions:
1. Fit the Cuisinart oven with the rack in position 2.
2. Add all ingredients in a large bowl and mix until well combined.
3. Transfer mixture in air fryer baking dish.
4. Set to bake at 325 F for 25 minutes. After 5 minutes place the baking dish in the preheated oven.
5. Serve and enjoy.
- **Nutrition Info:** Calories 265 Fat 20.7 g Carbohydrates 2.5 g Sugar 0.3 g Protein 17.4 g Cholesterol 90 mg

530.Easy Sweet Potato Fries

Servings: 2
Cooking Time: 16 Minutes
Ingredients:
- 2 sweet potatoes, peeled and cut into fries shape
- 1 tbsp olive oil
- Salt

Directions:
1. Fit the Cuisinart oven with the rack in position 2.
2. Toss sweet potato fries with oil and salt and place in the air fryer basket then place the air fryer basket in the baking pan.
3. Place a baking pan on the oven rack. Set to air fry at 375 F for 16 minutes.
4. Serve and enjoy.
- **Nutrition Info:** Calories 178 Fat 7.2 g Carbohydrates 27.9 g Sugar 0.5 g Protein 1.5 g Cholesterol 0 mg

531.Apricot Crumble With Blackberries

Servings:4
Cooking Time: 30 Minutes
Ingredients:
- 2 ½ cups fresh apricots, de-stoned and cubed
- 1 cup fresh blackberries
- ½ cup sugar
- 2 tbsp lemon Juice
- 1 cup flour
- 5 tbsp butter

Directions:
1. Preheat Breville on Bake function to 360 F. Add the apricot cubes to a bowl and mix with lemon juice, 2 tbsp sugar, and blackberries. Scoop the mixture into a greased dish and spread it evenly.
2. In another bowl, mix flour and remaining sugar. Add 1 tbsp of cold water and butter and keep mixing until you have a crumbly mixture. Pour over the fruit mixture and cook for 20 minutes.

532.Mushroom And Spinach calzones

Servings:4
Cooking Time: 26 To 27 Minutes
Ingredients:
- 2 tablespoons olive oil
- 1 onion, chopped
- 2 garlic cloves, minced
- ¼ cup chopped mushrooms
- 1 pound (454 g) spinach, chopped
- 1 tablespoon Italian seasoning
- ½ teaspoon oregano
- Salt and black pepper, to taste
- 1½ cups marinara sauce
- 1 cup ricotta cheese, crumbled
- 1 (13-ounce / 369-g) pizza crust
- Cooking spray

Directions:
1. Make the Filling:
2. Heat the olive oil in a pan over medium heat until shimmering.
3. Add the onion, garlic, and mushrooms and sauté for 4 minutes, or until softened.
4. Stir in the spinach and sauté for 2 to 3 minutes, or until the spinach is wilted. Sprinkle with the Italian seasoning, oregano, salt, and pepper and mix well.
5. Add the marinara sauce and cook for about 5 minutes, stirring occasionally, or until the sauce is thickened.
6. Remove the pan from the heat and stir in the ricotta cheese. Set aside.
7. Make the Calzones:
8. Spritz the air fryer basket with cooking spray. Set aside.
9. Roll the pizza crust out with a rolling pin on a lightly floured work surface, then cut it into 4 rectangles.
10. Spoon ¼ of the filling into each rectangle and fold in half. Crimp the edges with a fork to seal. Mist them with cooking spray. Transfer the calzones to the basket.
11. Put the air fryer basket on the baking pan and slide into Rack Position 2, select Air Fry, set temperature to 375ºF (190ºC), and set time to 15 minutes.
12. Flip the calzones halfway through the cooking time.
13. When cooking is complete, the calzones should be golden brown and crisp. Transfer the calzones to a paper towel-lined plate and serve.

533.Plum Cream(1)

Servings: 4
Cooking Time: 20 Minutes
Ingredients:
- 1-pound plums, pitted and chopped

- ¼ cup swerve
- 1 tablespoon lemon juice
- 1 and ½ cups heavy cream

Directions:
1. In a bowl, mix all the ingredients and whisk really well.
2. Divide this into 4 ramekins, put them in the air fryer and cook at 340 degrees F for 20 minutes.
3. Serve cold.
- **Nutrition Info:** calories 171, fat 4, fiber 2, carbs 4, protein 4

534.Pancetta And Asparagus With Fried Egg

Servings:x
Cooking Time:x
Ingredients:
- ½ lb. asparagus, tough ends broken off
- Salt and pepper, to taste
- 2 eggs
- 1 Tbsp olive oil
- ¼ pound pancetta
- 3 small shallots, sliced thin

Directions:
1. Heat olive oil in Breville smart oven.
2. Fry the pancetta, stirring frequently. Transfer to a plate.
3. Add shallots and cook for 2 minutes.
4. Add asparagus pieces and saute for several minutes.
5. Sprinkle with salt and pepper and continue to watch closely that asparagus is browned and cooked through.
6. Add pancetta back to the pan and stir together. Transfer to a plate.
7. Add a little oil if necessary and fry an egg in pan.
8. Top asparagus pancetta mixture with fried egg and season with salt and pepper.

535.Air Fried Apple Pie

Servings: 6
Cooking Time: 30 Minutes
Ingredients:
- 1 large apple, chopped
- 2 teaspoons of lemon juice
- 1 tablespoon of ground cinnamon
- 1 pie crust, refrigerated
- Baking spray
- ½ teaspoon of vanilla extract
- 1 tablespoon of butter
- 1 beaten egg
- 1 tablespoon of raw sugar
- 2 tablespoons of sugar

Directions:
1. Set the Instant Vortex on Air fryer to 350 degrees F for 30 minutes. Split the pie crust into two halves and spread into 8-inch greased pan. Combine apple with sugar, cinnamon, lemon juice, and vanilla extract in a bowl. Empty the apple mixture into the

pie crust and cover with the pie crust half. Seal the edges and brush the whisked egg on the top. Sprinkle the pie with raw sugar and place on the cooking tray. Insert the cooking tray in the Vortex when it displays "Add Food". Flip the sides when it displays "Turn Food". Remove from the oven when cooking time is complete. Serve warm.
- **Nutrition Info:** Calories: 368 Cal Total Fat: 6 g Saturated Fat: 0 g Cholesterol: 0 mg Sodium: 0 mg Total Carbs: 72.8 g Fiber: 0 g Sugar: 0 g Protein: 7.2 g

536.Cranberry Scones

Servings: 4
Cooking Time: 10 Minutes
Ingredients:
- 1 cup of fresh cranberries
- ⅓ Cup of sugar
- 1 tablespoon of orange zest
- ¾ cup of half and half cream
- 2 cups of flour
- ¼ teaspoon of ground nutmeg
- ¼ teaspoon of salt
- ¼ cup of butter, chilled and diced
- ¼ cup of brown sugar
- 1 tablespoon of baking powder
- 1 egg

Directions:
1. Set the Instant Vortex on Air fryer to 365 degrees F for 10 minutes. Strain nutmeg, flour, baking powder, salt, and sugar in a bowl. Blend in the cream and egg. Fold in the orange zest and cranberries to form a smooth dough. Roll the dough and cut into scones. Place the scones on the cooking tray. Insert the cooking tray in the Vortex when it displays "Add Food". Flip the sides when it displays "Turn Food". Remove from the oven when cooking time is complete. Serve warm.
- **Nutrition Info:** Calories: 219 Cal Total Fat: 19.7 g Saturated Fat: 0 g Cholesterol: 0 mg Sodium: 0 mg Total Carbs: 23.7 g Fiber: 0 g Sugar: 0 g Protein: 5.2 g

537.Coconut Pumpkin Bars

Servings: 16
Cooking Time: 28 Minutes
Ingredients:
- 2 eggs
- 1/4 cup coconut flour
- 8 oz pumpkin puree
- 1/2 cup coconut oil, melted
- 1/3 cup Swerve
- 1 1/2 tsp pumpkin pie spice
- 1/2 tsp baking soda
- 1 tsp baking powder
- Pinch of salt

Directions:
1. Fit the Cuisinart oven with the rack in position

2. In a bowl, beat eggs, sweetener, coconut oil, pumpkin pie spice, and pumpkin puree until well combined.
3. In another bowl, mix together baking powder, coconut flour, salt, and baking soda.
4. Add coconut flour mixture to the egg mixture and mix well.
5. Pour the bar mixture into the prepared baking pan and spread evenly.
6. Set to bake at 350 F for 33 minutes. After 5 minutes place the baking dish in the preheated oven.
7. Slice and serve.
- **Nutrition Info:** Calories 73 Fat 7.5 g Carbohydrates 1.6 g Sugar 0.5 g Protein 0.9 g Cholesterol 20 mg

538.Cinnamon Candied Apples

Servings:4
Cooking Time: 12 Minutes
Ingredients:
- 1 cup packed light brown sugar
- 2 teaspoons ground cinnamon
- 2 medium Granny Smith apples, peeled and diced

Directions:
1. Thoroughly combine the brown sugar and cinnamon in a medium bowl.
2. Add the apples to the bowl and stir until well coated. Transfer the apples to the baking pan.
3. Slide the baking pan into Rack Position 1, select Convection Bake, set temperature to 350ºF (180ºC), and set time to 12 minutes.
4. After about 9 minutes, stir the apples and bake for an additional 3 minutes. When cooking is complete, the apples should be softened.
5. Serve warm.

539.Banana S'mores

Servings: 4
Cooking Time: 4 Minutes
Ingredients:
- 4 bananas
- 3 tablespoons of mini semi-sweet chocolate chips
- 3 tablespoons of mini marshmallows
- 3 tablespoons of graham cracker cereal
- Aluminum foil
- Cooking oil spray

Directions:
1. Set the Instant Vortex on Air fryer to 350 degrees F for 4 minutes. Place the bananas on the aluminum foil sheet greased with cooking oil spray. Tear open the banana from one side to form a pocket. Top with the chocolate chips, marshmallows, and graham cracker cereal. Cover completely with foil and place on the cooking tray. Insert the cooking tray in the Vortex when it displays "Add Food". Remove from the oven when cooking time is complete. Serve warm.

- **Nutrition Info:** Calories: 249 Cal Total Fat: 11.9 g Saturated Fat: 0 g Cholesterol: 0 mg Sodium: 0 mg Total Carbs: 14.8 g Fiber: 0 g Sugar: 0 g Protein: 5 g

540.Currant Pudding

Servings: 6
Cooking Time: 15 Minutes
Ingredients:
- 1 cup red currants, blended
- 1 cup coconut cream
- 1 cup black currants, blended
- 3 tbsp. stevia

Directions:
1. In a bowl, combine all the ingredients and stir well.
2. Divide into ramekins, put them in the fryer and cook at 340°F for 20 minutes
3. Serve the pudding cold.
- **Nutrition Info:** Calories: 200; Fat: 4g; Fiber: 2g; Carbs: 4g; Protein: 6g

541.Apple Hand Pies

Servings: 6
Cooking Time: 8 Minutes
Ingredients:
- 15-ounces no-sugar-added apple pie filling
- 1 store-bought crust

Directions:
1. Preparing the Ingredients. Lay out pie crust and slice into equal-sized squares.
2. Place 2 tbsp. filling into each square and seal crust with a fork.
3. Air Frying. Place into the Cuisinart air fryer oven. Cook 8 minutes at 390 degrees until golden in color.
- **Nutrition Info:** CALORIES: 278; FAT:10G; PROTEIN:5G; SUGAR:4G

542.Vegetables Balls

Servings: 6
Cooking Time: 10 Minutes
Ingredients:
- 2 cups cauliflower florets
- 1 tsp paprika
- 1 tsp chives
- 2 tsp garlic
- 1 medium Parsnip
- 1 medium carrot
- 1 cup breadcrumbs
- 1/2 cup desiccated coconut
- 2 tsp oregano
- 1 tsp mixed spice
- 1/2 cup sweet potato
- Pepper
- Salt

Directions:
1. Fit the Cuisinart oven with the rack in position
2. Add all vegetables into the food processor and process until resemble breadcrumbs.

3. Add process vegetables into the mixing bowl.
4. Add all remaining ingredients into the bowl and mix well until combine.
5. Make small balls from the mixture and place in the air fryer basket then place an air fryer basket in the baking pan.
6. Place a baking pan on the oven rack. Set to air fry at 400 F for 10 minutes.
7. Serve and enjoy.
- **Nutrition Info:** Calories 131 Fat 2.7 g Carbohydrates 23.6 g Sugar 4.5 g Protein 4 g Cholesterol 0 mg

543.Orange Almond Muffins

Servings: 12
Cooking Time: 20 Minutes
Ingredients:
- 4 eggs
- 1 tsp baking soda
- 1 orange zest
- 1 orange juice
- 1/2 cup butter, melted
- 3 cups almond flour

Directions:
1. Fit the Cuisinart oven with the rack in position
2. Line 12-cups muffin tin with cupcake liners and set aside.
3. Add all ingredients into the large bowl and mix until well combined.
4. Pour mixture into the prepared muffin tin.
5. Set to bake at 350 F for 25 minutes. After 5 minutes place muffin tin in the preheated oven.

6. Serve and enjoy.
- **Nutrition Info:** Calories 273 Fat 24 g Carbohydrates 6 g Sugar 1 g Protein 2 g Cholesterol 75 mg

544.Effortless Apple Pie

Servings: 4
Cooking Time: 30 Minutes
Ingredients:
- 4 apples, diced
- 2 oz butter, melted
- 2 oz sugar
- 1 oz brown sugar
- 2 tsp cinnamon
- 1 egg, beaten
- 3 large puff pastry sheets
- ¼ tsp salt

Directions:
1. Whisk white sugar, brown sugar, cinnamon, salt, and butter together. Place the apples in a greased baking pan and coat them with the sugar mixture. Place the baking dish in your Cuisinart and cook for 10 minutes at 350 F on Bake function.
2. Meanwhile, roll out the pastry on a floured flat surface, and cut each sheet into 6 equal pieces. Divide the apple filling between the pieces. Brush the edges of the pastry squares with the egg.
3. Fold them and seal the edges with a fork. Place on a lined baking sheet and cook in the fryer at 350 F for 8 minutes. Flip over, increase the temperature to 390 F, and cook for 2 more minutes.

OTHER FAVORITE RECIPES

545.Sumptuous Beef And Bean Chili Casserole

Servings:4
Cooking Time: 31 Minutes
Ingredients:
- 1 tablespoon olive oil
- ½ cup finely chopped bell pepper
- ½ cup chopped celery
- 1 onion, chopped
- 2 garlic cloves, minced
- 1 pound (454 g) ground beef
- 1 can diced tomatoes
- ½ teaspoon parsley
- ½ tablespoon chili powder
- 1 teaspoon chopped cilantro
- 1½ cups vegetable broth
- 1 (8-ounce / 227-g) can cannellini beans
- Salt and ground black pepper, to taste

Directions:
1. Heat the olive oil in a nonstick skillet over medium heat until shimmering.
2. Add the bell pepper, celery, onion, and garlic to the skillet and sauté for 5 minutes or until the onion is translucent.
3. Add the ground beef and sauté for an additional 6 minutes or until lightly browned.
4. Mix in the tomatoes, parsley, chili powder, cilantro and vegetable broth, then cook for 10 more minutes. Stir constantly.
5. Pour them in the baking pan, then mix in the beans and sprinkle with salt and ground black pepper.
6. Slide the baking pan into Rack Position 1, select Convection Bake, set temperature to 350ºF (180ºC) and set time to 10 minutes.
7. When cooking is complete, the vegetables should be tender and the beef should be well browned.
8. Remove from the oven and serve immediately.

546.Taco Beef And Chile Casserole

Servings:4
Cooking Time: 15 Minutes
Ingredients:
- 1 pound (454 g) 85% lean ground beef
- 1 tablespoon taco seasoning
- 1 (7-ounce / 198-g) can diced mild green chiles
- ½ cup milk
- 2 large eggs
- 1 cup shredded Mexican cheese blend
- 2 tablespoons all-purpose flour
- ½ teaspoon kosher salt
- Cooking spray

Directions:
1. Spritz the baking pan with cooking spray.
2. Toss the ground beef with taco seasoning in a large bowl to mix well. Pour the seasoned ground beef in the prepared baking pan.
3. Combing the remaining ingredients in a medium bowl. Whisk to mix well, then pour the mixture over the ground beef.
4. Slide the baking pan into Rack Position 1, select Convection Bake, set temperature to 350ºF (180ºC) and set time to 15 minutes.
5. When cooking is complete, a toothpick inserted in the center should come out clean.
6. Remove the casserole from the oven and allow to cool for 5 minutes, then slice to serve.

547.Burgundy Beef And Mushroom Casserole

Servings:4
Cooking Time: 25 Minutes
Ingredients:
- 1½ pounds (680 g) beef steak
- 1 ounce (28 g) dry onion soup mix
- 2 cups sliced mushrooms
- 1 (14.5-ounce / 411-g) can cream of mushroom soup
- ½ cup beef broth
- ¼ cup red wine
- 3 garlic cloves, minced
- 1 whole onion, chopped

Directions:
1. Put the beef steak in a large bowl, then sprinkle with dry onion soup mix. Toss to coat well.
2. Combine the mushrooms with mushroom soup, beef broth, red wine, garlic, and onion in a large bowl. Stir to mix well.
3. Transfer the beef steak in the baking pan, then pour in the mushroom mixture.
4. Slide the baking pan into Rack Position 1, select Convection Bake, set temperature to 360ºF (182ºC) and set time to 25 minutes.
5. When cooking is complete, the mushrooms should be soft and the beef should be well browned.
6. Remove from the oven and serve immediately.

548.Potato Chips With Lemony Cream Dip

Servings:2 To 4
Cooking Time: 15 Minutes
Ingredients:
- 2 large russet potatoes, sliced into ⅛-inch slices, rinsed
- Sea salt and freshly ground black pepper, to taste
- Cooking spray
- Lemony Cream Dip:
- ½ cup sour cream
- ¼ teaspoon lemon juice
- 2 scallions, white part only, minced

- 1 tablespoon olive oil
- ¼ teaspoon salt
- Freshly ground black pepper, to taste

Directions:
1. Soak the potato slices in water for 10 minutes, then pat dry with paper towels.
2. Transfer the potato slices in the air fryer basket. Spritz the slices with cooking spray.
3. Put the air fryer basket on the baking pan and slide into Rack Position 2, select Air Fry, set temperature to 300ºF (150ºC) and set time to 15 minutes.
4. Stir the potato slices three times during cooking. Sprinkle with salt and ground black pepper in the last minute.
5. Meanwhile, combine the ingredients for the dip in a small bowl. Stir to mix well.
6. When cooking is complete, the potato slices will be crispy and golden brown. Remove from the oven and serve the potato chips immediately with the dip.

549.Dehydrated Crackers With Oats

Servings:x
Cooking Time:x
Ingredients:
- 3 tablespoons (20g) psyllium husk powder
- 2 teaspoons fine sea salt
- 1 teaspoon freshly ground black pepper
- 2 teaspoons ground turmeric, divided
- 3 tablespoons melted coconut oil
- 1 cup (125g) sunflower seeds
- ½ cup (75g) flaxseeds
- ¾ cup (50g) pumpkin seeds
- ¼ cup (35g) sesame seeds
- 2 tablespoons (30g) chia seeds
- 1½ cups (150g) rolled oats
- 1½ cups (360ml) water
- 1 large parsnip (10 ounces/300g), finely Grated

Directions:
1. In a large bowl Blend All of the seeds, Oats, psyllium husk, pepper, salt and 1 teaspoon ground turmeric.
2. Whisk coconut water and oil together in a measuring Cup. Add to the dry ingredients and blend well until all is totally saturated and dough becomes very thick.
3. Mix grated parsnip using 1 tsp turmeric and stir to blend.
4. Shape the first half to a disc and place it with a rolling pin, firmly roll dough to a thin sheet that the size of this dehydrate basket.
5. Put dough and parchment paper at the dehydrate basket.
6. Repeat steps 4 with remaining dough.
7. Hours and allow Rotate Remind. Place dehydrate baskets in rack positions 5 and 3. Press START.
8. Dehydrate crackers until tender. When prompted By Rotate Remind, rotate the baskets leading to back and change rack amounts.
9. Eliminate baskets out of oven and let rest for 10 minutes. Split crackers into shards.
10. Container for up to two months.

550.Easy Corn And Bell Pepper Casserole

Servings:4
Cooking Time: 20 Minutes
Ingredients:
- 1 cup corn kernels
- ¼ cup bell pepper, finely chopped
- ½ cup low-fat milk
- 1 large egg, beaten
- ½ cup yellow cornmeal
- ½ cup all-purpose flour
- ½ teaspoon baking powder
- 2 tablespoons melted unsalted butter
- 1 tablespoon granulated sugar
- Pinch of cayenne pepper
- ¼ teaspoon kosher salt
- Cooking spray

Directions:
1. Spritz the baking pan with cooking spray.
2. Combine all the ingredients in a large bowl. Stir to mix well. Pour the mixture into the baking pan.
3. Slide the baking pan into Rack Position 1, select Convection Bake, set temperature to 330ºF (166ºC) and set time to 20 minutes.
4. When cooking is complete, the casserole should be lightly browned and set.
5. Remove from the oven and serve immediately.

551.Crunchy And Beery Onion Rings

Servings:2 To 4
Cooking Time: 16 Minutes
Ingredients:
- ²/₃ cup all-purpose flour
- 1 teaspoon paprika
- ½ teaspoon baking soda
- 1 teaspoon salt
- ½ teaspoon freshly ground black pepper
- 1 egg, beaten
- ¾ cup beer
- 1½ cups bread crumbs
- 1 tablespoons olive oil
- 1 large Vidalia onion, peeled and sliced into ½-inch rings
- Cooking spray

Directions:
1. Spritz the air fryer basket with cooking spray.
2. Combine the flour, paprika, baking soda, salt, and ground black pepper in a bowl. Stir to mix well.
3. Combine the egg and beer in a separate bowl. Stir to mix well.
4. Make a well in the center of the flour mixture, then pour the egg mixture in the well. Stir to mix everything well.
5. Pour the bread crumbs and olive oil in a shallow plate. Stir to mix well.

6. Dredge the onion rings gently into the flour and egg mixture, then shake the excess off and put into the plate of bread crumbs. Flip to coat the both sides well. Arrange the onion rings in the basket.
7. Put the air fryer basket on the baking pan and slide into Rack Position 2, select Air Fry, set temperature to 360ºF (182ºC) and set time to 16 minutes.
8. Flip the rings and put the bottom rings to the top halfway through.
9. When cooked, the rings will be golden brown and crunchy. Remove from the oven and serve immediately.

552.Golden Nuggets

Servings: 20 Nuggets
Cooking Time: 4 Minutes
Ingredients:
- 1 cup all-purpose flour, plus more for dusting
- 1 teaspoon baking powder
- ½ teaspoon butter, at room temperature, plus more for brushing
- ¼ teaspoon salt
- ¼ cup water
- ⅛ teaspoon onion powder
- ¼ teaspoon garlic powder
- ⅛ teaspoon seasoning salt
- Cooking spray

Directions:
1. Line the air fryer basket with parchment paper.
2. Mix the flour, baking powder, butter, and salt in a large bowl. Stir to mix well. Gradually whisk in the water until a sanity dough forms.
3. Put the dough on a lightly floured work surface, then roll it out into a ½-inch thick rectangle with a rolling pin.
4. Cut the dough into about twenty 1- or 2-inch squares, then arrange the squares in a single layer in the basket. Spritz with cooking spray.
5. Combine onion powder, garlic powder, and seasoning salt in a small bowl. Stir to mix well, then sprinkle the squares with the powder mixture.
6. Put the air fryer basket on the baking pan and slide into Rack Position 2, select Air Fry, set temperature to 370ºF (188ºC) and set time to 4 minutes.
7. Flip the squares halfway through the cooking time.
8. When cooked, the dough squares should be golden brown.
9. Remove the golden nuggets from the oven and brush with more butter immediately. Serve warm.

553.Cinnamon Rolls With Cream Glaze

Servings:8
Cooking Time: 5 Minutes

Ingredients:
- 1 pound (454 g) frozen bread dough, thawed
- 2 tablespoons melted butter
- 1½ tablespoons cinnamon
- ¾ cup brown sugar
- Cooking spray
- Cream Glaze:
- 4 ounces (113 g) softened cream cheese
- ½ teaspoon vanilla extract
- 2 tablespoons melted butter
- 1¼ cups powdered erythritol

Directions:
1. Place the bread dough on a clean work surface, then roll the dough out into a rectangle with a rolling pin.
2. Brush the top of the dough with melted butter and leave 1-inch edges uncovered.
3. Combine the cinnamon and sugar in a small bowl, then sprinkle the dough with the cinnamon mixture.
4. Roll the dough over tightly, then cut the dough log into 8 portions. Wrap the portions in plastic, better separately, and let sit to rise for 1 or 2 hours.
5. Meanwhile, combine the ingredients for the glaze in a separate small bowl. Stir to mix well.
6. Spritz the air fryer basket with cooking spray. Transfer the risen rolls to the basket.
7. Put the air fryer basket on the baking pan and slide into Rack Position 2, select Air Fry, set temperature to 350ºF (180ºC) and set time to 5 minutes.
8. Flip the rolls halfway through the cooking time.
9. When cooking is complete, the rolls will be golden brown.
10. Serve the rolls with the glaze.

554.Oven Baked Rice

Servings: About 4 Cups
Cooking Time: 35 Minutes
Ingredients:
- 1 cup long-grain white rice, rinsed and drained
- 1 tablespoon unsalted butter, melted, or 1 tablespoon extra-virgin olive oil
- 2 cups water
- 1 teaspoon kosher salt or ½ teaspoon fine salt

Directions:
1. Add the butter and rice to the baking pan and stir to coat. Pour in the water and sprinkle with the salt. Stir until the salt is dissolved.
2. Select Bake, set the temperature to 325ºF (163ºC), and set the time for 35 minutes. Select Start to begin preheating.
3. Once the unit has preheated, place the pan in the oven.
4. After 20 minutes, remove the pan from the oven. Stir the rice. Transfer the pan back to

the oven and continue cooking for 10 to 15 minutes, or until the rice is mostly cooked through and the water is absorbed.

5. When done, remove the pan from the oven and cover with aluminum foil. Let stand for 10 minutes. Using a fork, gently fluff the rice.
6. Serve immediately.

555.Butternut Squash With Hazelnuts

Servings: 3 Cups
Cooking Time: 23 Minutes
Ingredients:
- 2 tablespoons whole hazelnuts
- 3 cups butternut squash, peeled, deseeded and cubed
- ¼ teaspoon kosher salt
- ¼ teaspoon freshly ground black pepper
- 2 teaspoons olive oil
- Cooking spray

Directions:
1. Spritz the air fryer basket with cooking spray. Spread the hazelnuts in the pan.
2. Put the air fryer basket on the baking pan and slide into Rack Position 2, select Air Fry, set temperature to 300ºF (150ºC) and set time to 3 minutes.
3. When done, the hazelnuts should be soft. Remove from the oven. Chopped the hazelnuts roughly and transfer to a small bowl. Set aside.
4. Put the butternut squash in a large bowl, then sprinkle with salt and pepper and drizzle with olive oil. Toss to coat well. Transfer the squash to the lightly greased basket.
5. Put the air fryer basket on the baking pan and slide into Rack Position 2, select Air Fry, set temperature to 360ºF (182ºC) and set time to 20 minutes.
6. Flip the squash halfway through the cooking time.
7. When cooking is complete, the squash will be soft. Transfer the squash to a plate and sprinkle with the chopped hazelnuts before serving.

556.Hot Wings

Servings: 16 Wings
Cooking Time: 15 Minutes
Ingredients:
- 16 chicken wings
- 3 tablespoons hot sauce
- Cooking spray

Directions:
1. Spritz the air fryer basket with cooking spray.
2. Arrange the chicken wings in the basket.
3. Put the air fryer basket on the baking pan and slide into Rack Position 2, select Air Fry, set temperature to 360ºF (182ºC) and set time to 15 minutes.
4. Flip the wings at lease three times during cooking.

5. When cooking is complete, the chicken wings will be well browned. Remove from the oven.
6. Transfer the air fried wings to a plate and serve with hot sauce.

557.Creamy Pork Gratin

Servings:4
Cooking Time: 21 Minutes
Ingredients:
- 2 tablespoons olive oil
- 2 pounds (907 g) pork tenderloin, cut into serving-size pieces
- 1 teaspoon dried marjoram
- ¼ teaspoon chili powder
- 1 teaspoon coarse sea salt
- ½ teaspoon freshly ground black pepper
- 1 cup Ricotta cheese
- 1½ cups chicken broth
- 1 tablespoon mustard
- Cooking spray

Directions:
1. Spritz the baking pan with cooking spray.
2. Heat the olive oil in a nonstick skillet over medium-high heat until shimmering.
3. Add the pork and sauté for 6 minutes or until lightly browned.
4. Transfer the pork to the prepared baking pan and sprinkle with marjoram, chili powder, salt, and ground black pepper.
5. Combine the remaining ingredients in a large bowl. Stir to mix well. Pour the mixture over the pork in the pan.
6. Slide the baking pan into Rack Position 1, select Convection Bake, set temperature to 350ºF (180ºC) and set time to 15 minutes.
7. Stir the mixture halfway through.
8. When cooking is complete, the mixture should be frothy and the cheese should be melted.
9. Serve immediately.

558.Caesar Salad Dressing

Servings: About $^2/_3$ Cup
Cooking Time: 0 Minutes
Ingredients:
- ½ cup extra-virgin olive oil
- 2 tablespoons freshly squeezed lemon juice
- 1 teaspoon anchovy paste
- ¼ teaspoon kosher salt or ⅛ teaspoon fine salt
- ¼ teaspoon minced or pressed garlic
- 1 egg, beaten
- Add all the ingredients to a tall, narrow container.

Directions:
1. Purée the mixture with an immersion blender until smooth.
2. Use immediately.

559.Enchilada Sauce

Servings: 2 Cups

Cooking Time: 0 Minutes
Ingredients:
- 3 large ancho chiles, stems and seeds removed, torn into pieces
- 1½ cups very hot water
- 2 garlic cloves, peeled and lightly smashed
- 2 tablespoons wine vinegar
- 1½ teaspoons sugar
- ½ teaspoon dried oregano
- ½ teaspoon ground cumin
- 2 teaspoons kosher salt or 1 teaspoon fine salt

Directions:
1. Mix together the chile pieces and hot water in a bowl and let stand for 10 to 15 minutes.
2. Pour the chiles and water into a blender jar. Fold in the garlic, vinegar, sugar, oregano, cumin, and salt and blend until smooth.
3. Use immediately.

560. Crunchy Green Tomatoes Slices

Servings: 12 Slices
Cooking Time: 8 Minutes
Ingredients:
- ½ cup all-purpose flour
- 1 egg
- ½ cup buttermilk
- 1 cup cornmeal
- 1 cup panko
- 2 green tomatoes, cut into ¼-inch-thick slices, patted dry
- ½ teaspoon salt
- ½ teaspoon ground black pepper
- Cooking spray

Directions:
1. Spritz a baking sheet with cooking spray.
2. Pour the flour in a bowl. Whisk the egg and buttermilk in a second bowl. Combine the cornmeal and panko in a third bowl.
3. Dredge the tomato slices in the bowl of flour first, then into the egg mixture, and then dunk the slices into the cornmeal mixture. Shake the excess off.
4. Transfer the well-coated tomato slices in the baking sheet and sprinkle with salt and ground black pepper. Spritz the tomato slices with cooking spray.
5. Put the air fryer basket on the baking pan and slide into Rack Position 2, select Air Fry, set temperature to 400ºF (205ºC) and set time to 8 minutes.
6. Flip the slices halfway through the cooking time.
7. When cooking is complete, the tomato slices should be crispy and lightly browned. Remove the baking sheet from the oven.
8. Serve immediately.

561. Buttery Knots With Parsley

Servings: 8 Knots
Cooking Time: 5 Minutes
Ingredients:
- 1 teaspoon dried parsley
- ¼ cup melted butter
- 2 teaspoons garlic powder

Directions:
1. 1 (11-ounce / 312-g) tube refrigerated French bread dough, cut into 8 slices
2. Combine the parsley, butter, and garlic powder in a bowl. Stir to mix well.
3. Place the French bread dough slices on a clean work surface, then roll each slice into a 6-inch long rope. Tie the ropes into knots and arrange them on a plate.
4. Transfer the knots into the baking pan. Brush the knots with butter mixture.
5. Put the air fryer basket on the baking pan and slide into Rack Position 2, select Air Fry, set temperature to 350ºF (180ºC) and set time to 5 minutes.
6. Flip the knots halfway through the cooking time.
7. When done, the knots should be golden brown. Remove from the oven and serve immediately.

562. Pastrami Casserole

Servings: 2
Cooking Time: 8 Minutes
Ingredients:
- 1 cup pastrami, sliced
- 1 bell pepper, chopped
- ¼ cup Greek yogurt
- 2 spring onions, chopped
- ½ cup Cheddar cheese, grated
- 4 eggs
- ¼ teaspoon ground black pepper
- Sea salt, to taste
- Cooking spray

Directions:
1. Spritz the baking pan with cooking spray.
2. Whisk together all the ingredients in a large bowl. Stir to mix well. Pour the mixture into the baking pan.
3. Slide the baking pan into Rack Position 1, select Convection Bake, set temperature to 330ºF (166ºC) and set time to 8 minutes.
4. When cooking is complete, the eggs should be set and the casserole edges should be lightly browned.
5. Remove from the oven and allow to cool for 10 minutes before serving.

563. Keto Cheese Quiche

Servings: 8
Cooking Time: 1 Hour
Ingredients:
- Crust:
- 1¼ cups blanched almond flour
- 1 large egg, beaten
- 1¼ cups grated Parmesan cheese
- ¼ teaspoon fine sea salt
- Filling:
- 4 ounces (113 g) cream cheese

- 1 cup shredded Swiss cheese
- $^1/_3$ cup minced leeks
- 4 large eggs, beaten
- ½ cup chicken broth
- ⅛ teaspoon cayenne pepper
- ¾ teaspoon fine sea salt
- 1 tablespoon unsalted butter, melted
- Chopped green onions, for garnish
- Cooking spray

Directions:
1. Spritz the baking pan with cooking spray.
2. Combine the flour, egg, Parmesan, and salt in a large bowl. Stir to mix until a satiny and firm dough forms.
3. Arrange the dough between two grease parchment papers, then roll the dough into a $^1/_{16}$-inch thick circle.
4. Make the crust: Transfer the dough into the prepared pan and press to coat the bottom.
5. Slide the baking pan into Rack Position 1, select Convection Bake, set temperature to 325ºF (163ºC) and set time to 12 minutes.
6. When cooking is complete, the edges of the crust should be lightly browned.
7. Meanwhile, combine the ingredient for the filling, except for the green onions in a large bowl.
8. Pour the filling over the cooked crust and cover the edges of the crust with aluminum foil.
9. Slide the baking pan into Rack Position 1, select Convection Bake, set time to 15 minutes.
10. When cooking is complete, reduce the heat to 300ºF (150ºC) and set time to 30 minutes.
11. When cooking is complete, a toothpick inserted in the center should come out clean.
12. Remove from the oven and allow to cool for 10 minutes before serving.

564.Air Fried Blistered Tomatoes

Servings:4 To 6
Cooking Time: 10 Minutes
Ingredients:
- 2 pounds (907 g) cherry tomatoes
- 2 tablespoons olive oil
- 2 teaspoons balsamic vinegar
- ½ teaspoon salt
- ½ teaspoon ground black pepper

Directions:
1. Toss the cherry tomatoes with olive oil in a large bowl to coat well. Pour the tomatoes in the baking pan.
2. Put the air fryer basket on the baking pan and slide into Rack Position 2, select Air Fry, set temperature to 400ºF (205ºC) and set time to 10 minutes.
3. Stir the tomatoes halfway through the cooking time.
4. When cooking is complete, the tomatoes will be blistered and lightly wilted.

5. Transfer the blistered tomatoes to a large bowl and toss with balsamic vinegar, salt, and black pepper before serving.

565.Sweet Cinnamon Chickpeas

Servings:2
Cooking Time: 10 Minutes
Ingredients:
- 1 tablespoon cinnamon
- 1 tablespoon sugar
- 1 cup chickpeas, soaked in water overnight, rinsed and drained

Directions:
1. Combine the cinnamon and sugar in a bowl. Stir to mix well.
2. Add the chickpeas to the bowl, then toss to coat well.
3. Pour the chickpeas in the air fryer basket.
4. Put the air fryer basket on the baking pan and slide into Rack Position 2, select Air Fry, set temperature to 390ºF (199ºC) and set time to 10 minutes.
5. Stir the chickpeas three times during cooking.
6. When cooked, the chickpeas should be golden brown and crispy. Remove from the oven and serve immediately.

566.Broccoli, Carrot, And Tomato Quiche

Servings:4
Cooking Time: 14 Minutes
Ingredients:
- 4 eggs
- 1 teaspoon dried thyme
- 1 cup whole milk
- 1 steamed carrots, diced
- 2 cups steamed broccoli florets
- 2 medium tomatoes, diced
- ¼ cup crumbled feta cheese
- 1 cup grated Cheddar cheese
- 1 teaspoon chopped parsley
- Salt and ground black pepper, to taste
- Cooking spray

Directions:
1. Spritz the baking pan with cooking spray.
2. Whisk together the eggs, thyme, salt, and ground black pepper in a bowl and fold in the milk while mixing.
3. Put the carrots, broccoli, and tomatoes in the prepared baking pan, then spread with feta cheese and ½ cup Cheddar cheese. Pour the egg mixture over, then scatter with remaining Cheddar on top.
4. Slide the baking pan into Rack Position 1, select Convection Bake, set temperature to 350ºF (180ºC) and set time to 14 minutes.
5. When cooking is complete, the egg should be set and the quiche should be puffed.
6. Remove the quiche from the oven and top with chopped parsley, then slice to serve.

567.Golden Salmon And Carrot Croquettes

Servings:6

Cooking Time: 10 Minutes
Ingredients:
- 2 egg whites
- 1 cup almond flour
- 1 cup panko bread crumbs
- 1 pound (454 g) chopped salmon fillet
- $^2/_3$ cup grated carrots
- 2 tablespoons minced garlic cloves
- ½ cup chopped onion
- 2 tablespoons chopped chives
- Cooking spray

Directions:
1. Spritz the air fryer basket with cooking spray.
2. Whisk the egg whites in a bowl. Put the flour in a second bowl. Pour the bread crumbs in a third bowl. Set aside.
3. Combine the salmon, carrots, garlic, onion, and chives in a large bowl. Stir to mix well.
4. Form the mixture into balls with your hands. Dredge the balls into the flour, then egg, and then bread crumbs to coat well.
5. Arrange the salmon balls on the basket and spritz with cooking spray.
6. Put the air fryer basket on the baking pan and slide into Rack Position 2, select Air Fry, set temperature to 350ºF (180ºC) and set time to 10 minutes.
7. Flip the salmon balls halfway through cooking.
8. When cooking is complete, the salmon balls will be crispy and browned. Remove from the oven and serve immediately.

568.Simple Butter Cake

Servings:8
Cooking Time: 20 Minutes
Ingredients:
- 1 cup all-purpose flour
- 1¼ teaspoons baking powder
- ¼ teaspoon salt
- ½ cup plus 1½ tablespoons granulated white sugar
- 9½ tablespoons butter, at room temperature
- 2 large eggs
- 1 large egg yolk
- 2½ tablespoons milk
- 1 teaspoon vanilla extract
- Cooking spray

Directions:
1. Spritz the baking pan with cooking spray.
2. Combine the flour, baking powder, and salt in a large bowl. Stir to mix well.
3. Whip the sugar and butter in a separate bowl with a hand mixer on medium speed for 3 minutes.
4. Whip the eggs, egg yolk, milk, and vanilla extract into the sugar and butter mix with a hand mixer.
5. Pour in the flour mixture and whip with hand mixer until sanity and smooth.

6. Scrape the batter into the baking pan and level the batter with a spatula.
7. Slide the baking pan into Rack Position 1, select Convection Bake, set temperature to 325ºF (163ºC) and set time to 20 minutes.
8. After 15 minutes, remove the pan from the oven. Check the doneness. Return the pan to the oven and continue cooking.
9. When done, a toothpick inserted in the center should come out clean.
10. Invert the cake on a cooling rack and allow to cool for 15 minutes before slicing to serve.

569.Ritzy Pimento And Almond Turkey Casserole

Servings:4
Cooking Time: 32 Minutes
Ingredients:
- 1 pound (454 g) turkey breasts
- 1 tablespoon olive oil
- 2 boiled eggs, chopped
- 2 tablespoons chopped pimentos
- ¼ cup slivered almonds, chopped
- ¼ cup mayonnaise
- ½ cup diced celery
- 2 tablespoons chopped green onion
- ¼ cup cream of chicken soup
- ¼ cup bread crumbs
- Salt and ground black pepper, to taste

Directions:
1. Put the turkey breasts in a large bowl. Sprinkle with salt and ground black pepper and drizzle with olive oil. Toss to coat well.
2. Transfer the turkey to the air fryer basket.
3. Put the air fryer basket on the baking pan and slide into Rack Position 2, select Air Fry, set temperature to 390ºF (199ºC) and set time to 12 minutes.
4. Flip the turkey halfway through.
5. When cooking is complete, the turkey should be well browned.
6. Remove the turkey breasts from the oven and cut into cubes, then combine the chicken cubes with eggs, pimentos, almonds, mayo, celery, green onions, and chicken soup in a large bowl. Stir to mix.
7. Pour the mixture into the baking pan, then spread with bread crumbs.
8. Slide the baking pan into Rack Position 1, select Convection Bake, set time to 20 minutes.
9. When cooking is complete, the eggs should be set.
10. Remove from the oven and serve immediately.

570.Dehydrated Honey-rosemary Roasted Almonds

Servings:x
Cooking Time:x
Ingredients:

- 1 heaping tablespoon demerara sugar
- 1 teaspoon finely chopped fresh rosemary
- 1 teaspoon kosher salt
- 8 ounces (225g) raw almonds
- 2 tablespoons kosher salt
- Honey-Rosemary glaze
- ¼ cup (80g) honey

Directions:
1. Place almonds and salt in a bowl. Add cold tap water to cover the almonds by 1-inch
2. (2cm). Let soak at room temperature for 12 hours to activate.
3. Rinse almonds under cold running water, then drain. Spread in a single layer on the dehydrate basket.
4. Dehydrate almonds for 24 hours or till tender and somewhat crispy but additionally spongy in the middle. Almonds may be eaten plain or roasted each the next recipe.
5. Put honey in a small saucepan and heat over Low heat. Put triggered nuts
6. At a medium bowl and then pour over warm honey. Stir To coat nuts equally. Add rosemary, sugar
7. And salt and stir to blend.
8. Spread Almonds in one layer on the skillet.
9. Insert cable rack into rack place 6. Select BAKE/350°F (175°C)/CONVECTION/10 moments and empower Rotate Remind.
10. Stirring almonds when Rotate Remind signs.
11. Let cool completely before storing in an airtight container.

571.Arancini

Servings: 10 Arancini
Cooking Time: 30 Minutes
Ingredients:
- $^2/_3$ cup raw white Arborio rice
- 2 teaspoons butter
- ½ teaspoon salt
- $1^1/_3$ cups water
- 2 large eggs, well beaten
- 1¼ cups seasoned Italian-style dried bread crumbs
- 10 ¾-inch semi-firm Mozzarella cubes
- Cooking spray

Directions:
1. Pour the rice, butter, salt, and water in a pot. Stir to mix well and bring a boil over medium-high heat. Keep stirring.
2. Reduce the heat to low and cover the pot. Simmer for 20 minutes or until the rice is tender.
3. Turn off the heat and let sit, covered, for 10 minutes, then open the lid and fluffy the rice with a fork. Allow to cool for 10 more minutes.
4. Pour the beaten eggs in a bowl, then pour the bread crumbs in a separate bowl.
5. Scoop 2 tablespoons of the cooked rice up and form it into a ball, then press the Mozzarella into the ball and wrap.

6. Dredge the ball in the eggs first, then shake the excess off the dunk the ball in the bread crumbs. Roll to coat evenly. Repeat to make 10 balls in total with remaining rice.
7. Transfer the balls in the air fryer basket and spritz with cooking spray.
8. Put the air fryer basket on the baking pan and slide into Rack Position 2, select Air Fry, set temperature to 375°F (190°C) and set time to 10 minutes.
9. When cooking is complete, the balls should be lightly browned and crispy.
10. Remove the balls from the oven and allow to cool before serving.

572.Dehydrated Vegetable Black Pepper Chips

Servings:x
Cooking Time:x
Ingredients:
- Spice mix for parsnip chips
- ½ teaspoon ground turmeric
- 1 teaspoon kosher salt
- ½ teaspoon ground white or black pepper
- Red wine vinegar glaze for beet chips
- 2 tablespoons red wine vinegar
- 1 medium sweet potato
- 2 medium parsnips
- 2 medium beets
- Spice mix for sweet potato chips
- ½ teaspoon dried thyme
- ½ teaspoon onion powder
- ½ teaspoon garlic powder
- ¼ teaspoon ground white pepper
- 1 teaspoon kosher salt
- ½ teaspoon kosher salt
- ½ teaspoon ground white or black pepper

Directions:
1. For the sweet potato chips, combine spice mix in a little bowl and set aside. Peel sweet curry then slice using a mandolin.
2. Arrange slices in One coating on the dehydrate baskets. Gently and evenly sprinkle with the spice mixture. Place dehydrate baskets in rack positions 5 and 3 and press START. Assess on crispiness and rotate trays occasionally, every 4--5 hours.
3. Chips should sense paper-dry and snap in half easily. For the parsnip chips, combine spice mix in a little bowl and set aside. Arrange pieces in a single layer on the dehydrate baskets. Lightly and evenly sprinkle with the spice mixture.
4. Dehydrate chips as per step 3, altering the dehydrate period to 6 hours. For the beet chips, peel beets then thinly slice using a mandolin. Arrange slices in a single layer on the dehydrate baskets. Lightly brush with red wine vinegar then lightly and evenly sprinkle with pepper and salt. Dehydrate chips According to step 3.

573.Dehydrated Bananas With Coconut Sprnikles

Servings:x
Cooking Time:x
Ingredients:
- 5 very ripe bananas, peeled
- 1 cup shredded coconut

Directions:
1. Place coconut in a large shallow dish. Cut Press banana wedges in the coconut and organize in one layer on the dehydrating basket.
2. Hours Put basket in rack place 4 and then press START.
3. Dehydrate for 26 hours or until peanuts are Dry to the touch but still garnish with a sweet, intense banana taste.
4. Let bananas cool completely before storing in an Airtight container for up to 5 months.

574.Asian Dipping Sauce

Servings: About 1 Cup
Cooking Time: 0 Minutes
Ingredients:
- ¼ cup rice vinegar
- ¼ cup hoisin sauce
- ¼ cup low-sodium chicken or vegetable stock
- 3 tablespoons soy sauce
- 1 tablespoon minced or grated ginger
- 1 tablespoon minced or pressed garlic
- 1 teaspoon chili-garlic sauce or sriracha (or more to taste)

Directions:
1. Stir together all the ingredients in a small bowl, or place in a jar with a tight-fitting lid and shake until well mixed.
2. Use immediately.

575.Chocolate And Coconut Macaroons

Servings: 24 Macaroons
Cooking Time: 8 Minutes
Ingredients:
- 3 large egg whites, at room temperature
- ¼ teaspoon salt
- ¾ cup granulated white sugar
- 4½ tablespoons unsweetened cocoa powder
- 2¼ cups unsweetened shredded coconut

Directions:
1. Line the air fryer basket with parchment paper.
2. Whisk the egg whites with salt in a large bowl with a hand mixer on high speed until stiff peaks form.
3. Whisk in the sugar with the hand mixer on high speed until the mixture is thick. Mix in the cocoa powder and coconut.
4. Scoop 2 tablespoons of the mixture and shape the mixture in a ball. Repeat with remaining mixture to make 24 balls in total.

5. Arrange the balls in a single layer in the basket and leave a little space between each two balls.
6. Put the air fryer basket on the baking pan and slide into Rack Position 2, select Air Fry, set temperature to 375ºF (190ºC) and set time to 8 minutes.
7. When cooking is complete, the balls should be golden brown.
8. Serve immediately.

576.Chocolate Buttermilk Cake

Servings:8
Cooking Time: 20 Minutes
Ingredients:
- 1 cup all-purpose flour
- ²/₃ cup granulated white sugar
- ¼ cup unsweetened cocoa powder
- ¾ teaspoon baking soda
- ¼ teaspoon salt
- ²/₃ cup buttermilk
- 2 tablespoons plus 2 teaspoons vegetable oil
- 1 teaspoon vanilla extract
- Cooking spray

Directions:
1. Spritz the baking pan with cooking spray.
2. Combine the flour, cocoa powder, baking soda, sugar, and salt in a large bowl. Stir to mix well.
3. Mix in the buttermilk, vanilla, and vegetable oil. Keep stirring until it forms a grainy and thick dough.
4. Scrape the chocolate batter from the bowl and transfer to the pan, level the batter in an even layer with a spatula.
5. Slide the baking pan into Rack Position 1, select Convection Bake, set temperature to 325ºF (163ºC) and set time to 20 minutes.
6. After 15 minutes, remove the pan from the oven. Check the doneness. Return the pan to the oven and continue cooking.
7. When done, a toothpick inserted in the center should come out clean.
8. Invert the cake on a cooling rack and allow to cool for 15 minutes before slicing to serve.

577.Supplì Al Telefono (risotto Croquettes)

Servings:6
Cooking Time: 54 Minutes
Ingredients:
- Risotto Croquettes:
- 4 tablespoons unsalted butter
- 1 small yellow onion, minced
- 1 cup Arborio rice
- 3½ cups chicken stock
- ½ cup dry white wine
- 3 eggs
- Zest of 1 lemon
- ½ cup grated Parmesan cheese

154

- 2 ounces (57 g) fresh Mozzarella cheese
- ¼ cup peas
- 2 tablespoons water
- ½ cup all-purpose flour
- 1½ cups panko bread crumbs
- Kosher salt and ground black pepper, to taste
- Cooking spray
- Tomato Sauce:
- 2 tablespoons extra-virgin olive oil
- 4 cloves garlic, minced
- ¼ teaspoon red pepper flakes
- 1 (28-ounce / 794-g) can crushed tomatoes
- 2 teaspoons granulated sugar
- Kosher salt and ground black pepper, to taste

Directions:
1. Melt the butter in a pot over medium heat, then add the onion and salt to taste. Sauté for 5 minutes or until the onion in translucent.
2. Add the rice and stir to coat well. Cook for 3 minutes or until the rice is lightly browned. Pour in the chicken stock and wine.
3. Bring to a boil. Then cook for 20 minutes or until the rice is tender and liquid is almost absorbed.
4. Make the risotto: When the rice is cooked, break the egg into the pot. Add the lemon zest and Parmesan cheese. Sprinkle with salt and ground black pepper. Stir to mix well.
5. Pour the risotto in a baking sheet, then level with a spatula to spread the risotto evenly. Wrap the baking sheet in plastic and refrigerate for 1 hour.
6. Meanwhile, heat the olive oil in a saucepan over medium heat until shimmering.
7. Add the garlic and sprinkle with red pepper flakes. Sauté for a minute or until fragrant.
8. Add the crushed tomatoes and sprinkle with sugar. Stir to mix well. Bring to a boil. Reduce the heat to low and simmer for 15 minutes or until lightly thickened. Sprinkle with salt and pepper to taste. Set aside until ready to serve.
9. Remove the risotto from the refrigerator. Scoop the risotto into twelve 2-inch balls, then flatten the balls with your hands.
10. Arrange a about ½-inch piece of Mozzarella and 5 peas in the center of each flattened ball, then wrap them back into balls.
11. Transfer the balls to a baking sheet lined with parchment paper, then refrigerate for 15 minutes or until firm.
12. Whisk the remaining 2 eggs with 2 tablespoons of water in a bowl. Pour the flour in a second bowl and pour the panko in a third bowl.
13. Dredge the risotto balls in the bowl of flour first, then into the eggs, and then into the panko. Shake the excess off.
14. Transfer the balls to the baking pan and spritz with cooking spray.
15. Slide the baking pan into Rack Position 1, select Convection Bake, set temperature to 400ºF (205ºC) and set time to 10 minutes.
16. Flip the balls halfway through the cooking time.
17. When cooking is complete, the balls should be until golden brown.
18. Serve the risotto balls with the tomato sauce.

578.Greek Frittata

Servings:2
Cooking Time: 8 Minutes
Ingredients:
- 1 cup chopped mushrooms
- 2 cups spinach, chopped
- 4 eggs, lightly beaten
- 3 ounces (85 g) feta cheese, crumbled
- 2 tablespoons heavy cream
- A handful of fresh parsley, chopped
- Salt and ground black pepper, to taste
- Cooking spray

Directions:
1. Spritz the baking pan with cooking spray.
2. Whisk together all the ingredients in a large bowl. Stir to mix well.
3. Pour the mixture in the prepared baking pan.
4. Slide the baking pan into Rack Position 1, select Convection Bake, set temperature to 350ºF (180ºC) and set time to 8 minutes.
5. Stir the mixture halfway through.
6. When cooking is complete, the eggs should be set.
7. Serve immediately.

579.Goat Cheese And Asparagus Frittata

Servings:2 To 4
Cooking Time: 25 Minutes
Ingredients:
- 1 cup asparagus spears, cut into 1-inch pieces
- 1 teaspoon vegetable oil
- 1 tablespoon milk
- 6 eggs, beaten
- 2 ounces (57 g) goat cheese, crumbled
- 1 tablespoon minced chives, optional
- Kosher salt and pepper, to taste
- Add the asparagus spears to a small bowl and drizzle with the vegetable oil. Toss until well coated and transfer to the air fryer basket.

Directions:
1. Put the air fryer basket on the baking pan and slide into Rack Position 2, select Air Fry, set temperature to 400ºF (205ºC) and set time to 5 minutes.
2. Flip the asparagus halfway through.
3. When cooking is complete, the asparagus should be tender and slightly wilted.
4. Remove from the oven to the baking pan.

5. Stir together the milk and eggs in a medium bowl. Pour the mixture over the asparagus in the pan. Sprinkle with the goat cheese and the chives (if using) over the eggs. Season with salt and pepper.
6. Slide the baking pan into Rack Position 1, select Convection Bake, set temperature to 320ºF (160ºC) and set time to 20 minutes.
7. When cooking is complete, the top should be golden and the eggs should be set.
8. Transfer to a serving dish. Slice and serve.

580.Roasted Carrot Chips

Servings: 3 Cups
Cooking Time: 15 Minutes
Ingredients:
- 3 large carrots, peeled and sliced into long and thick chips diagonally
- 1 tablespoon granulated garlic
- 1 teaspoon salt
- ¼ teaspoon ground black pepper
- 1 tablespoon olive oil
- 1 tablespoon finely chopped fresh parsley

Directions:
1. Toss the carrots with garlic, salt, ground black pepper, and olive oil in a large bowl to coat well. Place the carrots in the air fryer basket.
2. Put the air fryer basket on the baking pan and slide into Rack Position 2, select Roast, set temperature to 360ºF (182ºC) and set time to 15 minutes.
3. Stir the carrots halfway through the cooking time.
4. When cooking is complete, the carrot chips should be soft. Remove from the oven. Serve the carrot chips with parsley on top.

581.Sweet Air Fried Pecans

Servings: 4 Cups
Cooking Time: 10 Minutes
Ingredients:
- 2 egg whites
- 1 tablespoon cumin
- 2 teaspoons smoked paprika
- ½ cup brown sugar
- 2 teaspoons kosher salt
- 1 pound (454 g) pecan halves
- Cooking spray

Directions:
1. Spritz the air fryer basket with cooking spray.
2. Combine the egg whites, cumin, paprika, sugar, and salt in a large bowl. Stir to mix well. Add the pecans to the bowl and toss to coat well.
3. Transfer the pecans to the basket.
4. Put the air fryer basket on the baking pan and slide into Rack Position 2, select Air Fry, set temperature to 300ºF (150ºC) and set time to 10 minutes.
5. Stir the pecans at least two times during the cooking.

6. When cooking is complete, the pecans should be lightly caramelized. Remove from the oven and serve immediately.

582.Spicy Air Fried Old Bay Shrimp

Servings: 2 Cups
Cooking Time: 10 Minutes
Ingredients:
- ½ teaspoon Old Bay Seasoning
- 1 teaspoon ground cayenne pepper
- ½ teaspoon paprika
- 1 tablespoon olive oil
- ⅛ teaspoon salt
- ½ pound (227 g) shrimps, peeled and deveined
- Juice of half a lemon

Directions:
1. Combine the Old Bay Seasoning, cayenne pepper, paprika, olive oil, and salt in a large bowl, then add the shrimps and toss to coat well.
2. Put the shrimps in the air fryer basket.
3. Put the air fryer basket on the baking pan and slide into Rack Position 2, select Air Fry, set temperature to 390ºF (199ºC) and set time to 10 minutes.
4. Flip the shrimps halfway through the cooking time.
5. When cooking is complete, the shrimps should be opaque. Serve the shrimps with lemon juice on top.

583.Milky Pecan Tart

Servings:8
Cooking Time: 26 Minutes
Ingredients:
- Tart Crust:
- ¼ cup firmly packed brown sugar
- $^1/_3$ cup butter, softened
- 1 cup all-purpose flour
- ¼ teaspoon kosher salt
- Filling:
- ¼ cup whole milk
- 4 tablespoons butter, diced
- ½ cup packed brown sugar
- ¼ cup pure maple syrup
- 1½ cups finely chopped pecans
- ¼ teaspoon pure vanilla extract
- ¼ teaspoon sea salt

Directions:
1. Line the baking pan with aluminum foil, then spritz the pan with cooking spray.
2. Stir the brown sugar and butter in a bowl with a hand mixer until puffed, then add the flour and salt and stir until crumbled.
3. Pour the mixture in the prepared baking pan and tilt the pan to coat the bottom evenly.
4. Slide the baking pan into Rack Position 1, select Convection Bake, set temperature to 350ºF (180ºC) and set time to 13 minutes.
5. When done, the crust will be golden brown.

6. Meanwhile, pour the milk, butter, sugar, and maple syrup in a saucepan. Stir to mix well. Bring to a simmer, then cook for 1 more minute. Stir constantly.
7. Turn off the heat and mix the pecans and vanilla into the filling mixture.
8. Pour the filling mixture over the golden crust and spread with a spatula to coat the crust evenly.
9. Select Bake and set time to 12 minutes. When cooked, the filling mixture should be set and frothy.
10. Remove the baking pan from the oven and sprinkle with salt. Allow to sit for 10 minutes or until cooled.
11. Transfer the pan to the refrigerator to chill for at least 2 hours, then remove the aluminum foil and slice to serve.

584.Kale Chips With Soy Sauce

Servings:2
Cooking Time: 5 Minutes
Ingredients:
- 4 medium kale leaves, about 1 ounce (28 g) each, stems removed, tear the leaves in thirds
- 2 teaspoons soy sauce
- 2 teaspoons olive oil

Directions:
1. Toss the kale leaves with soy sauce and olive oil in a large bowl to coat well. Place the leaves in the baking pan.
2. Put the air fryer basket on the baking pan and slide into Rack Position 2, select Air Fry, set temperature to 400ºF (205ºC) and set time to 5 minutes.
3. Flip the leaves with tongs gently halfway through.
4. When cooked, the kale leaves should be crispy. Remove from the oven and serve immediately.

585.Hillbilly Broccoli Cheese Casserole

Servings:6
Cooking Time: 30 Minutes
Ingredients:
- 4 cups broccoli florets
- ¼ cup heavy whipping cream
- ½ cup sharp Cheddar cheese, shredded
- ¼ cup ranch dressing
- Kosher salt and ground black pepper, to taste

Directions:
1. Combine all the ingredients in a large bowl. Toss to coat well broccoli well.
2. Pour the mixture into the baking pan.
3. Slide the baking pan into Rack Position 1, select Convection Bake, set temperature to 375ºF (190ºC) and set time to 30 minutes.
4. When cooking is complete, the broccoli should be tender.
5. Remove the baking pan from the oven and serve immediately.

586.Chicken Sausage And Broccoli Casserole

Servings:8
Cooking Time: 20 Minutes
Ingredients:
- 10 eggs
- 1 cup Cheddar cheese, shredded and divided
- ¾ cup heavy whipping cream
- 1 (12-ounce / 340-g) package cooked chicken sausage
- 1 cup broccoli, chopped
- 2 cloves garlic, minced
- ½ tablespoon salt
- ¼ tablespoon ground black pepper
- Cooking spray

Directions:
1. Spritz the baking pan with cooking spray.
2. Whisk the eggs with Cheddar and cream in a large bowl to mix well.
3. Combine the cooked sausage, broccoli, garlic, salt, and ground black pepper in a separate bowl. Stir to mix well.
4. Pour the sausage mixture into the baking pan, then spread the egg mixture over to cover.
5. Slide the baking pan into Rack Position 1, select Convection Bake, set temperature to 400ºF (205ºC) and set time to 20 minutes.
6. When cooking is complete, the egg should be set and a toothpick inserted in the center should come out clean.
7. Serve immediately.

587.Baked Cherry Tomatoes With Basil

Servings:2
Cooking Time: 5 Minutes
Ingredients:
- 2 cups cherry tomatoes
- 1 clove garlic, thinly sliced
- 1 teaspoon olive oil
- ⅛ teaspoon kosher salt
- 1 tablespoon freshly chopped basil, for topping
- Cooking spray

Directions:
1. Spritz the baking pan with cooking spray and set aside.
2. In a large bowl, toss together the cherry tomatoes, sliced garlic, olive oil, and kosher salt. Spread the mixture in an even layer in the prepared pan.
3. Slide the baking pan into Rack Position 1, select Convection Bake, set temperature to 360ºF (182ºC) and set time to 5 minutes.
4. When cooking is complete, the tomatoes should be the soft and wilted.
5. Transfer to a bowl and rest for 5 minutes. Top with the chopped basil and serve warm.

588.Ritzy Chicken And Vegetable Casserole

Servings:4
Cooking Time: 15 Minutes
Ingredients:
- 4 boneless and skinless chicken breasts, cut into cubes
- 2 carrots, sliced
- 1 yellow bell pepper, cut into strips
- 1 red bell pepper, cut into strips
- 15 ounces (425 g) broccoli florets
- 1 cup snow peas
- 1 scallion, sliced
- Cooking spray
- Sauce:
- 1 teaspoon Sriracha
- 3 tablespoons soy sauce
- 2 tablespoons oyster sauce
- 1 tablespoon rice wine vinegar
- 1 teaspoon cornstarch
- 1 tablespoon grated ginger
- 2 garlic cloves, minced
- 1 teaspoon sesame oil
- 1 tablespoon brown sugar

Directions:
1. Spritz the baking pan with cooking spray.
2. Combine the chicken, carrot, and bell peppers in a large bowl. Stir to mix well.
3. Combine the ingredients for the sauce in a separate bowl. Stir to mix well.
4. Pour the chicken mixture into the baking pan, then pour the sauce over. Stir to coat well.
5. Slide the baking pan into Rack Position 1, select Convection Bake, set temperature to 370ºF (188ºC) and set time to 13 minutes.
6. Add the broccoli and snow peas to the pan halfway through.
7. When cooking is complete, the vegetables should be tender.
8. Remove from the oven and sprinkle with sliced scallion before serving.

589.Citrus Avocado Wedge Fries

Servings: 12 Fries
Cooking Time: 8 Minutes
Ingredients:
- 1 cup all-purpose flour
- 3 tablespoons lime juice
- ¾ cup orange juice
- 1¼ cups plain dried bread crumbs
- 1 cup yellow cornmeal
- 1½ tablespoons chile powder
- 2 large Hass avocados, peeled, pitted, and cut into wedges
- Coarse sea salt, to taste
- Cooking spray

Directions:
1. Spritz the air fryer basket with cooking spray.
2. Pour the flour in a bowl. Mix the lime juice with orange juice in a second bowl.

Combine the bread crumbs, cornmeal, and chile powder in a third bowl.
3. Dip the avocado wedges in the bowl of flour to coat well, then dredge the wedges into the bowl of juice mixture, and then dunk the wedges in the bread crumbs mixture. Shake the excess off.
4. Arrange the coated avocado wedges in a single layer in the basket. Spritz with cooking spray.
5. Put the air fryer basket on the baking pan and slide into Rack Position 2, select Air Fry, set temperature to 400ºF (205ºC) and set time to 8 minutes.
6. Stir the avocado wedges and sprinkle with salt halfway through the cooking time.
7. When cooking is complete, the avocado wedges should be tender and crispy.
8. Serve immediately.

590.Air Fried Bacon Pinwheels

Servings: 8 Pinwheels
Cooking Time: 10 Minutes
Ingredients:
- 1 sheet puff pastry
- 2 tablespoons maple syrup
- ¼ cup brown sugar
- 8 slices bacon
- Ground black pepper, to taste
- Cooking spray

Directions:
1. Spritz the air fryer basket with cooking spray.
2. Roll the puff pastry into a 10-inch square with a rolling pin on a clean work surface, then cut the pastry into 8 strips.
3. Brush the strips with maple syrup and sprinkle with sugar, leaving a 1-inch far end uncovered.
4. Arrange each slice of bacon on each strip, leaving a ⅛-inch length of bacon hang over the end close to you. Sprinkle with black pepper.
5. From the end close to you, roll the strips into pinwheels, then dab the uncovered end with water and seal the rolls.
6. Arrange the pinwheels in the basket and spritz with cooking spray.
7. Put the air fryer basket on the baking pan and slide into Rack Position 2, select Air Fry, set temperature to 360ºF (182ºC) and set time to 10 minutes.
8. Flip the pinwheels halfway through.
9. When cooking is complete, the pinwheels should be golden brown. Remove from the oven and serve immediately.

591.Roasted Mushrooms

Servings: About 1½ Cups
Cooking Time: 30 Minutes
Ingredients:

- 1 pound (454 g) button or cremini mushrooms, washed, stems trimmed, and cut into quarters or thick slices
- ¼ cup water
- 1 teaspoon kosher salt or ½ teaspoon fine salt
- 3 tablespoons unsalted butter, cut into pieces, or extra-virgin olive oil

Directions:
1. Place a large piece of aluminum foil on the sheet pan. Place the mushroom pieces in the middle of the foil. Spread them out into an even layer. Pour the water over them, season with the salt, and add the butter. Wrap the mushrooms in the foil.
2. Select Roast, set the temperature to 325ºF (163ºC), and set the time for 15 minutes. Select Start to begin preheating.
3. Once the unit has preheated, place the pan in the oven.
4. After 15 minutes, remove the pan from the oven. Transfer the foil packet to a cutting board and carefully unwrap it. Pour the mushrooms and cooking liquid from the foil onto the sheet pan.
5. Select Roast, set the temperature to 350ºF (180ºC), and set the time for 15 minutes. Return the pan to the oven. Select Start to begin.
6. After about 10 minutes, remove the pan from the oven and stir the mushrooms. Return the pan to the oven and continue cooking for anywhere from 5 to 15 more minutes, or until the liquid is mostly gone and the mushrooms start to brown.
7. Serve immediately.

592. Southwest Seasoning

Servings: About ¾ Cups
Cooking Time: 0 Minutes
Ingredients:
- 3 tablespoons ancho chile powder
- 3 tablespoons paprika
- 2 tablespoons dried oregano
- 2 tablespoons freshly ground black pepper
- 2 teaspoons cayenne
- 2 teaspoons cumin
- 1 tablespoon granulated onion
- 1 tablespoon granulated garlic

Directions:
1. Stir together all the ingredients in a small bowl.
2. Use immediately or place in an airtight container in the pantry.

593. Shawarma Spice Mix

Servings: About 1 Tablespoon
Cooking Time: 0 Minutes
Ingredients:
- 1 teaspoon smoked paprika
- 1 teaspoon cumin
- ¼ teaspoon turmeric

- ¼ teaspoon kosher salt or ⅛ teaspoon fine salt
- ¼ teaspoon cinnamon
- ¼ teaspoon allspice
- ¼ teaspoon red pepper flakes
- ¼ teaspoon freshly ground black pepper

Directions:
1. Stir together all the ingredients in a small bowl.
2. Use immediately or place in an airtight container in the pantry.

594. Traditional Latkes

Servings: 4 Latkes
Cooking Time: 10 Minutes
Ingredients:
- 1 egg
- 2 tablespoons all-purpose flour
- 2 medium potatoes, peeled and shredded, rinsed and drained
- ¼ teaspoon granulated garlic
- ½ teaspoon salt
- Cooking spray

Directions:
1. Spritz the air fryer basket with cooking spray.
2. Whisk together the egg, flour, potatoes, garlic, and salt in a large bowl. Stir to mix well.
3. Divide the mixture into four parts, then flatten them into four circles. Arrange the circles onto the basket and spritz with cooking spray.
4. Put the air fryer basket on the baking pan and slide into Rack Position 2, select Air Fry, set temperature to 380ºF (193ºC) and set time to 10 minutes.
5. Flip the latkes halfway through.
6. When cooked, the latkes will be golden brown and crispy. Remove from the oven and serve immediately.

595. Riced Cauliflower Casserole

Servings:4
Cooking Time: 12 Minutes
Ingredients:
- 1 head cauliflower, cut into florets
- 1 cup okra, chopped
- 1 yellow bell pepper, chopped
- 2 eggs, beaten
- ½ cup chopped onion
- 1 tablespoon soy sauce
- 2 tablespoons olive oil
- Salt and ground black pepper,
- to taste Spritz the baking pan with cooking spray.

Directions:
1. Put the cauliflower in a food processor and pulse to rice the cauliflower.
2. Pour the cauliflower rice in the baking pan and add the remaining ingredients. Stir to mix well.

3. Slide the baking pan into Rack Position 1, select Convection Bake, set temperature to 380ºF (193ºC) and set time to 12 minutes.
4. When cooking is complete, the eggs should be set.
5. Remove from the oven and serve immediately.

596.Parsnip Fries With Garlic-yogurt Dip

Servings:4
Cooking Time: 10 Minutes
Ingredients:
- 3 medium parsnips, peeled, cut into sticks
- ¼ teaspoon kosher salt
- 1 teaspoon olive oil
- 1 garlic clove, unpeeled
- Cooking spray
- Dip:
- ¼ cup plain Greek yogurt
- ⅛ teaspoon garlic powder
- 1 tablespoon sour cream
- ¼ teaspoon kosher salt
- Freshly ground black pepper, to taste

Directions:
1. Spritz the air fryer basket with cooking spray.
2. Put the parsnip sticks in a large bowl, then sprinkle with salt and drizzle with olive oil.
3. Transfer the parsnip into the basket and add the garlic.
4. Put the air fryer basket on the baking pan and slide into Rack Position 2, select Air Fry, set temperature to 360ºF (182ºC) and set time to 10 minutes.
5. Stir the parsnip halfway through the cooking time.
6. Meanwhile, peel the garlic and crush it. Combine the crushed garlic with the ingredients for the dip. Stir to mix well.
7. When cooked, the parsnip sticks should be crisp. Remove the parsnip fries from the oven and serve with the dipping sauce.

597.Classic Churros

Servings: 12 Churros
Cooking Time: 10 Minutes
Ingredients:
- 4 tablespoons butter
- ¼ teaspoon salt
- ½ cup water
- ½ cup all-purpose flour
- 2 large eggs
- 2 teaspoons ground cinnamon
- ¼ cup granulated white sugar
- Cooking spray

Directions:
1. Put the butter, salt, and water in a saucepan. Bring to a boil until the butter is melted on high heat. Keep stirring.
2. Reduce the heat to medium and fold in the flour to form a dough. Keep cooking and

stirring until the dough is dried out and coat the pan with a crust.
3. Turn off the heat and scrape the dough in a large bowl. Allow to cool for 15 minutes.
4. Break and whisk the eggs into the dough with a hand mixer until the dough is sanity and firm enough to shape.
5. Scoop up 1 tablespoon of the dough and roll it into a ½-inch-diameter and 2-inch-long cylinder. Repeat with remaining dough to make 12 cylinders in total.
6. Combine the cinnamon and sugar in a large bowl and dunk the cylinders into the cinnamon mix to coat.
7. Arrange the cylinders on a plate and refrigerate for 20 minutes.
8. Spritz the air fryer basket with cooking spray. Place the cylinders in the basket and spritz with cooking spray.
9. Put the air fryer basket on the baking pan and slide into Rack Position 2, select Air Fry, set temperature to 375ºF (190ºC) and set time to 10 minutes.
10. Flip the cylinders halfway through the cooking time.
11. When cooked, the cylinders should be golden brown and fluffy.
12. Serve immediately.

598.Mediterranean Quiche

Servings:4
Cooking Time: 30 Minutes
Ingredients:
- 4 eggs
- ¼ cup chopped Kalamata olives
- ½ cup chopped tomatoes
- ¼ cup chopped onion
- ½ cup milk
- 1 cup crumbled feta cheese
- ½ tablespoon chopped oregano
- ½ tablespoon chopped basil
- Salt and ground black pepper, to taste
- Cooking spray

Directions:
1. Spritz the baking pan with cooking spray.
2. Whisk the eggs with remaining ingredients in a large bowl. Stir to mix well.
3. Pour the mixture into the prepared baking pan.
4. Slide the baking pan into Rack Position 1, select Convection Bake, set temperature to 340ºF (171ºC) and set time to 30 minutes.
5. When cooking is complete, the eggs should be set and a toothpick inserted in the center should come out clean.
6. Serve immediately.

599.Air Fried Crispy Brussels Sprouts

Servings:4
Cooking Time: 20 Minutes
Ingredients:
- ¼ teaspoon salt
- ⅛ teaspoon ground black pepper

- 1 tablespoon extra-virgin olive oil
- 1 pound (454 g) Brussels sprouts, trimmed and halved
- Lemon wedges, for garnish

Directions:
1. Combine the salt, black pepper, and olive oil in a large bowl. Stir to mix well.
2. Add the Brussels sprouts to the bowl of mixture and toss to coat well. Arrange the Brussels sprouts in the air fryer basket.
3. Put the air fryer basket on the baking pan and slide into Rack Position 2, select Air Fry, set temperature to 350ºF (180ºC) and set time to 20 minutes.
4. Stir the Brussels sprouts two times during cooking.
5. When cooked, the Brussels sprouts will be lightly browned and wilted. Transfer the cooked Brussels sprouts to a large plate and squeeze the lemon wedges on top to serve.

600.Lemony Shishito Peppers

Servings:4
Cooking Time: 5 Minutes

Ingredients:
- ½ pound (227 g) shishito peppers (about 24)
- 1 tablespoon olive oil
- Coarse sea salt, to taste
- Lemon wedges, for serving
- Cooking spray

Directions:
1. Spritz the air fryer basket with cooking spray.
2. Toss the peppers with olive oil in a large bowl to coat well.
3. Arrange the peppers in the basket.
4. Put the air fryer basket on the baking pan and slide into Rack Position 2, select Air Fry, set temperature to 400ºF (205ºC) and set time to 5 minutes.
5. Flip the peppers and sprinkle the peppers with salt halfway through the cooking time.
6. When cooked, the peppers should be blistered and lightly charred. Transfer the peppers onto a plate and squeeze the lemon wedges on top before serving.

CPSIA information can be obtained
at www.ICGtesting.com
Printed in the USA
LVHW100155030921
696865LV00003B/24